Top Dog

Top Dog

J. David Pincus
J. Nicholas DeBonis

McGraw-Hill, Inc.

New York   San Francisco   Washington, D.C.   Auckland   Bogotá
Caracas   Lisbon   London   Madrid   Mexico City   Milan
Montreal   New Delhi   San Juan   Singapore
Sydney   Tokyo   Toronto

Library of Congress Cataloging-in-Publication Data

Pincus, J. David.
   Top dog / J. David Pincus, J. Nicholas DeBonis.
      p.   cm.
   Includes index.
   ISBN 0–07–050129-7
   1. Chief executive officers. 2. Executive ability.
3. Leadership. 4. Communication in management. I. DeBonis, J.
Nicholas. II. Title.
HD38.2.P53   1994
658.4'09—dc20   94–217
                                                    CIP

2 3 4 5 6 7 8 9 0 DOC/DOC 9 0 9 8 7 6   (hcp)
2 3 4 5 6 7 8 9 0 DOC/DOC 9 0 9 8 7 6   (scp)

ISBN 0-07-050129-7
ISBN 0-07-050188-2

*The sponsoring editor for this book was Philip Ruppel, the editing
supervisor was Fred Dahl, and the production supervisor was
Suzanne Babeuf. It was set in Frugal Sans by Inkwell Publishing
Services.*

Printed and bound by R. R. Donnelley & Sons Company.

This book is printed on recycled, acid-free paper containing a
minimum of 50 percent recycled de-inked fiber.

This book is dedicated to three sources of lasting inspiration.

First, to my uncle, **Ben Friedman**,
*who always told me the truth about who I was
and what I could become—
and whose advice and love set everything in the right direction.*

Second, to **Warren Bennis**,
*whose early humanistic work on leaders
helped me to see what hadn't been done yet
and what could be.*

And third, to all the **chief executive officers**—*past and present—
whose lives in the "hot seat" made this book possible,
realistic, and, we hope, worthwhile.*

In memory of
Ed Lewis,
*a dear friend whose "tough but fair" business wisdom
graces much of this book
and*
Rich Panich,
*a cherished friend whose life demonstrated
the real power of the human spirit*

J.D.P.

Contents

Part 3. How to Be an Effective Communicator: Transforming Chief Executive Officers into Chief Communication Officers

Part 4. Where Are We Going? A Look to the Future

Foreword: Communicating the "Vision Thing"

In *Top Dog*, authors J. David Pincus and J. Nicholas DeBonis have achieved a most astonishing thing. That is, they have crafted a timely and inspiring business book that hooks the reader as well as any thriller on *The New York Times* best-seller list. After all, how many business books include a compelling, fictional cliffhanger that keeps the pages turning long after you should have switched off the light?

Of course, this was something that Pincus and DeBonis *had* to do, for their audience can be a critical, demanding, astute, and cynical bunch. Of course, I'm referring to the CEOs and top echelon leaders of today's American corporations.

A tough audience, indeed.

Aside from the tremendous practical information it provides, the most valuable thing about *Top Dog* is that it delivers just the right message at just the right time. Why? Because today top executives in every industry are being judged not simply by the growth and profits they deliver to the bottom line, but by the visionary breakthroughs they are expected to generate.

Today, senior executives are being pushed to "tear down the walls." "To change the game." To create new markets and opportunities where none existed before. Speaking for myself, this "vision thing" requires a lot of energy.

And because it is so demanding, it becomes easy to lose sight of what is, has been, and must always be one of the most important roles that a CEO can play. That of communicator. Or, as the authors refer to the title, CCO, Chief Communication Officer.

Now, more than ever before, it is imperative that top business managers become world-class communicators. If we don't, the far-reaching visions we struggle so hard to create are destined to end up as nothing more than so many great secrets we share with only ourselves.

In 1988, we were about to introduce an initiative that would have one of two results: We would either become wildly successful, or we would jeopardize the future of our organization for many years to come. The initiative I'm referring to is our move to Value, that is, dramatically rolling back prices while providing customers with greater quality and service than ever before.

While research made it clear that Value was what customers wanted, no one in the industry was responding. We were about to be the first, and a great many people in our organization were skeptical, if not downright terrified.

But rather than let the doubts and concerns build, we took our message on the road—a three-week, 17-city tour in which I personally met with all our District Managers in a Town Hall format. There are times when the CEO is the only person capable of carrying the message. For me, this was one of those times.

The meetings weren't slick. Our notes were handwritten. And each presentation was more of a dialogue than a mandate from the mountain. We talked about our customers. About our vision. About risks and rewards. And finally, about the need for all of us to share in the vision and work together as never before.

By communicating in this way, our employees—from the field to the corporate office—gained a clear understanding of where we were going and, most importantly, what it would take to get there. The mission became shared. Understanding prevailed over fear. And our people took ownership in a tremendous way.

The result? Since 1988, the growth of Taco Bell has been dramatic and exciting. By taking the lead communication role, I was able to help motivate our workforce to embrace and act on the Value vision—a vision that has enabled us to effectively change both our company and the industry at large.

I'm pleased to say that this "vision thing" is still alive and well at Taco Bell today. And I feel we're still doing an effective job of communicating it to our management, to our Pepsico shareholders, to the press, and, most importantly, to our employees who turn vision into reality each and every day for the people who count most—our customers.

Yet, as *Top Dog* reminds us, we can never go far enough. And after reading this book, I'm inspired to redouble my efforts to communicate our vision, mission, and goals with even more clarity and completeness than ever before.

John Martin
President and Chief Executive Officer
Taco Bell Corp.

The Genesis of Top Dog

Imagine the horror. You're the chief executive of a major company attending an important meeting. Your second-in-command is called away for a moment, then returns ashen-faced. His news: Your company's last five quarters have been a lie. Reported profits never existed, and your books have been cooked for several quarters.[1]

That's the opening paragraph from a *Business Week* article written in March 1993. It describes what John J. Pomerantz, chief executive officer of women's apparel manufacturer Leslie Fay Cos., faced last February when outside auditors uncovered a scandal threatening the company's survival. And, claims Pomerantz, he knew nothing about it—until he heard it from the auditors.

Several months before the Leslie Fay case broke, we completed writing a fictional story about a CEO of a hotel company who confronts a remarkably similar "cooked books" situation—in facts and circumstances—to the one that shocked John Pomerantz. And, as you might expect, our story is part of this book, along with the nonfiction part based on years of research. From the outset, we sought to create a *realistic* story about a CEO enmeshed in a corporate crisis triggered by renegade managers who had juggled financial data. Little did we ever imagine that what we saw as realistic could possibly become *real*. But it did.

In this book, we discuss some of the realities of being a corporate leader today. Wait, make that *changing* realities. For life as a "top dog" today is dramatically different than it used to be. And that's what our story is about: *CEOs' need to change and the kinds of changes needed.*

[1]Lesly, Elizabeth, "Who Played Dress-Up with the Books?" *Business Week*, March 15, 1993, p. 34.

The CEO's Changing Role

Realizing the need to change is one thing. Actually changing is something else. But that's what CEOs, present and future, must do if they're to make it in a business environment where the people at the top are under fire as never before. Boards, stockholders, employees, consumer activists, government regulators, media, you name the group—they all want a bigger piece of the CEO and when they don't get it, guess whose scalp they come after? Indeed, the corporate landscape is littered with the ghosts of CEOs past—including those from the likes of General Motors, Time Warner, Kodak, Compaq, Goodyear, and Digital, to name a few—because their relationship with one or more key stakeholders fell apart.

Driving this accelerating trend is CEOs' failure to be adept leaders—that is, *relationship-builders*. Put another way, as we argue throughout the book, CEOs must better harness their inherent power as their organizations' chief *communication* officers, or "CCOs," to enhance their leadership role. We believe that communication and leadership are inextricably linked. A small, but expanding number of CEOs are beginning to understand how to play this communication-leadership role. You'll meet and hear from some of them in this book, as well as from some who are still learning the lessons of leadership.

Our central premise is that all managers, but especially CEOs, need to change the ways they communicate with critical stakeholders, particularly employees. We explore the implications of how and why the CEO's role has shifted from a "me boss, you worker" approach to one closer to "let us come reason together." My hope is that this book will motivate and guide you—whether you are a CEO now or aspire to become one—to evolve into the type of CEO-leader who can succeed in today's demanding marketplace.

A Book for All Managers

The book explores the topic of communication—strategically, tactically, conceptually, and psychologically—and, most importantly, communication's connection to leadership. Included are observations by us and a cast of hundreds, mostly CEOs, about the core principles all managers need to master in order to improve their communication effectiveness and consequently their supervisory performance.

The communication and human relations principles we highlight are universal—and apply to managers at all levels. The veteran CEO. The rookie CEO. The top manager. The middle manager. The first-line supervisor. And all those who carry a torch for the top job. To illustrate our story, we rely heavily on CEOs' own words and experiences, often condensing them into minicases.

Motivations Behind Top Dog

I first began to wonder about the "actual" impact of a CEO's communication style on workers and the bottom line when I was employee communication director at Marriott Corporation in the late 1970s. That same nagging curiosity sparked my doctoral research at the University of Maryland in the early 1980s.

After uncovering empirical evidence that top management communication does, in fact, influence employees' job attitudes and performance, I was hooked on wanting to learn more—and so the journey began.

This book is the culmination of a 10-year investigation into the chief executive officer's changing communication and leadership roles. We address what these changes are, why they are occurring and how CEOs can best prepare to adapt to them. The data forming the basis for our arguments and recommendations represent the results of a systematic program of research begun in 1982 and continuing to this day. Specifically, with the help of several colleagues, most notably Dr. Robert Rayfield, I conducted two national surveys of *Fortune* 500 industrial and service CEOs and interviewed a cross-section of 25 CEOs and COOs (and, in some cases, their top communication professionals) to learn how top executives view and practice their communication role.

Among the chiefs interviewed were senior executives such as Tom Clausen of the Bank of America; Hicks Waldron of Avon; Sandy Sigoloff of Wickes Cos.; Dick Schlosberg of *The Los Angeles Times*; Walter Williams of Bethlehem Steel; Phil Quigley of Pacific Bell; Henry Rogers of Rogers & Cowan; and Alexander Trowbridge of the National Association of Manufacturers. In addition, I talked with a number of younger, up-and-coming CEOs such as Carl Sardegna of Maryland Blue Cross/Blue Shield; Bruce Burtch of The William Bentley Agency in San Francisco; Jim Verney of Winchell's Donut House; Dr. Noel Hinners of NASA; and Tom Priselac of Los Angeles' Cedars-Sinai Medical Center.

When I'd gathered the information I needed to start writing, I was joined by colleague and friend Nick DeBonis, now a marketing consultant and professor at Emory University's Business School, who shared my zeal for the topic and the project. Working together, we discovered a rare kinship. The writing began in earnest on Labor Day, 1991.

A Different Kind of Book: Nonfiction/Fiction

This book isn't like any business book you've probably ever seen; it departs from the standard formula. We tell our story through two distinct voices. The first voice speaks through a nonfiction style, sharing facts and findings from studies and interviews, and offering insights and recommendations. The second voice—the voice that makes the book most different—speaks through a fiction style relating the story of CEO Arlen Burch Royster. We tell the story of Arlen's struggle to resolve professional and personal crises, and, through it all, what he learns about communication, leadership, and life.

Each fiction section puts into "real life" terms the "real" points made in the nonfiction section immediately preceding it; thus, we try to breathe life into our core messages through Arlen and the other characters. Our objective is to push beyond the numbers and quotations to delve into the CEO's mind, offering glimpses of how top dogs think and perceive, decide, and act.

I hope Arlen's story both educates and entertains you. Although he isn't real, he represents our interpretation of business reality. He's a composite of all we've learned about CEOs and contains bits and pieces from many of the top dogs we've talked to and come to know. Like many of his peers, Arlen wants more than anything else to be successful. To him, success means power and money. He was programmed from his MBA days to believe that success is measured by his rung on the corporate ladder and the size of his "compensation package."

Trained to be rational and make decisions by the numbers, while maintaining a proper distance from the "workers," Arlen became CEO at a time when management and leadership notions were being challenged and gradually reshaped. Control-driven management was in some companies being replaced by more collaborative approaches. At times, Arlen digs in his heels, resisting ideas he thinks threaten his traditional view of manager-employee relationships—just as many CEOs today are doing. But changing and adjusting are constants in contemporary organizational life, points deeply embedded in Arlen's story.

I hope the alternating fiction and nonfiction voices will make it easier and more enjoyable for you to "hear" the book's principles and practical advice.

J. David Pincus
Irvine, California

Acknowledgments

This was a project of unassuming and unintentional beginnings—and evolved into something I never imagined. Llike most complex projects, it seemed far simpler than it turned out to be. It took lots of help from lots of people. Nothing I say can adequately repay those who stood by me. I only hope each of them knows the depth of my gratitude.

Above all others, I'm forever grateful to my wife, *Karen Pincus*. My best friend, emotional backbone, and confidante, she always realized what this could be. It was her love and cherished counsel that kept me afloat when I thought I was drowning. Her keen editing eye saw all, and she willingly gave time she didn't have. You made all the difference, K. And to my children, *Jeff* and *Megan*, thanks for putting up with my spouting off about Arlen and for teaching me about relationships.

The best surprise was the arrival of *Nick DeBonis*, co-author, special friend, and fellow dreamer. His wit, creativity, and editor's pen were crucial during the writing phase of the journey. Nick, you made the ride a joy, especially bringing Arlen to life.

Invaluable contributions during the formative stages came from dear friend and colleague, *Bob Rayfield*, whose faith in me and the book never wavered, and whose efforts as a researcher, reviewer, and advisor helped shape many chapters. I'll always be grateful, Bob, for your comradeship and wise guidance.

Next is my alter-ego and ever loyal friend, *Bruce Burtch*, talented CEO-entrepreneur, whose infectious enthusiasm propelled me forward when I was stalled. BB, without you, I might never have "seen the book" and certainly never would have "been the book." Thanks for being there all along.

From my valued friend, *Steve Wood*, I received heartening words and selfless assistance in reviewing chapter drafts and crystallizing ideas. Steve, your intelligent, probing questions made huge differences on many of these pages. I'll never forget.

The mother's milk of any book is its informational foundation. Key assistance throughout the 1980s came from my kinsman and colleague, *Rick Knapp*, who believed so completely in the work that he convinced his employers, consulting firms William M. Mercer and Foster Higgins, to sponsor parts of the research. Dickie, thanks for being there and helping to keep the fires burning.

A number of former students/friends helped me collect new information, and to catalogue and make sense of the mass of data. I'll always be indebted to *Donn Silvis, Dawn Thurston, Terri O'Connor, Karen Von Elton*, and *Jeff Baker*.

So many of my friends and family put up with my star-gazing, whining, self-doubts, and hunger for feedback: *Mike and Sharon Meliker, Walter and Joan Gerson, Coral Ohl, Wendell Crow, Terry Hynes, Ed and Mady Lewis, Phil Stein, Jerry Keane, Tom Harrison, Larry Lieberman, Ted Smythe* and *Barry Pelissier*, who knows whence Arlen comes. My sister and brother-in-law, *Susan and Paul Azoulay*, were magnificent sounding boards for Arlen's character and story, especially on New York locations and landmarks. And to *Robert Cave-Rogers*, many thank-you's for teaching me about the complex publishing business. Thank you all for joining in the fun.

Perhaps the pivotal moment in bringing the book to life came when *Phil Ruppel*, publisher of McGraw-Hill's Professional Book Group, called to say "Let's go!" A moment I'll never forget, Phil. Thanks for taking the plunge and sticking by the original concept.

And, finally, I'd be remiss if I didn't recognize the people without whom this book would've been impossible—the hundreds of CEOs who participated in surveys and the 25 or so top dogs and, in some cases, their top communication professionals, who welcomed me into their organizations, and who patiently and candidly answered my many questions. A heartfelt thanks to *Ron Rhody*, colleague, friend and former senior VP at Bank of America, who graciously went out of his way whenever I asked for help.

J. David Pincus
Irvine, California

My participation in this challenging and personally fulfilling project would not have been possible without a number of people throughout my life, and three in particular: my wife and son, and the lead author.

Susan and *Andrew* provided not only support, but latitude, allowing me to borrow time from the family which can never be repaid. This book is as much a part of their legacy.

And I'm grateful to *David* for his selfless invitation to participate in his work. He taught me not only when to use a hyphen, but an important baseball ritual I call "first dog." His friendship has become and remains infinitely greater and more important than the scope of this book.

Thank you all.

J. Nicholas DeBonis
Atlanta, Georgia

PART 1

How We Got Here: The Changing Role of the CEO in a Changing Workplace

Prologue: "When 'It' Hits the Fan"

Wednesday, October 10, 6 a.m. Lost in thought, Arlen Burch Royster stood before the crystal-clear, eight-foot-high pane of glass that defined the outside wall of his office. He stared out as if in a trance, considering his suddenly uncertain future.

Wrestling with a procession of conflicting emotions—shock, uncertainty, anger, fear—the chief executive officer of Royal Accommodations knew that today would be the pivotal moment of his professional life. Since his meeting late yesterday with the auditors, he'd been trying to reconcile what they'd told him about the hotel and entertainment conglomerate he'd headed the past six years. He felt a sense of disbelief, of dread, beginning to overtake him.

From his executive-level vantage point 30 stories above New York's Central Park, Arlen visualized his neatly planned career turning into an out-of-control nightmare. Despite his fears, though, he remained determined to maintain control and not allow his self-doubt to show. The chairman was expecting him at 9 a.m. and he needed to have ready answers to the hard questions he knew he'd face.

The CEO wasn't usually in the office this early. But he wanted to meet with his management team before he saw the chairman. His secretary had called each member of his executive staff at their homes last night, but Arlen wouldn't allow her to tell them what the meeting was about. They only knew it was critical they be there. One had to take a red-eye back from Los Angeles. They had no way of knowing how much their lives and careers would eventually change after they heard the news.

Arlen turned back to his desk, which faced the outside glass wall. It was spotless except for a few papers neatly arranged in two piles. To the left of the desk was a comfortable conference area comprised of a soft leather couch and matching chairs, encircling a glass-topped brass coffee table. On the table were a telephone and a copy of *Great Hotels of the World,* which prominently featured Royal's San Francisco and Maui properties.

Immediately noticeable on the wood-paneled wall behind him was Arlen's prized collection of baseball memorabilia, including his framed mint-condition Mickey Mantle rookie card, saved for 20 years in a dusty shoe box from his childhood and currently worth upwards of $40,000.

"This'll turn the company upside down and inside out," he lectured himself. "What to do ...," he whispered softly. He pulled a legal pad out of the top drawer, snatched his Ben Franklin-style reading glasses from his vest pocket and began scribbling questions he'd been turning over all morning. They came faster than he could write. How do I tell my staff? How do we tell employees? What will Wall Street's reaction be? How could this happen here? He stopped, adding two thick exclamation points after the last question.

Next he printed "Media," and circled it several times. He then jotted a number of other questions: "Will the SEC fine us? Me? How will Royal's stock be affected? What about our expansion plans?" Arlen's pen drifted back to the "How could this happen here?!!" entry. He wrote, "Accountability!" next to it. "New managers?" was added to the list. He feared losing some of the bright, energetic, young managers and supervisors Royal had been recruiting the past few months.

In large block letters he wrote "COMMUNICATION???" He knew this would be critical in any damage control strategy. But he wasn't sure what to do. He wrote "Jamieson" next to it—his vice president of corporate communication and the person he most trusted at Royal.

Arlen stopped writing as his eyes drifted down to the lush, sprawling park below, awash in rich autumn reds and golds that seemed to explode under morning's undiluted sunlight. Now, the questions became more personal. He put the pen down, and reached for the lukewarm coffee he'd bought at the coffee shop downstairs, stood up slowly and walked around his desk to the window-wall.

Looking back at him was the reflected image of a man in his early 50s, 6 ft, 1 in., about 20 pounds overweight but evenly distributed over his solid frame. His oval, chubby-cheeked, clean-shaven face was normally dominated by alert, hazel eyes that exuded confidence and poise. Today, however, they appeared worried, almost forlorn. His wavy brown hair was dotted with gray flecks, especially in front, and his hairline receded in a V-shape at both temples. His flat, wide nose and thin lips gave him the look of a "modern-day Babe Ruth," a description given him by his closest friend, Barry Lewis, and one Arlen found amusing.

He began to unconsciously spin the silver cufflinks on his left sleeve, a nervous habit silently signalling that he was worried. He tried hard to concentrate on how this unthinkable mess would change the Royal Accommodations he knew. Then he thought about Stamps, the chairman.

"What's Jim going to think? Is he going to blame me? Have I let him down?" Royal's Chairman of the Board had been Arlen's mentor and major corporate good-luck charm since Arlen's early days at Mark Twain's "Americana Village" theme park in St. Louis. Then, after Arlen moved on to Open Seas Cruises where he promptly progressed to director of sales, Stamps lured him to Royal 12 years ago. The cagey Stamps enjoyed a well-earned reputation as a genius at spotting potential management talent. Just as Stamps had planned, six years after Arlen's arrival, he was appointed Royal's CEO, replacing Stamps, his self-appointed "godfather" who was elevated to chairman.

* * * * * * * * * *

"Well, the you-know-what must've hit the fan," said a familiar voice to Arlen's right. Rick Jamieson had slipped into the office. The digital clock on Arlen's desk showed 6:15. "The security guard says you came in by limo this morning. That's got to mean big trouble."

"What're you talking about?" Arlen shot back gruffly, gulping the last of his coffee. Although a chauffeur-driven limousine was available to the Royal CEO, Arlen preferred driving his own Cadillac to the office most days.

"You mean you really don't know? It's common knowledge around here that the only days you don't drive yourself are when something big's about to happen," Jamieson pointed out matter-of-factly, inching toward Arlen's desk.

Of his staff, only Jamieson could get away with being so flip when Arlen was under the gun. They joined Royal the same year and soon discovered they shared not only a love of business, but also a love of baseball.

"Didn't know people were so interested in my driving habits," Arlen said cynically, his attention remaining on the visible portion of New York's skyline.

"Oh, but they are. It sends us warnings that things ...," Jamieson paused momentarily, "that *big* things are about to happen." Arlen turned and gazed directly at Jamieson.

As always, Jamieson's manner was casual, yet out of the corner of his eye he noticed Arlen fidgeting with his cufflinks, the lucky pair he'd been given by Jim Stamps when Arlen had been appointed the youngest-ever vice president of marketing at "Americana Village." Rimmed with diamonds, the silver links replicated the park's original 1950s logo.

Jamieson went on, working hard to maintain his upbeat tone. "You'd be surprised how much of what you do is under the microscope. And the grapevine's faster than any new communication technology we could install. I mean, you don't realize your own power, Arlen ... just think, in a couple of hours, our people in California will be waking up to the news that Royster's limo was on the road this morning. By noon, the whole company will know."

As Arlen settled in behind his desk, he had that "presidential" look about him, a kind of "all-knowing" attitude he'd acquired over the years. He wore his customary three-piece suit, this one charcoal grey with white pin-stripes and an ABR-monogrammed shirt beneath a matching tie. Immaculately shined, as always, were his oxblood wing-tips.

Jamieson strolled to the glass wall, stopping where Arlen stood a few minutes before, and peered out. He was Arlen's sounding board inside Royal. Intelligent and funny, Jamieson, even at 45, still had the "boy next door" look: straight blond hair; aqua-blue eyes; and an easy smile that revealed perfectly straight teeth. What separated him from most other executives, Arlen believed, was his instinct for people and situations —knowing what, when, and how to say what needed to be said, as well as knowing when to keep quiet. He possessed that rare ability to hear not only words, but emotions—an ability Arlen envied.

Rotating away from the cityscape, Jamieson faced Arlen. "I know I'm here earlier than I needed to be. Thought you might want somebody to talk to before the meeting." Jamieson paused, then turned back toward the awakening city below. There was no response.

"Or I could go work in my office for half an hour." Jamieson was treading lightly, trying to get a handle on just how serious the problem was. Still, Arlen was silent. So he turned away from the glass and headed for the door. "Okay. See you in 30 minutes," he said with a brief wave.

As he opened the door, Jamieson looked back at the CEO. "Susan's here. Do you want some more coffee?" Susan O'Reilly, Arlen's secretary of 10 years, entered tentatively, her eyebrows rising at seeing Jamieson there. She nodded at him.

"Good morning," she said cautiously. Moving closer to Arlen's desk, she asked, "What do I need to do for the meeting?"

Arlen looked at Jamieson, but spoke to his secretary. "Just make sure all my appointments are cancelled and that there's plenty of coffee. And," he added, breaking off a half smile, "enough hemlock to go around."

Pivoting toward O'Reilly, Arlen missed the look of concern on Jamieson's face. She nodded and turned to go. Jamieson followed her to the door, grabbing the door handle to pull it closed behind him. Arlen's voice stopped him.

"Rick, wait a minute. Close the door and pull up a chair." He gestured to the conference area, got up from his desk, walked to the sofa and sat down. Jamieson quickly moved to the chair on Arlen's right, plopped down and leaned back expectantly.

"You're right. It is about to hit the fan big time. And it won't be pretty. I got a preliminary report late yesterday afternoon from the forensic auditors I brought in a few weeks ago." He stopped, unconsciously removing the cufflink from his left sleeve, his eyes remaining on Jamieson.

"Our books have been cooked." Arlen allowed the words to hang unexplained for a few seconds. "Fried is more like it," he added. "Maybe for several years. The full story's still being dug up, but it looks like we've over-reported several million dollars, at a minimum."

Jamieson sat up slowly, locking onto Arlen's cold stare. His playful demeanor had dissolved. He tried to whistle, but only silent air came out. "God help us," he muttered inaudibly.

Arlen's voice was calm, but filled with purpose. "The auditor isn't sure yet how widespread it is. But it looks like we've been unknowingly releasing phony financial information for the last two years or so." He tossed the cufflink from one hand to the other, sighing deeply. "If we don't handle this thing right, we'll be history before we realize what hit us."

* * * * * * * * * *

Hearing his own ominous words, Arlen was reminded of how much Royal—and he—had changed since he became CEO. Under his leadership, Royal Accommodations, a struggling, upstart enterprise with properties in 10 states when he took over as chief, had grown into one of the major players in the domestic hotel market. Today, the company operated upscale lodging facilities in 25 states, including Hawaii and Puerto Rico. During its growth spurt a few years back, the workforce doubled in size to around 63,000 employees.

Arlen felt enormous pride in Royal's hard-earned reputation as the "Mercedes-Benz" of the industry. For years, most Royal employees considered it a feather in their caps to have the Royal name on their resumes. During Arlen's initial four years at the top, the company opened new properties at a dramatic rate. To operate all these new hotels, young, inexperienced managers had been recruited, promoted, and transferred throughout the system at a furious pace.

During the late 1980s and early 1990s, however, the hotel industry suffered as the economy nosedived. Not only did Royal's expansion plans run into a brick wall, but occupancy rates and restaurant sales at existing properties plunged. Several resort hotels had to be sold or closed; for the first time in its history, Royal had to lay off employees at several sites, an act with enough symbolism to crush morale.

During the past two years, Arlen had yearned to rekindle the growth and sense of excitement Royal had lost. But as the economy continued to lag and business people pared back travel and off-site meetings, he'd been forced to freeze all new construction and initiate austerity programs across the company. He no longer thought in growth terms, merely survival terms. He suspended all pay raises and bonuses. Yet, compared to hotel chains of similar size, Royal was holding on better than most.

Strangely enough, it was during this dark period that Arlen first saw the company in a new light. It happened about 20 months ago, just after costs had been slashed and every expendable employee laid off at the 500-room Royal Surf Hotel in Maui, the hottest resort in the world a year earlier. But even after all the cuts, the property continued to lose money. Morale was alarmingly low; people were depressed, worried, and without hope. He didn't know what else to do. He'd voiced his frustration with the situation to Joyce Hadley, Royal's personnel manager, during lunch one day.

"Stop worrying only about the numbers and concentrate more on making our people comfortable and happy," she told him. "If they lose faith in the company," she insisted, "then we've really lost it all."

Although he didn't fully grasp the implications of her observation, the thought stuck with him for weeks after. It made inherently good sense to him when separated from everything else. Only, since nothing in business can ever be completely separate, he remained skeptical. Nevertheless, he agreed to experiment with some quality of worklife programs that claimed to revive workers' motivation. Early results were mildly encouraging, although inconclusive. Now he feared that the financial reporting fiasco would destroy his hopes of being able to start closing the psychological gap dividing managers and employees.

Coincidentally, at about that time and almost as if planned, Jamieson began pressing Arlen to get more personally involved in communicating with Royal's key constituencies, especially employees. He argued that the mystique of executive management as all-knowing and all-powerful was no longer. "You can't hide behind your desk anymore, Arlen. People today won't tolerate faceless executives they don't know and never see," Jamieson had told the doubting CEO last year when he resisted making a

Christmas videotape for workers on Royal's deteriorating business climate.

With Jamieson's and Hadley's words echoing in the far reaches of his mind, Arlen occasionally admitted to himself that the "employee experiment"—at least, he'd always thought of it in those terms—had fascinated the creative side of him. By no means was he a full-fledged believer in the value of the so-called "human" factor; nonetheless, Arlen's thinking had started to shift and he wasn't fighting it as he had in the past.

His subtle change in attitude emerged in real terms during a visit to Royal's downtown hotel in Atlanta a few months before. Arriving in late afternoon, he took off on an unannounced stroll through the property. When he wandered into the main kitchen, he found it in chaos: people screaming at each other and customers being ignored. The lead cook scheduled to work the night shift had just called in sick and nobody could find the restaurant manager to figure out what to do. His curiosity engaged, Arlen stepped in and offered to help, not identifying himself as the CEO. Then, in the whirl of conversations that followed, he somehow ended up wearing an apron and rubber gloves, working through a pile of dirty dishes. The regular dishwasher, a young Latino who'd been waiting for just such a chance to show-off his culinary talents, had talked Arlen into taking over his job while he did the cooking. Almost two hours passed before Arlen's relief arrived in the form of an embarrassed and apologetic general manager summoned from home by a perceptive assistant manager who recognized the CEO. Word of the top manager's escapade spread across the company like a runaway train.

For months after the incident, Arlen delighted in retelling the story, wholly unaware of his tendency to embellish the details. Ever since, he'd occasionally caught himself wondering whether the real power in a hotel company rested with those working the grills and check-in counters or with those holding meetings and shuffling papers in the executive suites and boardrooms.

* * * * * * * * * *

The phone startled Arlen, abruptly cutting off his daydreaming. He waited a few more rings before getting up and moving back to his desk. It was his private line, which only rang on his desk phone.

"Yes?" He paused while the message was relayed. "No, that's okay." Arlen put his hand over the mouthpiece, looked at Jamieson and said, "It's my wife." He went back to the phone. "Tell her I'm fine and I'll call her back after I meet with Stamps." He hung up.

"The vampires from the media are going to suck us dry on this one," blurted an agitated Jamieson. He jerked himself up from the chair and peered directly at the CEO. "How could this happen, Arlen? Our competitors will be dancing in the streets when they hear about this." Jamieson perched himself on the corner of Arlen's desk. He was universally liked, in large part for his even-tempered disposition and engaging informality. His ebbing anger was a subtle warning to Arlen of things to come.

"Wait a minute, Rick," Arlen said sharply, holding up both hands to stop him. "First things first. Before we worry about the press, we've got to figure out how bad it is, what's really going on, and what we can do about it. I want to be ahead of the press and everybody else on this thing. We can't undo what's happened, but we can sure as hell get our own house in order ASAP and make the best of a bad situation. That's your job. At this moment, only you, I, and the chairman know about this. At least I hope that's true."

Arlen's combative streak had been unintentionally goaded by Jamieson. Royal's top manager, like most key executives, lived for such career-making—or career-destroying—challenges, although he'd be hard pressed to ever admit it.

"And what about the ... what'd you call them? ... the *forensic* auditors you mentioned?" Jamieson queried. "What's that all about? Who's involved in this thing? How bad does it look?" Without any prompting, the investigative reporter lurking in Jamieson often reappeared at times like now.

"Well, it started as a bunch of small things that by themselves didn't mean anything," explained Arlen, "but over time they started to add up. For instance, earlier this year, my friend Barry Lewis attended a three-day conference at our Cincinnati hotel. When he got back, he kidded me about the restaurants there being out of both lobster and chicken. Then a couple of months ago, when I was going through several month's worth of customer response cards, I spotted a number of complaints by folks who couldn't get Chivas Regal, a big profit item, at our bars in Chicago and Milwaukee. Something smelled fishy, but I couldn't put my finger on what."

He paused, got up and drifted back to the glass wall. Jamieson swiveled in his chair to keep Arlen in sight.

"And remember the results of this summer's employee opinion survey? The unusually high negative ratings of managers at properties in the Midwest region? Those strange, almost cryptic comments about how supervisory managers were blind to what was happening right under their noses? We—I should say I—didn't take the time to follow-up." Jamieson's mind was racing ahead of Arlen's story, already anticipating questions the media would ask.

"The region's profit margin was better than most, which isn't saying much, yet in spite of that, the Midwest employees were the unhappiest in the company. I thought Keller had already talked to the regional manager and some of the general managers about what was going on. He assured me a month ago he'd investigate and find out."

Arlen's cufflink slipped from his hand and fell to the thick carpet, hardly making a sound. He bent and picked it up without missing a beat in his narration.

"Two weeks ago, I was hit by what an employee at our St. Louis property said in a transcript from one of the telephone hotline tapes. Unfortunately, by then, it was two weeks old. The comment was that thousands of dollars in inventory were missing and nobody was doing anything about it. Items that showed up on inventory lists were nowhere to be found when customers ordered them. Then I had Susan pull the customer response cards from the region for the past six months. And guess what? She found a string of similar comments so we went back a year and found even more."

Arlen started shaking his hands briskly, as if he were trying to awaken them. When he spoke, his irritation was evident in the rising pitch of his voice. "So I called some managers around the region. They told me they'd look into it and get back to me. I ended up having to call each of them back. They were stonewalling me. I called some of my old friends in the region—off the record, of course. Folks I worked with after I got here. Most I hired. While nobody had any proof, many sounded like they thought something was rotten in the system. But they didn't, or wouldn't, say anything concrete. It's what they didn't say that made me most suspicious, if y'know what I mean." Jamieson's eyes narrowed as a clearer picture of the crisis began to take shape.

"Keller and Grubner kept telling me not to worry. But damn it, I didn't like what my gut was telling me. I had to find out. I thought about asking our internal audit staff to investigate. But I couldn't be sure some of them weren't involved, so I contacted a CPA firm specializing in fraud investigations to check things out. I wanted an independent source just in case this eventually went public. They poked around and it looks like ...'"

A loud rap on the door stopped Arlen. Before he could move to get up, it opened and Michael Keller, wiry and trim from years of marathon running, leaned in. Arlen's and Jamieson's heads turned in unison.

"Well, I made it," he said, his strong bass voice breaking the silence his intrusion had caused. "Susan didn't catch up with me until 10 last night.

I was getting ready for bed—in downtown Los Angeles. And wham! Before I knew what hit me, here I am back in Manhattan. The wonders of modern transportation. Tell me, what'd we do, declare all-out war on Marriott?" The VP of operations' out-of-character attempt at humor failed to amuse either Arlen or Jamieson. After almost 30 years with Royal, where he started as a manager-trainee in Philadelphia, Keller was best known for his no-nonsense style and total lack of any sense of humor. No one, however, questioned his shrewdness when it came to organizational politics.

"Isn't Susan outside?" Arlen snapped, making no attempt to mask his annoyance.

"No, she's not there," Keller said. His dark, hawk-like eyes instantly surveyed the room. As usual, his wavy, greying hair was combed straight back, not a strand out of place. Keller knew his carefully conceived interruption wasn't appreciated, but he acted as though he didn't care.

Arlen walked over to Keller, blocking his entrance to the office. The CEO squared up and faced the taller man, only a few inches separating their faces.

"By the way, Mike, what's taking so long on getting back to me on the problems in the Midwest region?" Arlen queried, a tone of suspicion oozing into his voice.

"I'm working on it. I've been asking around and should have something soon." Keller waited for a complaint, an objection, an instruction—but none came. Using silence to induce information was a technique Arlen used frequently. It made people uncomfortable and Keller was no exception. "I'll probably have something next week," he offered quickly, then paused briefly to ponder his next words. "As a matter of fact, I was scheduled to be in Chicago today to nose around."

Arlen waited a moment, closely studying the crafty VP, considered by insiders to be the second most powerful figure at Royal. "I need it yesterday, Mike, but no later than 48 hours from now," Arlen ordered. Keller nodded and then looked at Jamieson for a hint about what was going on. None came.

"Why don't you two head to the conference room. I'll be there in a minute," Arlen said, starting to close the door. With that cue, Jamieson got up and headed for the door. Keller turned and slid out of the office, stopping long enough for Jamieson to catch up.

As he slipped on his suit jacket, Arlen faintly heard Keller ask, "What's up, Rick?"

* * * * * * * * * *

Arlen returned to his desk chair to collect his thoughts before encountering his staff. Leaning back, his eye wandered to the black and white photograph of his son that occupied the right-hand corner of his desk. It had been taken a year earlier at Glenn's graduation from the University of Miami in Florida, the last time they'd been together.

Arlen hated how strained their relationship had become. A relationship, he knew, made worse by his long hours and heavy travel. The latest issue they were at odds over was Glenn's intention to pursue a graduate degree in marine biology. A degree which Arlen thought useless in the real world of mortgages and car payments. And, of course, the more Arlen expressed his feelings, the more Glenn dug in his heels.

Arlen had always envisioned Glenn following in his footsteps. Glenn, on the other hand, wanted nothing to do with what he saw as his father's compulsion for authority and money. And Arlen made no secret of his disappointment with Glenn's career choice. As a result, communication between father and son had become superficial and often rancorous. They spoke by phone every so often, but it was mostly small talk about nothing important to either of them.

The irony of Arlen's inability to relate to Glenn, he realized, was that in his business life he'd begun to appreciate the value of candid, gut-level communication. But that new-found appreciation didn't seem to be helping him much with his son.

O'Reilly opened the door and announced softly, "It's time. Everybody's there." Arlen grabbed his notes and legal pad from his desk, and followed her out of the room. He felt both anxious and excited all at once, creating in him an eery sense of anticipation that had a faintly familiar feeling to it. He didn't know why, though. Then, without trying or any warning, Arlen's memory shot back to the precise moment 30 years ago when he last felt this way. Suddenly, it seemed like it was just yesterday.

It was during the NCAA baseball regional finals. He was the starting third baseman for the University of Virginia, which had never made it to the college world series. It was the bottom of the eighth inning, one out, bases loaded, and UVA trailing by a run. Arlen stood in the batter's box, nervous and exhilarated with his chance to be a hero, to make history, to catapult his team to glory. Then, to his utter disbelief, the third base coach flashed him the take sign—don't swing. Don't swing? It had to be a mistake! Heroes don't keep the bat on their shoulders when their moment arrives, he screamed silently. He doesn't really remember deciding to defy his coach, only that at the time he was certain everyone would later thank him for following his own mind.

Whenever he recalls the moment, which he does all too frequently, he can still see the downward spin on the sinking curve ball. He was sure he'd get a fastball. He realized his mistake too late. Fooled and badly off-balance, he dribbled the ball to the pitcher who started an easy double play, ending UVA's chance to reach the promised land. Instead of the years soothing his pain, it had grown worse over time. Ever since, he has desperately wanted a second chance, and his nerve endings were telling him this might be it.

Here he was again—facing a crucially important situation affecting many people he cared deeply about with the outcome riding on his performance. He cringed at the thought. Taking a deep breath to steady himself, he felt an adrenalin rush kick in as he headed to the conference room to take another turn at bat—for maybe the last time.

1

Being a CEO "Ain't" What It Used to Be

Many people today—in and out of business—are fascinated with the power, wealth, and glamour attached to chief executive officers, the CEOs of modern society. More and more young people aspire to become the powerful "top dogs" of corporate America, shunning the more traditional dream jobs like heart surgeon, U.S. president, movie star, or sports hero. A *Wall Street Journal* "Pepper ... and Salt" cartoon effectively captured this emerging fixation. A well-dressed, clean-shaven young man is seated across a large desk from a senior, mustached, balding personnel consultant who has asked the job applicant about his long-range career goals. Gesturing emphatically as he leans forward, the young man says with obvious pride, "Eventually, I'd like to get into *CEOing.*" Indeed, many managers dream of little else, according to a recent *Exec* magazine survey of 1500 lower and middle managers' on-the-job day-dreaming habits; three out of four admitted fantasizing daily about being the CEO of their company.[1]

What so many entry-level and future top managers today don't understand—like the young man in the cartoon—is that being a CEO isn't like they think it is, or what it used to be. But then, neither is the workplace nor the people in it.

Customers aren't what they used to be: They expect value-added service constantly or they'll run to a competitor. Employees aren't what they used to be: They're struggling to balance job and home life demands, and they're disillusioned with top managers who don't treat them as co-equals. Boards of directors aren't what they used to be: They're holding CEOs personally accountable for organizational performance and not hesitating to fire them if they don't deliver. Stockholders aren't what they used to be: They're more vocal and aggressive in trying to change managements that don't listen and respond to them. The competition isn't what it used to be: It's more global in scope and more cutthroat in style as companies scramble to capture greater market share. Even the media aren't what they used to be: They're more vigilant and critical in covering business, and they're demanding greater access to the CEO and other top managers.

With so many changes in motion, being a CEO "ain't" what it used to be either. And that's the focus of this book: to offer suggestions on how CEOs can modify their management and leadership styles to best operate in today's dynamic business environment. Our theme is that the CEO's communication role, particularly as it affects employees, has never been more crucial to corporate leadership. Regrettably, despite this fact, too many CEOs have failed to adapt their thinking and behavior to the diverse and demanding stakeholders whose support organizations desperately need. To adjust, CEOs need to be more sensitive to the complexities driving human behavior, and become more comfortable and skilled as communicators. *In a word, this book investigates the CEO's fast-changing communication role and examines what this new role means to the CEO's effectiveness as an organizational leader.*

In large measure, the book springs from the results of two nationwide studies of *Fortune* 500 chiefs supplemented by interviews with 25 CEOs of some of America's leading companies on how they view and practice their communication role. While the bulk of the findings are presented in Chap. 4, our analysis of the research results and their meaning appears throughout all nine chapters. In this opening chapter, we briefly discuss the key issues related to the CEO-as-communicator, each of which is treated more extensively in later chapters. The last section of this chapter tells the behind-the-scenes story of how Jim Verney of Winchell's Donut House used communication and human relations strategies to turn a loser into a winner.

The CEO's Roles Are Many and Varied

Top Executives Are Under Fire

CEOs used to be chosen for their ability to control, to organize, to plan, to give the right orders—in essence, to direct and manage everything and everybody. That approach worked quite well for a long time. But as times and people changed, the CEO's function began to subtly shift from one of day-to-day management to one demanding more direction-setting leadership. At the root of the trend, yet somewhat obscured, is a call for CEOs who understand the intricacies and nuances of human nature, and who know how to effectively use the communication process to reach and motivate people.

Enlightened CEOs realize that they must adapt their management styles to employees' and other stakeholders' increasingly critical perceptions of them. No longer is it acceptable for top managers to merely go through the half-hearted motions so as to appear that they care about establishing "meaningful" relationships with workers when they really don't. Employees will see through it and resent it. If workers don't believe and don't trust upper management, which is often the case today, then employee-management relationships will be tenuous, adversarial, and filled with suspicion. Employees' perceptions of upper-level executives can significantly influence employees' attitudes toward management and their work, as well as their loyalty and productivity. These topics are explored in Chap. 2.

One persistent source of employees' resentment of top executives is CEOs' skyrocketing annual salaries and fringe benefits packages. Top executives of America's largest companies take home on average around $650,000 a year, about 35 times more than the typical production worker and 20 times more than the average middle manager. And while the average American worker's pay increases by about 5 percent a year, top managers' salaries (not including incentives) grow by about 10 percent. Such striking pay differences have fueled many employees' suspicions of CEOs' and other top managers' real motives, aggravating the "us vs. them" mentality that can drive a productivity-stifling wedge between labor and management. "It's a motivational issue" that may threaten top executives' "ability to effectively lead the troops," says Ed Lawler, director of the Center for Effective Organizations at the University of Southern California.[2]

Responding to the public's soaring outcry against top executives' perceived hoggish pay packages and corporations' unwillingness to set any curbs, Congress passed new tax legislation limiting corporate deductions of a top manager's compensation to no more than $1 million, beginning in 1994. Such a loss in tax deductions can put a dent in a company's after-tax cash flow, especially if it means forfeiting deductions on several million dollars. The law, which has sent corporate tax attorneys scurrying to discover loopholes, applies the compensation cap unless pay is based on so-called "performance" criteria created by a committee of independent directors and approved by stockholders. While some organizations, like Microsoft, Quaker Oats, and Delta Airlines, have already won shareholder support for restructured performance-linked stock option plans for their top-rung managers, the message from Congress is incontrovertible: "Corporations, you'd better justify and control your top executives' compensation or we'll do it for you."

CEOs are perceived by some employees and business observers as willing to do almost anything—from justifying bad decisions to manipulating financial results—to earn jumbo bonuses and potentially lucrative stock options.[3] They're seen as thinking about themselves first and their employees and organizations second and third. Former University of Cincinnati President Warren Bennis, now a business professor at the University of Southern California, explains how many CEOs' priorities are shifting—and not necessarily for the better:

There was a time when CEOs were civic leaders and corporate statesmen. Today, they have no interest in anything but their own bottom lines ... American businessmen never had many moral imperatives, but they did feel some obligation to their employees, the towns they operated in, and the national economy. That's no longer true.[4]

Skeptical views of CEOs—like those held by the townspeople in the movie *Roger and Me* about General Motors' then CEO Roger Smith closing a plant in a small town in Michigan—can sabotage corporate leaders' plans to build committed, productive workforces. Traditional ways of relating to employees, customers, and stockholders often don't work in today's environment. Key constituencies are demanding a role, a voice, a chance to influence the kind of association they have with the people at the top.

As never before, CEOs find themselves under the harsh light of public scrutiny, making them vulnerable to criticisms that only a few years ago would've been considered corporate sacrilege. Although the glamour, wealth, and power are still there, the risks of sitting in the top dog's chair have increased several fold since the late 1980s. The darker side of CEO life is the rising susceptibility of being directly challenged by strident, organized groups of stockholders, boards of directors, consumer activists, and employees. Such challenges are no longer just possibilities, but probabilities. Distraught stakeholders are no longer content to merely express their dissatisfaction; they're ousting chief executives they believe haven't effectively represented their group's interests and/or the organization's overall best interests.

This trend was never more evident than during an extraordinary two-week period in early 1993 when a handful of chiefs of some of America's elite companies fell from grace like a row of teetering dominoes: James Robinson at American Express; John Akers at IBM; Paul Lego at Westinghouse Electric; Robert Stempel at General Motors; and Paul Kazarian at Sunbeam-Oster. This string of downfalls reflects a trend on the rise. Recent times have seen increasing numbers of CEOs banished from their executive suites at mighty corporations like Digital Equipment, Compaq Computer, Tenneco, Kodak, Time Warner, and Goodyear.

While each scenario is unique, underlying each top executive's demise was the failure to maintain a trusting relationship with one or more vital stakeholder groups. For instance, Paul Kazarian, the 37-year-old CEO of Sunbeam-Oster, was given a pink slip without any warning by the board only two weeks after receiving a bonus for his performance in leading the company's financial recovery. The reason? The board was lobbied hard by senior managers who threatened mass defections because they claimed that Kazarian, possessed of an intense work ethic, had for over a year demanded that they work unreasonably long hours seven days a week. Ironically, Kazarian's remedy to the company's economic woes became the instrument of his own destruction.

In the case of IBM, the toppling of long-time CEO John Akers appeared to have been rooted in the concerted efforts by exasperated, powerful stockholders, most notably institutional pension funds, who got fed up with the company's dwindling profits and market share. Ultimately, these giant stockholders harnessed so much direct pressure on IBM's board to bring in fresh leadership that the board was forced to dump Akers or risk a mass exodus of some of its largest stockholders.

At American Express, CEO James Robinson, touted for his brilliant stewardship of Amex's string of successes during the 1980s, faced a disillusioned board in early 1993 as the company's returns and stock price languished. Stockholders and Wall Street loudly voiced concern. Then, just when it appeared that Robinson would retire, thereby paving the way for a changing of the guard, he somehow convinced the board to bump him up to chairman and insert his personal choice for successor, Harvey Golub. This somewhat bizarre move provoked an instant wave of anger by disenchanted institutional stockholders and critical business media, who lashed out at the board for its lack of backbone. Within days, the vicious media barrage became too much for Amex to handle, so the board, populated by a number of former *Fortune* 500 CEOs, forced Robinson to clear out his desk.

Clearly, the CEO's role today is undergoing some dramatic and traumatic transformations. This rage, which we expect will intensify, suggests that the bloom may be off the CEO rose. The rewards, both tangible and intangible, and the lure of being a top dog are greater than ever, but so are the risks, especially if a company's bottom-line falters or if a CEO loses the backing of a principal constituency. Chiefs are in for a rough ride if they aren't able to change their many hats easily and frequently.

CEOs Must Be "Jacks of All Trades ..."

Over the past 30 years, the job of chief executive officer has simultaneously broadened in scope and increased in complexity. CEOs today need to be a blend of tough, get-it-done, bottom-line manager, and accessible, sensitive, inspiring leader—what *Business Week* has called a "compassionate tyrant."[5] The contemporary CEO is expected to have experience and expertise in multiple technical areas and handle a variety of different and sometimes conflicting roles: lawyer, lobbyist, accountant, public advocate, strategist, policymaker, conscience, economist, psychologist, administrator, futurist, politician, communicator, leader.

Finding individuals with the right blend of experiences and skills who can handle the multirole job of CEO can be an exercise in futility. The best CEOs may be strong in one or two, perhaps three, of the specialty areas, but never in all. Yet a "master of all trades" is what most boards, stockholders, and employees expect in a top executive today. Faced with the pressures of trying to be a corporate superman, many CEOs don't last in the job more than a few years before the organization becomes disillusioned with them or they become disillusioned with the job. Unless a CEO happens to be the company's founder—like Sam Walton of Wal-Mart who headed his company for almost 45 years until his death in 1992—or is the offspring of the founder—like a J. Willard Marriott Jr. of Marriott Corporation who took over from his father—CEO longevity has become as rare as four consecutive profitable quarters.

The swelling pressures on CEOs and their anticipated limited tenure in the position may help explain why top executives are demanding big compensation packages and laundry lists of expensive perks. With so much on the line and all the heat on them, many top dogs believe they deserve and earn every penny they get. Many employees are less convinced, however. This same "get it while you can" mentality is shared by other "short-timer" professionals, such as NFL players whose careers average about five years.

Life in the executive suite has changed slowly, methodically, inevitably, and with little fanfare. In fact, so gradually have these changes occurred that many inhabitants of the "big" office, including our fictional CEO Arlen Royster, never even noticed that life at the top "ain't" what it used to be. To grow and prosper, contemporary breeds of top dogs should be more responsive, collaborative, visible, inspirational, and communicative than their predecessors—and less authoritarian, isolated, secretive, rigid, and formal.

Old-line CEOs believed in the bottom-line, first, last, and always. New-line CEOs appreciate the bottom-line too, but they also recognize the hidden value of human resources. Modern-day chiefs are increasingly accepting of the notion that managing people's self-fulfillment is critical to business success. In many ways, contemporary "CEOing" represents a fundamental shift away from what *Fortune*'s Frank Rose calls "the old paradigm that numbers are all-important, that professional managers can handle any enterprise, that control can and should be held at the top." The contemporary paradigm, says Rose, "puts people—customers and employees—at the center of the universe and replaces the rigid hierarchies of the industrial age with a network that emphasizes interconnectedness."[6]

Today's CEO icons—like Iacocca, Trump, Morita, Perot, Ueberroth, Welch, Walton, Sigoloff, Clausen, Pickens, and Sculley—are more than just glorified green eyeshades dedicated to making money. They are powerful, influential, and enormously wealthy public figures who are, as *Business Week* noted in a cover story titled "The New Corporate Elite," beginning to "translate their personal wealth into public power ... moving outside their corporate cocoons into politics, education, and the arts. They are beginning to create their own style, serve as role models, take charge of the nation's institutions, and then set the agenda for the future."[7]

This phenomenon of CEO as emerging public figure was never more apparent than in the 1992 presidential campaign with the boisterous arrival of businessman Ross Perot on the national political scene. His acceptance by the American public as a legitimate presidential contender may have struck down the long-held belief that business executives are unworthy as candidates for America's top management job. Perot's visibility and outspokenness, plus his brash "can do" brand of rhetoric and natural charisma, opened many eyes to the prospect of business leaders serving as political leaders. His capturing of almost 20 percent of the popular vote may represent a dramatic shift in Americans' perceptions of CEOs as presidential material. With this apparent breakthrough, more chiefs of corporate America may soon come knocking on the White House door.

The business leaders of tomorrow will, as a routine matter, be expected to change personalities and hats at a moment's notice. The range of roles is already varied and demanding: business manager, book author, media personality, charity fundraiser, advertising pitchman, speechmaker, public advocate, and folk hero, to name just a few. That's asking much, maybe too much, of one person.

The CEO as Communicator-Leader

The nature and scope of the CEO's new leadership role are still evolving. Nevertheless, one fact is undeniable: The CEO's role is changing to one with increasing and more demanding communication and human relations responsibilities. This has been true concerning external stakeholders for some time now. Less obvious, however, is that CEOs today have an equally important responsibility to forge lasting relationships with internal groups. Employees have long asked—sometimes loudly and insistently—to receive more information directly from and to have a closer relationship with top-level managers, particularly the CEO. They're still asking today.

For too long at many U.S. companies, the chief executive officer has been a well-kept secret. The traditional perception of the CEO is that most of his (only one percent are women) time is spent tucked away in a spacious executive suite, poring over profit and loss statements. And then when he makes a decision, he *may* pass down an edict to other managers and employees in an awkwardly worded memo or secret meeting with his vice presidents. An exaggeration? Somewhat, maybe. Yet few business watchers would argue that such a perception doesn't persist today.

Those who fail to adapt their philosophy and style to the new business environment risk alienating the very groups that they most need to survive and prosper. To be sure, adopting a new approach to managing and leading is far easier to talk about than do.

CEO Communication Can Make a Big Difference

The implications of the top manager's new, expanded communication role are far-reaching, substantial, and touch all aspects of business. One such implication, which hits at the center of any relationship, is mutual trust. The division between upper management and line employees has created a widening and potentially debilitating "trust gap," writes *Fortune*'s Alan Farnham. This gulf, he argues, has developed because senior managers have turned a stone ear to employees' concerns and changing values.[8] Unless this worrisome situation is transformed soon, the long-term damage to manager-employee relationships could become irreparable.

A battery of recent studies by a host of management consulting firms reveals an alarming split "between what employees really want and what top management thinks they want," reports Farnham. The reason? Because senior executives, many who still cling to archaic management traditions, assume that today's employees are motivated by the same financial and job security needs as workers of 30 years ago. Not true. The solution? To begin closing the "trust gap," maintains Farnham, management must show respect for and recognize contributions by employees through "closer, more honest communication between employees and senior management."

Another implication of this rift is the CEO's ability—or as is more often the case, inability—to sound a drumbeat that all employees can hear, understand, and want to follow. Traumatic upheavals throughout the business world have triggered feelings of instability, insecurity, and uncertainty among workers about their work and personal lives. The swelling turbulence of the marketplace—set off by the continuing wave of restructurings, mergers, acquisitions, downsizings, buy outs, and bankruptcies—has turned employees' attitudes toward work and upper management inside out. Many feel lost, adrift, searching for a way to stabilize their topsy-turvy world. To fill this void, workers are looking to their leaders—the CEOs—to interpret what these unsettling times mean to their organizations and, most importantly, to their careers and families.

A third and perhaps the most compelling implication is that the CEO's communication activities do affect organizations' bottom-lines. That's what employees and CEOs themselves believe, according to surveys of more than 300 top executives completed for this book (discussed in greater depth in Chap. 4).[9] CEOs who don't accept the challenge of leading their organizations' communication efforts may eventually pay a steep price, believes Walter Williams, CEO of Bethlehem Steel. During an interview in his Pennsylvania office, he pointed out that carefully designed and executed communication can impact companies where it really counts: "When you have a good communication program going and you're really making an effort, you can see morale improve, you can see part of the business improve, you can see labor relations grievances go down and so forth. So you can measure to an extent what effect it has on the bottom line." But Williams, who resuscitated a dying company, also cautions that "communication is a constant effort. It's not a one-shot deal. It's a constant battle. It's still an unusual change for the organization. Not only the fact that the CEO believes in communication, but that all managers should believe in it. And it won't work if they don't."

Some CEO Eyes Are Opening, But Not Enough

These days, far more talk can be heard about the CEO's communication obligations than ever before. Some top managers have begun speaking out about how the communication components of the job influence the CEO's and the organization's effectiveness. For instance, Irving Shapiro, former CEO of DuPont, puts this influence into perspective: "A CEO is first and foremost in the human relations and communication businesses ... No other item on the chief executive's duty list has more leverage on the organization's prospects."[10] Retired GM Chairman Roger Smith suggests that communication "should be treated with as much thoughtful planning and attention to detail as quality, finance, engineering, and manufacturing."[11] And Harold Burson, former head of one of the largest public relations agencies in the world and a long-time counselor to CEOs, summarizes why communication has become so essential to the head honcho: "The communication process has become recognized by the CEO as absolutely critical to the accomplishment of his mission."[12]

Many CEOs remain blinded to the forces transforming the business landscape. Too many are unaware of their shifting responsibilities as "participative" managers, a focus of Chap. 2, and too many are unprepared and inadequately trained to play the role, explored in Chap. 9. CEOs of the 1990s must be more sensitive, responsive, and communication competent than were the top dogs of prior generations. Altered expectations by employees, stockholders, customers, and media make these characteristics mandatory. "Today CEOs are prime targets for anything from ambush media interviews to public floggings by shareholders to surly behavior from mutinous employees," writes Cliff McGoon, former editor of *Communication World*, a leading public relations trade journal. "The CEO's success or failure—as never before—depends on effective communication. And most are botching the job."[13] To most CEOs who entered the business world 20 to 30 years ago, this communication "stuff" is new and strange, much like a foreign language. Their business education never prepared or warned them about this part of the job. And because it is unfamiliar to them, they avoid communicating as much as possible, hoping it will either just go away or somebody else will do it. But that just won't do any more. Modern CEOs had better incorporate the communication "stuff" into their repertoires or they may not be around long enough to experience the other facets of the job.

A relatively small number of CEOs understand the top dog's "new" role and even fewer actually know how to play it. One CEO who appreciates the long journey ahead is Bill Davila, former president and CEO of Vons, a large grocery chain based in the Los Angeles area. "In the last 10 years, we've become much more interested in communicating with our employees," he said during an interview at Vons headquarters. "On a scale of 1-to-10, we're probably a 4. We're doing a lot, but have much more that we can do. I don't feel bad about that. I'd rather be at a 4 going to 10 than a 9 going to 10. We've got a tremendous opportunity."

The CEO's communication role doesn't exist in isolation of other aspects of the job; indeed, a close and influential relationship exists between a top manager's communication capabilities and leadership effectiveness—a key point analyzed in Chap. 3. The CEO holds the ultimate communication responsibility for clarifying in simple, understandable terms what makes an organization special, where it's going, why it's important to go there, and how people can help get it there. Central to the theme of this book is the need for CEOs to understand the vital communication-leadership linkage— because we believe it holds a large part of the solution to attaining long-term organizational success.

Too Many "Dinosaurs" Still Roam the Marketplace

Many popular business books, like the best-selling *In Search of Excellence*, focus on examples of how the "best" organizations do things. Unfortunately, such books can unintentionally create false impressions that a handful of glowingly positive examples are the norm. That's a danger we faced in writing this book. Highlighting only the most successful CEOs who happen to possess a flare for their communication role could create the inaccurate generalization that all CEOs are that way. Truthfully, many CEOs and other top managers remain stuck in prehistoric times when it comes to developing relationships, which is the name of the game today.

Underlying all our ideas and arguments is a core point we can't stress enough: *The CEO must earn employees' and other prime stakeholders' confidence and trust before any meaningful long-term relationships can be established.* That's exactly the challenge facing CEO Arlen Royster as he battles to protect Royal Accommodations' fragile position in the marketplace during the hotel company's crisis. More than that, though, Arlen must try to hold on to the support of Royal's major stakeholders—for they are his key to maintaining his own leadership position.

How can CEOs best build such relationships? The key is open and candid two-way communication, initiated by and involving the CEO. Binding relationships grow out of loyalty, a feeling of belonging, and a sense of sharing in making the future better. In discussing his arrival at Gerber Products as president and his ascension to CEO eight months later, Al Pergallini has come to appreciate the vital importance of CEO-employee communication in enhancing corporate loyalty. "The key is communication—making people understand exactly what you want them to do and when you want them to do it," he said after nine months as CEO.[14]

Employees today expect their CEOs—not their immediate supervisors—to be the trailblazers, leading the way and participating personally in shaping the future. "People are looking for a definition of what it is they're being asked to do, what the corporation's doing and where the corporation's going," explained Carl Sardegna, president of Blue Cross/Blue Shield of Maryland, during an interview in his suburban Baltimore office. "I and other people in top management become the focal point for that kind of definition."

The CEO's words and communication style slice deep into the hearts and minds of employees. Depending on employees' reactions to the CEO's performance, the effects may be positive or negative—but everything the CEO says or does will be noticed, discussed, and evaluated. "I've made dumb policies on the elevator by mistake," admits former *Los Angeles Times* Publisher and CEO Dick Schlosberg during a conversation in his office. "Someone asks me a question and I say, 'That's easy. Here's the answer.' And then I find out six months later what I said became company policy and I never even knew the issue had been teed up for me." The buck, to paraphrase Harry Truman, begins and stops with the top dog; most of what goes on in an organization can be traced back to the CEO's decisions and communication.

Unfortunately, many current CEOs resemble their ancestors of the 1940s and 1950s who preferred to hide behind closed doors rather than get out and press the flesh of workers, customers, and media. The result is a business world overpopulated with dinosaur-like chiefs who cling to neanderthal views of managing and communicating. On the brighter side, increasing numbers of corporate leaders are starting to catch up to the times. The pace may be frustratingly slow, but it is picking up a little steam.

A vivid example of a new guard CEO is Jim Verney of Winchell's Donut House. The story of his efforts to transform the organizational culture at Winchell's illustrates how top managers will increasingly be expected to operate, especially if they hope to win over cynical constituencies that can make or break their futures.

Jim Verney and Winchell's Donut House

The Problem—Correction, Challenge

Jim Verney had never faced a bigger challenge in his 14-year food service management career. When he became CEO of Winchell's Donut Houses in 1988, the once highly profitable 6000 employee, 700-unit chain owned by Denny's restaurant conglomerate was awash in red ink. Winchell's fortunes had tarnished in a big way. The donut giant's 3600 customers per week average in 1978 had plunged to 2200 10 years later. Revenues nosedived from $189.9 million in 1985 to $135.4 million in 1986. By 1987, the company reported an $11.5 million net loss. Winchell's major competitor, Dunkin Donuts, boasted a stock selling at $20 a share, while Winchell's sagging stock price, which had been valued at $18 in late 1986, had sunk to between $2 and $3.

Employees were worried and confused about their company's condition and future, and morale was dangerously low. The company had failed to keep up with the times and the competition, and was ripe for a buy out. So in 1987, with Winchell's net worth at a bargain basement value, TW Services, one of the nation's largest food service companies, purchased Denny's and El Pollo Loco restaurant chains, as well as 42 percent of Winchell's, thereby assuming the company's bloated debt. Within months, Carl Hass, a "numbers-oriented" manager, as Verney describes him, who had been hired as Winchell's president several months earlier, resigned just days before class-action suits were filed in federal courts against Denny's and Winchell's for alleged misleading information in the company's 1986 prospectus.

This was Winchell's dismal and deteriorating situation when, three months later, Jim Verney, former operations vice president of El Pollo Loco restaurants and engineer of the chain's skyrocketing growth from 15 to 100 units in four years, was named president and CEO of what appeared to be a sinking ship. Verney was brought in, promised Frank Salizzoni, chairman of TW Services, "to turn it around and make it a better company ... at least in the near term."

The New Approach

Verney's assessment of Winchell's problem was that management had lost touch with employees and customers, and that the once venerable industry profit leader needed a massive cultural overhaul. Organizational transformations take time and patience to accomplish, neither of which was in abundance as Winchell's reported a $6.2 million loss in the fourth quarter. Verney believed more than anything that what the company needed was to "win back customer by customer and donut house by donut house." His strategy rested on his ability as CEO to regain employees' trust in upper management. "If we don't deliver," he says, "the people will think we're pulling their chain."

The key to that strategy, says Verney, was for him and his management team to "over-communicate" the company's message to employees—that top management was committed to providing quality customer service and developing employees' self-esteem. Verney reasoned that if employees could be made to believe the new message, they would pass it on to customers.

One of his first moves was to gather together his corporate and field staffs for a major brainstorming session to redefine the company's mission and goals. From that meeting emerged a new mission statement that set the tone for the Verney program: "Winchell's will provide the best customer service and product quality, served by the friendliest employees in the cleanest donut shops in the donut bakery business, and develop pride and self-esteem in all employees." A mouthful to be sure, yet in one declarative sentence Verney captured his vision of the new Winchell's.

The mission, the product of a collective decision-making process that would mark the new CEO's style, drove all of Verney's and his team's decisions and actions. And Verney wasted no time throwing himself into his role as the leader-communicator. For instance, to make sure that nobody would lose sight of the company's redefined direction, he had the mission statement printed on laminated business cards and wall-size posters that were distributed to all restaurants. He changed some of the standard corporate language to better express his philosophy of the new Winchell's climate. He shed his formal title of CEO and replaced it with simply "leader." Employees were no longer referred to as "workers" or "employees," but "heroes," reflecting Verney's view of their role in Winchell's comeback and how he wanted them to see themselves.

To make the company's new mission less abstract and more concrete for Winchell's line employees, he broke down the ideas behind the revised mission into simple phrases. On the back of the "mission" business card and on posters was "The Winchell's Culture" redefined:

- RECOGNIZES the heroes in the donut shops
- PROMOTES equality and teamwork
- EMPHASIZES employee participation
- PROVIDES coaching for improved performance
- PROMOTES career development
- BELIEVES in a winning attitude
- STAYS honest and legal
- INSTILLS pride and self-esteem in everyone

The focus of each phrase was on Winchell's employees—oops, make that "heroes." Verney's hope was that by involving them in the comeback process, their sense of self-worth could be restored. To make some things happen quickly, Verney turned to a form of cultural "shock therapy" to coax from employees a quick, enthusiastic response that might, at a minimum, convince the new owners that his approach had merit and thus buy him and the company more time. More than that, he wanted to reincarnate the old Winchell's pride by triggering the competitive spirit that had catapulted the organization to the top of the donut industry.

The Seeds of the Verney Philosophy

Not wanting to lose any time kicking off the change process, Verney and his management team simultaneously set in motion a number of ambitious communication strategies. Key to this process was his personal and direct involvement in planning strategies, as well as implementing them. For him, playing the role of chief communicator was as natural as blinking. Blessed with an easy, disarming smile and an engaging personality, he knew he couldn't afford to be an armchair "leader" if this long-shot cultural change effort was to show meaningful results before the profit-minded new owners pulled the plug.

What separated Verney from most of his CEO counterparts facing a similar crisis situation was his long-standing belief in the power of communication to change people's beliefs and alter management-employee relationships. That belief took root in his psyche while he was an undergraduate at the University of Kentucky majoring in journalism and public relations. "It made me far more aware of my role as a communicator," says Verney, who somehow managed to complete his executive MBA at the University of Southern California while orchestrating Winchell's rebirth effort.

During several interviews, he revealed his two most influential role models: former Louisiana Governor Huey Long and super-salesman Zig Ziglar. In Long, Verney saw a leader who stayed close to his people and possessed a "communication ability to draw the masses together toward a common goal." Long's barnstorming talent in arousing a crowd's emotions captured Verney's imagination while he was a college student and still inspires him today. He frequently watches his personal videotape of the PBS documentary on Huey Long, which he says never fails to recharge his creative batteries. For the past 14 years, Verney has been motivated by the Zig Ziglar style of "taking complex, sophisticated topics and turning them into common, bite-size terms." Verney tries to emulate Ziglar's ability to tell stories and use analogies to illustrate his points, as well as Ziglar's gift for knowing "when to pause, when to speed up, when to laugh, when to cry." Verney admits that Ziglar's unique, flamboyant approach is "a little bit of theater," but, he adds immediately, "it's mostly good communication."

Empowering "Heroes"

One of Verney's deep-seated beliefs is in the value of sharing timely news and information with employees. "The good *and* the bad news," he stresses. He sees such openness between top management and workers as a precursor to employees being able to make informed and intelligent on-the-job decisions. And making decisions, Verney argues strenuously, should not be the exclusive domain of management. One of the knottiest issues he struggled with during the early days of Winchell's turnaround program was "empowering the heroes" to make decisions.

In many companies, employees want decision-making to be pushed downward; at Winchell's, however, according to Verney, "employees wanted to push decisions up. Too many people didn't want to make decisions. They just didn't seem to realize that the more decisions they make, the more highly regarded they are." Unlike many top dogs, Verney isn't squeamish about relinquishing some decision-making authority. Quite the contrary. He thinks it is "dangerous *not* to let employees make decisions." Although he readily admits feeling "some anxiety about delegating some decisions," he doesn't believe he needs to know about every one. "We have enough financial controls in place and receive sufficient weekly information on sales and customer transactions to keep us up-to-date," he adds. "The day-to-day decisions should be made by our people."

Launching the Change Process

Verney's first order of business was to get to know the people of Winchell's and solicit their ideas. To do this, he set up a series of 30 to 45 minute "two-way feedback" meetings at the corporate offices with groups of about 10 employees drawn from shops throughout southern California. He'd start by talking about his philosophy, role, and vision for the company. Then he'd ask each individual to tell him and his staff "about Winchell's pros and cons, and what they'd do to make the company better." At each of these meetings, Verney took his own notes and compiled a list of all suggestions. Then, armed with that list, he headed for the field to start meeting employees on their turf. He set up a travel schedule that took him into restaurants three days a week. He listened, he asked questions, he answered questions, he told his story when he could, and he moved among the people on the front lines. And he wasn't afraid to get his hands dirty.

On occasion, he found himself in shops during heavy traffic times and never hesitated to glaze donuts or work the cash register. "The only difference between corporate and restaurant folks is responsibility," he maintains. "We're real people, just like them. We laugh, we cry, all the same human emotions. If they see me doing what they do, hopefully I'm setting an example for them while showing them that we're more alike than different."

His operations background had sensitized him to worry more about sales and revenue than profitability, because, he explains, "If you take care of the people, the profit will follow naturally." So he made himself visible and available, spending 40 to 50 percent of his time in the field, seeking feedback, trying to rebuild management's credibility, and aggressively spreading the word of hope. Although you wouldn't necessarily detect it from Verney's hard-charging, positive demeanor, he never believed that convincing employees to trust him and his plan would be anything but an uphill battle. After all, Winchell's was unstable; it had changed presidents three times in 10 years, each one singing a different tune.

Why should Winchell's employees believe him? They were rightfully skeptical. Looking back, Verney believes that while some workers bought into the notion of the new culture from the start, most remained cautious, watching and waiting before deciding whether to commit themselves. They'd been "taken for a ride" too many times before. He was well aware that once he started down the cultural change road, there was no turning back if he was ever to be taken seriously.

Relying on the Personal Touch

The Verney approach was primarily fueled by his personal communication efforts. For instance, to recognize employees' contributions, he created a special event called "Spirit Day" during which Verney and his senior managers cooked a meal for corporate and field staff, and manufacturing people. While eating, employees were, of course, treated to hearing Verney chat about his vision of the new Winchell's.

When he was in the field, pressing the flesh and telling his tale, he tried to personalize his impact as much as possible. He believes that it's those one-on-one gestures that people remember most and are likely to share with other employees and customers. Being an amateur photographer, he carried his camera with him everywhere and didn't hesitate to grab a shot of Winchell's heroes doing their jobs, because "it makes them feel special." He'd then send a copy of the photo back to them several days later with a hand-written note saying something like "Enjoyed the time we spent together ... learned a lot from you ... stay in touch. Jim."

His person-to-person, informal style even carried over to the clothes he wore when he walked into a shop. Standard attire for him consisted of khakis and a company logo sport shirt. While this approach—his version of "management-by-walking-around," which he calls "management by *working* around"—made many Winchell's executives uncomfortable at first, Verney maintains that it helped tear down the invisible, intimidating barrier employees see separating them from management. His way was to never dictate or control, but to seek ways to support and build employees' commitment to the Winchell's mission.

A typical Verney field visit consisted of him sitting down with store managers for eyeball-to-eyeball "quality time" discussing what was on their minds. Verney deplored what he referred to as the "bird theory" field visit during which "upper management flies in, drops a load, and flies away in minutes to the next spot." So that the store manager could devote his full attention to their conversation, Verney usually brought along a regional or district manager whose job it was to handle the front counter while he and the store manager chatted privately.

Sometimes, not even Verney himself could believe the ripples his "MBWA" style sent through the ranks. For instance, one night he spent baking donuts with a number of professional bakers at shops in southern California so that he could better understand "what these heroes go through during a typical work shift." Wearing a baker's uniform and working side-by-side with them, Verney's self-education so tickled employees across the organization that thereafter the company grapevine periodically carried bogus sightings of the "leader" baking through the night.

As committed as he was to remaking Winchell's and as hard as he was willing to work, Verney knew he couldn't do the job himself. To maintain top management's continual presence in the field, he gently prodded his vice presidents to visit stores periodically to spread the word and obtain direct feedback about problems facing shop managers. "It's too easy sitting in an air conditioned office with pleasant music playing in the background, criticizing the guys in the field, because they can't get their reports done correctly and turned in on time," notes Verney. "Executives need to see for themselves how things really are. The more feedback they have, the better they'll be."

Integrating Media

Soon after he obtained a read of his heroes and the donut industry environment, Verney integrated a number of other media to supplement his face-to-face contact. The cruel reality was that, as the demands on his time increased, he couldn't get into the field as often as he wanted. As a supplement to—but never as a substitute for—person-to-person contact, he turned to "life-like" electronic communication channels such as video and telephone voice mail. Verney boasts that he's now become an avid voice mail enthusiast who can't resist sending daily messages to his staff on everything from leadership to performance appraisals. On some days when he's been out of the office, he may return to find 50 voice mail messages left for him. And no matter how much time it takes, he responds to every one of them within 24 hours, because he thinks "it'd be rude and unprofessional to do otherwise."

Video was a medium Verney saw as key to his creating an open communication, information-rich culture. "Since I can't be everywhere at the same time," he says, "video is one of the best ways for me to sort of do that." Verney's vision was to initially install video players in every training store and eventually in every unit throughout the Winchell's system. To his way of thinking, TV, although a step removed from the "real thing," is a familiar and comfortable medium for most people today, and offers the sender a chance to simulate the directness of nose-to-nose contact.

Verney differs from many other CEOs interviewed for this book in how deeply he thinks about the communication aspects of his decisions and policies. Moreover, he isn't afraid to spend his time and the company's money to get the important messages to employees. For example, during the kick-off phase of his turnaround program, he called a meeting of all 400 or so managers in southern California to discuss the company's new direction and draw them into the process. "I wanted to bring in all 700 managers from across the 14 states in which we had operations," he recalls. "Unfortunately, when a company is losing $11 million a year, that isn't cost-effective or smart business." The next best thing to being there was to videotape the meeting, edit it, and get it out quickly to all other managers and heroes so that they'd at least "get a feeling of what transpired" at the meeting.

An Uncertain Ending

Unfortunately, Jim Verney's long-term strategy to recraft Winchell's culture needed more time than he was able to give it. Before any significant effects of his efforts could be measured, the rules of the game changed. By mid-1989, TW Services, which had purchased a majority ownership position in Winchell's less than 18 months earlier, was no longer willing or able to commit the capital needed to help the company grow. Parent company TW Services was under siege from Coniston Partners, KKR and others. As rumors began circulating that Winchell's was on the chopping block again, Verney was given the go-ahead by TW Services' board of directors to seek a buyer for the beleaguered organization.

While this process was proceeding, employees' fears escalated. Meanwhile, Verney, concerned about leaks and rumors, shared all the information with them that federal securities laws allowed. He was determined that, regardless of how things turned out, he wasn't going to give worried employees any false hopes. He told them repeatedly that a buyer was being sought who was already in the food business, had the capital necessary to fuel the program they'd started and understood the problems of the donut business. He kept them abreast of developments right up to the time that Winchell's was sold for $40 million to a "turnaround specialist," Canadian conglomerate Shato Holdings Ltd.—a "good strategic buyer," Verney thought initially. Regrettably for Winchell's heroes and Verney, he concluded after some tough negotiating with Shato on a three-year contract that the risks-rewards ratio in the organizational climate he foresaw under Shato would undercut his philosophy, and he accepted an attractive offer to return to El Pollo Loco as its president.

When he talks about this decision, his mixed feelings surface. He was genuinely disappointed that circumstances didn't allow him to stay the full course to see his vision of the new Winchell's become reality, yet he takes satisfaction in what he and his team tried to do. "I regret we weren't able to see it through," he lamented during the second of three interviews, "but we went to all 16 markets and connected with every manager and employee. They knew we cared, they heard our message, and they got a glimpse of how things could be before the door closed. I know they took me seriously and trusted me —and morale did begin to improve."

Under the new ownership, 250 of Winchell's donut shops were sold to Pizza Hut, and many people from the corporate staff and top performing shops were laid off. Verney's frustration shows when he refers to Shato's "missed golden opportunity" to take advantage of the "human assets" his team had developed and primed for the long haul.

Post Post-Script

Verney thrived as President of El Pollo Loco (EPL), a Mexican-style fast food chain composed of 250 restuarants in four countries. His personalized communication came along with him. When he moved into the position, he spent almost two months meeting with managers at over 100 restaurants. "That time was crucial," he says, explaining that his purpose was to build relationships, open up communication channels, and get to know the EPL multicultural environment. To prepare himself for the tour, he started taking Spanish lessons so he could converse directly with many of EPL's "heroes" whose primary language is Spanish. As a result of what he learned during field visits, he launched an English language program called "English Sensaytions" for EPL crew leaders. Then in 1992, Verney moved to a North Carolina-based restaurant chain, Lone Star Steakhouse & Saloon, where his new title is—you guessed it—"leader." That story is for the next book.

Although it's impossible at this point to fully evaluate Verney's communication leadership effectiveness either at Winchell's or El Pollo Loco, his case offers a glimpse of how the CEO's communication role is changing. His hands-on communication demeanor and tight focus on relationship-building represents, we believe, what future CEOs will have to be if they want to be selected for the job and then survive it.

A Final Word

As increasingly visible and influential leaders of society, CEOs are attracting public attention and, in many cases, respect as never before. Some, such as Ross Perot and Peter Ueberroth and Lee Iacocca, view this trend as good for business. Observers like Peter Drucker are somewhat more skeptical of this movement, yet can't avoid acknowledging its impact: ". . . however short-lived, illogical, irrational, even undesirable it may be, it is a fact that business people are perceived as the leadership group in today's developed countries ... Business executives are inevitably leaders in their organizations, seen as such, perceived as such, judged as such."[15]

This book explains our thinking, grounded in years of research and analysis, about the importance of the CEO's evolving communication role. By understanding the nuances of this vital, emerging new role, top managers will be better able to adapt their leadership style to a changing generation of employees and an unforgiving, competitive marketplace.

In the chapters that follow, we take you on an excursion into some as yet unexplored regions of CEO and management life. Chapter 2 focuses on how and why the workplace and employees have changed in dramatic ways in the last 20 years, and what these changes mean to manager-employee relationships. Chapter 3 examines the concepts of communication and leadership, and shows why and how they are inescapably linked together. Chapter 4 lays out what we know about employees' and top dogs' views of the CEO's communication role, and presents an overview of our strategic model of CEO communication. Chapters 5 to 8 describe in detail and illustrate each of the model's four principles (consistency, compassion, organization, selectivity) and what they mean to CEO communication. And finally, Chap. 9 peers into the future, examining how the CEO's leadership role is likely to grow and change.

Returning to Arlen ...

In the prologue, a troubled CEO, Arlen Royster, was introduced as he tried to grasp the implications of a perplexing "cooked books" scandal involving field managers' misreporting of financial information that poses a threat to his career and his company—Royal Accommodations, a major hotel chain. He knows he can't escape the ultimate responsibility for the crisis—the blame as well as the resolution. Yet, at this point he is completely overwhelmed by the magnitude and complexity of the problem facing him. He knows that the crisis can be managed, but he's just not sure how best to do it.

Arlen, like many of his real-life contemporaries, isn't convinced that communication and human relations strategies will make much of a difference in leading his company out of its predicament. As we rejoin him, he's about to break the shocking news to his vice presidents at an emergency sunrise meeting at Royal headquarters.

"Opening Pandora's Box"

Wednesday, October 10, 7 a.m.   Arlen burst into the executive conference room and stopped just inside the door, pleased by what he saw.

Usually, people were scattered around the room in pairs or threesomes, casually chatting and sipping coffee or tea. Several minutes would pass before they'd find their seats and quiet down. This morning, however, every person was already in place, sitting silently, strained expressions on their faces. His eyes swept the room, then he sat down.

Arlen laid his notes on the table and leaned forward, resting on his forearms. His movement drew the staff's immediate attention. He liked that; it reinforced his sense of control. He scanned the table clockwise from his left, taking a moment to make eye contact with each person. Like Arlen's office, the cylindrical conference room had a floor-to-ceiling outside glass wall, though on the opposite side of the building from Arlen's office on the 30th floor. The translucent, burnt orange curtain was drawn, casting a muted hue over the room. Fourteen high-back leather chairs ringed the oak conference table.

"Okay, you know there's something going on or you wouldn't be here this early. It's major. So let's get to it."

Arlen's resonant voice carried easily throughout the room. He spoke more slowly, more deliberately than usual. It bought him time to gauge reactions. Unconsciously, he reached for his cufflink and began spinning it. He inhaled deeply before launching into his monologue.

"I learned late yesterday afternoon that it looks like a number of our hotels in the Midwest region manipulated their books the past two years, maybe longer. In other words, we've been publicly reporting false financial information. I can't say anything for certain yet, but it appears we've been claiming net profits about 10 percent above actual. Don't yet know how many dollars that represents, but it could be as much as $40 or $50 million. What this means to things like dividends, bonuses, pay raises, bank credit lines, etc., isn't completely clear yet.

"The bottom-line, people, is that this will be interpreted by the media and others as Royal's management ... us ... lying to our stockholders, the SEC, our employees, the public—to ourselves—about the financial health of Royal Accommodations." Arlen quickly surveyed the group around him. No one moved.

"The culprits appear to be our own managers. I don't yet know how many or who." Expressions of disbelief began registering on the faces looking at him, some more than others. "We'll have to disclose this as soon as we're sure of our information. I'm trying to buy us a few days so we can be prepared for the avalanche of questions and accusations that'll follow. Needless to say, the implications are as big as they get. I can't think of anything more damaging to the company—and to our futures. Nothing."

The shock of the news was taking hold; mental wheels were spinning wildly throughout the room, but still no one spoke. Arlen looked at Jamieson, who was doodling furiously on the pad in front of him. Now that he'd divulged the headline, the CEO moved quickly to the details before the shock dissolved into panic. He wanted them focused on what had to be done, not on what might happen. He raised his voice slightly.

"Needless to say, this could undermine everything we've been trying to do to get back on the growth curve. This kind of thing puts us under a dark cloud that makes everything difficult. People won't trust us. And winning back that trust will be the biggest challenge this company's ever faced. It *can* be handled, though. But it's going to take time ... time we don't have right now. Get ready to be scrutinized, individually and collectively, up one side and down the other. We won't be in control of our lives—or our destinies—for a while."

Arlen had just inadvertently revealed his greatest fear: being out of control. He hated admitting he'd lost control, but he knew it was undeniable. "What we do, or don't do, over the next few days will make us ... or break us.

"Okay, we're facing a potential disaster here. But it doesn't have to be, not if we use our heads and don't run off half-cocked. Think of this as just another business challenge. In a strange sort of way, it's an opportunity to show our employees, our stockholders, even our customers, present and potential, what kind of managers we really are. But we've got to move fast. We've got to grab the initiative before we're forced on to the defensive."

As he talked, Arlen's composure was evident in his steady voice and fluid, punctuating gestures; shortly after he'd started talking, he'd stopped fingering his cufflinks. His unemotional, yet intense approach seemed to be having its intended impact. No signs of panic yet. Subconsciously, he wanted his staff to share his inner excitement for the personal and organizational test in front of them.

The phone on the coffee table near the door rang right on cue. It startled some, its intrusion unexpected. Heads turned to look at Susan O'Reilly as she caught it on the second ring. Her voice was barely audible, but her body language revealed annoyance with the caller. The words "only for an emergency" were loud enough to be heard. Arlen had turned halfway in his chair to pick up the exchange behind him. She looked over at him cautiously and said, "It's Ed Hines. He says you do want to talk to him."

Arlen pushed his chair back and stood up. "Excuse me, folks, this shouldn't take long." He stepped to the phone, turned his back toward his staff, purposely blocking their ability to eavesdrop. O'Reilly returned to her spot at the table. She began logging in the meeting's attenders on her steno pad. Over the 10 years she had worked with him, Arlen had come to rely on and value both her polished organizational skills and savvy business instinct. As the gatekeeper of the CEO's schedule, she controlled access to him, which gave her genuine power. Office gossip over the years had romantically linked her, an attractive 37-year-old brunette and tennis buff, with some of Royal's top executives, including Arlen. But she painstakingly kept her social and professional lives separate.

As she mechanically wrote down the names of those around the table, she wondered who among them might be behind the "cooked books" and who could be counted on to help Arlen solve the mystery. Across from her, to the left of Arlen, was John Grubner, the chief financial officer. Everything about him was gray, from his drab three-piece suits to his cardboard personality. O'Reilly wondered how it was that this financial whiz from Yale hadn't spotted anything out of line. He had to be squirming, she thought.

Next to Grubner was Joyce Hadley, VP of human resources management. Arlen had recruited Hadley three years ago to be Royal's manager of personnel. Then just six months later—which raised many eyebrows—he promoted her to VP of a broader-based and newly named HRM department responsible for everything from recruitment and compensation to union relations and training. O'Reilly admired Hadley for what she'd done with the opportunity given her.

As she took her silent roll call, O'Reilly picked up snatches of Arlen's phone conversation behind her. His voice had taken on a raw edge to it. "Are you absolutely sure, Ed?" she heard him say, and then a moment later, "Let's double check that, okay?" She could see Keller and the others straining to catch his words.

Rick Jamieson, VP of corporate communication, was at the far end of the table. A well-kept secret was O'Reilly's attraction to him. She knew it was mutual, but he'd never tried taking it further. They flirted occasionally, but she knew anything more could end up hurting her, although she'd had second thoughts recently after hearing that Jamieson's divorce from his 15-year marriage had been finalized. As she wrote his name, Jamieson looked up at her as if he'd heard her thoughts.

On O'Reilly's right was native New Yorker Joe Coletto, Royal's head legal counsel. Short and stocky with blubbery jowls, a jovial personality, and a full gray-white beard, Coletto had the look of a Brooks Brothers version of Santa Claus. Behind that jolly-looking exterior, though, was an incisive, quick mind that could unravel the most convoluted legal issues. O'Reilly never understood why Coletto had stayed at Royal for close to nine years; she'd often heard the water cooler gossip about his turning down lucrative offers from several venerable Wall Street law firms that had tried wooing him with offers twice or three times what he currently earned.

As O'Reilly looked up at Gloria Bernard, Arlen's lowered voice cut in. "Don't stop there, Ed, if there's even the slightest chance it's spilled over ...," he said, glancing over his shoulder at his silent and increasingly impatient staff. Before turning back, Arlen said, "I can't do anything until we have verifiable information. Keep digging."

O'Reilly refocused on Bernard, who was hired to be Royal's first vice president of investor relations, a department Arlen created three years ago to help fuel the company's planned growth. Her coming had created a slight stir in the company, as she was Royal's first-ever African-American VP. When the stagnating economy destroyed capital sources, Arlen brought in Bernard who, armed with her Harvard MBA and stints at Mellon Bank and Shearson-Lehman, would pump up Royal's visibility on Wall Street to attract some of the big institutional investors. A stickler for fashion and style who understood the nuances of each, Bernard was striking in her designer ensembles and perfectly applied make-up. Slightly on the reserved side, she generally preferred to listen than to talk, although she rarely passed up an invitation to expound on her ideas for enhancing Royal's position with the big league money moguls.

O'Reilly turned slightly to catch sight of Robert Azoulette at the far end of the table. The marketing VP always looked like he just walked out of a TV commercial. He had coal-black wavy hair, an expertly-trimmed mustache, and he walked with a regal air. His custom-tailored Italian suits and matching silk ties fit flawlessly on this confirmed bachelor. Arlen had lured Azoulette—who was fluent in French, Spanish, and German—three years earlier from a successful European hotel chain to spearhead Royal's planned international expansion. Unfortunately, Royal's fiscal difficulties had gotten in the way. Consequently, Azoulette had grown increasingly restless and frustrated with the delays and broken promises, and he didn't always suffer his disappointment in silence. O'Reilly recalled a meeting where company-wide austerity measures were being discussed when Mike Keller suggested cutting the marketing budget. Azoulette pounced all over him, acidly telling an open-mouthed Keller he'd layoff his people only after "you forfeit your next bonus."

O'Reilly could tell that Arlen's conversation was ending. He hadn't said much for a few minutes other than an occasional "uh-huh," "okay," "tell me more." The group couldn't help but hear Arlen when he asked loudly, "Are you sure about that, Ed?" The tension thickened with each passing minute.

As she looked up, O'Reilly noticed Mike Keller, vice president of operations, staring coolly at her as though he were reading her mind. She instantly looked away. He'd made it clear to the others long ago by sitting directly opposite Arlen that he considered himself second-in-command and heir to the Royal throne. His reputation in the regions was as a tough, demanding manager who got the job done no matter what it took. A number of the VPs suspected his often self-serving, ulterior motives, but they couldn't help but respect his ability to make the hard calls when necessary and get results fast, which showed up in tangible ways, like in their bonus checks. Therefore, most, including Arlen, silently tolerated his rough-and-tumble management style.

* * * * * * * * *

O'Reilly looked at her watch and routinely recorded 7:20 in her notes. Arlen put the phone down and paused, speedily reorganizing his thoughts.

According to Hines, head of the outside audit team, the investigation turned up a file containing a copy of a six-month-old memo to Keller from an assistant manager at the Minnesota property outlining her belief that the hotel's profits were being "juggled by the general manager." In the same file was Keller's hand-written reply thanking her and assuring her he'd look into it immediately. In the note, Keller had asked her to keep everything to herself until he got back to her. Curiously, noted the auditor, the assistant manager had resigned, without any explanation, a month later.

Arlen did a slow about-face, his gaze spinning directly to Keller. It was a cold, hard, focused look, very unlike Arlen. Heads turned in unison for Keller's reaction. He stared back at Arlen for several seconds. Then, not wanting a confrontation just yet, he broke off eye contact.

With that, Arlen returned to his chair, sat upright, interlocked his fingers like he was about to pray, and resolutely faced his staff. As his thoughts crystallized, he scanned the room in which so many of his decisions as CEO had been debated, argued, and shaped. The wall opposite him was a beautiful mural of North America with each of Royal's hotels and restaurant sites designated by a color-coded magnet. The map, which served as a sort of corporate scoreboard, had been Arlen's idea after he became CEO, a time when Royal was growing like an Iowa cornfield after a rain. At first, the addition of each magnet prior to staff meetings triggered mock drum rolls and spontaneous applause. Originally a source of pride, the magnet game was now working in reverse. As properties closed, removing magnets from the map had become a harsh and unpleasant reminder of how quickly things can change in the hotel business, or any business for that matter. The third wall, opposite the door leading into the conference room, was set up for audiovisual presentations. It included a remote-controlled, rear-view projection screen, and a 56-inch, high-definition monitor fed by a sophisticated cable system.

"Sorry for the interruption," Arlen said. "But it looks worse than I first thought. That was Ed Hines, chief of the forensic audit team I hired a few weeks ago. After working practically round-the-clock this past week, he's confirmed that the bookkeeping scheme isn't confined to one region, but may be company-wide." As he delivered the worsening news, Arlen's eyes closed and his head tilted backward, perhaps his subtle way of seeking divine intervention.

For several seconds, no one moved or spoke. Then, as the shocking revelations sank in, reactions came one after another. "Dammit," Coletto spit out under his breath. Grubner tossed his eye glasses onto the table. They slid across the table's smooth surface, spinning to a stop in front of Susan O'Reilly. "I don't believe it," he protested limply. O'Reilly pushed the glasses back. Bernard looked across at Hadley, rolling her eyes toward the ceiling in disgust. Keller's pen tapped a rhythmic staccato on the pad in front of him, like he was transmitting an SOS to anybody who would listen. His eyes shifted from Arlen to Grubner and back.

"I think this might be a good time to take my vacation," Azoulette cracked with a nervous laugh. "Starting tomorrow." When nobody bit at his humor, his smile evaporated.

Jamieson was the first to move. He pushed back his chair, stood and walked along the glass wall, passing behind Arlen on his way to the coffee. He poured a cup, faced the group and took a sip.

"All right," Jamieson said finally. "I guess I'll ask the question that's on all our minds. How could this have happened here and none of us knew about it?" Arlen was glad he hadn't been the one to raise the $64 million question. No one said anything before Jamieson had returned to his chair.

"Why did you bring in outside snoopers to begin with? I know they weren't scheduled to be here," broke in Grubner, his face showing how worried he was. He shushed the others while he bored in on Arlen. "I'd heard something about some accountants being here, but I thought it had to do with the annual report. I didn't give it much thought."

"You weren't supposed to," Arlen said pointedly. Keller immediately locked Arlen into his sights, trying to assess what the CEO really knew, or thought he knew. Arlen stared back, expressionless.

"Wait a minute," Hadley interjected stridently, raising her voice above the others. "How come this is the first we're hearing about it? Who's responsible for this?" She looked at Arlen, imploring him to give answers.

Keller jumped in before Arlen or anyone else could answer. "We all know, Joyce, that the board of directors must ultimately accept responsibility," he said pompously. And then, to add to his sting, "And allocate blame."

He peered straight at Arlen again. "Arlen, does the board know about this yet? I think they should, don't you?" He smiled faintly.

Arlen's corporate bones told him that Keller was baiting him—and that behind his smokescreen he was hiding something. But Arlen instantly reminded himself that he didn't know anything for sure—yet.

"Well, I'd like to go back to ...," began Coletto.

Arlen held up an open hand, stalling the attorney in mid-sentence. "Okay, okay," Arlen interjected, forming the time-out sign with his hands. "Let's stay on track. There isn't time for speculation and the finger-pointing can come later. Let me tell you what we do know." Keller sat back, content that the incriminating questions had been raised.

He recounted the red flags that had prompted him to bring in the auditors. As he spoke, O'Reilly slid a sheet of paper across the table to him. It was a handwritten listing of the questions asked and by whom. He skimmed the list.

"Now, to answer Joyce's question about how this happened, here's the gist of what I know and what I *think* happened. According to what the auditors learned, some hotel managers shifted profits, often from quarter to quarter, to guarantee that their profit and loss statement showed them meeting profit goals. During poor quarters, they'd cover the shortfalls with money from healthy quarters they'd stashed in bogus accounts. And during good quarters, when their revenue exceeded goal, they'd divert the surplus profits to those hidden accounts until the monies were needed. This way, they were always right on target, regardless of their actual revenue picture.

"For example," he continued, quickening his pace, "let's look at Minneapolis. In each quarter last year, reported earnings went up 5 percent, which was right on goal. But profits weren't actually that high. At the end of the first quarter, they were 2 percent over goal. So they simply delayed invoicing and carried that money over to the second quarter. In essence, they banked it for a rainy day.

"In the second quarter, they were again ahead of projections, so they again delayed invoicing. They also prepaid some suppliers for purchases not yet delivered but recorded the expense as current. But in the third and fourth quarters, earnings fell well below the 5-percent objective—which meant the rainy day had arrived. So in the third quarter, they rolled out the hidden profits from the first two quarters. At the close of the fourth quarter, when decisions about bonuses were being made, the secret account was empty. So they falsely inflated inventory figures to be able to report meeting the 5-percent increase. They did this believing they'd make it up in the first two quarters of this year."

Arlen decided to cut to the chase. "What this all means is that lots of important decisions were being made based on profits and earnings that didn't really exist. Year-end incentive bonuses were paid out based on phantom profits. Some managers were promoted based on false financial performance of their units. And investments were made based on fake earnings. Stock prices were probably artificially inflated as a result, not to mention the banks that gave us credit lines based on those figures."

Gloria Bernard cut in, "If a bunch of managers would go to this much trouble to manipulate profits, why wouldn't they report better-than expected earnings, rather than merely meeting goal? I mean, they'd make bigger bonuses that way, right? If these guys were so greedy, why didn't they grab all they could for themselves and run?"

"I think I can answer that," piped up Bob Azoulette, shifting in his chair toward Bernard, who was on his left. "We had a situation like this when I was in France. Managers reported the excess profits one year. And they got their bonuses. Then the company came back and set higher targets the following year. No one could meet them. So there were no bonuses. In fact, some of the managers lost their jobs because they couldn't deliver. The logic caught on that there was no advantage to reporting earnings above goals. It only made it harder the next time around." Azoulette glanced at Arlen for a stop or go sign, but got neither, so he kept going.

"The managers realized that doing better than expected was actually a disadvantage. So they tried to find ways to meet goals without ever exceeding them. Sometimes that meant involving other employees and suppliers. Failure to meet goals was pure death. But so was exceeding them. So managers felt like they were caught between the proverbial rock and a hard place."

"But why would they do this?" Bernard persisted. "It doesn't appear to be the Ivan Boesky or Michael Milken sort of malicious greed. These guys were just trying to earn what they were expected to earn, right? The money wasn't going directly into their pockets. Royal's financial assets weren't being stolen *per se*, were they?"

The question, a perceptive one, hung in mid-air for just a moment. "I and the Securities and Exchange Commission beg to differ, Gloria." The distinctive thick New York accent was Joe Coletto's, the company's legal conscience. "They did put money in their pockets when they cashed bonus checks they wouldn't have earned if they hadn't lied. That's stealing in my book. They had to realize it would come back to haunt them. Or … or …" Coletto's train of thought came to a sudden halt; he'd just been struck with a new thought, one he hesitated to share. As an attorney, he made his living by avoiding saying anything he couldn't prove or might not be able to justify later. But before he could stop himself, the words fell out of his mouth. "… or they might've been led to believe upper management didn't really object to this 'harmless' manipulation and thus tacitly sanctioned it. It certainly wouldn't be the first time in history that sort of thing has happened. Remember Ronald Reagan and the Iran-Contra affair?"

Coletto's subtle observation hit a bull's eye with the group. Arlen sat back in his chair, content to observe for the moment. He saw Keller's eyes sprint toward Grubner, who met them with a nervous pair of his own. Keller looked suspiciously at Coletto. Hadley and Jamieson exchanged raised eyebrows. Several long seconds passed before Azoulette retook the floor.

"After a while you can't get out of the cycle, robbing Peter to pay Paul. One day, though, no matter how careful you've been, the numbers catch up to you." The marketing VP's interpretation captured the essence of why people who know better sometimes disregard what they know is right.

Arlen looked at Bernard and asked, "Does that answer it?" She nodded affirmatively, though her perplexed eyes said something different.

Arlen turned to Keller. "Do you have anything to add, Mike? Did we leave anything out?" His tone was curt, accusatory.

Caught slightly off-guard, Keller said, "Don't think so. Makes sense to me, in a perverted sort of way."

Coletto then frowned at CFO John Grubner and gently probed. "Tell me, John, is all this really possible without you or anybody on your staff or our regular outside CPA firm detecting it?"

Grubner fidgeted nervously with his tie, avoiding any eye contact. Then, with a note of impatience, he said, "Of course it is. Almost anything can be done with numbers if you know what you're doing."

A tiny smile appeared on Arlen's face, noticed by Jamieson. Keller's head snapped in Grubner's direction, his wide-eyed expression chastising the comptroller for his thoughtless remark.

"Okay, John, I'll grant you that," admitted Coletto, readying his next question in the verbal poker game now underway. And there was nothing Coletto loved more than a late-night poker bust or good debate. "But what're the chances of something like this happening over a two-year period without *anybody* noticing something out of place?"

"Like I said, Joe, anything's possible if you know how to play the game," retorted Grubner, looking down at his clasped hands. Realizing he couldn't allow the veiled accusation to go unchallenged, he decided to take on Coletto. "Joe, if I didn't know you better, I might think you were suggesting I or members of my staff were somehow knowing parties to this fiasco. You aren't saying that, are you, Joe?" Grubner peeked over at Arlen, who sat motionless, listening, before returning to Coletto.

Coletto shrugged, but said nothing. "Are you, Joe?" Grubner probed again, louder, provocation in his voice.

"Of course not, John. Just asking a hypothetical question—a question which you still haven't answered."

Grubner wasn't sure what to do next. He looked to Keller for help.

Like an actor taking center stage, Keller permitted the silence to stretch. He pushed back from the table, got up and walked behind Azoulette and Bernard. He had everybody's attention. He started slowly.

"You all know what we're facing. The economy's gone south. The competition's gotten a lot tougher the last couple of years. We've all been under tremendous pressure to just hold our own. We've often been given the impression that it hardly mattered how we succeeded—just so long as we did." Keller stopped behind Coletto and faced Arlen, who looked up stoically, stroking his chin.

As Keller continued, his gestures became more animated, his tone more biting. He'd long ago convinced himself the board had erred six years ago when it selected Arlen over him. This was now his chance to correct the wrong done him by mounting a frontal assault on Arlen's unavoidable accountability.

"We've been running ourselves ragged to meet the tough goals *you* set," he said, pointing intensely right at Arlen. "Everything out of your mouth was growth and bottom-line. Then it was layoffs and closing facilities. There was never any choice. It was either meet the quarterly goals or take a hike." Keller was enjoying the moment. Out of the corner of his eye, he saw Grubner nodding in agreement.

Keller then returned his focus to the group. "And all the lip service you gave these so-called 'people programs' was great eyewash for the board and Wall Street, Arlen. But the real game is and always has been played at the front desks and in the restaurants and bars. Beating up on the competition was the only thing that mattered to you. How many times did you tell us that if you looked good, we all looked good? So much for that theory."

Arlen refused to engage Keller as the VP pressed his attack. "And when we met his lofty, unrealistic goals, none of you complained. None of you complained when you cashed your bonus checks. None of you complained when *The Wall Street Journal* did that big story touting Royal as the next coming. And none of you complained when Arlen took his bows on our behalf before the board. Let's face it, we were all taking our cues from the 'top dog' himself." The "top dog" label had been inadvertently given to Arlen by board chairman Jim Stamps during the news conference announcing his appointment as CEO.

Keller abruptly swiveled back around and strode back to his chair and sat down, clearly pleased with himself.

"What are you trying to say, Mike? Just spit it out, why don't you!" Arlen was already annoyed. He thought he knew what Keller's answer would be, but he wanted him to say it to the group.

"Whether you did it intentionally or not, Arlen, you put unreasonable pressure on every manager in this company to deliver unreasonable earnings figures—just so you could look pretty in front of Stamps and the board," said Keller tersely. "You really shouldn't be surprised ... at any of this ... because success at Royal means pleasing you, whatever it takes."

"Really, Mike? I always thought that pressure was part of life up here on the 30th floor," Arlen countered. Then he paused, checking each of his VPs for reactions. "What do the rest of you think? Do you agree with Mike's claim?"

The silence told him he shouldn't take anything for granted. It was Jamieson, always the diplomat, who spoke first. "It wasn't Arlen's or any one person's doing. We all sat around this same table developing corporate goals we knew were necessary to get us out of the hole.

"And I don't remember you, Mike, or you, Joe, or you, Joyce, or you, Gloria, or any of you challenging those goals at the time." He looked directly at each executive as he said their name. "We knew there was no other way. And we knew about the pressure. We all accepted it. Isn't that why they pay us the big bucks?" he asked rhetorically.

Out of the corner of his eye, Arlen saw O'Reilly pointing to her watch. He glanced at his gold Seiko. It was 7:45, time to retake control and wrap up. Before anybody could answer Jamieson's query, Arlen jumped back in, refocusing matters on the here and now.

"All right. This is serious and time's getting away. Let's get back to saving Royal, shall we?" Arlen didn't see Keller's sarcastic smirk.

The group quieted and looked at the CEO. "Let's put this thing in perspective. Yes, it'll probably cost the company millions of dollars. And make no mistake, there's going to be accountability. But far more important right now is to control the damage and try to hold on to our key constituencies, like the board, our employees, the stockholders and, of course, our guests, present and future. If they think we're crooks or incompetent, then we'll never make it to the next annual report."

Arlen sounded almost like an evangelist looking to save his flock from evil. His intense eyes mirrored the passion he felt. This was vintage Arlen, which he rarely exposed. The words came from his gut. When his convictions merged with his underplayed ability to persuasively articulate them, Arlen Royster could be a compelling leader.

"Our corporate integrity, credibility, reputation—those are the things that have kept us on top. Our employees and customers trusting us. That's why we've done well. But we'll be left at the starting gate if we can't attract the supervisory people we need to run our operations. If they think we're running a house of cards that's about to collapse, we're through. Royal's good name has to be our top priority."

Jamieson cut in. "Did anybody know anything about this before today? If we can't be honest with each other, we're gonna have one helluva time convincing anybody else," he argued. He didn't really expect any response, although he searched their faces for a sign, any sign. Not even Keller blinked.

"Arlen's right, y'know. This is about holding on to as much of our credibility as we can," Jamieson emphasized, moving around the end of the table, past Keller, before stopping in front of the wall map, which served as a powerful backdrop for this discussion about Royal's future.

"Something like this, that smacks of fraud, is a slur on all management in this company." He spread out his arms. "But mostly on us."

* * * * * * * * *

At 8 a.m., Susan O'Reilly leaned over and tapped the face of Arlen's watch. "All right," he said, closing off conversation. "I'm seeing Stamps in a few minutes. This was a pretty good beginning, all things considered. But we're a long way from understanding what this mess is all about. Think of time as our enemy. The next 48 hours are crucial to our getting through this. So here's the drill."

His words came fast now. "The auditor's preliminary report should be in my hands by noon Friday. We have to let our employees know what's going on. And we'll need to disclose this to the public, so we have to develop plans for communicating the situation to the world."

Arlen's directives were laid out in sequence, pausing after each one only long enough to make sure each person had time to write them down. "One: Standby for word about our possibly reconvening early tomorrow morning.

"Two: Mum's the word until we get the formal report from the auditors. For the next 24 hours, this subject is off-limits to anyone other than us. And I do mean anyone."

"How the hell are we supposed to do that?" Azoulette asked.

"It'll smell like a cover-up," Jamieson nodded. "People know we're meeting. You don't think they're going to wonder what's really going on? Remember the grapevine?"

Coletto, the attorney, jumped back in. "We've got to be careful about partial information seeping out before a public announcement. We don't want to prematurely or inadvertently expose the company or ourselves to potential liability. We should hold the lid tight on any public statements until we know everything."

"This isn't a cover-up," Arlen said firmly, another flash of annoyance showing briefly. "We're just trying to buy some time so we're sure we know what's going on and can plan our strategy. It'll all be coming out sooner than we'd like. Just be careful. Please.

"Three: I want each of you to outline recommendations on how your department should handle this thing. Think short- and long-term. Think strategic and tactical. Consider everything. I want the outlines to Susan by 5 today. I'll look at them tonight. By noon Thursday, we have to have things in place." He waited until everyone looked up.

"Four: I'll want to meet with some of you individually today or tomorrow. Let Susan know your schedules so I can reach you day or night.

"Five: At tomorrow's meeting, we'll decide what we ought to do next and start doing it." The list completed, Arlen asked for questions. There were none.

"One final word," he said seriously, standing up. "Remember, your one and only priority right now is this: Once the word gets out and it all hits the fan, we won't have time to sit around this table and contemplate our next move. All we'll have time to do is react. So we've got to nail down a solid strategy and assign tasks before Friday."

The meeting obviously over, the VPs began to sort and stack their papers. Jamieson passed a page of notes to Hadley. Azoulette and Bernard talked quietly at their seats. Keller had started for the door when he heard his name.

"Mike, when I get back from seeing Jim, let's meet. Susan'll buzz you." Arlen's tone was flat, business-like. "As you wish," said Keller, immediately shifting his focus back to Grubner, who was hurrying toward him.

Arlen pushed his chair under the table. "Wish me luck," he said off-handedly to no one in particular. "I need all I can get—I'm about to open Pandora's box."

Turning to leave, he spotted Keller and Grubner huddling in the far corner. Keller's hand was on Grubner's shoulder and the two were smiling at each other.

O'Reilly recorded the time in her notes—8:17.

2

A New and Different Workplace

Since the mid-1980s, sweeping social and political changes have reshaped the world order. The penetrating cries of self-determination and democracy—heard from China to South Africa to Germany—have brought down governments and changed people's ways of life in every corner of the world, from the USSR to Gaza. Many of the images are unforgettable. A Chinese student, armed with a flower, staring down a government tank in Peking's Tiananmen Square. Nelson Mandela emerging from a Johannesburg prison after 30 years, his fist thrust triumphantly into the air. East and West German students standing atop the Berlin wall, tearing down with their bare hands a global symbol of Cold War oppression.

People the world over are claiming their fundamental right to control their own destinies. Former Soviet leader Mikhail Gorbachev spoke of this core change in 1988: "We would be making a great political blunder were we not to pay attention to the very profound changes in the mood of the world public . . . people have started to feel their will . . . and they have begun to do something about it."[1]

Powerful social and economic forces are reshaping not only the international political landscape, but the business marketplace as well. The workplace has been turned upside down by a series of cataclysmic trends: A world once split apart by nationalism is now seeking cooperation through globalism. A society once defined by its ability to manufacture hard goods is now characterized by the quality of its services and information. A marketplace once controlled by centralized, authoritarian management is coming under increasing pressure to allow employees to manage themselves. A workforce once dominated by blue collars seeking security is now driven by white collars seeking self-actualization.

A new generation of employees has arrived with expectations far different—and in many ways, far greater—than its ancestors. Unlike their post-Depression era grandparents and Baby Boomer parents who defined success in economic terms, the new generation of employees defines success in self-fulfillment terms. As corporate managements try to figure out how to adapt to this new and different era, a new and different workplace is taking shape.

In this chapter, we explore some of the powerful demographic and psychographic trends that are transforming workers and the workplace. And we analyze how management is responding—or, in some cases, not responding—to these changes with new approaches, most of which are driven by a need to improve communication and relationships between managers and employees.

A New Breed of Workers

Today's employees are better educated and more savvy about business and economic issues than prior generations. They bring a fresh perspective to work and organizational life. And with life expectancy rates rising, these workers are bearing more of the responsibility for caring for their aging, dependent parents. For years now, women have been assuming new and different roles at home and in the workplace as more and more pursue careers—a trend that has turned work and lifestyles upside down. By the year 2000, they are expected to outnumber men in the workforce.

This development alone has spawned a host of new and increasingly complex issues—such as dual-income families, single parents, and child care—that are transforming the work and personal lives of men and women alike. Many Americans—four out of 10 reports a recent Roper poll—are putting leisure activities and family time ahead of or at least on an equal par with work, an attitude shift that is forcing changes in the way people and corporations are organized and managed.[2]

Employees today view management quite differently than did their parents or grandparents, whose overriding concern was having a steady job and paycheck. Today's workers want to be respected as individuals with rights and as human beings with personal lives. In essence, workers want managements that are willing to address employees' desire to pursue professional aspirations, and help them resolve the nagging conflicts between career and family.

Not too long ago, employees' work and home lives were separate and not necessarily equal. Work dominated. Problems at home were the employee's sole responsibility, and management expected workers to keep their personal problems out of the workplace, feeling neither an obligation nor a desire to assist. In today's fast-changing world, however, the dividing line between home and work has blurred considerably. Consequently, workers' home-life problems are impacting the workplace in ways never before imagined. Employees expect top management to assist them in solving their organizational *and* home-life problems in hopes of creating an "employee friendly" work environment.

Clearly, the traditional manager-worker relationship is shifting dramatically from one dominated by the manager to one where supervisor and employee share responsibilities. This trend emerged time and again in interviews with CEOs completed for this book. After analyzing those conversations and other secondary data, we pinpointed four workplace issues that top managers believe are most important to employees.

1. *Employees want managers who invite them to be participants in workplace decisions.* "Our workers want to know what's going on with their company," explains Bill Davila, former president of California-based Vons Grocery Company. "They want to know why their company makes the decisions it does. They want to feel that they're a part of the enterprise—and that they're well informed. Then they can become more involved. They're begging for more and better information." The value of employee feedback is gradually gaining believers among the upper echelons of corporate America. Phil Quigley, president and CEO of Pacific Bell Telephone Companies, tells why he thinks employee feedback is essential today. "We have a participative environment that includes programs with two-way communication. To the degree we're able to lift some of the mystique about how we make decisions about our future, I think a better informed employee is a happier employee. And in the long run we're a better company."

2. *Employees want managers who share information with them openly during good and bad times.* Walter Williams, CEO of Bethlehem Steel in Pennsylvania, a former millworker himself, knows how important this is to workers. "When they decided to close down the Lackawanna steel plant [in the mid-1980s] three days after Christmas, I said I would handle the whole thing," he recalls. "For something that far-reaching, I just couldn't pass it off to someone down the line, like a plant manager. The people of that community deserved upper management talking to them. So I went to Lackawanna, where I began my career and had lived for nine years, and met with the people, the media, and the local community. I had an obligation to do this myself—as the CEO and a human being. I couldn't let somebody else do it."

Pacific Bell's Phil Quigley talked about employees' soaring need for information from management during times of great change, and how that need affects workers' performance. "We're undergoing a cultural change in our business. And when changes are occurring as fast as they are, people need to be informed," he notes. "The bottom line [for employees] is, 'How's it going to affect me and my family?' Giving them information to help reduce their uncertainty allows them to focus a bit more on the job."

3. *Employees want managers who are sensitive and responsive to their personal and professional needs.* Herb Stein, founder and chairman of H&E

Hardware Stores, a successful chain in the desert area north of Los Angeles, talks about his reaction to a general manager's complaint about the high cost of labor. Stein, who says he considers his employees "part of my second family," seems to genuinely care about his people's feelings. "If someone is hurt, then I'm hurt," he says. "The general manager was complaining yesterday because our minimum wage is now up to $4.25. I said to him, 'Have you bought a piece of fruit lately? A damn peach is 49 cents. What the hell are you beefing about?' So I said, pay it. It's not the money the company will make that's important. What's important is creating an industry where people can make a living and enjoy their families." Then, smiling, Stein adds, "Of course, that's not good capitalism, is it?"

4. *Employees want a relationship with management based on partnership, not "powership."* Jim Verney recalls one of his early impressions when he became president of Winchell's Donut House. "The employees said that the corporate office was a kingdom unto itself. Rather than the corporate office serving the donut stores, it was the other way around. So we started to invert the corporate pyramid so that the president is on the bottom where he or she should be, and the hero is on top in the number-one spot." He saw his function as reinforcing field managers who "really are Winchell's to a person buying donuts." Employees needed to know that there was a Jim Verney, but they didn't need to see or hear from him every day. "I'm a cheerleader and communicator," he says. "I'm the rah-rah guy who, in many ways, sits on the sidelines rooting the organization on to bigger and better things. I try to inspire people to stretch to meet ambitious goals."

The key to creating a teamwork atmosphere between employee and employer is found in one word: *trust*. Unfortunately, the workplace is dominated by mistrust, particularly from the employee's perspective, because managers won't give up some of the control traditionally perceived as sacred to management's domain. Says Secretary of Labor Robert Reich: "Managers got to where they are because they were good at controlling. It's a little scary for them to give up that control. There's a lot of distrust between workers and managers out there."[3]

The Invasion of Stress

New values and new lifestyles bring with them certain costs that employees, as well as employers, must pay. As people today attempt to live their professional and personal lives in peaceful coexistence, they must make some difficult and oftentimes conflicting choices. Workers, whether they wear a white or a blue collar, are frustrated in their seemingly futile attempts to balance their career and family responsibilities. Those frustrations are made worse for aspiring young managers who must face roadblocks to advancement as beleaguered companies prune staffs and compress bureaucratic structures. Left unchecked, workers' rising sense of futility can further damage an already fragile employer-employee relationship. This ever-present tension has spawned a new workplace enemy: *stress*. Stress has invaded America's workplaces and homes like the plague.

Caused by a battery of overlapping pressures, stress is real, it is harmful, and it is expensive—literally and figuratively—to both employer and employee. More and more employees are suffering the harmful effects of on-the-job stress-induced illnesses or conditions (such as, heart disease, alcoholism, suicide) which, in turn, push up already skyrocketing health care costs. In California, for example, workers' compensation claims on mental stress-related illnesses have shot up a whopping 700 percent over the past decade. "Stress is the most pervasive and potent toxin in the workplace," argues Leon Warshaw, executive director of the New York Business Group on Health, a business compendium concerned with health care.[4]

Many companies today, confronted with escalating global and domestic competition, are restructuring their organizations to boost productivity. Whether it be a downsizing, a merger, an acquisition, a leveraged buyout, a "de-layering," or a Chapter 11 reorganization, such changes create worries and debilitating uncertainty for those affected, especially workers who lose their jobs, but also for those left behind who fear they may lose their jobs. Traumatic forms of job-related uncertainty, better known as stress, pose a constant danger to employees' state of mind and physical well-being.

Quite naturally, such dangers can impair employees' on-the-job performance, which is an ongoing concern of productivity-conscious employers. Competition-obsessed top managements are bearing down hard on employees, pushing them to do more, to do it better and to do it in less time. Such pressure on employees to achieve unrealistically ambitious goals, often called "overtasking," can push some workers to cheat or behave unethically—as may have been the case with the Royal Accommodations managers who, due to pressure applied by CEO Arlen Royster, misreported financial results in order to hit stringent bottom-line targets.

Pressure and uncertainty have become as much a part of working as time cards and lunch breaks. Observes Tom Clausen, former chairman and CEO of Bank of America, during an interview in his San Francisco office: "You can't keep reducing staff and saying, 'We're not going [to do that anymore.]' You and I come to work tomorrow morning and Ron's gone. What happened to him? He's been de-employed. But we liked Ron. We enjoyed working with him. We miss him. Our morale is low. [The worry becomes], 'Who's next?' Everyone thinks, 'Ain't going to be me, I hope.' But they're never sure."

A major stress point in many employees' lives today is their constant efforts to juggle the overlapping demands of home and work. The dominance of this issue was confirmed in 1993 when the Families and Work Institute reported results of a five-year study encompassing 3000 employees that found that one of the "most important" reasons workers took their current job was its positive effects on their family life.[5] Nothing typifies this flourishing dilemma better than the child care issue—the number one concern in the workplace today. With the number of working parents escalating, concerns over child care preoccupy not just employees, but employers as well. The effects of anxiety over child care touch parent-employees in various ways: lower productivity, higher absenteeism, and more grievances.

Los Angeles Times reporter Harry Anderson describes what many workers whose employers don't offer on-site child care facilities grapple with each day: "Virtually every employer is hearing horror stories. *The long commute:* an hour to the day care center in the morning and half an hour from there to work—then reverse in the evening. *The fear:* a baby sitter disappears or quits. *The worry:* a parent is caught in traffic and won't be able to pick up a child before the center closes. *The panic:* a child is ill but too far away for the parent to rush over from work. *The frustration:* knowing that the only real solution may be to quit work and cut back your standard of living."[6]

As the child care movement has gained momentum, most employers have been pushed to respond in one way or another. A recent study by management consultant Hewitt Associates of more than 800 large companies found that two out of three companies offer some form of child care assistance.[7] Some companies, including giants like IBM, American Express, and Allstate Insurance, are forming networks of child and elder care services for their employees' families, a collective attempt to address the critical shortage of such services.[8] Most encouraging, however, is that more and more companies are realizing that they need—indeed, some view it as a responsibility—to help employees cope with caring for their children. Others, however, still see child care as a wasteful expense wholly unrelated to employees' worklives, a perspective heard only occasionally these days.

Increasing numbers of senior executives see child care and other issues affecting job performance as prudent long-term investments. At Johnson & Johnson, a recent internal study of the effects of company work-family programs over a two-year period showed that managers became more understanding of their employees' needs and more helpful to employees in finding ways to meet those needs. In addition, employees now feel more comfortable bringing up family or personal issues, and are more apt to stay with J&J as a result. A supportive immediate supervisor is one of the key factors in reducing so-called "negative spillover" from the job to home life, says Ellen Galinsky, co-president of the Families and Work Institute.[9]

The child care issue is but one example of how American management is responding, albeit slowly and reluctantly, to employees' changing needs and expectations. Looking down the road, the signs are positive and hopeful. Nevertheless, the road ahead will be long and bumpy.

Management Behavior
Changes "Glacially"

History teaches us that change will continue to "occur glacially, so slowly as to be almost imperceptible to the average worker," says Bob Baker of *Los Angeles Times*. Regrettably, his pessimistic prediction for the next decade offers little hope for these trends uncoiling any faster than a snail's pace. "It's likely that the 1990s will see more debate than resolution of issues like employee involvement and work versus family."[10]

Employees are often disheartened by management's sluggish efforts to adapt corporate policies and practices to their needs. It sometimes seems that top managers would rather talk about changes instead of making them. Many employers, even knowing employees' altered values and lifestyle preferences, have resisted relinquishing or even sharing control of the workplace with employees. Corporate managers, many of whom worked most of their careers to gain the manager title, cling to the belief that authority and control are rights they've earned through their hard work and loyalty.

As is true in most bureaucratic institutions, conservative-thinking managers are likely to initially resist the idea of changing their style to accommodate the so-called "new breed" of employees—a breed eager to get involved in helping manage their organizations. Such unresponsive management can, intentionally or otherwise, create disillusioned and low-performing employees. Years of research tells us that employees who are dissatisfied with the way managers treat them will be less productive, less loyal, and less committed to their organizations, and more apt to leave.

Furthermore, as management's role in the workplace changes, many fear losing their long-sought positions of authority, which to them define success. Therefore, they cling to tradition, to the passe belief that title bestows power, that managing means controlling and directing. What they really fear, says Harvard's Rosabeth Moss Kanter, is "a loss of power because much of their authority used to come from a hierarchical position. Now that everything seems negotiable by everyone, they are confused about how to mobilize and motivate staff."[11]

Many of the changes espoused by employees effectively blur the faint line distinguishing managers from nonmanagers. It's no wonder, then, that managers are not clamoring to install new systems they fear will make them obsolete. As a result, fundamental changes in organizational life come about slowly and often painfully, usually exacerbated by managers' defiant opposition. After more than 20 years of preparing for the vaunted "changing workplace," The Commission on the Skills of the American Workforce (a nonprofit task force co-chaired by former Secretaries of Labor Ray Marshall and William Brock), estimates that only "one employee in 20 works for a company with a serious program in place to redesign jobs so its people can increase their skills and work smarter."[12] That's not to say that such changes won't eventually happen on a wide-scale basis. For the time being, however, progressive employers face an ongoing challenge to simply attract and retain required skilled labor.

To meet that challenge, some top managers are taking the initiative, though hesitantly, to redesign the workplace in hopes of solidifying employees' eroding sense of corporate loyalty; strengthening employees' commitment to the organization's goals; increasing employees' job satisfaction; and helping employees learn to control stress-related problems. As Baby Boomers make room for Baby Busters, those 50 million Americans approaching or in their 20s, employers must try to forge relationships rooted in personal challenge and growth rather than money and titles.

Bank of America's former CEO Tom Clausen, long portrayed by the media as tough and insensitive, describes the essence of the "new" manager-employee association. "We're nothing without employees," he says. "We're not an institution of $95 billion of assets or x millions of dollars in profit. We're an organization of people. The only real resource we have is people. And in the financial services industry, the company with the best people is going to win."

Even though the pace of change may be frustratingly slow, it is beginning to pick up steam. The business literature is ripe with stories and examples of organizations that have incorporated new and different work designs and cooperative labor-management strategies. Some are formal redesigns of organizational structures. Some embody new legal arrangements. Others offer financial incentives or ownership stakes to employees. Some attempt to make organizational life easier and more flexible for employees. Still others seek to make work more challenging and interesting. Each trend, in one way or another, represents an effort to improve how managers and employees work together and relate to one another.

The Rise of "Participative Management"

A handful of companies have launched workplace experiments designed to cater to employees' changing values. Many others are talking about joining the movement. The preeminent general strategy for reaching this new plateau is called "participative management," a broad-based idea spawned years ago as a response to employees' desire for greater involvement in workplace decisions.

The participative management philosophy seeks to methodically dismantle the old, top-down manager-employee relationship. In real terms, the general notion of participative management spans a continuum of differing employee involvement strategies. At one end are low-involvement or passive approaches, such as suggestion boxes and telephone hotlines. At the other end are more complicated and aggressive high-involvement strategies, such as employee stock ownership plans and employee representatives on boards of directors. Along the continuum are participative management alternatives such as quality circles, labor-management committees, flextime, job sharing, job rotation, and gainsharing. The major difference distinguishing one program from another is the quality and quantity of input employees have to workplace decisions.

The goal of all participative management approaches, regardless of where they fall on the continuum, is to draw employees into the decision-making and managing processes in meaningful ways. To do that, lines of communication need to be opened and information needs to be shared vertically and horizontally. Two strikingly different case examples should help illustrate the scope and diversity of approaches covered under the generic participative management umbrella: self-managing work teams and employee stock ownership plans, known as ESOPs for short.

The Teamwork Approach

Self-managing work teams, more commonly called "superteams," consist of small groups of employees, usually between 10 and 30, who act as entrepreneurial work units. Generally speaking, these groups handle a set of interrelated—or cross-functional—tasks focused on a certain aspect of the business, such as billing or manufacturing. As the term implies, when a superteam is working effectively it manages itself in every aspect of worklife—including scheduling, training, profit targets, hiring and firing, quality improvements, and even establishing its own compensation strategies. The theory behind self-managing teams is to push decision-making down to those who know the business best and empower them with ultimate responsibility for their work. This, so the thinking goes, should increase employees' perceptions of self-fulfillment and control of their own professional destinies.

Self-managing superteams reflect a substantial change in the labor-management balance of power. In a team environment, employees are no longer told what to do and expected to do it. Now they have to think more for themselves, organize themselves, share information among themselves, and solve problems for themselves.

This concept, like most that fall under the participative management rubric, is fraught with controversy because managers perceive it as diluting their control and power. That fear may partially explain why this form of participative management hasn't caught on at more companies. A recent survey of 476 *Fortune* 1000 companies conducted by the American Productivity & Quality Center (AP&QC) in Houston found that only about seven percent of the workforce is presently organized into superteams.[13] Current signals suggest, however, that the number of organizations willing to try self-managing teams will grow substantially during the remainder of the 1990s. Half of those companies responding to the AP&QC survey said they plan to use superteams in the near future.

It's no wonder. Early results from companies using self-managing teams, manufacturing and service firms alike, reveal dramatic productivity improvements and increasingly satisfied employees. At General Mills, for instance, productivity at plants using superteams is as much as 40 percent higher than at other traditionally organized factories. After being asked by the CEO, blue-collar teams at Johnsonville Foods in Wisconsin decided to support a plant expansion program, even though it meant they had to work harder for a while. The teams studied the problem, said yes, and productivity is up 50 percent since 1986.

Aetna Life & Casualty sharpened its customer service and reduced the need for many of its middle managers after structuring its home office into superteams. The highly publicized joint venture between General Motors and Toyota at GM's Fremont, California plant has used employee-run teams to turn out more cars with 2000 fewer employees compared to a conventionally organized operation—and the cars are rated among the highest quality in the United States.[14]

A major reason for the encouraging impact of superteams, say experts, is because teams made up of a cross-section of people with varying skills and hailing from different parts of the company can effectively break through bureaucratic walls that isolate functions to get a job done.[15]

Another key to the process of self-managing is the open-mindedness of the people participating—that is, being flexible and receptive to new ideas and workplace changes. This sort of approach can prompt changes in the workers themselves as well as in the work environment, including how employees do their jobs and relate to others in their organizations; how middle and upper-level managers accept new roles; how team members learn new skills; and how workers take responsibility for their own decisions. In addition, employees are more likely to share information with one another, listen to others' suggestions, and consider what's best for the team.

Superteams are unwritten contracts between management and employees intended to alter their workplace relationship. This new type of labor-management arrangement is designed to pull back some of the reins of control in management's hands. Much of that control grew out of management's hoarding of information by constricting the lines of communication between managers and employees, and between employees and other employees. By definition, self-managing teams trample on these old-line ways of managing.

The teamwork approach is far more sophisticated than it might seem. Thomas Kuczmarski says that just relabeling work units and patting workers on the head doesn't do it. "In most companies, multidisciplinary teams are just lip service, because companies don't provide the right motivation and incentive.

Most top managers think people should just find 20 percent more time to work on a new team project. It's a very naive and narrow-minded approach."[16] Moreover, it isn't enough to form new groups of workers and tell them to do things their way. Teamwork represents a far deeper recognition by management of the need to turn their organizations upside down and transform the basic ways work gets done, ranging from reward systems to communication systems to performance appraisal systems. To make the team philosophy work demands patience and a whole new way of thinking about how managers and employees ought to relate to and communicate with one another.

The Employee Ownership Approach

Another example of participative management in action is the employee stock ownership plan, or ESOP. With this approach, employees are substantially more involved in running their organizations than they are as members of superteams, which usually limit workers' participation to concerns with day-to-day operational issues. In contrast, ESOPs give employees a direct financial stake in their companies, partially tying their fortunes to the company's bottom-line performance.

Because of the financial incentives built into ESOPs, employees' motivation and productivity should, promise proponents, increase substantially as the natural, divisive conflict between company and employee economic interests are reduced by sharing the financial risks. As with superteams, this new employee-ownership role should give workers more of a say in decisions affecting their companies.

ESOPs are, by their very nature, more complicated to operate than superteams. For instance, how superteams are structured and how they operate is based solely on the company's discretion. There are no established standards or legal regulations. That's not the case with employee stock ownership plans.

The ESOP movement has taken root in the American business landscape in recent years. Upon entering the 1990s, the National Center for Employee Ownership reported that there were about 9000 ESOPs incorporating about nine million employees nationally.[17] In the last couple of years alone, about 200 public companies set up ESOPs, including such powerhouses as Anheuser-Busch, Lockheed, Procter & Gamble, Polaroid, and Avis.[18]

The early results of ESOPs have been very encouraging. ESOP companies have generated more jobs and higher sales growth than their non-ESOP competitors. Ten-year projections suggest that companies with ESOPs will generate 46 percent more jobs and a sales increase 40 percent higher than they would have without employee ownership, according to the National Center for Employee Ownership.[19] The impact is revealed on the P&L statement as well as in employee attitudes. Take the case of Brunswick Corporation, which established an ESOP in 1983. Sales per employee jumped 50 percent by 1988. This improvement, explains William McManaman, vice president for finance, spills over to how employees feel about themselves and the company, "The ESOP has improved morale of our employees by creating a sense of ownership and has had a definite impact on productivity."[20]

The effectiveness of ESOPs as a participative management tool has been suspect at times. On occasion, ESOPs have been used as a defense against unfriendly takeover attempts and as a means to escape bankruptcy. That was exactly the scenario involving department store giant Carter Hawley Hale, which filed for bankruptcy in early 1991.

Several years earlier, the company—a takeover target of several aggressive competitors—shifted 45 percent of its stock to its employees in hopes of staving off further buyout attempts. To the employees, the ESOP was presented as a way to directly support their company and, assuming that the stock's value grew as expected, to better their own financial positions. Carter Hawley also created an employee savings plan; those funds were used to buy more shares of company stock. In theory, these financial maneuvers were suppose to benefit everyone, but especially the company's employees. Everything was, of course, contingent upon Carter Hawley Hale stock remaining healthy. Unfortunately, that didn't happen. A share of stock tumbled from $14 in 1989 to $2 in 1991.

When the company was forced to file for Chapter 11 protection, many of its employees were shocked when they lost their jobs and learned that their nest eggs and retirement accounts had practically been wiped out. Some employees expressed their anger over the company's failure to explain to them the risks inherent in the savings plan when it was initially offered. Many Carter Hawley workers steadfastly argued that they never fully understood the potential risks and rewards ratio of their ESOP because management failed to adequately communicate that information to them. To what extent is that management's responsibility? In retrospect, many employees believe that their participation in company affairs had been little more than an illusion.

Employee ownership without real participation in organizational matters is not likely to gain employees' commitment. Overall, employee-owned companies using participative approaches show an 11 percent faster growth rate than those that don't, reports the National Center for Employee Ownership. But when ownership and genuine participation are combined, as car renter Avis has done, the effects can be extraordinary. Avis, which initiated a 100 percent ESOP among its 23,000 employees in 1987, has seen dramatic improvements in operating profit, market share, employee morale, productivity, and customer service (customer complaints went down 35 percent).

The reason for this upgraded performance was not the installation of the ESOP alone, explains Avis CEO Joe Vittoria, but the continuous two-way dialogue it forced between managers and employees. Avis has, for example, created employee participation groups that meet monthly at each of its company-owned sites. These groups have license to suggest new ideas for improving any aspect of the company's business. And to further bolster the participative process, Avis provides training in people skills for its managers. "If people think improved productivity just takes giving shares to employees, they're wrong," says Vittoria. "A big part of my time is spent meeting with employees."[21] The real key, claims the CEO, is "how you involve the employees, how you maintain a dialogue, listen to their input, and use it."[22]

Although ESOPs are more legally and administratively complex than self-managing teams, the two approaches share the common objective of bringing employees more into the mainstream as full-fledged, empowered participants of their companies. If clumsily administered or misunderstood by employee-owners, ESOPs have the potential to disappoint or hurt those intended to benefit; if adeptly applied, ESOPs can energize and meaningfully involve employees in their organizations. Crucial to the effectiveness of ESOPs or superteams or any other form of participative management is open and candid communication among organizational members.

"Participative management" as a concept and a practice symbolizes the core changes driving today's workplace. As a concept, few managers would argue with the efficacy and appropriateness of employees participating in shaping their work environment. As a practice, however, participative management has been slow to grab hold in the workplace. To date, slightly less than 10 percent of all employees are part of any kind of a participative management program. Across the board, American employees still feel left out, dissatisfied with the way top management treats them. Recent evidence, however, offers encouragement that more employers may be willing to experiment with some form of systematic employee participation.

Communication: At the Heart of Participative Management

For any participative management strategy to work effectively, managers and employees have to trust each other. A trusting relationship is built on understanding and credibility; that is, each party knowing the other party's needs and motivations, and believing unequivocally that what the other says is true. Forging trust, never easy to do or to do quickly, demands consistent, candid, two-way communication that opens the door to understanding and, thus, credible relationships.

By intention, participative management "forces" labor and management to work closer together, to share information, and, most significantly, to communicate directly and frequently in ways long considered by American managers inappropriate or a waste of time. The success or failure of a participative management venture is largely dependent on managers' and employees' communication effectiveness over time, maintains Max DePree, CEO of furniture-maker Herman Miller. "There may be no single thing more important in our efforts to achieve meaningful work and fulfilling relationships than to learn and practice the art of communication."[23]

At the heart of the participative management ideology must be management's willingness to listen to employees' ideas and suggestions, and employees' belief that their voice will be heard and their recommendations considered. "Participative management guarantees that decisions will not be arbitrary, secret, or closed to questioning," says DePree. But, he quickly cautions, participative management doesn't imply that management should arbitrarily relinquish its role as the ultimate decision-maker. "Participative management is not democratic. Having a say is different than having a vote."[24] Employees who have a say—that is, true participation in managing their worklives—are much more likely to give their loyalty.

A Final Word

The tightly structured workplace and the passive workforce of the 1970s and 1980s are no more. Employees today do not resemble generations past whose major worry was pay and stability; in contrast, contemporary workers are motivated by self-actualization and a need to be involved in workplace decisions. Also, major demographic shifts have spawned a workforce frustrated with trying to juggle the stressful demands of work and home. These emerging, new employee attitudes and concerns demand sensitive, "shared" approaches to managing—that is, cooperative, participative management models that depend on give-and-take forms of communication between managers and employees.

Returning to Arlen ...

As Chap. 1 ended, Arlen was breaking the news to his executive staff about Royal's fraudulent financial reporting crisis. As expected, most were shocked and disbelieving. Mike Keller, VP of operations and long-time Royal veteran, immediately pointed the finger of blame at Arlen, claiming that it was the unrelenting pressure the CEO put on Royal managers to meet unrealistic bottom-line goals that practically forced them to manipulate revenue results. Communication VP Rick Jamieson argued that the entire executive staff, not Arlen alone, must accept responsibility. Arlen ordered that mum's the word for now and that each VP should start drafting plans for handling the crisis.

As we rejoin Arlen, he is about to meet with Royal's patriarch-chairman, Jim Stamps. While expressing his understanding of Arlen's precarious position, Stamps assures the CEO of his support for now—but reminds him in no uncertain terms that his support is contingent upon something positive happening very soon.

"Some Bets Are Worth Losing"

Wednesday, October 10, 10 a.m.   Arlen was emotionally and mentally drained, and it wasn't even lunch time yet.

He moved slowly down the hallway toward his office, the usual spring in his step missing. The energy rush he'd felt during the early morning staff meeting had abandoned him.

The meeting with Jim Stamps, Royal's chairman, had been trying. It had been terribly uncomfortable rehashing the forensic audit team's findings with his boss and mentor. Their talk had sapped Arlen. Stamps' parting comment had not reassured him much; he knew the politically savvy Stamps would support him only as long as he believed it prudent to do so.

"I know you're on top of things, Arlen, and you know I'm behind you as much as I can be," Stamps had said, raising his 270-pound bulk from the oversized chair behind his desk. "But if I can't show the board something tangible very soon," he warned, pausing and exhaling a weighty sigh, "or at least offer up a plausible explanation or a symbolic head or two, we may be out on the street. Am I making myself clear?"

"Loud and clear, Jim," Arlen said after a moment, a lump forming in his throat. With that, Stamps fell back into his chair, looking suddenly older and more haggard than his 67 years.

Now, as Arlen entered the friendly confines of his own office, his thoughts returned to Mike Keller. "What do I do about him?" he whispered to himself, removing his suit jacket before slipping behind his desk but not sitting. He couldn't shake thinking about something Keller had said during the staff meeting. In spite of Keller's motives, Arlen knew he was right about one thing: The CEO must ultimately answer for a company's actions.

He'd have to figure out what to do about Keller a little later. Right now, he was worried—for himself and the company—right down to his toes. The stakes couldn't be any higher. Despite his deep concerns, though, he felt turned on by the enormity of challenge before him. He couldn't explain this strange, illogical sensation, but he was enjoying the excitement he felt. Maybe it was his need for self-renewal, for recapturing the thrill of accomplishing something important he'd thrived on during his climb to the top. Lately, he'd felt bored with his work, his mind often wandering during meetings and his patience short when his staff made typically human mistakes.

Finally giving in to his mental fatigue, he collapsed into his high-backed orthopedic chair, his wife Andrea's gift to him when he attained the CEO title. Seconds later, just as his eyes were closing, the blare of his private line cut into the silence he'd just begun to enjoy. After two bursts, he hit the button on the speaker box.

"Royster."

"You're a tough guy to reach, Mr. CEO. Forget about me?" Andrea's lilting, high-pitched voice was tinged with annoyance. Instantly, he felt guilty.

"Sorry, Andy. I haven't had a moment to myself since Jamieson popped in on me early this morning. I've been trying to figure out a way to save this place—and me—from going the way of the buffalo." Arlen realized that Andrea wouldn't be calling him now unless there was a problem.

"What's up?"

"First, tell me how things are going there."

"Could be better. Could be worse, I guess. The fingers are being pointed ... in my direction. Not surprising. Solid information is scarce and all hell's about to break loose. Other than that, it's just another day at the office," he quipped. He rubbed his eyes vigorously, one with each hand, wishing he could make things appear differently.

"Do you know what you're going to do yet?" asked his wife and counselor of 26 years. She knew his every idiosyncracy and could read his words, tone, and non-verbal signals like nobody else. His tenseness didn't escape her.

"Nope. Not yet. Still talking to people and waiting for more information. Keller smells dirty and I think he's planning to come after me. He wants to be CEO so badly, he'd sell his soul to the devil for it," he said, a thumping headache pinching at his temples.

"Sounds like something Glenn would say about you," retorted Andrea, subtly switching the subject to their son. As she knew he would, he went for the bait.

"Jeez, Andy, don't make me feel any worse than I already do," Arlen pleaded. "How is that stubborn son of ours, anyway? Did you hear from him?" Deep down, Arlen hoped the answer was no. He wasn't sure he could handle Glenn's problems as well as his own right now. "Is everything all right?"

"I spoke to him this morning, a few minutes after you left. He's okay, I guess, except that he's really bothered about his uncertain future. The last conversation—or should I say argument—you and he had didn't help much."

In a flash, Arlen relived the ugly quarrel they'd had on the telephone last week. Guilt and regret tugged at him. Glenn always seemed to pick the worst times to push his father's hot buttons. And, Andrea had to admit, he never passed up a chance to do so.

"It didn't do much for my sleep that night either," Arlen recalled with some irritation. He shifted forward, resting on his knuckles face-down on the desk blotter.

"That kid fights me at every turn," he said, shaking his head in disgust. "I don't know why you think he wants my advice when I know damn well he doesn't give it a second's thought. I think he actually enjoys fighting with me, Andy.

"Of course he doesn't," she responded gently. "Listen, Arlen—you've just become immune to his feelings, his point of view. For two years now, I've heard you say over and over how hard you're trying to better understand your employees. That they're so different from you. And all the things you're trying to get inside their heads. The same's true about Glenn. Doesn't your own flesh and blood deserve at least the same from you?"

The question rudely confronted him, making his head pound even more. Then, her voice softer but firmer, Andrea said to her husband, "My dear, you may think you know your son, but you don't have a clue. You've lost touch with him."

The words "lost touch" crashed down on Arlen. He'd heard them three years ago, spoken with almost the same disturbed tone. And then, as now, he hated the feeling of failure they aroused in him. In an instant, his memory transported him back three years, when his accuser was Joyce Hadley during an unplanned conversation that would change forever the way Arlen managed.

* * * * * * * * *

He and Hadley had been on a flight together from New York's JFK to San Francisco. Arlen had been annoyed when he learned he'd have to fly commercial because the Royal-owned Lear jet was grounded for engine maintenance. The CEO was on his way to the annual conference of The Hotel Management Society at the St. Francis Hotel in downtown San Francisco. He was to be one of four panelists in a plenary session exploring the question: "Have American Hotels Lost Their Way?" Hadley was traveling to the Bay City to kick off a week of visits with Royal's regional personnel directors on the west coast.

They sat side-by-side in the roomy first-class section of the United Airlines 747 jumbo jet. The day before, Hadley—hired three months earlier to be Royal's corporate manager of personnel—learned accidentally that she and her boss were on the same flight. Immediately realizing her rare opportunity to hoard his attention, she wasted no time upgrading her coach ticket to first class.

Unbeknownst to Hadley, Arlen actually welcomed her companionship. He'd wanted to spend more time with his new head of personnel, but his unrelenting schedule as CEO of a fast-growth company kept him constantly on the go, rarely in New York for more than a few days at a time. He saw the flight as a chance to catch up and assess how she was handling the job.

Bringing Hadley to Royal was a real coup for Arlen. Only 35 at the time, Hadley was on the fast track at General Electric where she had spearheaded creation of an aggressive "new look" affirmative action program. After several months of courting her, Arlen finally convinced her to join Royal and help him "set the hotel industry on fire."

Her pleasant, round face exuded a fiery energy, centered by her wide, absorbing hazel eyes and bordered by shoulder-length auburn hair. She was, in many ways, the consummate professional woman of the '90s, plagued by the push-pull of her professional responsibilities and her desire to have more time with her two-year-old son and husband.

For the first hour of the trip, they chatted about general company news and Hadley's impressions of Royal's somewhat outdated approach to "personnel," an unfashionable term Hadley wanted to change—and she didn't waste time trying to do so. Shortly after take-off, as they sipped orange juice, the new personnel manager recommended that her department be renamed "human resources management" as soon as possible. "I'd like to raise the subject at our next staff meeting … of course, only if you've no objection," she informed her boss.

Hadley's directness pleased him. That's what had impressed him about her in the first place: She could speak her mind pointedly, without antagonizing. He thought she would shake things up at Royal. He didn't realize, though, that one of the first people she'd shake up would be him.

About two-and-a-half hours into the flight, following a lunch of shrimp cocktail and filet mignon, Arlen began leafing through a draft copy of a confidential report on a new retirement program he and the company's Compensation & Benefits Committee planned to distribute to Royal's board the next week for review. An outside benefits consultant had evaluated Royal's package against its primary competitors and concluded that "Royal's benefits program lagged far behind its three major competitors." Most persuasive to Arlen, however, was finding that "Royal was losing current and prospective employees, particularly entry-level manager-trainees, as a result of negative perceptions of the company's outdated benefits package." The long-run implications of that finding made it clear to Arlen that things had to change.

But there was considerable uncertainty over which parts of the benefits plan should be altered and which should remain intact. Of course, every new benefit costs the company millions of dollars. The issue had grated on his nerves for months now. He had stalled making a decision—until a few weeks ago. With the Compensation & Benefits Committee pressuring him for a response, he reluctantly gave in to his own indecision and agreed to go along with the consultant's recommendation to bolster the life insurance, disability, and retirement components of the package. He wasn't comfortable with the changes, but he couldn't put his finger on why. His discomfort had followed him around for weeks.

"Joyce, I probably should've talked to you about this some time ago," said Arlen, enjoying her eagerness. "But time hasn't been on my side lately. I'd like you to look over this proposal to change our employee benefits package and let me know what you think. Would you mind taking a few minutes now and giving it a quick read?"

"Sure. No problem. I heard something about this from a few people in my department and wondered when you'd mention it."

As she reached for the 10-page report, her eye was pulled to the bright red "CONFIDENTIAL" stamped in the center of the cover sheet. Then, after hesitating a few seconds to consider her next move, she decided to complete her thought.

"Frankly, I was wondering about your confidence in me as time passed and you didn't run this by me. It clearly falls into my area," she said protectively, avoiding looking at him. She was testing Arlen and he knew it.

He looked out the window, half noticing the multicolored geometric patterns of passing farmlands below. Then he looked directly at her. "Confidence in you? That's not in question," he said firmly, convincingly. "Not at all. It's just that I didn't want to dump something this big ... I mean ...

uh ... this sensitive in your lap so soon after you'd arrived. I figured you at least needed enough time to learn where the bathrooms are and who's who."

Just then, the captain's voice boomed over the PA system telling them they were about to enter some turbulent air and should return to their seats and fasten their safety belts. Sure enough, as the pilot signed off, the ice cubes in Arlen's glass tumbler began clinking as it started sliding off the tray. He grabbed it just as it was about to plunge into his lap. The entire cabin shook violently for a few seconds before the air smoothed out.

Arlen realized how weak his impromptu explanation sounded. He wasn't sure why he hadn't talked to her sooner. He really did believe in her ability. At least, he thought he did. Maybe he just wasn't used to her being at Royal yet. Or maybe he was embarrassed over his indecision. Not feeling in total control, not having the right answer at the ready, always made him uneasy. He couldn't explain it.

He swiveled back toward the window and heard Hadley click on her overhead reading light.

* * * * * * * * * *

Twenty minutes later, Hadley finished reading the report. She placed it on her lap and looked to see if Arlen was awake. His eyes were open, although drooping. He appeared to be lost in himself, looking but not seeing. She intruded, "Arlen, can we talk now?"

Slightly startled, Arlen's head jumped back as he refocused on Joyce, straightening his vest and crossing his legs in her direction. "Sure, Joyce. Sorry. I was really somewhere in those clouds out there," he admitted, pointing with a hitchhiker's thumb-out gesture. "I'm all ears. So what do you think of what we're considering doing?"

"Well, to tell you the truth," she began hesitantly, "and excuse my bluntness, but I think it really misses the mark. It doesn't address the sorts of needs employees ... Royal's employees ... have today. I really doubt that a large portion of our people would get too excited about more retirement benefits they wouldn't need for 20 or 30 years when they're struggling to meet child care and mortgage payments today."

A bit taken back, Arlen didn't miss a beat. "But this represents a multimillion dollar investment by Royal in our employees and their families' future security," he explained, sounding a little defensive.

"Don't get me wrong. This is a very generous investment by Royal," she said appeasingly. "I applaud those efforts. And I do recognize the need to beef up the benefits package. I just think it's misdirected. The way it's structured won't be seen by most employees as having much current value to them."

Hadley waited for Arlen to counter. When he didn't say anything, she added firmly, "And, unfortunately, that means Royal won't get much bang for its big bucks."

Almost as if on cue, a stewardess broke in and asked if they'd like an after-dinner cordial. Arlen begged off, preferring a diet Coke. Hadley decided on a chocolate liqueur; her biggest weakness was chocolate and she made no excuses about it.

As the stewardess left to get the drinks, the CEO's eyes came alive, darting rapidly from Hadley to the report and back again. "Wait a minute, Joyce. What do *you* think our employees want ... or should I say need?"

She began to answer, but Arlen quickly flicked up a hand to forestall her. "We looked long and hard at what they've told us they prefer," he defended. "I reviewed the data from our last survey myself. This plan sure as hell wasn't thrown together over coffee one morning. There's no question most of them want more to put into their nesteggs. With the dough we're sinking into the pension plan, our people ought to be dancing in the streets."

Arlen was quite animated now. Hadley didn't know him well enough then to realize how much he loved playing devil's advocate. It was one way he collected information and found out if people truly believed what they were telling him. The stewardess, not wanting to intrude, silently placed the drinks before them and drifted away.

"How long ago was that survey done?" she probed delicately, her voice and eyebrows rising.

"Oh, I'm not exactly sure. It's not that old. Maybe four years?" His shoulders scrunched forward in an indifferent shrug, indicating he didn't think the age of the data mattered much.

"Actually, it was five years ago," she corrected him, holding up five outstretched fingers. "I checked on it shortly after I joined Royal." He knew then that she'd been anticipating, or hoping, they'd have this conversation. "And the survey included only about 42 percent of all employees, most of them from old-line eastern cities like New York, Philadelphia, Chicago, and Boston. No properties from San Francisco, Dallas, Atlanta, or San Diego were even included."

Arlen felt a slight twinge of embarrassment. He hadn't known. "Really? It's been that long, has it?" Arlen asked, trying to sound nonchalant. He was impressed she'd checked the facts. He was beginning to think she had staged the entire conversation.

"As slowly as things move in a company the size of Royal, that doesn't strike me as being that long ago." Arlen was testing her convictions now. He leaned back, folded his arms, and waited.

She hesitated, peering at him. He was stone-faced. "Arlen, that's just not so," she said. "Five years can be a lifetime of changes when it comes to people's lives ... work lives as well as personal lives."

She saw in Arlen's eyes a flicker of encouragement, so she pushed on. "Just think about these facts, which I checked out last week," she said matter-of-factly, her pace gaining speed. "Over the past five years, Royal's workforce has increased in size by 35 percent. Most of these new employees are under 30, which has lowered the average age of a Royal employee from 34 five years ago to 32 today."

Arlen was amused—both at the statistic and at Hadley's initiative.

"Here's another one. The turnover among salaried employees over that same time period has averaged 29 percent a year. And among hourly employees, many of whom are part-time or not necessarily career-oriented, it's 43 percent."

She slowed her pace to drive home the next point. "People working in this company are constantly changing. To make any major decision without knowing what they think—today!—is to risk blowing the company's future." She stopped and focused on his face, which had turned pensive.

"Some interesting facts, Joyce," responded Arlen. "I'm listening. Please keep going." She nodded, her enthusiasm growing.

"Everything I've read and observed over the past five or six years screams out about how people have changed, especially the young and the very old," Hadley insisted. "Their drives and values and lifestyles are dramatically different than workers of years ago. What worked with the previous generation just won't do the trick today. Employees want to be treated differently. And they need different benefits."

Then, cupping her hands together and shaking them to drive home her point, she said, "I know I'm right about this. I know I'm right." Arlen liked her sincerity, her fire. He pressed her in another direction.

"Are you that different today from who you were five years ago, Joyce?" He was baiting her again. "I really doubt you are."

"I'm probably not a good example. But truthfully, I'm nothing like I was five years ago. Just ask my husband. My friends. I see my career in a totally different light today than when I was single and free of the obligations I have today, like dragging a whining two-year-old all over town searching for decent day care. That takes every ounce of leftover energy I have—and that's not saying much."

Unknowingly, Arlen had touched a nerve. "And the way I see myself career-wise has come full circle. Ten years ago, I was struggling at GE just to be accepted as a professional. Too many top-level managers, all men of course, questioned whether women, much less women with children, should be working at all." Her lips parted to continue, but she stopped herself. Arlen thought he understood and actually empathized with what she was saying, but he wasn't about to bite into this prickly pear.

He proceeded diplomatically, still trying to induce her to convince him that the new benefits package proposal was a mistake. "Sure things have changed some. And hopefully for the better. But people are people and they change awfully slowly."

"I think that depends on how you define slow," shot back Hadley, brushing her hair back over her shoulder. "Month to month, things don't change much. But over five years, people can do 180 degree flips. And it's easy to miss those changes if you aren't looking for them."

With her last sentence, her voice turned softer, more pacifying. She seemed to know instinctively how far to go to awaken him to what he needed to hear without losing him. "The truth is, Arlen, and I hate to be the one to tell you this, but you and most of your staff have ... have ... lost touch ... with your employees."

Arlen was stung where it hurt most—in his ego. The words "lost touch" tumbled over him, rudely assaulting his self-confidence. He wasn't used to his underlings speaking to him so bluntly, so critically, so ... so honestly. Was she being insubordinate? He thought he should be angry or resentful or hurt. He should put her in her place. But, inexplicably, he felt none of those emotions. "Why not?" he asked himself.

Then, from out of nowhere, it hit him like an undetected left hook to the chin. He realized what had been bothering him for months about the benefits package, but had eluded him until this very instant. It was so obvious. So simple. Yet he'd been unable—or unwilling—to see it. All the input he received on how to shape the benefits package had come from senior managers, all men and all over 45 who worked at headquarters. Most of them, like himself, saw the world through their eyes only, though they'd argue to the death they put employee interests ahead of their own.

"It's human nature to want your view to be the world view," continued Hadley eagerly, gently. "We all do it. At the risk of being blunt, Arlen, I

think that your committee has done a wonderful job convincing itself what
it thinks employees want—or maybe what it thinks employees should want."

Arlen's little inner voice told him that Hadley was probably right. The
employee opinion data, which Arlen had relied on to make his decision,
was out-of-date. It had simply been easier not to bother collecting new data.
Arlen wondered about the outside consulting firm. Why didn't those
high-priced consultants advise him as Joyce was now doing?

Things were suddenly clarifying. He felt somewhat revived, back in control.
The fog that had blinded him on this issue for so long was lifting. "So what
course of action do you propose, Ms. Hadley?" queried Arlen, his face
brightening. He thought he knew what she'd say. And now he welcomed it.

"Well, sir," she mimicked in a similar high-brow tone. "Hold off on
implementing the new benefits package. Keep an open mind. Let me do
a fresh survey of employees." She was watching him closely. Arlen appeared eager for more. "Give me about $25,000 and a month to get it done,
and I promise you accurate, up-to-date information showing how Royal
employees view the company and the world *today*."

"How about three weeks?" Arlen smiled sheepishly, always relishing a
good negotiation.

"Now I know why you've been so successful, Arlen. Never accept the
first offer," Hadley said, a broad grin replacing her intense expression. "I
think I can live with that," she added playfully. "But let's really make this
interesting. How about a little side wager?"

Arlen's curiousity was engaged. "You really are willing to put it on the
line, aren't you?" kidded the CEO.

"You bet I am," said Hadley. She swallowed hard, then ran her fingers over
her dark grey wool skirt. He thought he saw a hint of hesitation in her eyes.
But any reluctance she might've felt vanished as soon as she spoke.

"If the results of this survey show—no, make that convince you," she said,
her confidence ascending, "that Royal employees see their needs differently than you think they do, you agree to let my department conduct an
annual employee opinion survey for the next three years, no questions
asked." She crossed her arms. She'd just taken the mountain to Moham-
med. But for good measure, she added, "And, of course, you'll increase
my budget accordingly to do it."

"Of course," agreed Arlen sarcastically, willing to play along a little
longer. "But how will we agree that I've been ... convinced?" he asked, his
eyes narrowing as he studied her.

After a few seconds passed, she had it. "We'll define convinced as you willingly agreeing to change the mix of benefits in this package," she announced, holding up the report.

"You really are a gambler, aren't you?" shot back Arlen. "You're willing to leave the decision solely to me, eh?"

"Yes, I am," she said without a hint of hesitation. "You're a man of your word and I think a man of enormous good sense," she patronized, demonstrating her poise. "And," she appended, her grin widening, "I know you can't pass up a bargain when it stares you right in the face."

"Okay, what do you give up if I'm not convinced?"

"If I'm wrong … ," she paused, her voice drifting off as her mind spun in circles," … I'll agree not to press you to do another employee opinion survey for … for two years. In fact, I'll do the next one in three years without any additional budget."

"Are you serious about this?" She was giving away more than was necessary to make her point or win her position, he thought.

"Completely," she said firmly, slightly defiantly. "Do we have a deal?" He had the feeling that behind her poker face was a fair share of insecurity and doubt. If there was, he noted, she camouflaged it well. She seemed to have a sixth sense about how far to push, without falling over the edge.

"Sure, why not?" said Arlen magnanimously, extending his hand. "But let's keep this between us for now, okay?" Arlen couldn't help but feel he'd just stuck his own neck out pretty far and he didn't want the second-guessing to start prematurely.

"Deal." She reached for Arlen's hand and they shook vigorously. He felt a slight dampness in her palm. They each dropped back into their cushy seats, pondering for a moment the unusual business arrangement they'd just consummated. Then he turned toward her.

"Do you play much poker?" he inquired, a twinkle forming in his eyes. "I think maybe we ought to stop in Vegas on the way back—and find out just how lucky you really are."

"Nah. Gambling for money isn't nearly as intriguing as putting your ideas where your mouth is. Know what I mean?" She was enjoying this, Arlen could see. He peered out his sun-drenched window and realized he was too.

Hadley got up and said to him, "Excuse me just a minute, Arlen. I've got to make a call to New York, to a research firm I've used. Suddenly I have something important to talk to them about."

Her energy and enthusiasm buoyed Arlen's spirits. His curiosity was already rising about what the survey would reveal. Actually, he was far more nervous that the data might not convince him.

* * * * * * * *

Three-and-a-half weeks later, Arlen was pleased—and relieved—to admit to Hadley she'd won the bet. Following her thorough and adeptly argued presentation on the research firm's findings, everyone in the conference room, especially Arlen, was convinced the benefits package needed to be restructured. Slide after slide of data revealed new insights into what made Royal's employees tick.

Thanks to the research firm's manipulation of the data by various demographic, psychographic, cultural, and geodemographic categories, Arlen and the committee were treated to a new perspective on Royal's workforce. The survey, supplemented by a series of focus group interviews spanning all levels of the company, brought employees' concerns alive in compelling ways. For example, the video clips of employees speaking their minds about what was most important to them in deciding where to work made them more than statistics, but flesh and blood individuals who cared about Royal and cared even more about their families.

Arlen commented to Hadley later how moved he was by one young Hispanic bellman from Dallas who'd said in slightly broken English, but with intensity, "This company gave me a chance, a real chance, to become somebody when nobody else would. I'll never forget that. But I have six mouths to feed, and a mother and four brothers back in Mexico who depend on me for money every month. I'll do what I have to do to keep my job. If you ask me whether I'd rather put money away for a rainy day or have it in my pocket today so I can pay for babysitters and doctor bills, I don't have to think very long about it."

About midway through the presentation, Arlen had looked over at Hadley, who'd been intently watching him, and gave her a thumbs up sign. She smiled graciously and bowed her head deferentially.

Six months later, at Arlen's initiative and with no resistance from the board or any executive staffer, Joyce Hadley's department was renamed Human Resources Management and six months after that, she was promoted to vice president. One of her first hires was the company's first full-time director of employee research.

* * * * * * * * *

An irked voice penetrated through Arlen's flashback, immediately pulling him back to the here and now.

"Arlen ... Arlen, are you listening to me? I said you've lost touch with your son." Andrea was miffed at her husband's lengthy silence, his preoccupation with something, or somebody, else. "What do you have to say about that?" she demanded. He wished he knew.

PART 2

What We Know: The Link Between Communication and Leadership

3
Redefining Communication— The Essence of Leadership

Although not visible to the naked eye, most U.S. businesses today have hung on their front door a large help wanted sign. Those signs spell out corporate America's ongoing search for the rarest of individuals: the corporate leader. They symbolize business' call for a new type of CEO, one who understands both how to manage the bottom-line and how to motivate an eclectic work force. Finding in one individual those dual sets of capabilities is every organization's hope, but is as rare as a Lee Iacocca or a Peter Ueberroth.

The American marketplace is in turmoil, reeling from escalating global competition, a worsening skilled labor shortage, and a fast-changing, diversi-fied work force—factors which, when taken together, demand more flexible, give-and-take forms of organizational leadership. Consequently, the need for multitalented CEO-leaders has never been greater as the marketplace turns more complex and cutthroat, and employees become more disillusioned with management and insecure about the future. But the unavoidable question confronting U.S. business is: Are there sufficient leaders-in-waiting capable of succeeding in the "new wave" marketplace?

For years, we've heard about the widening "leadership gap" in corporate America. Harvard's John Kotter has characterized most U.S. firms today as being "over-managed" and "under-led."[1] His point is that top management has relied too much on control, bureaucracy, and top-down authority. We've all heard the horror stories about companies aimlessly adrift in the cross-currents of an unforgiving business environment because they lack a captain to keep the ship on course. There are other stories about American managers' fixation with delivering short-term profits at the expense of long-range growth. And there are still other stories about the profitable companies which won't stay that way because their top managers lack the vision and human relations skills needed to inspire others and gain their allegiance. Clearly, a business imperative of the 1990s must be to develop a new legion of top executives— individuals who thrive on big challenges, who can handle constant pressure, and who relish a high-profile job. For those with the interpersonal and administrative talents for that brand of leadership, the route to the top can be non-stop.

In this chapter, we analyze the concept of leadership and how it fits into today's business world. We also examine the allied concepts of communication and leadership and analyze how they help shape manager-employee relationships. To illustrate some of our points, we look at the leadership styles of three national leaders: Lee Iacocca and his transformation of Chrysler, and the contrasting leadership/management styles of former Presidents Ronald Reagan and Jimmy Carter.

Transforming CEOs
Into "Leaders"

Being appointed a CEO doesn't guarantee that a person will, in fact, be a leader. Leadership capabilities are neither God-given nor automatically acquired with status, title, or experience. If those skills could be obtained by divine intervention, then every pope would possess the charm and magnetism of John Paul II. Similarly, if they came attached to the CEO title, then every top executive would have the persuasive ability of Ross Perot. More accurately, leadership is learned and earned over time, dependent on how others perceive a leader's personal attributes, view of the future, and treatment of others.

Abraham Zaleznik of Harvard argues that corporate top managers have fallen prey to what he calls the "managerial mystique" of believing that wielding power and creating bureaucratic structures makes for good leadership. He maintains that "the mystique requires managers to dedicate themselves to process, structures, roles, and indirect forms of communication,"[2] and forces them to ignore the crucially important human side of organizational life and the more direct forms of communication that can draw people together. An abundance of executives suffer from this "managerial mystique"—an unfortunate truism that has deterred the development of many top managers into human relations-oriented leaders.

Why is there such a shortage of competent corporate leaders? Simply put, most professional managers don't understand what leadership is or how to use it.

They've been trained to manage technical systems, not to lead people. CEOs see themselves as their company's super *manager*: the planner, the organizer, the controller, the problem-solver. They don't see themselves as *leaders*, except perhaps by virtue of their title. But, of much greater concern, is that they don't know how to act as leaders. The manager's job description says nothing about being a role model, a trend-setter, a visionary, or a voice for change. The idea of being a leader is foreign and fuzzy to most CEOs. Few actually distinguish—intellectually or otherwise—between their management and leadership obligations. As a result, most are ill-equipped for the responsibilities of organizational leadership.

What does it take to be a leader today? The attributes change from organization to organization and situation to situation. One size leader does not fit all organizations or situations. Like human beings, organizations move through a series of life stages. At each stage, the organization's problems require different sorts of solutions. Depending on the stage and the problems, the leadership style needed will shift accordingly. For example, a company in the throes of bankruptcy probably needs a bold, decisive CEO, one with authoritarian tendencies and expertise in finance and accounting. On the other hand, an organization poised to enter new markets with new products probably needs a CEO with a penchant for flexibility and risk taking, and who has a strong sales/marketing and customer orientation.

Contemporary CEOs are expected to be more than financial or operations wizards who make wise decisions behind closed doors. They're also expected to be able to sell those decisions to diverse organizational stakeholders and gain their buy-in. The job has shifted from one emphasizing technical skills to one stressing a mix of technical and human relations talents. In his book, *The New CEO*, George Steiner says a CEO's capabilities need to be far broader today than in the past, especially in the noneconomic and nontechnical areas of business. As CEOs get more involved in shaping public policy and employee relations strategies, they necessarily are forced to assume high public profiles.[3]

Business needs CEOs who believe not only in making money but who also want to make people happy in their worklives. *Business Week* describes the metamorphosis of the CEO's broadening responsibilities:

> Not long ago, the chief executive was responsible for three things: making money, setting strategy, and grooming a successor. Today, CEOs who do only that won't be doing it for long. What's necessary is a repertoire of roles that aren't being taught in business schools. The CEOs who get to the head of the corporate class will be able to play them all: tough cost cutter, dynamic corporate communicator, hands-on manager, sophisticated financier, a motivator of employees.[4]

A generalist who's also a multitalented specialist—that's the schizophrenic expectation of CEOs today.

The Essence of Leadership

Leadership may not have any universally accepted definitions, but everybody seems to want their top managers to be perceived as leaders. Is there really a difference?

During his unsuccessful presidential campaign, former Governor Michael Dukakis persistently claimed that the pivotal issue confronting Americans was "the L word," meaning leadership. His triumphant opponent, one-term President George Bush, referred to "the V or vision thing." Whatever terms or acronyms are used, there's little question that leadership, whether applied to politics or business, has captured the American public's imagination. This was never more apparent than in CEO Ross Perot's surprisingly strong, grassroots presidential bid, a phenomena perhaps reflecting the American electorate's longing for new and different types of political leadership.

Book stores today are overrun with titles on various aspects of leadership and management. Major business publications such as *Fortune*, *Business Week*, and *Harvard Business Review* can't seem to publish an edition without a story on some new perspective of leadership or the "how to's" of management. This explosion of interest in leadership has generated mounds of new and revealing information on a long misunderstood subject. But understanding such an abstract and complex concept remains elusive.

What is this thing we call leadership? Most of us are hard-pressed to define it, but we'd probably claim to know a leader when we saw one. Are leaders those individuals we anoint to head governments or social movements or moral causes? Or are they people, regardless of position or background, to whom we're inexplicably attracted and believe in because of the irresistible force of their personality and/or ideas?

Think about it. When asked to name the leaders you most admire, what names jump to mind? Franklin Delano Roosevelt? Saddam Hussein? Gloria Steinem? Martin Luther King? Margaret Thatcher? Jesse Jackson? Boris Yeltsin? Gandhi? George Bush? Adolf Hitler? Mother Theresa? Ralph Nader? John F. Kennedy? Bob Hope? Jesus Christ? Abraham Lincoln? Is a leader larger-than-life, a doer of great things, a great communicator, a conqueror of evil?

Perhaps before trying to define leadership, we should look at what a typical leader does. Former President Harry Truman said leadership is "the ability to get other people to do what they don't want to do, and like it."[5] In his book, *Prisoners of Leadership*, psychologist Manfred Kets de Vries suggests that leadership is akin to leading the charge or sounding the drumbeat for others. He thinks leadership should "create new visions and unleash and channel the untapped talent that exists at every level of an organization ... for the challenges of tomorrow. As catalysts for change, [leaders] have to set this process in motion."[6] Truly inspired leadership can unleash the latent power of the human spirit, and when that happens, which isn't often, there may be no greater force for change in any business setting.

Until recently, the topic of leadership was rarely spoken in the same breath as business terms like profit, return on investment, and employee relations. After all, so the argument went, business needs great managers, not great leaders. But as businesses struggle to survive and names like Sam Walton, Frank Lorenzo, Donald Trump, and Jack Welch become as common as Richard Nixon, Jesse Jackson, Robert Redford, and Nolan Ryan, business people are starting to think more about the elements of leadership and how they differ from management.

Leadership vs. Management

During the past 20 years, both internal and external pressures have contributed to the burgeoning need for stronger business leadership. "Most firms didn't need much leadership—until the 1970s," says Harvard's John Kotter. But as business became "more competitive, more volatile, tougher," he argues, the old ways of managing became inappropriate and ineffective. Something else was needed: leadership.[7] As we discussed, not only is the business environment changing, so are the people inhabiting the workplace—people who don't respond well to the old ways of managing or doing business. By the early 1980s, point out researchers Richard Ruch and Ronald Goodman, workers were becoming angry with and alienated from top-level management in droves, thus creating a crisis in leadership.[8]

Although leadership and management are related and equally necessary to a business organization, they differ in objectives, functions, and skills. These distinctions reveal some of the intricacies of the CEO's increasingly complex role—a role that's shifting from a management to a leadership orientation. The explanations of how leadership differs from management are legion and diverse. Viewed collectively, however, certain patterns emerge.

USC's Warren Bennis studied this issue for many years and insists that there's a "profound difference—a chasm—between leaders and managers." He describes the core difference this way: "managers doing things right, while leaders do the right things." More precisely, he says that "managing is about efficiency. Leading is about effectiveness. Managing is about how. Leading is about what and why. Management is about systems, controls, procedures, policies, structures. Leadership is about trust—about people ... Leadership looks at the horizon, not just the bottom-line."[9]

In contrast, Kotter sees leadership and management as separate, albeit complementary, organizational systems. In his view, management "is about coping with complexity," about bringing "order and consistency" to organizational life. In contrast, he sees leadership as "coping with change." Leadership doesn't attempt to bring order; it attempts to bring a sense of purpose and direction so that people will be better able to adapt to changes within the workplace.[10]

Although many researchers have studied the meaning and practice of leading, their varying findings illustrate how elusive the concept is. Consider how several prominent business scholars define leadership similarly—yet differently. Kotter sees leadership as comprised of three complementary *factors*: (1) establishing direction, (2) aligning people, and (3) motivating and inspiring people.[11] Bennis and colleague Burt Nanus, in contrast, frame effective leadership in terms of four *strategies*: (1) attention through vision, (2) meaning through communication, (3) trust through positioning, and (4) deployment of self through positive self-regard.[12]

How do you compare these definitions? Notice the variations in language and emphasis, beginning with leadership "factors" vs. leadership "strategies." Each refers to the long-range aspect of leadership, which Kotter calls "direction" and Bennis and Nanus term "vision." Other differences also stand out; for example, Kotter's factors appear to stress the leader's need to influence or create change in other people, while Bennis and Nanus focus more on the leader's personal characteristics, namely trust and positivism. Interestingly, of the many definitions we reviewed, only Bennis and Nanus explicitly singled out communication as an integral component of leadership. Most leadership paradigms indirectly address some aspect of communication, usually its message delivery role, but don't necessarily explain those aspects in communication terminology.

A number of other definitions emphasize the leader's personal attributes and objectives. That was the case in 1988 when *Fortune* magazine, prompted by the Bush-Dukakis debate over how to resolve the national leadership crisis, developed a cover story that analyzed the essentials of corporate leadership. *Fortune*'s "seven keys to business leadership" were: (1) trust your subordinates, (2) develop a vision, (3) keep your cool, (4) encourage risk, (5) be an expert, (6) invite dissent, and (7) simplify.[13] Again, the common term is vision. Communication seems to underlie leadership by simplifying messages and seeking feedback by inviting dissent.

Another slightly different way of viewing leadership is offered by Zaleznik. He sees a leader's major function as being an organization's shepherd of new and innovative ideas. "Whereas managers focus on process," he says, "leaders focus on imaginative ideas. Leaders not only dream up ideas, but stimulate and drive other people to work hard to create reality out of ideas."[14]

What does all this tell us about leading and managing? True leadership seeks to instill in followers a belief in a leader's ideas and integrity, and belief in the future. A leader's thinking embraces—or should embrace—all aspects of organizational life, from employees' dreams to an organization's products and structure, emphasizing the long-range implications of decisions. Managing concentrates on the limited picture of the here and now, the details involved in getting the job done today. These distinctions are clearer on paper than they are in reality. On the job, the line between leading and managing is blurry at best. The difference, says Kotter, is that managing *controls* people by pushing them in the right direction; leading *motivates* them by satisfying their basic human needs to achieve and belong.[15]

All leaders must manage at times and all managers must lead at times. The higher one ascends in an organization, the more one must lead and the less one should manage. In real time, however, the two notions are practically indistinguishable; the differences rest more in an executive's reading of a situation and how to handle it, which usually will involve mixing and matching certain management and leadership principles.

Unfortunately, there is no sharply defined set of management rules and another set of leadership rules. Knowing when to change hats (figuratively speaking, of course) is what separates the average executive from the excellent one. Leading and managing serve organizations in different ways. Over the long haul, though, leadership determines, maybe more than any other function, an organization's success, says Russell Palmer, former dean of the Wharton Business School: "Leadership is the prime difference between a lot of successes and failures. We have a lot of managers—short-term, control-oriented, report-oriented. Leaders think longer-term, grasp the relationship of larger realities, think in terms of renewal, have political skills, cause change, affirm values, achieve unity."[16]

Which comes first, leading or managing? This is a chicken-and-egg question, but there does seem to be a logical order. Learning to manage is usually the first step, a necessary precursor to leadership. Supervisory personnel who aspire to the top positions in corporate America must first walk as managers before they can hope to run as leaders. An effective executive should understand the subtle differences, and be able to manage systems and lead people. Would-be leaders who aren't able to *manage* their human and physical resources constructively are unlikely to survive as leaders for very long. Some are able to make that transition, others aren't.

Leader-Manager vs. Manager-Leader: Reagan and Carter

Take the case of President Jimmy Carter. His inability to shift from a manager's to a leader's perspective may have been a major reason for his unanticipated departure from the White House after only one term. Originally a naval officer and nuclear engineer, Carter gained national prominence largely on the strength of his reputation as a professional manager while serving as two-term governor of Georgia.

As President, he received high marks for his long hours devoted to the details of running the bureaucratically-bloated federal government. He was said to be an accomplished planner, budgeter, strategist, meeting conductor, memo writer, and negotiator. He much preferred to involve himself in management-oriented activities which he could do at his desk or in a conference room. In public settings, however, he often appeared nervous and stiff, such as during nationally televised speeches or news conferences.

Carter's greatest triumph as President—convincing Egypt's Anwar Sadat and Israel's Menachem Begin to put aside generations of hatred and war to pursue a new era of peace—was achieved behind closed doors, hidden from public view and media scrutiny. Yet his well-intentioned communication campaign (such as media interviews, televised and community speeches) to gain the American people's support for his human rights crusade and his efforts to gain the release of the American hostages held in Iran failed to inspire public confidence in either his leadership or his policies. A strong manager, Jimmy Carter lacked the public charisma and the public communication skills necessary to win people's "minds and hearts." As a result, he was seen by a majority of Americans as a weak leader and was soundly defeated by Ronald Reagan, a man who was seen by many citizens as the epitome of a public leader.

Carter, who held a leadership position but who's strong suit was managing, might be labeled a "manager-leader;" Reagan, who's strength was publicly communicating his vision for America, is the flip side—a "leader-manager." It's been widely reported, for example, that Reagan avoided many of the day-to-day technical details of running the Oval Office. He preferred to delegate such matters to his staff and focus his attention on the big picture. A common perception of the former actor and governor was that he was unfamiliar with and uninterested in the specifics of his administration's policies. Apparently, he delegated most of the detail work of government to his staff. It was not surprising, then, that he was far less tuned in to how his advisors and cabinet chiefs managed their departments than was Jimmy Carter.

Although relatively uninvolved in the intricacies of managing, Reagan, dubbed by some as the "Great Communicator," commanded an avid and faithful following through both his terms as president. Due to his masterful use of language, his unflinching emphasis on fundamental "American" values, and his polished stage presence, Ronald Reagan was able to win widespread public support for his positions and causes. His prepared, polished manuscripted public speeches, memorable for his thespian's flare for timing and cadence, were always delivered flawlessly and persuasively. This leadership aura he enjoyed led to his being dubbed the "Teflon President," because of his uncanny ability to prevent any negative news from sticking to him.

The American public swept Ronald Reagan into office in 1980 and kept him there in 1984. The majority of citizens believed in him, at least until the Iran-Contra affair. And even then many of his faithful refused to admit even the possibility that their leader had mismanaged an illegal international operation. What the President knew, what he should have known, when he knew it, and why he directly or tacitly attempted to circumvent Congress are among the many unanswered questions that could eventually affect Reagan's place in history. Public evidence seems to suggest that Reagan might have over-delegated and under-managed his staff throughout his eight years in office. Ultimately, leaders cannot escape responsibility for their staff's misman- aged actions as their own. After all, that too is part of leadership: knowing when to accept the heat and when to deflect it. That knotty question nags at Arlen Royster's sense of guilt as he sorts out his share of responsibility for his lower-level managers' mismanagement even though he didn't learn of their mistakes until after the fact. What's fair? What's right? What's reality?

The CEO of any organization, be it the president of the United States or the chairman of IBM, is expected to be the corporation's leader-manager first and always. Good leaders, of course, are expected to be good managers. In contrast, many effective managers lack the ability to lead. The reason? They don't know how to relate to people; that is, they don't know how to communicate effectively.

Leadership = Relationship-Building = Communication

Historically, a CEO's major imperative was to manage the organization's bottom-line. Social and human factors have been, in large measure, either downplayed or delegated to underlings to handle as they see fit. As the CEO's role has been transformed over the years, renewed emphasis has been placed on the need to better manage the human side of business. Put another way, top executives are expected to assume an increasing responsibility for *developing productive working relationships* with influential internal and external groups, such as employees, customers, government officials, media, stockhold- ers, and Wall Street analysts.

This relationship-building responsibility has somewhat reduced the CEO's administrative-oriented managing obligations and expanded the human rela- tions-oriented leading aspects of the job. CEO Max DePree of Herman Miller believes that corporate leaders need to construct bridges between their organizations and key stakeholder groups: "Leaders need to foster environ- ments and work processes within which people can develop high-quality relationships—relationships with each other, relationships within work groups, relationships with clients and customers."[17]

A recent study by researchers at Case Western Reserve University asked 24 chief executives to describe their roles. The CEOs reported that "the familiar rubric of 'plan, organize, control ...' that used to define their jobs has given way to the more subtle injunction to 'manage meaning.'"[18] That finding echoes Bennis and Nanus' argument that leaders must "influence and organize meaning for the members of the organization."[19] Incumbent upon the CEO, suggest Bennis and Nanus, is to shape—through communication—constituents' understanding of the organization and where it is going.

Based on our intensive review and analysis of the large and growing body of literature on leadership and management, we believe that *leadership and communication are hand-in-glove processes sharing the common purpose of forming and crystallizing meaningful relationships.* This core finding defines the perspective we bring to our examination of leadership. The leadership and communication processes share the identical objective of building relationships; however, the types of relationships each seeks to establish are different.

The communication process aims to create relationships of *understanding*: understanding of purpose, understanding of message, understanding of source, understanding of expected outcome. The leadership process differs slightly, seeking to construct relationships of *commitment*: commitment to leader, commitment to organization, commitment to cause, commitment to stay committed. Most people would argue that understanding usually precedes commitment. The logic suggests that one must understand the meaning of an idea or a person or an organization, before being able or willing to commit to it. In practical human terms, understanding and commitment may just as likely occur simultaneously or in the reverse order. Separating communication and leadership in real terms is difficult; they are allied processes that overlap in many ways. Perhaps we ought to further define communication and leadership before going on to how they operate in tandem.

Further Defining Communication

Our definition of communication as a relationship-building function may surprise you. To most business professionals, the term "communication" implies "information" and not much more than that. Most CEOs, as our survey data showed, see communication as having a primarily information exchange purpose. More to the point, they see communication mainly as management sending information to employees, with substantially less emphasis on employees sending information to management.

Such a constricted view of communication, while common, is fundamentally inadequate and denies the broader relationship-building value and potential of the human communication process. That's not to say, of course, that information about job and organization isn't essential to employees' productivity. It is. It's just that too many CEOs see communication with employees as strictly an information routing function. If information transmittal is defined as communication's prime directive, CEOs will see it as a purely administrative function and probably delegate the responsibility for it to third parties (such as supervisors who may not think it important) who will treat it accordingly (like a stuffy memo). Moreover, if communication is viewed as simply the distribution of information, management is likely to ignore taking steps to address employees' desire for more meaningful *relationships* with managers, from first-line supervisors to the top dog.

Wal-Mart offers a good example of how the information dimension of communication differs from the broader objective of shaping relationships. A key to Wal-Mart's amazing business growth from a small niche retailer 20 years ago to the largest and most profitable retailer in the world has been its emphasis on acquiring and sharing information about the business with managers and line employees. The company boasts a huge technological network of information systems, ranging from a private satellite system for sharing daily sales data with vendors to videoconferencing capabilities in most stores.[20]

The information generated by these systems allows Wal-Mart managers to make business decisions faster and better than its competitors. Moreover, company managers share and discuss information about the company's progress and problems with employees. This openness with so-called "management information," a practice resisted by many U.S. corporations, helps Wal-Mart establish a foundation of trust with its workers. Other less information-dependent forms of communication were embedded long ago in the Wal-Mart culture by founder Sam Walton, who steadfastly believed in (and personally practiced!) listening to employees and celebrating their successes as ways of earning their loyalty and trust. "Mr. Sam," as he was affectionately called by employees, said over and over that "if you had to boil down the Wal-Mart system to one single idea, it would probably be communication."[21] Notice he said communication, not information.

Further Defining Leadership

To repeat, our notion of leadership is: seeking to instill in followers a belief in a leader's ideas and integrity, and belief in the future. But that general definition does not adequately capture all the vital components we identified earlier and that are central to leadership as a relationship-building process. The four factors we pinpointed are:

1. *Developing a shared vision* of the future (such as understanding stakeholders' needs and expectations, developing a common mission, and communicating it).
2. *Trust* in the leader (such as encouraging stakeholders' belief in the leader's business and moral credibility).
3. *Initiating* and *managing* the change process (such as providing the necessary fiscal and human resources so that the organization can fulfill its mission).
4. *Empowering* and *motivating* employees (such as showing sensitivity to the changing corporate culture and employees' concerns, and to the nature of the changing manager-employee relationship).

In some ways, communication and leadership are similar in concept and function, despite obvious variations in the terminology associated with each. Only when the two concepts are viewed side by side and contrasted do their similarities and differences become clear.

Communication and Leadership: Working Together

Communication and leadership overlap and interlock as concepts and as practices. To demonstrate how inseparable communication and leadership are, and to illustrate how the two processes work in concert, we explore how each of the four central factors of leadership we identified fit into a relationship-driven notion of communication.

First, "developing a shared vision of the future" is tantamount to the initial step in the communication process—that of establishing an overall goal or objective. Creating a vision of the future means offering employees a futuristic target that should, if persuasively presented, motivate them. This envisioning process can have powerful effects on workers who can see the same future their leader sees. Top-level executives who can paint mental pictures have the power to forge employees' understanding and commitment.

Research tells us of the potent effects of creating and communicating a common vision; nevertheless, doing so requires top managers with a grasp of communication strategies. In their research on leaders, James Kouzes and Barry Posner found that "... managers say that inspiring a shared vision is the most difficult [leadership] practice to learn ... and the most difficult to apply."[22] They maintain that a leader can bring life to an abstract vision through the choice of language, a positive communication style, personal charisma, and a sincere belief in the vision.

Second, the "credibility of and trust in leader" factor directly parallels the credibility of source factor essential to effective communication. This factor may be the most crucial to both communication and leadership, and it provides the basis for all other leadership characteristics.[23] If the source of the message can't be trusted, then the message itself will be ignored, dismissed, or selectively misinterpreted. In *Fortune* writer Kenneth Labich's review of leadership, he concluded that "the key to making a high-commitment organization work is mutual trust between top executives and employees. The ability to engender that trusting relationship has become the number one leadership test."[24]

Third, "initiating and managing the change process" parallels the typical implementation phase of the communication process, which seeks to deliver messages designed to change a target group's attitudes and behavior. This factor encompasses the leader's managing of human and physical resources;

that is, recognizing people's need for order and supplying them with the information and support to perform their jobs and solve problems. CEOs faced with broader spans of control and more demands on their time are being compelled to delegate responsibilities and shift accountability to others. But CEOs would be ill-advised to delegating managing of certain functions, such as developing the company's strategic direction or maintenance of key organizational relationships. Those are part of the CEO's primary job.

Fourth, the "empowering and motivating employees" component of leadership reflects CEOs' sensitivity to shifting corporate cultures and the evolving nature of management-employee relationships. "Each employee is, to a remarkable extent, the organization in miniature," explains Warren Bennis in *Why Leaders Can't Lead*. "The top person must understand this and be something of a social anthropologist in addition to being an architect, in order to know, maintain, and even alter the culture."[25]

This factor also addresses the participative management and employee empowerment movements permeating the workplace today. Top managers who draw employees into the mainstream of company activities and workplace decisions can earn their loyalty and spark their motivation. Jay Conger of McGill University says that leaders must first convince employees—through their management and communication styles, reward systems, and design of jobs—that they hold much of the power to control their work environments and create their own job satisfaction.[26] But to accept this belief, employees have to be convinced of the organization's (that is, top management's) commitment to such programs—convincing which can only come from the top.

There is a distinct logic pattern to the interdependent communication-leadership connection. People need and want to understand what and who they're being asked to follow and commit to. Effective communication can create that understanding. A leader, therefore, communicates to shape that understanding so that he or she can eventually gain commitment and long-term loyalty.

For analytical purposes, we discuss communication and leadership as separate concepts, though in reality, they are far more alike than they are different. Where leadership begins and communication ends, and vice versa, is sometimes imperceptible; they blend together as natural allies seeking to establish meaningful relationships. Stated another way, true leadership is impossible without a strong communicator-leader.

Lee Iacocca: Leading Chrysler's Comeback

One of the better examples of a modern-day corporate leader-manager is Chrysler's Lee Iacocca, arguably the most recognized, analyzed, and criticized CEO of modern times. Iacocca rose to national prominence in 1980 when, as the new chairman of financially devastated Chrysler Corporation, he unabashedly led America's third largest car-maker from the brink of ruin to profitability in just a few years. And he did this in broad public view, practically inviting the hordes of eager skeptics to challenge him so he could use their doubting words to motivate Chrysler employees to push on and save their company.

With bravado and single-minded determination, as well as an acute sensitivity to people's feelings and perceptions, Iacocca, an engineer by trade, used both his managerial and leadership talents to spearhead one of the most miraculous turnarounds in American business history. In a matter of months, he convinced all of Chrysler's key publics that the company could manage itself back to financial health. His arguments about saving jobs and Chrysler's importance to America gained Congress' commitment to guarantee $1.5 billion in loans to the teetering company. Those guarantees, of course, opened the banking industry's doors to cash-starved Chrysler. He then had to win employees' commitment to fight an uphill battle to return the company to respectability and somehow make them believe they could do it. By selling them and their unions on Chrysler's ability and potential to produce a better car that would sell in America, he saved the company millions of dollars in daily operating expenses by convincing employees to give back some of their salaries and fringe benefits. He solidified his personal credibility when he reduced his salary to one dollar a year until the company turned a profit.

At the same time, he was pressing Chrysler's engineering staff to complete the long-awaited production of the company's new K-car line, the line which Iacocca argued would put the company back in the game. As the K-cars began rolling off the production line, Iacocca, a "super salesman," burst into America's living rooms as Chrysler's spokesperson and cheerleader in a series of hard-hitting TV advertisements. In those ads, he personally made performance and service promises beyond anything ever seen in the auto industry. Interestingly, he accepted this highly visible—and exposed—role despite his own personal inhibitions and social insecurities. In playing the public spokesperson role, Iacocca reluctantly put aside his shyness and fear of TV cameras, and went on to establish himself, and thus Chrysler, as one of the most recognized names in business.

The company's confidence in its ability to recover and build better cars was embodied in Iacocca, the brash, articulate leader-manager. Up to that time, CEOs of major American companies rarely, if ever, appeared as pitchmen in their corporations' advertisements. But despite his initial resistance to performing in the ads, he subsequently agreed. The results were immediate and dramatic. Iacocca's gritty personality and down-to-earth, persuasive style catapulted him to folk hero status while Chrysler's message won over millions of American car-buyers. As the chairman's name recognition skyrocketed, the auto company's sales started to accelerate too.[27] The rest, as they say, is history.

For the next several years, Chrysler's amazing comeback from potential disaster made it a role model within the American business community and elevated Iacocca to America's quintessential leader. His new found fame and credibility—enhanced by his frequent public and media appearances, his books, and his involvement in national causes such as the Statue of Liberty restoration project—no doubt accounted for much of Chrysler's rise from the ashes. Over time, it became difficult to separate Chrysler Corporation from Lee Iacocca. His name was bandied about several times as a possible candidate for the Democratic presidential nomination. Because of his spreading appeal, he was in big demand; he even appeared on TV shows such as "Miami Vice" in its hey-day.

Iacocca reached the pinnacle of his leadership of Chrysler's revival in a televised public ceremony held at the Washington Press Club in 1983 when he announced that Chrysler would repay the guaranteed loans seven years before they were due.

The Iacocca leader-manager phenomenon is remarkable on several grounds. First, the Iacocca case illustrates the need for integration between leadership and management strategies and skills. Corporate leaders must be able to balance the daily, technical demands of management with the broader, public demands of leadership. During Chrysler's comeback, Iacocca worked internally to build a corporate infrastructure and a motivated workforce that could produce quality cars efficiently. At the same time, his emerging high profile helped build the public's belief in Chrysler as a viable corporate entity (and in Iacocca as its CEO). Shifting between the internal and external leadership and management responsibilities is not easy; it demands versatility, flexibility, and a thorough understanding of one's objectives and capabilities.

Second, this case points up the fragility of being perceived as a leader, and how difficult it is to maintain the delicate balance between leadership and management obligations. Since Chrysler's reincarnation in the mid-1980s, the shine on Iacocca's star has lost some of its glow. A failed marriage hurt his personal image. Controversy over his dual roles as chairman of both the private Statue of Liberty Foundation, a fundraising arm, and the federal Commission for the Restoration of the Statue of Liberty, which spent the funds, raised some questions among officials in the Republican White House about the ethics of his management oversight. His candid public observations about the Japanese auto industry, even taking into account Chrysler's joint venture with Mitsubishi, caused some critics to label him a "Japan-basher"—perhaps an unfair characterization, but damaging nonetheless. And his public *mea culpa* in accepting responsibility for the Chrysler managers who illegally turned back odometers in demonstrator cars, although handled adeptly, did little to strengthen his and Chrysler's public standing.

But the most damaging criticism of all may have been the finger that was pointed at Iacocca for allowing his attention to be diverted from managing

Chrysler during the late 1980s when, critics argue, he lost sight of Chrysler's best interests and didn't realize that "the days are over when he could sell cars through the sheer dint of his personality."[28] Perhaps he was swept up by the lure of his own fame, a human failing any leader is subject to. Nevertheless, he was blamed for the company's plummeting sales.

Third, placing so much of its reputation in one person—even one as popular and powerful as Lee Iacocca—was risky because of the potentially vulnerable position it put Chrysler in. If an established leader falters or leaves the company, then the company may suffer serious damage to its position in the business community. A corporate reputation takes years to attain, but can be lost in the blink of an eye. In Iacocca's case, his charisma bolstered Chrysler's bottom-line. "Public perception that Lee Iacocca ought to be president sells cars and trucks," says Jim Tolley, former vice president of public affairs.[29] But the perception of Chrysler—or any company—being a one-man band can no doubt hurt the company eventually. To guard against that prospect, Iacocca and Chrysler's board developed a strategy to reduce the downside effects of Iacocca's planned retirement, originally set for 1992 but later postponed to 1993, explains Tolley.

Fourth, the success of Lee Iacocca illustrates the tight fit between communication and leadership. His success as a leader was a direct outgrowth of his effectiveness as a communicator, and his skill in winning stakeholders' emotional and financial support. People believed in him and his company's plight because his message had merit and he articulated it persuasively. He understood from the outset that Chrysler's turnaround hopes rested on his ability to convince employees, congressmen, customers, dealers, and others to believe in his vision of Chrysler's future and in his ability to make that vision a reality.

His direct, candid, enthusiastic approach to communicating his message—in his ads, speeches, articles, and books—helped create understanding of Chrysler's predicament and its commitment to rebuild the company at a time when it could barely meet its payroll. Iacocca won workers' loyalty, despite their enormous trepidation about their jobs and future, by communicating with them honestly and frequently about how things really were—and what they could be. "The only way you can motivate people is if you communicate with them," wrote Iacocca in his first book.[30]

Finally, the Lee Iacocca case demonstrates how strong communication provides the basis for the kind of leadership that can form and strengthen human relationships. He drew on people's beliefs in their company, in its mission, in its CEO-leader, and in their hope for better times. "Leadership is a relationship," say Ruch and Goodman. "It's a way of interacting—of communicating—with other individuals according to certain rules adhered to by both leaders and followers."[31] Iacocca led and managed Chrysler through his vision of what the company still could be. Because his powerful, engaging personal style spurred employees, stockholders, customers, and Congress to believe in him and his message (that is, understanding and commitment), they were willing to follow him and form a relationship on the uncertain journey ahead.

A Final Word

"American corporate leadership is clearly in a state of crisis," observe Ruch and Goodman. "Communication is the pathway out of this crisis, and top management is the focal point for the effort."[32]

We couldn't agree more. Effective business leaders are rare because business people are rarely effective communicators. CEOs strive to be perceived as credible, caring leaders of people, and efficient, fair managers of resources. But to be a true leader-manager requires a special individual: a competent and versatile communicator who can win over diverse constituencies, and who can resourcefully manage people's job needs and personal aspirations. Only those executives fitting this description of a leader-manager should bother applying for the glut of CEO jobs opening up throughout corporate America.

Returning to Arlen ...

At the close of Chap. 2, Arlen Royster immersed himself in a flashback of his famous bet with VP of HRM Joyce Hadley that he could identify Royal employees' needs and desires as accurately as a scientifically administered attitude survey. Although he happily lost the bet, he learned a lot about his employees and their changing values and problems, and learned what he still needs to learn. After returning to present day, he is bluntly reminded by his wife, Andrea, about another party the CEO needs to understand better: his son, Glenn. Arlen's callous reaction to Glenn's career aspirations has put their already precarious relationship in further jeopardy.

In the upcoming section, Arlen comes face-to-face with his career-long fear of public speaking and his classic ideas about leadership—and, let's just say, the old top dog teaches himself a few new tricks.

"Telling It Like It Is"

Wednesday, October 10, 11:00 a.m.   Arlen's image stared glumly back at him from his private washroom mirror. For a fleeting moment, he saw his father's face, wrinkled and drawn, absent the alertness of the countenance he had shaved just six hours before. He wrung out the plush washcloth and buried his face in its warmth.

Keller had just left Arlen's office after a tense 20-minute confrontation. Arlen's head reverberated with his nemesis' accusations. "Admit it," Keller had charged. "This isn't just a matter of greed, which is what most people will assume when they hear about a bunch of corporate types manipulating financial figures. It's a case of trying to please the boss at all costs—pardon the pun. You're to blame for this disaster, Arlen. Nobody but you. And now you have the nerve to act horrified at what your managers did!"

"I am horrified, damn it," Arlen responded angrily. "These people cheated and they lied. I've never, repeat *never*, implied that that sort of behavior was ever acceptable or would be condoned. Don't tell me they did this just to please me, Mike."

"Okay, maybe not to please you, Arlen." Keller's tone was mocking. "But you never let up about how Royal and every employee's future was tied to hitting those impossible bottom-line numbers. Well, they heard you. Now it's your turn to be accountable."

Arlen massaged the swollen sinus areas over his eyes, then dropped the washcloth to the counter top and reached for a dry towel. Opening the door of the medicine cabinet, he absent-mindedly reached for the bottle of Tylenol he knew was there. Popping the lid, he dumped two onto his palm, threw them into his mouth, and washed them down with a glass of tap water. His eyes again caught his twin in the mirror, still peering back at him.

"Is the pressure I put on my people that unreasonable?" he wondered. "Pressure is as much a part of business as buying and selling. If pressure is permitted as an acceptable excuse for being dishonest or unethical, then we won't be able to tell the crooks from the good guys."

He wanted to believe what he was arguing to himself and simply dismiss Keller's accusations, but he couldn't.

"People handle pressure in different ways," he lectured himself. "Who's to say what's too much? Maybe Keller's right—maybe I am to blame." Abruptly and for no apparent reason, Arlen decided this wasn't the time to beat himself up. There'd be plenty of time for that later. He hit the light switch on the way out of the washroom and sat back down at his desk.

Maybe he'd underestimated Keller. Reaching for the phone, he pressed the autodial key for Barry Lewis' private line. CEO of a Manhattan-based publishing house, they'd been close friends since their college days together. They relied on each other for counsel, personal and professional. And while Lewis' no-holds-barred advice was at times tough to accept, Arlen valued his candor and respected his judgment, which was more on target than off. He needed him now.

"Lewis," Lewis answered in a clipped monotone.

"Barry, I know you're busy, but I really need to talk," Arlen said with just enough pleading in his voice.

"Yeah, sure, Arlen. Be right with you. Just give me a minute." A click was followed by soft elevator music. Lewis returned in a moment.

"So, what's up?" Lewis asked, his tone business-like. Arlen briefly summarized Royal's predicament, ending with his concerns about Keller.

"Keller's trying to cast me as the scapegoat and him as the savior. He thinks the board will vote me out and him in."

"Is he right?" asked Lewis matter-of-factly.

"I doubt it," Arlen said unsurely.

"So what's the problem?"

"I think he can muster some support. With things getting worse by the minute, the board and everyone else will soon come looking for someone to blame. And the CEO's frequently handy."

"Get rid of the guy," Lewis advised, baiting Arlen to make his case. "Tell him to clean out his desk."

"Unfortunately, I can't do that. I need a rationale. And I may have unknowingly blown it when I asked him to check out some potentially explosive information I think he's purposely keeping from me. He's stalling, which makes me awfully suspicious about what he's up to that I don't know about."

"What about the books? Somebody had to be juggling them. How about the CFO, what's his name, Grubner? How could he *not* have known?"

"He should've," Arlen said, quickly considering Grubner's possible motives, "and maybe he did. If so, he's gone. But he's not the one I'm worried about right now. He's not as politically savvy as Keller, but I think they may be teaming up."

"All right, then fight fire with fire. Gı␣ ᵇner and Keller must've or should've known, right? Hold them responsible for not knowing," Lewis suggested.

"Can't do that. If they should've known, then I should've known, too. At this point, I have no hard proof either of them knew or did anything wrong. And I may never." His voice trailed off.

"But he might be able to nail me. He doesn't need concrete proof," Arlen said, shaking his head and upping his volume. "People don't need verifiable facts to get the CEO. They only need to manufacture perceptions that others accept as gospel. That's the card Keller's trying to play. And I can't say he's completely wrong."

"How could you have known?"

"I don't know. By listening better maybe. People were sending me signals, but I was too damn busy building an empire to hear them. Somebody's got to be held accountable. And you know who that is. When the Yankees lose, who gets fired, the players?"

"Whoa, pardner. Slow down a minute. As usual, you're holding yourself responsible for everything. I don't see a big red S on your chest, do you? It's not your job to be in every city, every day, holding every manager's hand. Give yourself a break, damn it." Arlen squeezed the phone tighter.

"Do you think I should accept *sole* responsibility for every typo in every book my company publishes?" Lewis asked.

Arlen laughed, the tension eased for a moment. "Hell, no. I know you can't read. But suppose one of your assistant editors lets a book slip through that you learn later was based on falsified data. Who's your board gonna come after?"

Lewis thought for a moment. "I can't be everybody's eyes and ears. When a mistake happens, I'm held accountable for correcting it and making sure it doesn't happen again. The editor's gone and I look for a better one."

"Ultimately, though, Barry, if the screw-up's big enough, your board's not going to go after your staff. They come for the guy at the top, who they put there. It may not always be fair, but that's how it works."

"Look, forget about fair and right and wrong. If that's your main concern, you should've become a priest," Lewis chided. "Business and life don't work that way. How many of your principles have you had to compromise to get where you are?" Arlen had never reconciled the age-old business dilemma of expediency vs. morality.

"The critical issue now is the board. Where does Keller stand with it? And where's Stamps? With you?"

"Sure he is, for now. But even he can't protect me by himself if the board thinks I'm to blame." Arlen kneaded his throbbing temples.

"What's the board count?" Lewis quizzed.

"It's probably three for Keller and three for me, including Stamps. The other three I don't know."

"Don't let yourself get diverted by the politics," Lewis advised. "When's the next scheduled board meeting?"

"Three weeks from now, but Keller won't wait that long. He'll want to strike while he thinks I'm most vulnerable."

Just then, Arlen's private intercom buzzed. "Hang on a second," Arlen said to Lewis, hitting the intercom button. "Yes, Susan?" Arlen listened, looking at his watch. "Okay, tell him to come on in." Arlen punched Barry's line.

"I've gotta go," he said to Lewis. "Bob Azoulette's here. We're heading over to the Castle for my big speech at noon."

The door opened and Azoulette stepped in. Arlen waved him toward the desk.

"Watch your back with Keller," Lewis warned. "You know what Don Corleone always says," Lewis continued in a cotton-mouthed whisper, referring to *The Godfather*, which the two had seen together and constantly cited lines from. "Keep your friends close and your enemies closer. And never let anyone outside the family know what you're thinking."

Arlen laughed softly. "Good advice, padron. Ciao." Arlen hung up and turned to Azoulette, who smiled mechanically and glanced at his watch.

As Arlen slipped on his suit jacket and headed to the elevator with Azoulette by his side, his mind switched to the speech he was about to deliver. A slight wave of nausea rocked him as the elevator slid downward. His dread of speaking in public, which bordered on outright fear, went back to his MBA days. Arlen had been a member of a project team in a student competition to develop an off-season marketing package for Mark Twain's "Americana Village" theme park, situated on the Los Angeles-Orange County border. The culmination of the semester-long project was a 30-minute presentation to the theme park's then-director of marketing, Jim Stamps, and a representative of the park's public relations firm. Arlen was pressed by his team into being the lead presenter. He'd argued against the assignment, but to no avail—the others were just as uptight about standing up in front of others. He remembered wisecracking that no one had ever told him this was part of managing.

When the time came, his anxiety got the better of him, and his presentation was mechanical and stumbling. He perspired so much that it showed right through his collar. At one point, he'd dropped his note cards and took what seemed like an eternity to pick them up and refind his place. His group came in third out of four. Later, Stamps sought him out at the reception held for the participants.

"Young man, that was one of the worst presentations I've ever seen," Stamps said in his booming voice, a big smile splitting his face. "Next time take a shot of Wild Turkey before you start. Works for me. But I liked your ideas. You fielded questions well and knew your subject better than you presented it. And I couldn't help but notice how much your team members look up to you."

He handed Arlen a business card and said without emotion, "Give me a call," before turning away. Arlen was thrilled by Stamps' attention, and more than curious about the door that had been opened for him. As fate so often does, his call to Stamps the following week changed his life forever. Thankfully, Arlen noted to himself, he hadn't screwed up a speaking assignment to that extent since then, although the memory sent chills up his spine whenever he thought about it, which always seemed to happen just before he was about to speak in public. His fight was to not be swallowed up by his own paralyzing anxiety.

The elevator stopped at ground level and the two executives ambled out onto the glistening marble floor stretching across the lobby, now teeming with lunch-goers moving in every direction. Azoulette stayed close to Arlen as they headed for the revolving doors.

"You know," Arlen said, "I've given a lot of these lunchtime speeches. But I never eat the meal because my stomach's always churning. Practice makes you better, but it doesn't make you comfortable.

"And today, with this crisis staring us in the face, I've really got reason to worry. Come Friday, all these people I'm talking to today will know about our dirty laundry and will judge me—and Royal—by my words today. Here I am spouting off about leadership when my company's credibility is about to be put on public trial."

They pushed through the slow spinning doors and headed for the street where Jeffrey Andrews, Arlen's chauffeur and aide, was waiting with the Royal limousine. As Arlen slid into the spacious towncar, Azoulette wondered whether his boss really was as insecure as he sounded or simply seeking reassurance.

Leaning into the car, the marketing VP looked at Arlen and said in the most positive tone he could muster, "Hey, I've seen the speech. It's good stuff. You'll get rave reviews." He then climbed in, Andrews closing the door behind them, and a moment later the car nudged its way into bumper-to-bumper Manhattan traffic for the five-minute drive to Royal's flagship property on the opposite side of Central Park, known as "The Castle," coincidentally the site of Arlen's speech.

The CEO flipped open the leather-bound folder containing his speech and began to read. "Take your time, Jeff," Arlen gently ordered Andrews through the window divider, as he started scanning his written opening remarks. "I'm in no hurry."

* * * * * * * * * *

Wednesday, October 10, noon. "... we are pleased to have him present the keynote address at this year's annual conference."

Introducing Arlen was the association's President, Wendell O'Shaughnessy, a tall Irishman with curly gray hair and a top executive with Woods Hotels International. If he could have gotten away with it, Arlen would have backed out so he could focus on Royal's problems—except that the International Association of Hotel Executives (IAHE) represented virtually every major player in the lodging industry. Comprised of top-level people from member companies, the influential IAHE served as a lobbying arm and public advocate for the large hotel chains.

He had accepted the invitation to speak almost eight months ago. Backing out at the last minute would have been the ultimate professional discourtesy and would have personally embarrassed Azoulette, Royal's official representative to the IAHE. It was Azoulette who had nominated Arlen as the keynote speaker, considered a rare honor, and then battled through several sticky meetings of the program committee to nail down the invitation. It might also have served as a warning signal that something was awry at Royal.

The lights in the banquet room dimmed. Busboys and waiters hovered around the outside edges of the room, waiting to finish clearing dessert dishes. "His topic," O'Shaughnessy continued, "'The Changing Face of Leadership in the Hotel Industry for the 21st Century,' is most appropriate today as we gear up for the exciting and frightening challenges in the decade ahead." Arlen flinched when he heard the title said aloud, all too aware that many of the executives in the audience were as or more experienced than he was.

The speech was completed a week ago by Charles Doransky, a young go-getter on Jamieson's staff with a gift for turning a phrase. The speech represented Arlen's surface thoughts about executive-level management and Doransky's interpretation of those thoughts, plus lots of research on the concept of leadership. The manuscript had been worked over mercilessly by Jamieson and Doransky through three rewrites. As usual, Jamieson wanted Arlen to do several dry runs, but the agile CEO always found an excuse to avoid doing any or would consent to one cursory practice session, as had been the case for this one. Right now, though, Arlen wished he'd followed Jamieson's advice.

Before he'd learned about the cooked books situation, he had been pleased with the speech, comfortable with its quota of thoughtful platitudes and witty phrases. But now that he was about to confront the eye of Royal's brewing storm, he wondered if the manuscript contained anything useful about real leadership and how to make it work. As the words rolled around in his head, he kept thinking the speech had the too familiar cadence of so many other formula convention speeches he'd heard.

Unable to stay focused on his speech, Arlen's mind kept drifting to Royal's dilemma and his nagging insecurities about what to do. Was he really a leader or just another executive who talked a good game? The answer to that question seemed as far away as he wished he was.

* * * * * * * * * *

"... Royal, a rising star in the industry." Arlen realized that O'Shaughnessy's introduction was winding down.

"Since Arlen Royster became CEO six years ago, he's been so busy building his company—often at the expense of many of us in this room, I might add—that he's not been able to join us very often." O'Shaughnessy winked at Arlen who didn't miss the subtle dig, but was too overcome by nerves to care. He nodded and smiled obligingly.

Looking at those closest to the slightly elevated head table, he could see Azoulette studying him from the far-right table. He was glad to see a familiar face. Jamieson, unseen by Arlen, had slipped through the back door, accompanied by an eager and jittery Charles Doransky. They stood together in the shadows of the far corner of the cavernous ballroom, purposely out of Arlen's line of sight.

O'Shaughnessy paused as he approached the final segment of his intro. "Ladies and gentlemen. A man of energy. Of vision. A worthy competitor.

The chief executive officer of Royal Accommodations. Mr. Arlen Burch Royster." He stepped back from the podium and gestured to Arlen on his right. The spotlight in the back of the room swung to pick up Arlen as he stood.

He grabbed his speech and unconsciously ran his fingertips down his vest buttons to check that his tie was straight and all was buttoned. His arms and legs felt heavy. The natural shot of adrenalin he usually felt before a speech was missing.

Despite O'Shaughnessy's big build-up, the post-introduction applause was light and brief. Arlen shook O'Shaughnessy's extended hand, turned to the audience and laid his text on the podium. He started with a formal, required greeting to those seated at the head table. That obligation done, he reached for the speaker's water glass. He felt parched already. After taking a long, slow sip, he glanced down at the top page and began, still struggling to find the energy and vision O'Shaughnessy said he possessed.

"First, let me thank all of you for giving Royal the business this week—that is, by choosing The Castle for this prestigious gathering. The 100-percent occupancy rate is much appreciated." The throwaway quip, intended by the speechwriter to be given off-the-cuff, was delivered stiffly and fell flat. Against the back wall, Doransky's head sagged. He started to whisper something to Jamieson, but was silenced by the VP with a finger to his lips. He was trying through mental telepathy to deliver Arlen a sense of rhythm.

Arlen looked up, the strain he felt evident on his face. He considered trying an ad lib, but quickly thought better of it. He went right back to the text, but couldn't find his place for several seconds. Jamieson rolled his eyes and pushed his head back against the wall.

"It's no news that our industry is in the doldrums. We like to blame the downturn on the economy. The lack of consumer spending. But that's not where we ought to be pointing our fingers." He stabbed his index finger at the audience, then gradually turned it back on himself.

"The real responsibility, ladies and gentlemen, lies with those of us in this room. Never before has the hotel industry needed leadership from us as it does today." His eyes caught the written instruction in the manuscript to pause after the last statement, so he did, somewhat clumsily, and too abruptly. His voice had no emotion or feeling to it.

"Leadership. That's our key to unlocking the door of opportunity. We here today have the power and the skills to lead our beleaguered industry out of its depression and enter the twenty-first century with hope and enthusiasm."

Again, his pause was artificial, his heart clearly not in his words. "What is this thing we call leadership?" he asked, his voice rising slightly as instructed in his script. He answered in a tense monotone. "Harry Truman," Arlen read, his eyes pinned to the script, "said leadership was the ability to get other people to do what they don't want to do and like it."

Doransky, his facial color growing whiter, poked Jamieson gently on the arm. "That was terrible," he whispered. In the single rehearsal Arlen had reluctantly agreed to, they coached him to pause after the second "to do" and deliver the "and like it" as a snappy, upbeat punchline. But today he didn't pause and didn't vary his vocal inflection at all.

Arlen stopped and looked up from the text, scanning the tables. People were still sipping coffee and talking quietly, many only half listening. His flat delivery inspired neither his audience nor himself. Displeased with his performance but at a loss how to improve it, he drifted back to the safety of his prepared notes.

"World War I hero Alvin York was once asked by a West Point cadet why a platoon leader is always at the head of the line of soldiers charging up the hill. York's terse response—'Son, have you ever tried pushing a string?'"

Arlen paused again, this time obeying the written direction—"the dummy card," he said to himself—in his manuscript. Azoulette and Jamieson, from their separate vantage points, noticed him reaching for his left cufflink. Azoulette wondered if his professional coup in setting up the keynote address for Arlen was about to backfire. Jamieson feared that Arlen was giving in to the pressure.

As the pause reached an uncomfortable length, the background drone gradually quieted. Many whispered conversations stopped as heads turned to see what was wrong with the speaker. Arlen remained frozen in place, expressionless. He thought about what the balance of the text included. It was, he reminded himself, exactly the thoughts he'd thrashed out with Jamieson and Doransky, and had approved. But now it all seemed wrong; it wasn't what was really in his mind, or his heart. "Well, what now?" he thought. After about 20 seconds, which seemed more like 20 minutes to most there, he looked up, apparently ready to speak again. "If I'm gonna fall on my face," he told himself, "it might as well be on my own terms."

"Weeks of work have gone into this speech." His tone was measured, cautious. "It's certainly relevant and, I think, worthwhile material. And if it were delivered effectively, you'd probably see its relevance and appreciate it. Bob Azoulette or I will be happy to share copies of this carefully polished manuscript with you."

To the audience's complete astonishment, Arlen stepped away from the podium and returned to his place at the head table, tossing the manuscript away. It landed on top of his untouched dessert. Then he took off his jacket and hung it on the back of his chair. Looking directly at Azoulette, who sat transfixed at what he was seeing, Arlen winked. As he made his way back to the podium, he unfastened his cufflinks and began rolling up his sleeves. Doransky gulped, his eyes pulled to the discarded manuscript he'd ghosted, now turning soggy from the baked Alaska underneath it. Jamieson watched Arlen closely, speculating on the CEO's next move.

* * * * * * * * * *

Arlen leaned heavily onto the podium with both forearms and gripped the front edge. "I've never been much of an extemporaneous speaker," he said, his voice more intense and controlled now. "That text I just dumped on my food has always been what got me through a speech. I usually feel lost without it. A bright, young speechwriter worked long and hard with me to shape my thoughts into articulate sentences."

Jamieson turned to Doransky, whose eyes were still glued to Arlen, and gently nudged him. Doransky turned his head slightly and nodded.

"But what I'd really like to do is share with you what I'm feeling and thinking right now about this slippery topic of leadership. What I think it means and how it can be used effectively. Because nothing is more important to the future of our industry."

The room was silent now. Arlen's transformed demeanor was carefully noted by Karen-Elaine Marshak of *The Wall Street Journal*, sitting at an outside table near the back. She picked up her chair and moved it closer to the front. She hadn't been using her tape recorder, but now laid it on her lap and hit the record button.

Arlen took the mike out of its gooseneck stand, walked to the left side of the podium and leaned against it with his right elbow. His throat was parched. "Feel free to take off your coats and get comfortable," he directed his listeners. Arlen looked at his watch. "Just give me 15 minutes and we'll wrap this thing on time." He cleared his throat as he felt a rush of adrenaline finally punch into his system.

Suddenly the CEO felt an odd, almost out-of-body sensation overtake him. He was suddenly floating above the podium, looking at the person speaking, someone who looked and sounded like him, but couldn't be him because this person looked relaxed as he spoke, not uptight as he always was. This person—"is that really me?"—was walking the long-feared tightrope without a net for the first time.

He was running on pure instinct and reflex. Later, he'd look back and wonder what happened. Whatever it was, it felt cathartic, uplifting, the words just seemed to flow naturally. The audience was fascinated by this strange metamorphosis occurring in front of them. They now wanted to listen to this man to see if it was real.

Not even Jamieson had ever seen this side of Arlen, this stripped-down version of him, actually baring his soul in public to strangers. Neither Arlen nor Jamieson could have known how crucial Arlen's speech would be to Royal's dubious future.

* * * * * * * * * *

"In the last 48 hours, ladies and gentlemen, I've been doing a lot of thinking about what leadership really means. I came here today to tell you about the many lofty ideas I have about what makes for superb leadership. But they're up here," Arlen said, raising his right hand over his head, "when I think we need to talk down here," holding his left hand chest-high. He could feel the audience focus exclusively on him, and it felt good. He unconsciously slowed his pace.

"Leadership, in my opinion, is an illusion we believe we possess ... almost like a birthright ... simply because we managed to climb our way to the top rung of our organizations. That sort of leader-follower bond is weak, rooted in quicksand. If we rely solely on our titles and our need to control, our people will only goose-step to our commands for so long before they throw us out." Arlen took a small step closer to the edge of the riser and peered out, inviting through his expression a response, any response.

"Do you see what I'm trying to get at?" he challenged rhetorically. "The illusion of leadership is the need we as CEOs or vice presidents have to demonstrate *our* authority," his said, his right hand forming a fist that he shook intensely. "This illusion, though, often blinds us to the needs and desires of the very people we need to motivate and inspire to follow our lead.

"I thought I could learn about leadership by reading books and listening to others, many of them so-called experts. That's useful, sure, but they can't give us what only we have ..." He stopped, his unfinished thought forming in his head. "... Experience." He paused again, searching for more words. "I guess it's a bit like trying to describe marriage, or sex, to somebody else. It's interesting to listen to others describe it, but until you try it yourself, you really don't know." He smiled and panned the room in an instant. The faces, many with sheepish grins, seemed friendly and eager for the first time.

"Here's what I think I've learned about the meaning of leadership. First of all, leading involves two parties: the leaders, that's us, and those we're trying to lead." The words and thoughts were coming naturally now, as though he'd been anointed by a divine being. Jamieson, relieved, mumbled to Doransky, "I've never seen him like this. I just hope he remembers what he's doing, because we're gonna need it again—very soon." Doransky nodded reflexively, his eyes remaining on Arlen.

Arlen moved back behind the podium, dragging the mike cord behind him. "If you're searching for the 1-2-3 step formula of leadership, good luck to you. It doesn't work that way, even though I wish it did," he said, emotion filling his eyes. "People and organizations—and the chemistry that pulls them together or pushes them apart—are always different. It's the leader who has to align his mental image of the future with people's desires, hopes, dreams, and fears. Only through that alignment of leader and followers can a common cause be shaped."

As the words pumped out of him, the pace of his speech picked up, as did his vocal pitch. At this point, he leaned over the podium toward the audience, the muscles in his neck taut, straining to get closer to them. "True leadership in the hotel industry or any industry, must begin with the leader's genuine belief in the power of the human spirit to solve business problems. Then, if those human energies are to be harnessed, the leader has to be able to earn people's trust in his judgment and his vision as their ... their messiah.

"It's always amusing to speculate about what leadership is and isn't. But actually being accepted as a leader may well be the toughest thing in all of business. Why do I say that? Because employees have been brainwashed to believe that those of us in authority don't care about them, and have little or no interest in trying to relate to them. To tear down the wall that's divided us from them for so very long, I know of only one way."

Arlen looked from table to table. He tightly wrapped both hands around the microphone and stretched out his next words. "By building better relationships with the people who matter most—our own people, our employees.

"How do you do it? Actually, it's so obvious and simple, most of us never see it." He felt in control again, at last. "By communicating with them. Really communicating, eyeball-to-eyeball." He slowly moved away from the podium and stepped down from the raised stage, dragging the mike cord behind him, and moved to within a few feet of the front row of tables.

"Communicating candidly. Communicating frequently. And communicating up, down, and across your organization. To do that, you've got to tear down the invisible blockades that have for too many decades divided management and labor. The first step is to get inside your employees' heads so you can communicate with them on their level, about things *important to them*. To find out what they think, you have to ask them. That's easier said than done, and it takes time, thought, and some money. All in short supply, I know."

He then stepped back on to the stage, drawn again to the security of the podium, where he stopped just long enough to daub his perspiring forehead with his handkerchief. A moment later, he again moved out from behind the podium, the mike held below his lower lip, instinctively knowing what he wanted to say next.

* * * * * * * * * *

"Let me tell you a story about the father of a young woman I met when I was in the MBA program at the University of Southern California. It's been a long time since I last talked to her, but I've never forgotten the anecdotes she shared with me. Until recently, I don't think I really appreciated their meaning. Her name is Lilly Danielle.

"When Lilly was a child, her father was president of the Allegheny Galvanized Processing Company outside of Pittsburgh, a manufacturing firm with about 250 employees, many of whom were immigrant Russians and Italians. I recall Lilly telling me, her pride obvious, that her dad never put on airs with his employees and they respected him because of that. He didn't play 'me president, you worker.' He really got down to the workers' level when he walked around the plant and talked to them about their concerns, and shared his with them. And he always looked them straight in the eye when he talked to them.

"Lilly's dad also taught her to always get information from the best source available—which isn't always management. One time, in the middle of a meeting with executives from other companies, he was asked some production questions he couldn't answer. So, instead of trying to tap dance around the issue or offer lame excuses, he picked up the phone and called the shop floor to speak to the foreman. Later, some folks thought he embarrassed himself and exposed his ignorance with such a 'demeaning' move. But Lilly never thought so. And neither do I."

At this point, the room was still, broken only by Arlen's penetrating voice. "I don't know why, but Lilly's stories about her father have stayed with me all these years. Until recently, I don't think I truly understood their meaning. He was a CEO who didn't hide under his desk. He saw value in his workers beyond their productivity rates. And he wasn't afraid to talk frankly to them and encourage them to speak that way to him. He was a leader, pure and simple."

A weariness had now crept into Arlen's body, the adrenalin rush having petered out. The quick, high-energy hand gestures visible at the start of his impromptu speech had given way to more subdued, less frequent hand movements. He pressed forward, shifting his focus somewhat.

"But the people at the top—you and me, ladies and gentlemen—can't do it alone. Managers at every level have to assume their own distinctive communication roles—roles that, if they're to be effective, must complement, not conflict with, one another. And it all begins and ends with the … the top dog. It's got to cascade down from the CEO to all layers of an organization. Your people, wherever they are in the organization, have to believe management is an ally and not the enemy—or you'll never win."

Jamieson had become enthralled. He'd never before seen Arlen with such natural timing, rhythm, and word selection. And his emotions, usually buried, were readily exposed for all to see and react to. The audience seemed to be accepting this stranger. "Lilly's dad knew what was important to his workers because he made it his business to find out. He told them, without pulling any punches, when things were bad and why, as well as when things were good and why. It's that kind of openness and honesty on which healthy relationships are built. I'm no psychologist, but common sense tells me Mr. Danielle had the right idea."

Arlen stopped hastily, feeling like he'd run out of things to say. He drifted back to the lectern, snapped the microphone into place and lowered his eyes. From somewhere deep within him, more thoughts and words bubbled up.

"Simply put, relationships are built on good communication," he said in a more subdued tone. "But we don't have any more time for communication, right? Nonsense! If you don't, you'll soon have plenty of it as you look for a new job. Our offices have become glass offices, unable to shield us from those constituencies, particularly employees and customers who expect us—and rightfully so—to be visible and accessible, to be our organization's chief communication officers, or CCOs." Arlen remembered reading about the notion of CCOs in an article Jamieson gave him a few weeks ago.

"Our organizations are judged in large part by what the number one person says and does," Arlen said, wishing he didn't really believe it. "We can't hide from scrutiny in the comfort of our executive suites any longer. The only way to win the support of your employees and customers … " He was losing his train of thought, so he recycled his statement. "The only way to win their support is to open up with them and … and … get naked together." Surprised and curious expressions appeared instantly; a snicker or two could be heard. Arlen kept going.

"I saw a cartoon recently that depicted a naked executive, except for his tie, standing at the head of a waist-high table in a glass conference room as other executives, fully clothed, look on. Out the window, you can see people in nearby buildings looking out their windows into the glass-walled office. In the caption, one executive is saying to another, 'Do you want to tell The Emperor or should I?'" Light laughter sprinkled the room.

"The cartoon originally caught my eye because it depicted the idea that the CEO—or should I say emperor—can't afford to get caught with his clothes off. But I don't think that's the real meaning. What I think it really means is that leaders today have to tell it like it is and want to be told how it is—and can't be afraid, if you'll excuse the expression, to get naked with the truth."

Then, trying to drive home his point, Arlen fixed on several faces and, purposely mixing metaphors, said, "The moral to the story, as I see it, is that top executives who work in glass offices *are* really emperors without clothes." He allowed his convoluted riddle to float unexplained for a moment before going on.

"I guess what I'm trying to say is that we're on the firing line by virtue of the positions we hold. We can't escape the spotlight—no matter how hard we try. We can't say one thing and then do another—and hope to get away with it. We're out there for all to see, so we might as well open up the lines of communication, share what we know and ask for the same in return. Because if people don't know us, they won't trust us, and if they don't trust us, they won't believe in us. And if they don't believe in us, our relationships will be hollow and meaningless. And we'll have failed as leaders. Creating meaningful relationships is what leadership is all about." He was searching for a way to close.

"We act like we're emperors of our own kingdoms. But the truth is the walls are glass. We can't hide. Eventually, people will see us without our clothes on ... which is pretty much how I feel right now," he said slightly embarrassed, throwing his arms wide open and grinning sheepishly.

The audience provided Arlen's exit by starting to applaud spontaneously. Scattered at first, the ovation built slowly. A few stood up as the house lights came up to normal. The applause had the same effect on Arlen that a hypnotist's finger snap has on a subject leaving a trance. He felt exhausted and elated all at once. Then, as the applause continued, he returned to his seat, rolled down his sleeves and put on his jacket.

* * * * * * * * *

Minutes after Wendell O'Shaughnessy's farewell, the noise level in the banquet room increased steadily as people reacted to Arlen's talk. O'Shaughnessy was the first to reach Arlen, who was soon surrounded by others on the dais. Azoulette pushed his way through the group to stand at Arlen's side. Jamieson and Doransky slipped out the back door unnoticed.

At one of the front row tables, a precarious balancing act was underway. *Journal* reporter Karen-Elaine Marshak was furiously scribbling notes while simultaneously surveiling the group surrounding Arlen, waiting for an opening to jump in. She held the miniature tape recorder to her ear, seeking reassurance she'd gotten a clear recording. She smiled to herself, recalling her attempt to duck this boring assignment—figuring it was just another rubber chicken lunch listening to some cookie-cutter executive read a speech. The dignitaries who'd been hovering around Arlen drifted away, leaving only Azoulette near him. She saw the CEO look at his watch and say something to Azoulette as they beelined for the exit. Jumping up, she slung her purse over one shoulder, stuck her pen between her teeth, grabbed her notebook and recorder, and took off in pursuit. Before she could reach Arlen, he was intercepted.

"Arlen, wonderful speech." The familiar voice came from behind him. He turned to see a smiling Bruce Mahoney, patriarch of the U.S. hotel industry and founder of Mahoney Inns & Resorts, Royals' chief competitor. Mahoney offered his hand and the two men shook warmly. "Great gimmick, that off-the-cuff act," he said wryly. Mahoney winked mischievously, a gesture with meaning only to Arlen and Mahoney. The two shared a well-hidden secret that could affect both their companies' future. Mahoney, through a headhunter, had recently approached Arlen about becoming the CEO of Mahoney Inns & Resorts. "Or was it a well-planned act?"

"Does a good magician give away his secrets?" Arlen said, a naughty twinkle in his eye. "How are you, Bruce?" Arlen was aware that Azoulette, who'd taken a step back, was watching them curiously. Arlen didn't know that Mahoney had been the association's first choice for keynoter until Azoulette's lobbying had won Arlen the honor.

"Fine, Arlen. Just fine," Mahoney said, studying him. He leaned a little closer. "Give me a call—soon." Mahoney then turned to greet O'Shaughnessy, who had approached him.

As Arlen and Azoulette moved toward the door, their path was deliberately blocked. "Mr. Royster, I'm Karen-Elaine Marshak with the *Journal*. I need just a minute of your time—a few quick follow-up questions, please." He was instantly hit by her sizzling smile, which seemed a perfect match with her reddish hair and dancing green eyes.

Before Arlen could respond, Helen Casey, Royal's media relations manager, a short, fast-talking New Yorker who'd been sent by Jamieson to coordinate any media coverage or inquiries, stepped in front of Marshak. "I'm sorry, Mr. Royster," she said apologetically. Turning abruptly to face Marshak, her eyes flashed anger at being put in such an awkward position in front of her CEO, but said sweetly, "Karen-Elaine, you already have a copy of the speech. I thought we agreed you'd work through me for anything else."

"Sorry, Helen, but I couldn't find you," Marshak said in an indulgent tone. The dig was obvious. "Mr. Royster was on his way out and after that marvelous speech," she said, playing up to Arlen, "I just had to ask a couple of quick questions." Casey, who had had her share of run-ins with Marshak in the past, wasn't buying the reporter's sugar-coated charade. She reached for Marshak's arm when Arlen, sensing the tension, stepped in.

"Thanks, Helen," he said, gently pulling her around, away from Marshak. "No harm done. I can spare a couple of minutes if Ms. Marshak doesn't mind walking with me to the car."

"Fine. Great," said Marshak, her mock frown instantly replaced with a smile, pushing her way past Casey.

"If that's okay with you, Mr. Royster," Casey remarked, not allowing her irritation to show. "Karen-Elaine, if there's anything else you need ... " Marshak threw an off-handed wave over her shoulder as she walked away.

As Arlen turned toward the exit, people continued to stop him to offer kudos on his performance. For the first time since he'd learned of the crisis, he wasn't thinking about it. Ten minutes later, the trio finally advanced to the hallway and headed for the main lobby to the right of the convention area.

"Tell me honestly," Marshak started. "Was that for real? Or were you just scamming the audience?"

Arlen stopped. He looked at her eager, attractive face, trying to figure out if she was serious or just baiting him. With the generous mood he was in, he gave her the benefit of the doubt, for now.

"I'm not good enough to rehearse that and pull it off," he told her honestly. "My words and my feelings were as real, maybe even more real, as they've ever been. I don't know if I said anything new or whether anyone in the audience learned anything. But I know I learned a lot." He resumed walking.

"What *did* you learn?" Marshak popped back, opening her notepad as she hustled to catch up. She had to quick-step around Azoulette to get alongside the CEO. Arlen stopped suddenly, taking in one of the most alluring hotel lobbies anywhere in the world. It was elegant and expansive, a traditional open area unlike many contemporary lobbies where space is purposely compressed to discourage milling around. The Castle's lobby featured large crystal chandeliers, thick and well-cushioned carpets, and numerous alcoves and sitting areas with comfortable chairs and coffee tables. Arlen always thought the lobby was as inviting for its classic decor as for its intimacy. On those occasions when he had to stay overnight in the city, he stayed in one of the Castle's penthouse suites, if it wasn't sold.

Marshak took advantage of Arlen's delayed departure. "Do *you* really get naked in front of your staff, Mr. Royster?" The way she said it turned the metaphor into something which both amused and embarrassed Arlen. He wondered whether his verbal imagery had been overdone and had diminished his real message.

"Maybe 20 years ago," Arlen rejoined, patting an imaginary paunch.

"That would have been something to see," she quipped, playing off his embarrassment. "I was speaking figuratively, of course."

"Not often enough," he responded, warming to her wit and directness. "It's harder to do than most people imagine. Getting naked—speaking figuratively, of course—runs counter to what most of us business people are trained to do. Being open—truly being open and honest—has its risks and dangers."

"Like answering a reporter's questions?" The challenge was deliberate. Arlen smiled and looked at his watch, deferring an answer. It read 1:25. Realizing her time was running out, Marshak checked her notes.

"Where'd you find that cartoon you referred to? I'd like to use it with my story."

"*Playboy*—a couple of months back," he responded, catching Azoulette's eye and motioning to the front doors. After jotting a notation in her spiral notepad, Marshak scurried to catch up with Arlen and Azoulette.

The revolving door spit the three onto the sidewalk in quick succession. "Mr. Royster," persisted Marshak, trying to position herself to slow down Arlen's departure. Azoulette moved around them and stepped into the limo door being held open by Jeffrey Andrews. "I'd like to do something more in depth on you and your ideas. I'm fascinated with your notion of communication somehow being a part of leadership. Could I do an interview?" She spoke rapidly, closely watching for any change in his expression. His thoughts were already back on his and Royal's crisis.

"I'm pretty tied up the next couple of weeks," he said.

"Well, I'd like to get on this while it's hot. I'd only need about an hour of your time. I really think there's an interesting story here." Arlen could see she wasn't easily dissuaded. But he was uncomfortable with the thought of his ideas being interpreted, and perhaps misstated, especially once the news of the cooked books situation got out.

"Maybe you should talk to Helen or Rick Jamieson. I've really got to go." He slipped into the car as Andrews closed the door behind him. Before Marshak turned away, the smoked-glass rear window silently lowered and Arlen's head popped out. "By the way, how often do you people at the *Journal* read *Playboy*?" he asked friskily. She was caught off-guard.

"Obviously, not often enough," she laughed, but the towncar had already pulled away.

Years ago, Arlen realized that a major advantage of Royal's headquarters location was its proximity to Central Park. He saw its natural serenity—its gentle, wooded slopes and meandering walkways, in daylight, of course—as a welcome counterpoint to the city's otherwise harsh personality. He'd adopted the park as his haven from the strains of business; when he needed time to think, to sort things out, this was where he went.

"Jeff, I've still got about 10 minutes. Let's take a quick pass through the park."

4

The Making of Chief "Communication" Officers

By 1990, the St. Louis Cardinals baseball team, winners of three pennants in the 1980s, had plummeted to last place. Dal Maxvill, general manager (akin to chairman of the board) of the club, knew what the team needed to begin the long climb back: a new manager. He wanted a manager who could take a group of downtrodden veterans and upstart rookies and make them believe they could win—without alienating them. Maxvill didn't expect much in this person, only the wisdom of Solomon, the patience of Mother Theresa and the diplomacy of Henry Kissinger. Above all, he wanted a manager who could communicate with players of different ages and backgrounds—and a leader who could rekindle their passion for the game and restore their respect for themselves and management.

Maxvill's search lead him to one person: former player and manager Joe Torre. At the time, though, Torre was a TV commentator—and not looking to make a job change. But Maxvill, impressed with Torre's articulate on-air manner and long-honed baseball sense, appealed to his insatiable appetite for self-challenge. And somehow, he convinced the former batting champion to trade in the serenity of the broadcast booth for the turmoil and controversy of the dugout.

It didn't take long for things to improve. Within two years, merely the blink of an eye in franchise turnaround terms, things were looking up for the perennial pennant-contending Cardinals. They were near the top of the standings, the players were performing near their potential, and Maxvill had signed Torre to a multiyear contract, thus assuring the organization of his proven leadership for the long-term. Torre, who claimed to have softened his former carrot-and-stick management style, succeeded where others had failed, said Maxvill and the Cardinal players, because of his "live and let live" communication style.

He's honest. "Joe doesn't shoot with a crooked stick," explains Maxvill. "When he tells a player something, that's the way it is. Players will work their butts off for somebody like that." *He's direct.* "There were times when Whitey [Herzog, the prior manager] wanted to say something to you, he'd do it through the newspapers," says former Cardinal pitcher Joe Magrane. "If Joe has something to say to you, he does it face-to-face." *He has very few rules and only insists on one thing from his player-employees—play hard.* "In Atlanta, I had all these rules, like you couldn't play golf, you couldn't go swimming," Torre says. "But I've learned you can't baby sit them. I told them, 'You're adults, do what you want. But I want to see it on the field.'"[1]

Truthful, open, noncontrolling—these are the attributes of effective communication, effective relationship-building. Joe Torre, a member of management, gained a level of trust with his players, members of labor, rarely achieved in this age of free agency and multimillion dollar contracts. GM Dal Maxvill probably wouldn't classify Torre as anything other than a good baseball manager. Yet when he sought somebody who could relate, rather than dictate, to the players, he was actually looking for a so-called leader, meaning a strong communicator who understands the complexities of human behavior.

Joe Torre's straight-from-the-hip, person-to-person, reward-for-performance style symbolizes the shift underway in many organizations from command management to collaborative management. As this trend takes root in American business, some CEOs are realizing the need to learn new human relations and communication skills—or risk personal and organizational failure. Phillip Hawley, CEO of Carter Hawley Hale Stores, explains why: "Our ability to communicate effectively, as opposed to just communicating, makes a big difference in results—and that's true internally as well as externally."

Put more directly, a CEO today needs to be a CCO—a chief communication officer. Being a CCO means that a CEO will assume the organization's key communication leadership role; that is, a *communication strategist* who grasps and relies on the communication process, and a *communication tactician* who knows how and when to employ different types of communication. The CEO's communication role is far more difficult and demanding than most business people realize. The importance of the CCO role shouldn't be underestimated, particularly as CEOs come under increasing scrutiny by boards, stockholders, employees, and consumer groups to account for their decisions.

How well are CEOs doing as CCOs? How do employees perceive CEOs as communicators and leaders? How do CEOs view themselves as communicators? What communication strategies should CEOs rely on to play this role? In this chapter, we share what we've learned in seeking answers to those and other related questions. We start with a look at how employees view CEOs as managers and communicators, and how those perceptions impact organizational life. Then we focus on highlights from research on how CEOs see their communication role. Finally, we outline the four principles comprising a new strategic model of CEO communication—which offers a framework for evaluating and increasing CEO communication and leadership effectiveness. Each principle will be fleshed out and illustrated through examples and case studies in Chaps. 5 through 8.

How Employees View
Top Management

Until about 20 years ago, management research concentrated on trying to understand the employee-immediate supervisor relationship. It was common wisdom that how an employee felt about his or her immediate boss—in practical terms, the employee's definition of management—held the key to explaining an employee's feelings about work and worklife in general. After all, prevailing thinking suggested and research confirmed, employees are closest to, most influenced by, and most want to please their direct supervisor.

Little attention was paid to studying other manager-employee relationships until about the early 1970s. That's when a study of several thousand General Motors hourly employees at 14 different plants found that workers' perceptions of supervisors, while important in determining job satisfaction, is not as influential as how employees view *upper management*. This revelation exploded the long-held belief that employees' views of their *immediate supervisors* was the single dominant force shaping their attitudes toward their job and organization. This meant that employee attitudes were being recognized as the complex, multidimensional human reactions they really are—reactions that are not easily explained or altered.

Later research probed this notion further, discovering that employees don't see management as a single entity, but differentiate among levels and categories of management. Ironically, this same thinking doesn't seem to hold true for managers, many of whom still see and treat employees as all wearing the same hat all the time.

It's clear to us now that employees want and expect to have different relationships with different levels of management. More precisely, they see their immediate supervisor in one light and their CEO in another. With their supervisor, employees assume they'll have frequent, direct, in-depth contact about their personal concerns and the nitty-gritty, everyday issues related to the job. With a CEO or top-level manager, workers anticipate less frequent, more indirect or mediated communication that is focused on big-picture issues, such as new corporate policies or future directions. Building on these findings, subsequent research uncovered a new fundamental principle embedded in the workplace: the *quality of communication* between employees and managers, from front-line supervisors to vice presidents, is a crucial factor reflecting—and determining—whether a relationship is healthy or sick.

How healthy has this relationship been? Over the past 25 years, employee attitude surveys have reported remarkably consistent findings. Workers have said they're generally pleased with their communication with immediate supervisors, but quite unhappy with communication with top management. In study after study, employees have described upper-level executives as communicating poorly and infrequently, talking down to them, addressing trivial issues only, not listening to or caring about their ideas, and not being candid with them. For example, when employees have been asked which sources don't communicate with them often enough, their response is always the same: immediate supervisors *and* top managers. Regrettably, the research tells us, things haven't improved much in recent years.

The costs of weak, insensitive communication efforts by CEOs and other top managers can be substantial in both human and financial terms: dwindling job satisfaction, reduced productivity, higher turnover, absenteeism, and weak contact with customers. Research conducted in a variety of organizational settings encompassing thousands of workers, much of it sponsored by consulting firms and professional organizations, has uncovered compelling evidence that employees' perceptions of management communication (supervisory and top management) are directly linked to employees' job satisfaction and work performance.

Moreover, the need and desire for more communication with top management increases as employees' distance from the top of the hierarchy increases. Studies have consistently shown that the further employees are from the top, geographically and psychologically, the less satisfied they are with top management's communication performance.

The central point is this: Employees will become frustrated and less productive without recurring, open, and two-way communication with the people at the top—and, if such communication doesn't improve over time, people will more likely flee the organization. If the problem holds such serious implications, why don't more top managers recognize and adapt to it?

Survey results pinpoint a communication gap between employees' perceived communication needs and top managers' perceptions of employees' needs. CEOs and other top managers often think they know what employees want, but, most of the time, they don't. And the reason for this gap? Top management hasn't listened well, say employees. As a result, corporate chiefs are losing touch with their people, many of whom are losing faith in top management (as Arlen Royster is being accused of having done with his employees and his son). Regrettably, the gap is widening. And what's even worse is that the communication gap has spawned what *Fortune* magazine has termed the *trust gap*, which threatens to drive a dangerous wedge between employees and CEOs.[2]

How CEOs View Themselves

It is apparent that employees aren't pleased with CEOs' inadequate communication efforts and they desperately want things to be better. But as important as the employee viewpoint is, it's only half the story. How important do CEOs think their communication role is? How do they define it? How do they practice it? Do they take it seriously or delegate it to others? How much time do they devote to it? What's behind their feelings and perceptions?

Until recently, answers to these questions were nowhere to be found. Then David Pincus designed the first nationwide study to find out how *Fortune* 500 industrial and service CEOs define and practice their communication role, focusing heavily on CEOs' communication relationship with employees. This comprehensive study, cosponsored by New Jersey-based management consultants Foster Higgins and the International Association of Business Communicators, a major professional trade organization, was completed in 1987.[3] Two years later, a follow-up study was completed, with the support of Foster Higgins. One especially valuable finding that emerged from the two studies—which collectively revealed remarkably consistent results—was a general profile of the typical CEO as communicator.[4]

A Profile of the CEO-Communicator

This profile offers a composite snapshot of over 300 *Fortune* 500 chief executive officers' perceptions of the communication process and how they use it in their jobs. The archetypical CEO-communicator, almost always male, looks something like this:

1. *Demographics*. He's middle-aged (around 55; other studies suggest the average age is decreasing), has been a CEO for about eight years, runs an industrial company of about 12,000 far-flung workers, and has previously held management positions in operations and/or sales and marketing.

2. *Attitudes*. He believes strongly that the CEO's communication with employees positively impacts employees' performance and attitudes as well as the organization's bottom-line, and that the top executive's communication role is unique and special, unlike any other manager's.

3. *Media habits*. He's most comfortable and effective using face-to-face types of communication, and tries to avoid written and mass forms of communication whenever possible.

4. *Feedback.* He believes in the value of employee feedback and uses mostly informal means to obtain it (such as conversations, meetings).

5. *Time communicating.* His time spent communicating with organizational members, which averages about 20 percent of his work day, is gradually increasing and would be more if not for so many other demands on his time.

6. *Target publics.* However, his communication with line employees is relatively infrequent when compared to his typical communication patterns with top and middle management, professional and technical staff, and the board.

A fascinating overview of the *average* CEO-as-communicator, we think. But as with any profile, you only get the headlines. There's always much more behind it that isn't readily apparent—unless you dig deeper. Pincus conducted 60 to 90 minute personal interviews between 1988 and 1991 with 25 CEOs at a cross-section of mostly large, U.S.-based organizations, which included banks, government agencies, industrial firms, communication organizations, and retail chains. Comments and observations from these corporate leaders, who captained such influential organizations as Bank of America, Bethlehem Steel, NASA, Avon, the *Los Angeles Times*, Pacific Bell, and Cedars-Sinai Medical Center, are interspersed throughout this book. In a number of cases, interviews were also conducted with the organization's top communication or public relations professional to better understand the organization's overall communication system and how the CEO fit into it. A listing of all the top executives interviewed is in the appendix.

In the following pages, we present a synopsis of the survey and interview results, along with our interpretation of their meaning.

How Do CEOs Define Communication?

Despite the gathering momentum of the participative management movement in the workplace, CEOs still see internal communication in largely top-down, informational terms. More than half (53%) agreed that the primary purpose of employee communication is sending information to employees; a third (37%) disagreed, and the rest (10%) weren't sure. If communicating doesn't mean information sending, then what does it mean? A number of CEOs talked about their desire to design an organizational culture that encourages open communication—up, down, and laterally. Among those who see communication as more than information distribution was a CEO of a large corporation who said: "It's my responsibility to encourage an environment in which employees feel free to take risks, participate, grow with the corporation. I'm trying to remove barriers which prevent them from doing their best job."

Bank of America's former chairman, Tom Clausen, sees communication as a sort of ebb and flow between top management and all employees, regardless of their position. He cites the example of how this approach worked effectively for him and the VPs on his senior management council. "Communication isn't a one-way monologue. To get buy-in, it's got to be a discussion. Everyone has to be given an opportunity to speak and contribute. No passive observers allowed, only active participators."

Tom Priselac, chief executive officer at Cedars-Sinai Medical Center in Los Angeles, views communication as a perpetual process of mutual influence, shaped as much by what's said as what isn't said, meaning the ever-present nonverbal nuances contained in every glance and gesture. "Communication occurs constantly," he says. "At the risk of sounding metaphysical, it occurs when a manager walks down the hall, or through the look you have on your face, or by the spring in your step. That may sound a little odd, but it's those subtle signals that go beyond the routine or formal types of communication ... that a manager must realize communicate as much as anything."

How Do CEOs See Their Communication Role?

There's no question that CEOs believe *intensely* in the power of their own communication. Eighty to 90 percent said they believe their communication activities positively influence employees' job satisfaction, job commitment, and job performance—as well as profitability. Most agree with Dick Schlosberg, former *Los Angeles Times* Publisher and CEO and executive VP in the Times-Mirror organization, that CEO communication makes a difference: "Top management communication absolutely impacts the bottom-line, performance, objectives, where the company's going, what people do. I'd be surprised if any top manager thought differently."

Most CEOs interviewed expressed a personal sense of responsibility for shaping the nature of the communication climate and culture in their organizations. Robert Dockson, former chairman of California Federal Savings Bank, addresses this point: "The CEO is responsible for communication. If communication is poor in a company, it's the CEO's fault. He has no one to blame but himself. If he's arrogant, undignified, if he lacks a simpatico with the lowest-ranking member of the organization, then he's not doing his job. The job of communicating is as important as his strategy decisions, his goal-setting, and his ability to win employees' commitment. Without good communication, people won't feel they're a part of an organization."

The fact that three out of four (74%) CEOs see their communication role as unique and different from other managers is intriguing. If CEOs see their communication obligations as different, what are those differences? Generally speaking, CEOs said that all managers, regardless of title or scope of responsibilities, have distinctly defined communication duties and obligations. In other words, each category of management—first-line supervisors, middle managers, and top managers—is expected to assume a communication role that is different in certain ways from every other category of management. Looking at this another way, CEOs envision a system of coordinated managerial communication in which each manager, playing his or her particular role, supports every other manager. A CEO of a large company in Pittsburgh explains the difference in the top manager's and other managers' roles: "The role of the CEO is to provide the vision ... interpretation of that vision is the responsibility of operating unit managers." The top executive of a New Jersey-based industrial firm adds, "The CEO must set the tone, but total communication is the role of every supervisor."

CEOs see their communication leadership role differing from other managers when it comes to particular types of topics or issues. Most CEOs (70%) see themselves as being the lead communicator on issues with organization-wide implications (such as layoffs, year-end reviews, product recalls). In contrast, they see other top and middle managers assuming the driver's seat on issues most directly related to workers' job needs (such as new benefits program, changed overtime policy). CEOs demonstrated a far greater sensitivity to the importance of who is communicating (that is, source credibility) than anticipated.

CEOs expressed mixed feelings about how bold and visible they ought to be in the CCO role in general. When asked if they thought they should be their company's primary spokesperson, only half said yes. Their reasons vary, however. Some just don't feel comfortable in that role; others don't think they're qualified or experienced enough to play it convincingly. But the trend appears to be toward more CEO-spokespersons. "There's less and less tolerance for CEOs hiding behind the corporate veil," explains the CEO of a Houston-headquartered service company. A 10-year top dog points out why: "The increased demand for accountability by corporations makes it imperative that the CEO be the public point-man."

Differences in age, type of organization, and managerial experience appear to influence how CEOs view their communication role. For instance, statistical analysis of the survey data showed that older and more experienced CEOs place *less* value on the CEO's communication role than their younger and less experienced counterparts. The data also revealed that CEOs of industrial companies and those with little or no sales/marketing management experience are much less likely to believe in the impact of the CEO's communication role than chiefs of service firms and those with lots of sales/marketing experience.

How Much Time Do CEOs Spend Communicating—And Is It Enough?

Do CEOs' optimistic attitudes about their communication role translate into the amount of time they actually spend communicating? Clear-cut answers to this sticky question are elusive, according to the facts and the CEOs themselves.

The typical CEO commits about 18 percent of his time to internal communication. That's up slightly, they report, but is less than what they'd like it to be (23%).

While the ideal or optimum amount of time varies from CEO to CEO, organization to organization, and situation to situation, there seems little question that CEOs are being pulled in criss-crossing directions these days, forcing them to constantly reevaluate their priorities and reallocate their precious time. Logic suggests that the highest priorities should get the most time. The data reinforced the logic: CEOs who believe more strongly in the value of communication commit more time to playing their communication role.

Which Media Do CEOs Prefer and Consider Most Effective?

The average CEO communicates most frequently and effectively through informal, interpersonal media, such as casual conversations, meetings, and forms of MBWA (management by walking around). In contrast, top managers prefer to avoid—due to their discomfort and lack of faith in their effectiveness—mass forms of communication, such as video and other types of electronic media. To illustrate, 8 out of 10 chief executives see themselves as very effective with face-to-face types of communication. But their self-confidence drops considerably when it comes to written or mass media. Only 4 out of 10 rated themselves strong with written communication, and just 2 out of 10 did so with mass media.

These findings suggest a good news-bad news condition. The good news is that interpersonal communication, the strong suit of CEOs, is considered to be the most direct and immediately effective way to build credibility and relationships. A CEO of a New Orleans-based service firm says there will be "more and more emphasis on frequent contact with all levels of employees and more day-to-day, hands-on management." The bad news is that person-to-person types of communication necessarily limit the number of employees a CEO can reach quickly and simultaneously. In a small company, that may not be a problem, but in large organizations—the target of the surveys—heavy use of interpersonal communication, particularly when used in place of or to the exclusion of other media, can isolate a top manager from the majority of employees.

On the other hand, mass media are cost-effective and time-efficient. They offer the potential of high visibility and broad exposure—attractive features to those who seek a public spotlight and a deterrent to those who don't. Says a veteran CEO of a large midwestern industrial firm: "A greater emphasis on technology has made timeliness possible. Through the video medium, I've been able to take a greater personal role in communicating with employees." But for the most part, CEOs are uncomfortable with mass media, because they're unfamiliar and inexperienced with them. In addition, top managers are frightened by mass media's potential to magnify, distort, and expose. By dodging or underusing mass distribution methods of communication, CEOs of large and geographically dispersed operations restrict the type of relationship they can have with employees, most of whom rarely, if ever, see or have direct contact with them.

Not surprisingly, CEOs of larger organizations (10,000 or more employees) hold significantly more positive views of the usefulness of mass media and rely on them much more than top managers of smaller organizations. This may reflect the growing pressure on CEOs of big, complex organizations to use mass communication technologies to reach and nurture relationships with employees, despite top dogs' preference for interpersonal forms of contact.

Who Do CEOs Communicate with Most Frequently?

Do chiefs' communication practices parallel their attitudes? Do they give employees or stockholders or boards their fair share of attention? Once again, their behavior doesn't seem to jive with their intentions.

When asked to indicate how frequently (daily, weekly, monthly, quarterly, less than quarterly) they communicate directly with 13 key stakeholders, CEOs disclosed that they communicate most regularly (that is, daily/weekly) with other managers: top managers (98%), professional/technical staff (59%), and middle managers (45%). Next in line were three outside groups: customers (43%), other CEOs (34%), and community leaders (27%). However, two crucial internal groups—employees and boards of directors—receive only occasional attention from CEOs; only 2 out of 10 (22%) top managers said they communicate with workers and boards weekly or daily. And only slightly more than a quarter (27%) of them report communicating with employees less than once a quarter. At the bottom of the CEO's "hit list" are shareholders (12%), media (11%), and union leaders (2%).

CEOs' relatively infrequent communication with their own workers seems to defy top executives' passionate belief that their personal communication with employees strongly influences employees' attitudes and performance, and the company's bottom-line. How can we explain this apparent incongruity in CEOs' attitudes and behavior? Are they merely saying what they think they're expected to say?

During in-depth interviews, many CEOs said that no single group, however influential, justifies more than a minor portion of a CEO's constricted time and overloaded schedule. To do otherwise would not only be impractical, but unfair to the many other groups vying for the top manager's attention. When pressed for reasons why employees were so low in the pecking order, CEOs were at a loss to explain. "That's just the way it is" seemed to be the prevailing attitude. CEOs don't seem to know how much communication with employees is enough, only that they'd like it to be somewhat more than it is now.

We believe that most CEOs don't communicate with their people often enough or effectively enough. There's a touch of irony in that conclusion given that no group is more vital to an organization's prosperity than its own members. Without workers' commitment and loyalty, success is a pipedream. Top managers appear to agree—philosophically, at least. They say their communication with employees makes a difference to employees and the organization's effectiveness, and that employee input improves management decisions.

Yet, in the same breath, they admit communicating more frequently with community leaders and other CEOs than they do with their own people. Those findings are puzzling and challenge sound business logic. Such discrepant findings, however, point up CEOs' ongoing dilemma about what their communication role should be. How much time is enough time to be effective in the role remains a question still begging for an answer. Clearly, a universal formula prescribing how a CEO's time ought to be ideally allotted to communicating with certain groups seems neither possible nor practical.

How Do CEOs Obtain Feedback?

An area offering insight into CEOs' gut-level feelings about employees' place and value in organizational life is what they think about and how they use feedback from employees. This dimension of the CEO-employee relationship may represent the crucial dividing line between CEOs who define communication as information-sending (one-way) and those who see it as relationship-building (two-way).

Genuine two-way or symmetrical communication, rare in corporate America, requires a leader willing to not only listen to people up and down an organization, but one who will also make changes based on that feedback. As a top manager of a consumer products giant in New York says, "Communication—to be effective—must be two-way. I just can't talk to them, I must also listen."

A CEO who regularly seeks input from employees is sending an important unspoken message to them: "You're an important member of this enterprise and I welcome and need your ideas and suggestions—which I'll seriously consider, thus involving you in the decision-making process." Conversely, those who don't solicit input or try, but aren't believed to really want it, are sending the opposite message.

CEOs are big believers (94%) in the proposition that employees possess information important to CEO decision making. This finding is encouraging; it reflects a dramatic step forward in CEOs' perceptions of employees' utilitarian role in organizational life. Explains Richard J. Knapp, a principal and manager of the Cleveland office of management consultant William M. Mercer, during a telephone interview: "Twenty years ago, most chief executives felt that employees were there to do the work and not the thinking. Fortunately, recent evidence shows that CEOs' attitudes are changing. American business has been infamous for imposing a solution on employees before telling them there's a problem. No wonder they're often resentful and question management's judgment."

CEOs' preference for interpersonal communication surfaced again when they were asked which forms of feedback they consider most effective—casual conversations (57%) and employee meetings (39%). Rated a distant third were formal employee attitude surveys (29%). One in 10 said the grapevine was a highly effective method for feedback. And the least useful channel of feedback was reported to be the suggestion box, rated as very effective by only five percent of CEOs.

Once again, these findings appear to serve as red flags, revealing what may be CEOs' lukewarm desire for and willingness to seek and use employee input. They say they believe unequivocally in the value of feedback, yet they mainly rely on unsophisticated and somewhat unreliable sources of bottom-up input. It seems curious that managers trained to trust empirical evidence over human perceptions would be content making organization-wide decisions based in part on chance conversations and meetings with unrepresentative small groups. Yet, that appears to be the case.

Several explanations are possible. It could be that CEOs are giving the socially acceptable response, but don't really mean what they say. Or it might be that they do believe what they say, but don't have the tolerance for the time-consuming and imprecise nature of attitude research. Then again, these conflicting findings may merely mirror many CEOs' often inaccurate belief that they instinctively know their people better than they really do. Survey results uncovered that CEOs of larger organizations (10,000 or more employees) place significantly more value on formal methods of feedback, such as employee attitude surveys, than top executives at smaller companies.

The CEOs interviewed seemed to understand why feedback from employees can help them do a better job. In theory anyway, the more information CEOs have about a target audience, the more responsive and sensitive their decisions ought to be. It sounds simple enough—which is usually a sign of danger. For executives indoctrinated from "day one" to believe that a good manager should know all the answers and that asking for help from others, particularly workers, is a sign of weakness, accepting employee feedback as valuable is not an easy admission.

Top managers' attitudes toward feedback, also known as two-way communication, are monitored closely by other managers and workers in an organization. Those attitudes send clear signals whether or not the upper echelon of an organization really encourages or discourages employees to offer input upstairs. Whatever the CEO says and does—or doesn't say or do—sends a message throughout an organization as to what's important.

Bruce Burtch, president of The William Bentley Agency, a small product development firm in San Francisco, tells the story about his executive-father's long-standing reliance on employee involvement in organizational matters.

"My dad always taught me to get information directly from the source, even if others thought it humbling. On one occasion, during a meeting in Ohio, he was asked a question about some production figures he didn't know the answer to. I watched him pick up the phone and call a plant in Pittsburgh to talk to the shop steward. Some of the other people in the meeting were startled. They asked my dad, 'You don't know?' He answered, 'I don't presume to know. That's not my job. But I've got a guy right on the shop floor who does know.' That's always stuck in my mind."

Feedback can be as simple as a phone call or as complex as a system-wide survey. What's required, though, above the investment in time and money, is a zealous belief in the value of feedback. Some, like Robert Jones, have actually been accused of taking the principle too far. Jones, president of JP Hotels, a 14-property chain based in Clearwater Beach, Florida, believes sincerely in customer feedback. He's gone so far as to post all his telephone numbers—office, home, and mobile—in every room of every hotel, urging travelers to call him with complaints. "Sometimes my wife thinks I'm crazy," he says, only half joking. But guests seem to be taking him up on his offer; calls average about one a day and run the gamut from complaints about watered down drinks to skeptics calling to see if he really answers his own phone. He recently added a second mobile phone so he can call a hotel while talking to a guest and get instant action.[5]

Survey data indicated that less experienced CEOs believe more in the value of employee feedback than those who've been CEOs for some time. Why would veteran CEOs be so much more skeptical about input from workers than rookie top managers? It could be due to fundamental differences in philosophies and business school training between old and new guard CEOs. Or it could be explained by senior CEOs' frustration with trying to communicate with employees over the years—without much success or positive feedback on their efforts. It's probably safe to predict that future CEOs will probably be more aggressive than their predecessors in soliciting input from employees and seriously considering that input in corporate decisions.

How Do CEOs Assess Themselves As Communicators?

Do top dogs view themselves as strong communicators? Surprisingly, they appeared less confident in their own communication effectiveness—as well as their professional staff's capabilities—than might've been expected. To illustrate, while they see the purpose of employee communication as primarily distributing information to workers, half of the CEOs (49%) admitted that employees aren't getting enough information from management to do their jobs effectively.

Perhaps even more troubling, though, is that one out of three (34%) chief executives said he *doesn't know* if employees are receiving enough job-relevant information. CEOs should know. They must know. Because if they're uninformed about what employees know and don't know, and what they want and need to know, then CEOs' decisions on employee relations issues will be made somewhat blindly.

Moreover, CEOs don't think they're particularly credible sources in employees' eyes. About one of three CEOs (35%) admit that their employees don't believe CEOs communicate with them candidly and honestly. Without trust in the messenger's integrity and veracity, messages are likely to be rejected. "The need for open, frequent, direct, creative communication" from the top person, says a young CEO from New York, "will continue to grow and will be much more important in the future."

A Quick Recap

Based on survey and interview findings, the typical CEO of a large company strongly believes communication efforts positively impact employees' outlook and the organization's financial picture. In contrast, he's less certain about the effectiveness of his own organization's formal communication program. He sees the CEO's communication role as special and atypical, and defines employee communication in largely "information-sending" terms. The average CEO communicates with employees only sporadically, wishes it were more frequent, and claims to believe in the power of employee feedback, which he obtains mostly through informal means. He's essentially a face-to-face communicator who avoids contact through mass media whenever possible.

When all is said and done, as the survey and interview findings exposed, CEOs' "talk" about communication is well ahead of their "walk." They say they believe in communication's human and economic value, yet they practice it as if they're not really convinced—or maybe CEOs, like many other managers, don't yet know how to be effective communicators. Most current top managers, as well as those who aspire to become chiefs, probably need some help in figuring out how to be a chief communication officer. Enter the C-C-O-S model.

A Formula for CEO Communication: The C-C-O-S Model

We offer that help in a new model for effective CEO communication. The model is comprised of *four* principles—two behavioral and two strategic—that, we believe, capture the essence of what competent CEO communication is all about and which offer a blueprint for crafting sound CEO communication plans. As luck would have it, the formula contains four principles whose first letters form the acronym C-C-O-S, the designation for **C**hief **C**ommunication **O**fficer**S** ... and stand for ...

- **C**onsistency—aligning CEO words and actions, and internal and external messages.
- **C**ompassion—being empathetic to employees' concerns by listening sensitively to their feedback.
- **O**rganization—integrating CEO communication with other managerial and organization-wide communication, and matching sources, messages and media.
- **S**electivity—strategically deploying the CEO-communicator for maximum impact and to reinforce other managers' communication.

Consistency and compassion represent CEO *behaviors* or *characteristics* that are the basis for the CEO's credibility, vital to establishing trust. Organization and selectivity refer to the core *strategic* or *tactical* components of CEO communication, both essential to implementing a CEO communication plan. The four principles combine to create a CEO communication system. And as in all systems, each principle is notable for its singular value, yet when the four principles are merged and integrated, the result is a strategy substantially stronger than if the principles operated separately. Each principle is dependent on every other principle; if one principle is weak, then every other principle will be weakened proportionately.

This set of principles should guide the formation of CEO communication strategy—although which principle or principles should dominate the strategy will vary with CEOs, organizations, and circumstances. A hypothetical example should help illustrate the dynamic alliance among these factors. Let's say a CEO gave a speech to stockholders claiming that the company's prospects look strong for the next year. Two days later, the CEO, speaking to a gathering of workers at one of the company's plants, warned that next year will be a "downer" and that layoffs are inevitable. Since both of the CEO's speeches were reported in the company's daily news update distributed to all employees, the contradictory messages didn't stay a secret very long. The employees' perception was of a top manager "speaking out of both sides of his mouth."

Obviously, the CEOs' messages were contradictory (inconsistency), thereby damaging the CEO's and the organization's credibility with employees (lack of compassion). Betraying the consistency principle exposes the CEO's lack of a thoughtful communication plan (organization) and the poor timing—and thus, weak impact—of the speeches (selectivity). In many ways, applying these principles may seem more like common sense than behavioral science. That may be true. But unfortunately, violating common sense principles is far more common than makes any sense. The model provides a framework, a guide if you will, for constructing CEO communication strategy and a built-in criteria for subsequently evaluating the strategy's effectiveness.

In the next four chapters, we describe and break down each principle in detail, using case examples and CEOs' comments and anecdotes to illuminate how these principles can best be employed by CEO-communicators.

Before moving ahead, though, a couple of cautions about using this or any other model. First, no model, however detailed or precise, can be applied *carte blanche* to "real time" situations. Models like this one are not intended to be "quick fixes"; the model must be adjusted and reconfigured to fit a particular CEO's style and each organization's circumstances. Second, as already noted, no principle operates in isolation within a system and, depending on the situation, each principle will at times play a dominant role and at other times a supporting role. Determining these core principles' relative roles is a key step in shaping overall CEO communication strategy. Therein lies the heart of the value of the C-C-O-S model.

A Final Word

The C-C-O-S model is intended to assist CEOs in becoming more competent communicators—and thereby stronger corporate leaders. But what exactly is a competent communicator? That's tough to say, because communication has many looks and structural arrangements. Communication strategy weaves together objectives, situations, strategies, target audiences, messages, and media—and one organization's or CEO's strategy hardly ever looks just like another's.

Such strategy doesn't fit a single, universal formula; it's a kaleidoscope of elements, forever forming different patterns as situations and circumstances change. The right combination, if there ever is one, comes from the strategist's reading of the situation and knowledge of the communication process. This model offers counsel to CEOs and their professional staff members as they search for the right mix of behavioral and strategic factors to make a CEO an effective CCO and corporate leader.

Returning to Arlen ...

As Chap. 3 closed, Arlen was leaving Royal's Castle Hotel off Central Park, buoyed by his out-of-character triumph as keynote speaker to a gathering of prominent top hotel executives. Despite his career-long fear of public speaking, Arlen inexplicably tossed aside his manicured speech, rolled up his shirtsleeves and turned what began as a fumbling, embarrassing performance into a compelling, impassioned extemporaneous talk about communication and corporate leadership.

His candid and persuasive commentary captured the attention of an aggressive, attractive reporter for *The Wall Street Journal*, Karen-Elaine Marshak, who was covering the luncheon speech. She had pressed Arlen for a follow-up interview. Minutes after the speech, he was congratulated by Bruce Mahoney, industry celebrity and founder of Mahoney Inns & Resorts, who secretly began recruiting Arlen a few weeks before. As we rejoin the busy CEO, he has just returned to Royal headquarters and is about to enter into a conversation with the company's chairman, Jim Stamps, that will rattle his faith in Stamps and exacerbate his own guilt over his role in Royal's mess.

"Sometimes an Emperor Without Clothes"

Wednesday, October 10, 1:30 p.m.   Strutting confidently into Susan O'Reilly's office, Arlen Royster was noticeably more upbeat than when he'd left a few hours earlier.

The quick excursion through Central Park hadn't eroded Arlen's emotional high following his surprise, impromptu luncheon speech. While pleased with himself, he was also perplexed over his own out-of-character behavior, an aberration he couldn't explain. "It must have been pure instinct taking over," he thought, searching for some sort of logic where none existed.

O'Reilly, his executive secretary, looked up from her desk. Standing in front of her was a relaxed-looking Arlen, a satisfied grin on his face. "I'm back," he announced. "So, what new crises have come up in the last hour or so?"

"Was your speech cancelled or something? I expected you to look like you just had a root canal," she wisecracked, puzzled by his ebullient mood.

"Are you kidding?" he said sarcastically, feigning surprise. "I may take my act on the road ... especially after the reviews come in."

He turned and walked into his office, leaving O'Reilly to scramble out from behind her desk to follow him, confused by his enigmatic behavior. "Where's the manuscript?" she asked, closing the outer office door. Arlen usually couldn't wait to hand her his speeches for immediate filing. It was a ritual he followed, simulating his unshackling himself from a dead-weight ball and chain.

"Don't know. Didn't use it today." He smiled again and took off his coat, tossing it on the back of the couch to the side of his desk. O'Reilly grabbed it, brushed it off, put it on a hanger, and hung it on the coat rack near the door.

"What happened?" she pressed.

"I have a feeling you'll read all about it in the *The Wall Street Journal* tomorrow," he teased. Arlen rifled through the organized stack of opened mail and routine paperwork she had placed on his desk. He marveled at her efficiency. Almost every item had a post-it note from her telling him what she'd done or suggesting how he ought to handle it. He always thought of her as his own Radar, the perceptive company clerk from "M*A*S*H" who could anticipate his commanding officer's words just before he said them.

"Okay, don't tell me," she said, sounding a little piqued, making a mental note to check with Azoulette about what really had happened.

"I don't want to rain on your parade," she continued, "but I think something rotten is going on around here." He looked at her blankly, as if to say, "Tell me something I don't know—or suspect."

"I overheard Phyllis make a lunch date for Keller with Marcia Gross and Donn Lieberman," O'Reilly said, referring to Keller's secretary and two members of Royal's board of directors, each long-time critics of Jim Stamps and Arlen, who they saw as Stamps' "boy." "And Grubner's been holed up in Keller's office all morning."

In a split second, Arlen's confidence disintegrated. "That doesn't surprise me," he said flatly, hiding his ebbing doubt. "He sure didn't waste any time, did he?"

Arlen moved to the glass wall, his train of thought derailed. He could pick out Royal's Castle Hotel in the distance, easily identifiable by the unsightly satellite dish anchored on its roof. He was drawn back to his curious public speaking experience, which in retrospect, was terrifying but also thrilling. "It's a very thin line that separates fear from excitement," he thought, remembering a line he'd once heard daredevil Evil Kneivel say during a TV interview after he'd scaled 15 Mack trucks on his flying motorcycle.

Someone knocked softly on the door and, without waiting for an invitation to enter, opened it and strode in. It was Jim Stamps, Royal's large-framed, burly chairman. It was unusual for him to come to Arlen's office, especially if they hadn't set an appointment. He marched up to the CEO and bellowed jovially, "How'd the speech go, Arlen?" Stamps— with his 270-pound bulk, flabby jowls, and full head of fluffy white hair—was often mistaken for Tip O'Neill. "Sorry I wasn't able to be there."

"Read about it in *The Wall Street Journal*," Susan shot back before Arlen could answer. "That's all he'd tell me," she followed-up, firing a quick frown at Arlen as she moved toward the door. "Gentlemen." It was her exit cue.

"Susan," Arlen's voice stopped her, "thanks for the information." She swiveled in his direction, nodded, and flashed a quick smile, and then pulled the door closed behind her.

* * * * * * * * * *

"So, how did the speech go?" Stamps inquired, lowering himself onto the leather couch. "I don't want to wait for tomorrow's *Journal*." His tone indicated it was time for business, that deadlines were encroaching.

"I didn't spill the beans if that's what you're worried about," Arlen answered, slipping into the chair facing the couch. Stamps shook his head to dismiss Arlen's paranoia, still waiting for an answer.

"It was ..." Arlen paused, searching for words to describe his odd experience. Finally, he gave Stamps a shortened, no-frills version of his performance, purposely neglecting to recount his improvised, stream-of-consciousness remarks.

"Too bad I didn't see it in real time," Stamps said sincerely, "but I've been on the phone all morning with various members of the board, telling them about our little problem." Stamps enjoyed disarming people with understatements. He peered intently at Arlen. "Maybe it's my Scottish blood," he said, slipping into the brogue of his youth, "but I've got a ken, as my grandfather would've said, that something's rotten in Denmark." Susan had used the same word a few minutes earlier, Arlen thought.

"So I hear. What exactly is rotten?" Arlen probed, purposely repeating the word while holding back his own information until he'd heard more from Stamps, who possessed an uncanny feel for boardroom politics. Arlen could see his mentor was worried. He hadn't taken Mike Keller's threats all that seriously at first, figuring they were mostly bravado. The apprehensive expression on Stamps' face said otherwise; Arlen had better not underestimate the VP of operations' political support and daring.

Stamps shrugged, then told Arlen that, while the board members he'd reached were very concerned about the accounting imbroglio, most weren't willing to discuss their views or recommendations, which was in itself highly unusual. "I'd like to know what the hidden agenda is," the chairman speculated, shifting his rotund torso to look straight at Arlen's. Now it was the CEO's turn to share information.

"What did Lieberman and Gross say?" Arlen queried.

"They weren't in. I tried reaching them a few times, but no luck."

Arlen sat forward on the edge of his chair, suddenly more alert. In his mind, he reviewed bits and pieces of information he'd accumulated during the day—Keller and Grubner's confab following the staff meeting; Keller placing the blame on him several hours earlier; O'Reilly's intelligence about Keller and Grubner hatching something; and Keller's lunch meeting with Gross and Lieberman. All at once, the full mosaic formed in Arlen's fast-revolving mind. An instant later an expletive formed softly on his lips as the fragments fell into place.

The shreds of data he'd collected were now lining up into an alarming logic: Keller had shown only mild surprise at the false revenue reports and wasted no time placing full responsibility at Arlen's feet, while never once accepting any himself. He acted almost as if he'd been planning for this moment for a long time.

"What're you talking about? You know something, Arlen. Let's hear it," Stamps demanded. Arlen rose from the chair and walked to his favorite spot in front of the glass wall, peering into the distance. After a few seconds, he turned back. Neither man spoke at first.

The thoughtful CEO drifted back to his chair, stood behind it, his vacant expression revealing only that he was preoccupied. "Nothing's for sure," he told himself, "but there is an underlying, twisted logic to the pattern." Arlen being Arlen, he hesitated to say anything based on such flimsy proof, but he suspected Stamps held similar hunches.

"I think we're probably thinking the same thing, Jim," he began, still standing, but now leaning forward with both palms locked tightly on the back of the chair. "I think we may have a mutiny brewing. Keller had lunch today with Gross and Lieberman and so much as announced to me earlier that this office won't be mine for much longer. Interesting timing, eh?"

Stamps reacted visibly, shaking his head briskly and grumbling loudly. "Just what we need," he complained. "More politics with the board. What's Keller's angle?"

"That I'm responsible for everything because of the bottom-line pressure I put on everybody," Arlen said, settling into the chair next to Stamps and crossing his arms. He recounted in detail his earlier confrontation with Keller when the VP all but threatened to take things public if Arlen didn't step aside.

"And who knows, Jim, he may be right," Arlen suggested, unfolding his arms and running his hands over the arms of the chair. "Maybe I did trigger this mess."

"What the hell are you talking about?" Stamps shot back with sharp annoyance. "When I asked for someone's head earlier today, I didn't want you volunteering yours."

"Who do you think the board's going to hold responsible, Jim? The hotel managers or me? The underlings or the guy who's supposed to set the example?" Arlen sounded a little like a courtroom prosecutor arguing before a skeptical jury.

"Don't flatter yourself, Arlen. No CEO's responsible for his people's illegal activities unless he overtly encourages or openly condones them," countered Stamps, playing the senior counselor role. "You didn't do either, did you?" Before Arlen could say anything, Stamps zoomed ahead with the subtlety of a runaway train. "You're not every employee's keeper. No one expects you to be. Except maybe you. These managers went over the line because they're naive, stupid, or greedy ... or maybe all three. Who knows, maybe Keller encouraged them or made them think you wouldn't mind.

"Sure, maybe you made some mistakes," he pushed, without pausing for a breath. "Everybody does. Did you do anything unethical? Or illegal? Did you ask any of your people to do anything unethical or illegal? They did this on their own and they damn well knew it was wrong."

"Won't the board ask why I didn't see it coming or know about it sooner?" Arlen pressed.

"If you carry your logic to its extreme, then I'm the one who's responsible. Or maybe the board itself." Stamps' response was strident. Arlen hadn't thought of it that way.

"But you're not ...," he began.

"No, I'm not, Arlen," Stamps broke in firmly. "I don't see it that way. Where do you draw the line?"

Arlen's powerful sense of guilt wouldn't allow him to patently accept Stamps' effort to absolve him of responsibility. "I think the board draws it with the CEO. Jim, you know that's the strategy Keller will play with his friends on the board." Arlen ran his fingers up and over his grey-streaked brown hair to the back of his neck, where he began a gentle massage.

"Let me worry about the board right now. You worry about doing your job and let me do mine," said Stamps, pointing a stubby finger at Arlen.

"I know you're trying to take me off the hook, Jim," Arlen replied. "And here I am trying to stick the dagger in my own heart." He recalled Stamps telling him one time he had an overactive sense of responsibility, which was his personal albatross.

Arlen halted for a moment. "Ah-h-h-h. I don't know what to think. It's been a hell of a day. So far," he tagged on.

"Look, Arlen," Stamps said impatiently. "Let's put this in perspective. Right now we're not sure who's responsible for what. Or who should be held responsible for what. You? Keller? Me? The board? The managers who screwed around with the books? Don't assign or accept responsibility yet, okay? That could hurt everybody—and make Keller's case for him." For a man so overweight and slow-moving, thought Arlen, Stamps sure is quick and nimble in other ways.

"And if you think you're responsible—which I don't think you are—then you've got to try to fix things immediately. Otherwise, you may never get the opportunity." Stamps sank back into the couch, his suit jacket springing open to reveal burgundy suspenders stretched over his protruding midsection. They stared at one another, each contemplating the next moves in this high-stakes game of corporate chess.

* * * * * * * * *

Arlen's private line buzzed, ending the lengthening silence. He leaned forward and pressed the button with no number. "Yes?"

Stamps started to stand, pressing his left forearm on the arm of the couch to hoist himself from the soft leather chair. His body left a deep, rounded recess. He lumbered to the wet bar at the far end of the office, still turning over his thoughts. He grabbed a tumbler, dropped in a few ice cubes and unscrewed the cap on a bottle of Dr. Brown's diet cream soda. With glass in hand, he strode to the transparent wall, keeping his back to Arlen to camouflage his eavesdropping.

"How'd you get this number?" The reply obviously didn't please Arlen. "You mean *The Wall Street Journal* has my private number?" At the mention of the newspaper, Stamps turned with a look of concern. He inched toward Arlen, focusing intently now on Arlen's expression.

"No, it really isn't convenient. I'm right in the middle of a meeting." Arlen's annoyance came through in his clipped tones. "I don't suppose it would do any good if I asked you to throw this number away?" He stopped again for the caller's response.

"That's blackmail," he replied a little more congenially. At the word "blackmail," Stamps nearly choked on his drink. Arlen picked up a pen and began to print block letters on the pad in front of him, unaware that Stamps was next to him. Stamps leaned in and could see "MARSHAK," which Arlen proceeded to underline and draw a circle around. "I said I'd think about the interview." He paused.

"Well, talk to Rick Jamieson's office about that. I told you to set it up with his office. It's gonna be a few days before I can even think about it." Arlen looked up and noticed Stamps peering at him, his raised bushy eyebrows asking, "What gives?" The CEO held up one finger as he listened, indicating the conversation was ending. Then, suddenly, he smiled.

"As long as you're not writing it on the bathroom wall there at the *Journal*," he laughed. "And, yes, I'm still fully clothed—and planning to stay that way for now."

After a short pause to listen, Arlen apologized for his abruptness and ended with a friendlier "Bye now." He replaced the phone in its cradle and leaned back, his smile remaining.

"Who the hell's Marshak?" quizzed Stamps, concerned any time *The Wall Street Journal* and Royal were mentioned in the same sentence. "And what was that about blackmail?"

Arlen explained that Marshak was following-up on a conversation they'd had after his luncheon speech and wouldn't take no or even maybe for an answer.

"Why isn't Jamieson handling that?" asked Stamps. "You're sure she doesn't know anything about our ..." He searched for the right phrase. "... our little accounting problem."

"Not unless Keller's called her," Arlen cracked. Seeing that Stamps wasn't amused, he admitted, "Okay, bad joke. She's interested in doing a profile on me. She's aggressive. But I think she's harmless." He couldn't resist a final quip. "So far."

"What are you going to do when this thing does break and the media are all over us like a bad suit?" Stamps asked, lowering himself once more onto the sofa, carefully balancing his soft drink.

"I don't know if we'll have any choice but to come clean and swallow our medicine like good little managers."

"You could still end up looking dirty," Stamps cautioned.

"I know," Arlen acknowledged. "But I can't control much of what the media think and say. Though I'll try. Eventually they'll move on to another story. Our employees will stay, though ... I hope."

He stood up and began aimlessly pacing the floor. "It's like Rick said in the staff meeting this morning. We can't afford to lose our own employees' faith in us. Which is what Keller's claiming will happen." He was standing behind and directly above Stamps now, speaking to the top of his head.

"The only way we'll be perceived as credible by our own people is not to treat them like airheads. If we aren't bone honest with them, they'll see through us in a second—and then we've lost." Arlen was thinking out loud as much as he was talking to Stamps.

"The employees are one thing," Stamps interjected. "The media's another."

"But we can't say one thing to our people and another to the outside world. We'll look two-faced."

"That's my point exactly," argued Stamps, jabbing the index finger of his free hand at Arlen. "If you give the full story to the employees, then intentionally or not, you're giving it to the press." Stamps pushed himself forward to place his empty tumbler on the glass coffee table. He remained balanced on the front edge of the sofa. "Sometimes keeping your mouth shut—even if you're criticized for it—is a better strategy than telling only part of the story. No matter what we say or don't say, those scavengers in the media hear what they wanna hear anyway. It scares me to death that our employees, stockholders, and customers may do the same thing."

Arlen, now standing to Stamps' right, considered the chairman's perceptive point for a moment. "Our first priority has to be our employees, because without them to make the business go, the stockholders and customers will just go away," he said softly. He leaned down, bringing his face almost eye-level with Stamps. "What about the time you brought in a management consulting firm to the Village to help bolster employee productivity and save jobs?"

Arlen was referring to when Stamps was CEO at Mark Twain's "Americana Village" theme park and Arlen was a management intern. At the time, the park was losing money and Stamps was under heavy pressure to do something fast to fix it. Taking the initiative, he brought in a noted management consulting firm, Brian Lauren & Associates, to take a hard look at how the park's operations and bottom-line could be improved—quickly.

"I seem to remember you coming clean with employees then. You were up front about how tough things were and told them what would have to be done to turn a profit, and assured them the consulting firm's presence posed no threat to anyone's job. Your big announcement at the all-employee meeting nixed rumors about the consultants being management's Trojan horse. Let's see, as I recall, after your meeting with employees, you then wrote a column in the company newsletter explaining your decision," Arlen reminded him, ticking off each point on one of his fingers. "I think," Arlen concluded, "that the same forthcoming, open type of strategy is best here."

He sat down with a thump, crossed his legs and absently picked an imaginary piece of lint off his pants. His gaze returned to Stamps, whose half-closed eyes disguised the brain energy he was expending. Almost imperceptibly, the pear-shaped body of Royal's figurehead executive slid back on the couch, his attention now on his own thoughts. Nearly 20 seconds passed before he spoke again. "I know you think you've proved your point," Stamps began, his eyes never leaving Arlen. "But you're actually making my case for me. Things aren't always what they seem."

"We've known each other for a long time, Arlen. But you never knew that all of that public posturing about efficiency and productivity was just to ..." Stamps searched for the right word "to camouflage ... no, let's call a spade a spade, to cover up ... the real reason the consulting firm was brought in."

Stamps methodically and unemotionally told Arlen the real story, beginning with how he had no choice but to lop off jobs to rescue the financially failing park from likely extinction. He wanted to forestall the panic and legal threats that would've followed if he'd publicly admitted the park's precarious financial condition and his intention to institute mass layoffs. Instead, he decided to use a big-name outside firm as the vehicle to do what he knew he had to do.

In actuality, a deal had been worked out with Brian Lauren & Associates before the consultants ever set foot in the park. The trumped up plan called for the consultants to do what consultants do—nose around, review records, interview key employees, look busy and then a month or so later announce their recommendations. Stamps admitted that the secret deal allowed him a way to cut positions without alarming or hurting people any more than was necessary, while minimizing damage to his leadership position. "Merely a case of the ends justifying the means," Stamps insisted without any regret, rubbing his eyes vigorously. He stopped and studied his fingernails, purposely avoiding looking at Arlen.

"And, although some suspected, nobody ever really knew," Arlen concluded, shaking his head in disbelief. "I guess you got away with it, didn't you, Jim?" He remembered that in the months following the management firm's initial report and recommendations, Americana Village underwent large-scale changes in organization streamlining, as the consultants labeled it, resulting in hundreds of workers being transferred, displaced, offered lower paying jobs, or pushed into early retirement. Yet, the reduction in force went largely uncriticized by the press or unions, because, as Stamps put it, "everything appeared to be above board, supported by sound business logic, and not that unusual."

Arlen wasn't sure if he was reacting more to his surprise at Stamps' flimsy ethics or his surprise at his own naivete. Stamps' next comment cleared it up. "No, I didn't get away with it," sighed Stamps. "A confidential memo I'd written to Johnny Lauren, president of the consulting firm, describing our little plan somehow fell into the hands of one of my department managers, a power-hungry type much like Keller."

Anticipating Arlen's question, Stamps quickly went on. "It doesn't matter who. But this individual used that memo to blackmail me. For promotions. For raises. Eventually for an early pension … and more." Arlen ran down the people he could remember at the park then, but none rang a bell.

"Even when he wasn't working for me," Stamps admitted sonorously, his eyes blinking furiously, "I always knew there was someone out there who could destroy me with a phone call to the press." Stamps again looked at Arlen. "Can you imagine what would've happened if that memo had been leaked?" He paused. "Like I said, Arlen, I think you just proved my point for me."

"Jim, if you could turn back the clock and do it again, would you act any differently?" asked Arlen, a trace of moral indignation slipping in.

"I don't know. Probably. It might be harder to pull off today, though. Employees are savvier. The media are sitting on our shoulders constantly. But the logic I relied on then would still apply. That much hasn't changed, I suppose."

"Workers these days sure as hell know a lot more than we think they do," said Arlen.

"But some things never change," Stamps scolded. "Allowing employees too much latitude can be dangerous. Only we at the top have the full picture. Don't forget that. The world of business politics hasn't changed as much as you might think."

Arlen turned philosophical. "It doesn't always matter what we do or how well we do it. People see things as they want to see them, not as *we* want them to." His piercing tone was losing its edge.

"You're right," agreed Stamps. "I was afraid employees wouldn't understand what we had to do to survive and many, especially the good ones, would leave. I didn't want to hurt people. But giving out partial information allowed us to keep the enterprise intact and hold on to the majority of jobs. If I'd come clean from the beginning, everybody would've given us up for dead and gone elsewhere."

Stamps had said enough.

"So what you're saying, Jim, is that half-truths and twisting information are okay as long as the ends justify the means," pressed Arlen, purposely baiting the chairman.

"No, dammit, I'm saying it was smart business. In that case, it was a matter of survival." Seeing he was making no progress with Arlen, Stamps stood, grabbing the lapels of his jacket. "I know you, Arlen. You want me to admit I was wrong and I'd do it differently now. You know I don't second guess myself, it's an unhealthy practice." He turned and walked toward the door. Arlen stood up quickly and moved with him.

"My mistake was in getting caught," Stamps quipped, briefly flashing a guilty grin. "Makes me sound like Richard Nixon, doesn't it?" Arlen said nothing as he reached for the door handle.

"You've got to look at the total business picture, my friend," resumed Stamps. "You can't be concerned about just one person or one group. It's never black and white. What really matters is whether people feel secure and have hope that things'll get better."

Arlen started to open the door, but Stamps pushed it closed and leaned against it. "I'm going to call Lieberman and Gross," he stated. "It should be a much more interesting conversation now that I know about their lunch with Keller."

"I'll do what I can with the board, but our necks are stuck out on this one," Stamps warned in a fatherly tone. "I know we'll have to release the information once the auditor's report comes in on Friday. We could wait until Monday or Tuesday. But then the danger of this leaking increases …"

"So what're you telling me?" Arlen interrupted.

"Be careful," growled Stamps, straightening and letting Arlen open the door. "I know times change. Styles change. But be careful. For all our sakes."

He looked hard into Arlen's fatigued eyes, the CEO's determination evident. "Keep me informed," said the elder man, gently touching Arlen's shoulder before walking out. As Arlen closed the door, he could hear Stamps joking with Susan O'Reilly before he trundled out.

Arlen swung past the coffee table and instinctively picked up Stamps' empty glass and placed it in the sink. Then he began pacing in front of the outer glass wall. As usually happened, in a few minutes, he was drawn to the picturesque Central Park scene beyond, vibrantly alive in a kaleidoscope of sun-drenched reds and yellows and oranges.

Stamps is of the old management school, Arlen thought, brainwashed from business school on about the potential dangers of being too open with anybody outside the inner circle. Arlen liked to think he'd grown more trusting of others, especially employees, during the past couple of years. Now he was torn between the philosophy of "naked communication" he'd talked about in his speech and his contradictory inclination to keep his mouth shut.

"I seem to be talking about changing a lot more than I'm actually changing," he admitted a little ruefully. "I too am a product of the old school."

As he continued walking back and forth along the outer edge of the glassed-in office, his introspection deepened. He knew the type of executive—and the type of human being—he wanted to be. But he also knew that merging his wishes with his behavior wasn't something that came easy to him.

Just then, the phone rang out, jarring him from his self-evaluation.

* * * * * * * * * *

"Are you busy, Joe?"

Joe Coletto, Royal's head legal counsel, looked up from his desk and saw Gloria Bernard, VP of investor relations and youngest member of Arlen's executive staff, standing in his doorway.

"No, no," Coletto answered, hastily disentangling himself from the papers on his desk and pushed his chair back so hard it hit the wall.

"Come on in, Gloria." Coletto pulled out two chairs from under his small, round conference table and waited until Bernard was seated before lowering himself into the other chair. He eyed Bernard, who was wearing a sharply tailored, dark green suit over a white silk blouse. "What's up?" he asked.

"Keller tried twisting my arm to join his move against Arlen, during our walk back to the office after lunch," she announced, smoothing her skirt. As the only African-American vice president, she was ever-sensitive to others' perceptions of her and her position. Coletto, her unofficial mentor, was one of the few people she was comfortable sharing her feelings with.

After the morning staff meeting, she'd talked with him about how things would likely play on Wall Street, her territory. He'd suggested they get away for lunch and discuss it. They'd gone to Coletto's favorite place, Nana Ziroli's, a traditional Northern Italian restaurant near Radio City Music Hall, featuring home-made minestrone and an assortment of authentic pastas.

On her way back from the restaurant bathroom, Bernard had spotted Mike Keller engaged in deep conversation with Marcia Gross and Donn Lieberman, two of Royal's board members, in a far corner of the crowded restaurant. When Keller spotted her, he quickly hustled over to her and Coletto's table, all smiles. Bernard had muffled her discomfort when Coletto took his usual direct approach.

"Interesting timing, Mike, you meeting with board members today of all days. Anything we should know about?"

Avoiding the question, Keller sounded an ominous note. "Royal's in serious trouble and somebody's got to do something about it," he said, harping on the theme he'd initiated that morning. "We need to plan now so that when Humpty Dumpty falls," he said, not hiding his disgust, "we're ready to put the pieces back together again."

As Bernard and Coletto started to leave Nana Ziroli's, Gross and Lieberman buttonholed Coletto to talk about some relatively unimportant legal issue. As soon as Coletto was diverted, Keller fell in beside Bernard for the jaunt back to Royal headquarters.

"I think he planned it that way," Bernard told Coletto drolly, knowing that Keller couldn't have known that they were going to be at the restaurant. "It gave him the perfect chance to try and work on me without any interference."

"What do you mean, work on you?" probed Coletto, softening the question so it didn't sound like an interrogation. "What'd he say?"

"It's probably not so much what he said, but how he said it. Maybe what he hinted." She stopped and deliberated for a moment. "He seemed cock-sure he'll be taking over soon. And, as he delicately put it, he wanted me to know I'd be a 'valued counselor and strategist' on *his* staff."

"Mike's an experienced and adept boardroom gamesman, Gloria. He can be slippery," Coletto said, stroking his full white beard. "I'd never trust him to tell me the whole truth about anything. He's no Arlen, as far as I'm concerned."

Bernard looked confused—and unconvinced. "But, Joe, I'm not so sure Arlen isn't to blame, at least partially. To escape from this mess, we need somebody at the controls who'll be believed. The SEC and most others will assume management's guilty until hard proof to the contrary surfaces. Say one wrong thing now and it's all over."

"Don't worry about it," Coletto said calmly, gently placing his hand on her forearm. "As long as Arlen's in the driver's seat, I have faith we can survive. He's a straight shooter. If I were a betting man," Coletto added, the sparkle in his eyes revealing his poker player's intensity, "I'd put my money on Arlen every time." He once confided to Arlen during a business trip that nothing in life was more exciting for him than coming home a winner in the wee hours of the morning.

Seeing that Bernard still had her doubts about Arlen's leadership, Coletto hitched his chair forward until his knees were almost touching hers. "Let me tell you a story that may help you understand why I trust Arlen," Coletto began in his thick Queens accent. "I was one of Arlen's first hires after he became CEO. He's the reason I came here. There's a side to Arlen not many people know."

Shortly after Arlen became VP of operations at Royal, he inherited a gigantic problem. The Teamsters union had gained the right to hold an election at Royal's flagship hotel. Polls showed employees were 3 to 1 in favor of voting in the union. In those days, Coletto explained, Royal didn't put much into personnel problems. But the company was so obsessed with keeping out unions that it spent whatever it took to win, even if that meant doing business under the table. For instance, if the company wanted to get rid of a particularly vocal prounion employee, a quiet buyout might be offered. In one case, Coletto recalled, an influential union booster "mysteriously" saw his personnel records changed over-night to reflect three additional, unearned years of service—thus allowing him to retire with full benefits several weeks before the election was to be held, as long as he agreed to keep his mouth shut and leave the hotel immediately.

"Anyhow, Arlen was the chief firefighter—the numero uno 'bombero,' as the Hispanic workers called him—sent in to salvage the election for Royal." Coletto leaned back, lacing his hands behind his head and keeping his eyes trained on Bernard, who was becoming enthralled with this inside glimpse of Arlen and Royal history.

"I was working for a law firm representing the union at the time. So Arlen was my adversary. We locked horns during some tough bargaining sessions. At first, I didn't know him well enough to trust him, but after a few days of negotiating, I could see he was a straight shooter and I started giving him the benefit of the doubt."

Arlen wouldn't give up, no matter what the polls showed, recalled Coletto. He listened and brought an objective perspective to the bargain-ing table, a stark contrast to his predecessors' doggedly biased and unbending views. Six weeks later, the union won, but by only 10 votes.

"Arlen's team lost the election, but his honesty, his directness, his integrity impressed me. And I guess he saw some of the same things in me. Although we didn't see each other for a number of years after that election, when I was approached by a headhunter about coming to Royal, I met with him, he made me an offer I couldn't refuse, and I've never regretted it. I've stayed mainly because of Arlen," Coletto concluded, releasing his hands from behind his head and leaning forward.

"Lemme get this straight, Joe. You're telling me I should be comforted by a story about a guy who *lost* a union election?" she chided a little caustically. "A loser? That's supposed to make me feel better?"

"Look, Gloria, Arlen hasn't won them all. Show me a CEO who has," Coletto said, trying hard to placate her. "But give me somebody I can trust and who has his head on straight—and I'll give you a winner most of the time. I like those odds."

"Okay, counselor," she sighed. "I'm still not sure I know what's really going on here. I'll wait and see how things go. Thanks, Joe. I do feel a little better." She smiled and got up to leave.

As she was closing the door, Coletto reached across his desk for the phone. He punched in "1," Arlen's inter-office number.

PART 3

How to Be an Effective Communicator: Transforming Chief Executive Officers into Chief Communication Officers

5

Consistency—The Heart and Soul of Credibility

Scenario 1: In late 1992, David Glass, CEO of Wal-Mart, the nation's largest retailer whose advertisements proudly proclaim its policy of buying goods from American manufacturers, appeared on NBC-TV's "Dateline" to discuss Wal-Mart's "Made in the USA" marketing campaign. Shortly after the segment began, Glass told reporter Brian Ross, "We can make merchandise in this country as efficiently and as productively, and for every bit the value available anywhere else in the world."

Moments later, Glass was shown a videotape of rows of young children assembling clothing in what looked like a sweat shop in Bangladesh. Ross asked Glass whether Wal-Mart does much business with firms in Bangladesh that employ children. "To my knowledge," responded Glass, "we don't buy from any vendor that uses child labor." The next scene was Ross standing in that same factory in Bangladesh, explaining that on this day he saw three floors of children, some as young as nine years old, making shirts and putting Wal-Mart labels on them. Ross said that the manager of the factory told him he'd been doing business with Wal-Mart for over a year, and that Wal-Mart buyers had been to the plant.

The next visual was of a fire two years earlier in that same factory in which 25 workers, many of them children, died because exits had been blocked. Ross pointed out that less than a year after the fire, Wal-Mart gave this factory a big production contract. Next, Glass is seen saying, "Yeah, there are tragic things that happen all over the world." Ross countered, "That's all you have to say about it?" And Glass, obviously embarrassed and struggling for words, says, "I—I don't know what else I would say about it." At that point, a Wal-Mart vice president halted the interview and David Glass left the room.[1]

Journalistic tactics aside, the image left in the minds of millions of viewers, including many Wal-Mart employees and customers, was of a mortified and speechless CEO claiming that his company believes fervently one way while its actions reveal something quite different. Such inconsistencies between a company's stated priorities and its actual practices can cause not only red-faced embarrassment to the CEO, but also a drop in the company's public standing.

Scenario 2: Also in 1992, Pete Wilson, the beleaguered governor of California, faced the prospect of a multibillion dollar budget deficit in a state that mandates its annual budget be balanced. Early in the year, he proposed to the state assembly that the budget be brought in line through cuts in existing state programs rather than by tax boosts. Speculation was that Wilson figured the Democratic-controlled assembly would never support such cuts, which would likely cause a budget stalemate and thereby fuel popular backing of Wilson's ballot measure shifting budget powers from the legislature to the governor during fiscal crises.

When, to the governor's surprise, the Democratic legislators agreed to most of his plan, he lashed back by criticizing as "phony" the same planks of the Democrats' plan that were contained in his original proposal. For example, Wilson blasted the Democratic budget proposal as unbalanced, while his own Department of Finance reported that it actually showed a small surplus. And he attacked his opponents' call for exempting the state's big programs from budget trimming, while arguing at the same time that public education—by far the state's biggest ticket program—should be spared from any cuts.

Wilson, characterized by Assemblyman Steve Peace as "the most confusing human being" he's ever seen in politics, hurt his own and the state's cause with his waffling statements and behavior on the state's priorities.[2] One news commentator wrote that the governor "contradicted himself and misstated some facts, and in the process confused legislators and sent the public a mixed message of what he stands for." Wilson's inconsistencies might be chalked up to normal political rhetoric and posturing; however, they did little, if anything, to improve the state's budget situation or the governor's reputation. In fact, the budget impasse between Wilson and the Assembly caused California to operate without an official budget for seven weeks, forcing the issuing of IOUs in place of checks to many employees and vendors. And the governor's state-wide initiative to shift budget powers from the legislature to his office was soundly defeated.

These two scenarios are sad but true examples of different violations of the principle of consistency. Lack of consistency can cause serious damage to CEOs' and their organizations' credibility. And once credibility—that is, the degree to which a person or institution is believed and trusted—is jeopardized as in these cases, recapturing lost confidence is extremely difficult, if not impossible.

In this chapter, we probe the principle of consistency, exploring its many dimensions and applications, and why it is the heart and soul of a CEO's and an organization's most indispensable ally: credibility. First, we delve deeper into the concept of consistency and clarify its meaning. Then, we identify its various subparts and illustrate how each part contributes to the larger concept. And, finally, we outline a case involving the CEO of a national camera store chain that demonstrates how the absence of consistency at the top can harm customer relations.

A Simple, Yet Perplexing Concept

Among the four principles comprising our C-C-O-S model, consistency may be the most complex and least understood, yet none is more fundamental or critical to CEO communication. At first glance, you might think that being consistent is a pretty simple concept: doing the same thing, the same way, time after time. Put that way, consistency does appear to be a simple idea, with few complications. Realistically, though, what seems simple in the abstract can be far more complex in practice. And that's certainly the case when the concept of consistency is placed in an organizational setting and viewed through the CEO's eyes.

A Working Definition

In the most basic terms, consistency is meaning what you say and saying what you mean, all the time. This notion is at the root of effective CEO communication, because it is *the* principal determinant of a CEO's credibility, a vital dimension of leadership. The logic goes something like this: Being credible means being believed; being believed means being trusted; and being trusted is the basis for establishing meaningful relationships. And, as is clear in the two scenarios, credibility is fragile, easily fractured if a CEO is perceived to be speaking out of both sides of his or her mouth, or acting inharmoniously based on prior promises and actions. Even our fictional CEO, Arlen Royster, must constantly struggle with his inconsistencies, as he can't seem to reconcile his willingness to listen to and understand his employees with his unwillingness to do the same with his son, Glenn—an inconsistency his wife, Andrea, won't let him forget.

Credibility can take years to earn, yet can be lost in a split second, with an innocent or unintended slip of the tongue or one small misstep. A case in point is former Los Angeles Dodgers executive Al Campanis. Long-considered a strong proponent of racial equality in baseball, he told "Nightline's" Ted Koppel, during a show marking the 50th anniversary of Jackie Robinson's breaking of baseball's color barrier, that African-Americans didn't "have the capacity" to manage. The resulting public outburst was so vehement that Campanis, a respected executive in baseball circles, was forced to resign prematurely, because his mere presence had become an untenable liability to the Dodgers organization and the game of baseball.

Yet total consistency is rarely attainable. Every day, CEOs and other managers must navigate ticklish situations where being 100 percent consistent with prior statements and actions may be impossible, or, on occasion, inadvisable. When the audiences, settings, problems, and circumstances change, so must the message, the language, and the solution. The trick is to make the necessary adjustments in communication and actions without straying too far from people's perceptions of what you stand for. If you drift too far, you may be seen as being inconsistent and no longer believable. "Credibility doesn't automatically transfer from one person to the next," notes Ron Rhody, former senior vice president of corporate communication and external relations for Bank of America. "You can't transfer the acceptance a worker has for the current CEO to a new CEO, who may have earned his spurs before taking over, but must always reearn those spurs in his new chair."

The CEO = The Organization = The CEO

The CEO's credibility and the organization's credibility are inextricably linked; in fact, they're inseparable. Each rubs off on the other and, if perceived positively, becomes a highly prized organizational asset. When the top dog speaks or acts, it's the organization speaking and acting, and vice versa. Employees, stockholders, customers, and the media take their cues from the CEO, forming their impressions of the organization based on what the chief executive says and does.

"When people think about the Times Mirror Company, they think about (CEO) Bob Eruburu and the high standards he sets, the quality of the individual he is, the values he shares," contends Dick Schlosberg, *Los Angeles Times* publisher and CEO, during an interview atop the *Times* building in downtown Los Angeles. "And it's not hard to figure out who people think about when they think of Chrysler."

As an organization's primary tone setter, a CEO's attitudes and behaviors will invariably be reflected in an organization's people and, subsequently, to vital external publics. "It's easy for a CEO to underestimate his profound impact on the organization, how it perceives itself, and how it's perceived," says Schlosberg. A CEO's consistency or inconsistency will touch employees at all levels, particularly those in regular contact with customers, as you'll see up-close in the Sharp Vision Camera case later in the chapter. If a CEO is considered credible, people will listen and believe what they hear. But when a CEO isn't credible, people will tune out and turn off. And when top management's credibility is damaged, the entire organization suffers.

The Dimensions of Consistency

Consistency is the core ingredient of credibility. To achieve true credibility, a CEO must be consistent in thought, language, and actions, and in every aspect of business life. Consistency isn't a single concept; it's really a number of elements all rolled together to form the concept. If one of those elements is weak, then all the other elements will be weakened, as will be the overall concept. As we see it, consistency is composed of five different, interrelated dimensions, each of which we'll examine.

1. *Consistency of objectives.* The CEO's words and actions, and internal and external messages, are in alignment with organizational objectives and other management communication efforts.
2. *Consistency of words and actions.* The CEO's behavior is congruous with previously stated messages to key audiences, and managers throughout the organization are sending the same messages and acting accordingly.
3. *Consistency of style.* The CEO's approach to communication is, to the greatest extent possible, direct and candid, and includes soliciting feedback from stakeholders.
4. *Consistency of priorities.* Audiences and issues that the CEO says are important are treated as such; for example, employees and other key internal constituencies receive crucial information about the organization from the CEO or another top manager before it's released to external audiences.
5. *Consistency of roles.* The CEO is the organization's chief communication officer and, as such, is the primary spokesperson on the most important organizational matters, whether communicating with internal or external audiences.

Consistency of Objectives

To ensure that a CEO's communication is aligned with overall organizational objectives, the CEO should be included—preferably as an active participant—in the planning of the company's communication program. To do this, the organization's senior communication professionals must regularly monitor and evaluate the CEO's communication performance and capabilities so the top executive's best role(s) can be considered in all business decisions. As usual, establishing the same objectives throughout any organization begins with the CEO, but must carry over to all other employees.

Jim Verney, former CEO at Winchell's Donut House, made certain that each employee was given a wallet-size, laminated card containing Winchell's mission statement clearly stating the company's main objectives. A poster-size version of the statement was hung in the public area of each store. And Winchell's vendors were sent cards, too. The statement eventually came to be more than just hollow words; its meaning seeped into Winchell's culture. Indeed, Verney defined much of his role as reinforcing that culture.

"Any time I spoke to a group of our people, I talked about the statements," Verney recalls. "It was crucial for me to reinforce what the district manager, the region manager, and the vice president of operations were saying, and what they were trying to accomplish in the field." Even realizing the pressing need to publicize the company's new mission statement as widely as possible, Verney also realized the gamble he was taking if the company failed to live up to its promises. "If we didn't deliver, people would think we were pulling their chains. Senior management has to be credible. It has to build up trust. If we put these mission statements and culture cards out there, then we'd better live up to them."

Keeping objectives in sync in a large organization can be as difficult as keeping a group of school children together on a field trip. During lagging economic times like now, many top executives have felt employees' and stockholders' wrath when the dual objectives of job security and new investment clash. That was the case in late 1992 when IBM, long touted for its unwritten lifetime employment policy, announced a $6-million commitment to sponsor the IBM OS/2 Fiesta Bowl in 1994 and 1995.

Taken alone, it wasn't an unusual business decision for a company of IBM's size and reputation. Indeed, some might applaud the move as a brilliant marketing decision to try to regain lost market share. However, the announcement of the sponsorship came only days after the company revealed its plan to chop 25,000 jobs and close operations around the world in order to add $6 billion to its bottom-line.[3] Many confused and upset IBMers did little to muffle their outrage when they learned of the company's seemingly conflicting company objectives. No doubt the hailstorm of criticism resulting from this decision only added to then-CEO John Akers' battle to keep his job, a fight he lost not long after.

Consistency of Words and Actions

Being intentionally consistent in approach is important, but it's merely the first step. Nothing speaks louder about a CEO or an organization than the CEO's actions and how they line up with his or her words. Much of the time, a CEO's most powerful message—positively or negatively—is his or her behavior, or misbehavior. Frequently the targets of critics, CEOs cannot easily dodge public finger pointing, whether they're leading the annual stockholders meeting or speaking to a Rotary club. Or attending a National Hockey League game, as Disney CEO Michael Eisner found out at the opening exhibition game of

Disney's expansion team, the Mighty Ducks. Eisner, an avid hockey fan, spent part of the evening fending off criticism of family-oriented Disney's decision to back a sport that condones fighting. While personally deploring fighting for fighting's sake, a distressed Eisner was forced to defend his company's perceived inconsistent belief in family values and its financial support of a violent sport. Eisner cleverly downplayed the criticism, stressing that players are penalized for fighting and showcasing Disney's plans to sponsor youth hockey programs that teach nonviolent ways of resolving conflicts.[4]

Whatever the setting or situation, the CEO's behavior, from subtle hand gestures to televised policy statements, will send intentional and unintentional signals to stakeholders watching and listening, not to mention all those who will read or hear about it later. For instance, a CEO who inadvertently fails to acknowledge an employee in an elevator can cause spasms of insecurity in the snubbed worker and all those the person tells later. For CEOs, both the little and big things mean a lot.

A Gesture That Counted at Delta

The CEO's behavior can have a big influence on organizational strategies, particularly because of how employees tend to react to even small gestures from the top. Delta Airlines' Chairman and CEO Ronald Allen's largely symbolic gesture during a critical time for the company demonstrates this point. In 1992, Delta faced the greatest financial crisis in its 65-year history. Buffeted by fare wars that hurt virtually all domestic airlines, the Atlanta-based carrier posted losses of $506.3 million. To save $375 million in fiscal 1993, Allen imposed a five-percent cut in staff, which resulted in layoffs of thousands of workers; he froze salaries; and he reduced health and vacation benefits for Delta's 78,000 employees. The airline also asked its union pilots to defer a five-percent pay raise, but they declined.

At the same time he launched this tough austerity program, Allen was drawing a much-publicized salary of $575,000, the result of a 21-percent pay raise voted him by Delta's board of directors. According to industry analysts, the raise was intended to bring Allen's $475,000 salary—modest by industry standards and only two-and-a-half times more than the $184,000 earned by Delta's top pilots—more in line with the salaries of other airline executives. Perhaps such a move would have seemed wholly reasonable during normal times. But, in the face of such huge company losses and so many employees losing their jobs, the board's action was viewed by many as ill-timed and ill-advised.

So in late August, 1992, Allen, in a move designed to demonstrate the seriousness of the situation, asked the board of directors to rescind his pay raise, thereby cutting his salary by $100,000. Whether this was intended as a challenge to the pilot's union or simply an attempt to do the right thing, Allen's action, despite its modest monetary savings to the company, nevertheless won him high praise for his sensitivity. In effect, he was demonstrating his belief, through his behavior, that no employee, regardless of rank or title, was any better or more privileged than any other employee.

For Appearance's Sake at Wickes

In a similar vein, Sanford "Sandy" Sigoloff, former chairman and CEO of conglomerate Wickes Companies, has for years been an avid collector of Porsche automobiles, the classic German sports car. He had never before hesitated to drive one of his Porsches to work—that is, until Builder's Emporium, a Wickes-owned and operated national chain of building supplies and hardware, went into bankruptcy. When that happened and until the company recovered, Sigoloff, known for his skill in curing desperately sick organizations, drove a Honda to work. He didn't want anyone wrongly assuming that, while asking employees to work longer hours, forgo pay raises, and trust him to lead Builder's Emporium back from the dead, he was joy-riding around town in a company owned Porsche.

To Sigoloff, it was essential that his behavior never be perceived as different from the way he was asking his employees to behave. When you're the person at the top and everyone is watching, little things can mean a lot, and may very well become exaggerated or blown out of proportion precisely because it is the CEO. "Is that being sensitive to the common misperceptions?" asks Mike Sitrick, Sigoloff's one-time senior vice president of communications who now runs his own crisis management firm. "You bet it was. Sandy wanted to make sure that all of our communication, including his behavior, was consistent, and that it adequately reflected the reality of the situation. It wasn't an accident."

A CEO's actions should never be accidental; they should always be purposeful. The same is true of the CEO's *messages* to the organization's stakeholders. Messages and behavior must reinforce one another, and, as usual, it starts with the CEO, who is the precursor for all that follows.

Consistency of Style

Effective CEO-communicators seem to instinctively understand that honesty and candor are essential to a leader being consistent and, thus, believable. Telling the whole truth, without any embellishments or euphemisms, is a worthy goal which, for a variety of legal and other reasons, isn't always possible in business settings. How *consistently* honest and candid a CEO is, however, will go a long way toward determining whether target constituencies listen and believe what they hear.

A sad example of a CEO who lost his job because his personal style clashed head-on with his organization's goals is William Aramony, former head of United Way of America. Amid allegations that he misused the charity's funds to feed a lavish lifestyle and hire family and friends, Aramony's public standing crumbled almost overnight and he was compelled to resign under siege. Several months later, Aramony observed that his major mistake was not paying enough attention to how his actions or personal style could have been perceived by people working for or contributing to the United Way.

Candor Has Many Meanings

Candor implies forthrightness: unreserved, honest, sincere communication. A worthy goal not always possible to reach. Top managers often feel constrained by circumstances, or potential legal liabilities, or fear of being misquoted or misunderstood. Thus, total candor is viewed as a dangerous prospect to many business people. Sometimes managers may be less than candid in order to spare others' feelings by softening what might otherwise be a harsh, hurtful message. Or, as some top managers believe, silence has its rightful place in the organizational communication strategy continuum.

Somtimes called "strategic use of ambiguity," *not* communicating is thought to buy much-needed time for an organization—to gather facts or recompose itself, hold off negative effects for as long as possible or to prevent giving away organizational plans or intentions prematurely. Strategic silence, however, may also create an information void that will be filled by misinformation and rumors not easily corrected when communication resumes.

It's this very dilemma of keeping the organization's mouth shut or opening it wide that confronts Arlen Royster, our imaginary CEO. His indecision is over how much candor is enough and appropriate. On one hand, his top legal advisor, Joe Coletto, advises him to come down with a case of lockjaw to limit any potential legal liability. On the other, his principal communication specialist, Rick Jamieson, counsels him to spill his guts to enhance his own and thereby Royal Accommodations' credibility. As most top managers do, Arlen sought a middle ground position he was comfortable with—or at least could live with.

Candor is not absolute, either in the abstract or in reality. There are degrees of candor, ranging from the unvarnished truth to what an audience "absolutely needs to know." Who's to say just how candid a CEO should be in each and every situation? It's a judgment call that shifts with each scenario. We believe that the more candor, the better, in most situations. But absolute candor is a luxury few top dogs believe they can afford. The essential point is this: Whatever degree of candor is used with one audience ought to be used with all audiences.

The CEO can't afford to act one way with one group and another way with another group. If that happens, the resulting confusion can dilute, if not destroy, the impact of the intended message. "If you went to two meetings at which I was speaking, you'd see the same person, not two different people," says Dick Schlosberg, publisher of the *Los Angeles Times*. "A talk at a recognition breakfast meeting for a branch sales office wouldn't be unlike what I would say at a security analysts' lunch. I'd talk pretty much the same way, be pretty much the same person."

Being consistently candid to the greatest extent possible can help CEOs avoid having to remember various and sometimes contradictory versions of the same message. If a CEO's messages vary significantly in their degree of candor—such as telling Wall Street that the company had a "moderately good year" while telling employees, in hopes of motivating them, that the company had an "off year"—the result is likely to be confused and skeptical audiences who don't know which message to believe, or whether to believe the CEO at all. "I have one rule I pass on to everyone in my organization," explains Bethlehem Steel's Walter Williams. "That the strategy for communicating with all audiences is to be candid, up front and honest, and portray an image of integrity. I never try and peanut anybody. I never try to give anybody double talk. Because then when I talk to somebody else, I never have to worry about remembering what I said before."

Consistently straightforward communication is embedded in management's operating procedures at Los Angeles-based Vons Grocery Company. "We're honest not only with our customers and our suppliers, but most importantly with our employees," emphasizes Bill Davila, Vons' former CEO and still its chief spokesperson. "Employees don't have to agree with you. They don't have to fall on their knees and give hallelujahs. But if they believe you're honest, then they'll listen to what you have to say. And if you ever lose that trust, then I don't care what you communicate to them, you're not going to be effective."

Sometimes communication must be brutally blunt to penetrate the psychological barriers stakeholders construct to tune out or filter unpleasant messages. That was the sort of scenario facing Bethlehem Steel's Walter Williams when he wanted to be certain that workers understood what the company was trying to accomplish to stay in business. "Our strategy can be summed up in two words—to survive," he told them. "And in order to survive, we're going to cut your compensation, cut your benefits. We're going to improve quality. You're all going to go to management development schools to improve labor relations in this plant."

How much candor is enough candor—or too much candor? "I'm not going to spill my guts about things that are company confidential," admits Williams. "If I can't talk about something, I say so. I say that to my workers, I say that to the financial community." To put everything that needs to be said into a 25-minute talk and be completely candid isn't easy or always recommended, acknowledges Avon's retired top dog Hicks Waldron. "We always let the bad news hang along with the good news. Although, when it's all over, it's not what's said that's important. It's what's taken out of the meeting that's important." Frequently, what employees will remember more than what was said or how it was said is whether the CEO was honest, frank, and treated them like adults and colleagues.

An aspect of candor with powerful repercussions on a top manager's credibility is the ability—and willingness—to fess up to mistakes. Admitting publicly that something is screwed up or that someone screwed up and accepting responsibility for it is perhaps the ultimate honesty. While such admissions don't excuse the wrongs being acknowledged, they are likely to be perceived as self-effacing and humbling human acts that should arouse forgiveness—as long as the same mistake doesn't occur repeatedly.

When some of Chrysler Corporation's managers were discovered to be surreptitiously turning back odometers on demonstrator cars, Lee Iacocca faced the bad news swiftly and without flinching. Instead of attempting to defend or explain away a blatantly dishonest practice, the up-front CEO accepted responsibility for his managers' indiscretions and openly admitted that the guilty managers were "wrong" and "stupid." And he gave his personal assurance to the public that it wouldn't happen again. His public confession immediately defused what could have easily blossomed into far greater injury to the carmaker's reputation.

Another chief executive who hasn't hesitated to admit either his or his organization's blunders is Bill Clinton. After being publicly chastised for delaying some air traffic at Los Angeles International Airport while he got a haircut from a famous hair stylist on board Air Force One, the president conceded during a televised "town meeting" it was a "boner" and a "mess up." Had that been an isolated instance, he might've been praised for his candor and excused for such a trivial miscue, dubbed "Hair Force One" by detractors. Unfortunately, though, it was but one in a series of miscalculations and inconsistencies by the president and his staff at the time (such as dismissal of White House travel office employees; withdrawal of Lani Guinier's nomination as assistant attorney general), and merely served to further aggravate his already smarting public reputation. When asked to interpret his credibility problem on a morning news show, the president placed the burden of correcting matters on himself, echoing sound advice for many top managers, "I have to find a better way of communicating."[5]

Candor Also Means Feedback

Employee research over the years has consistently revealed that workers are critical of top managers for sugar-coating information they share with employees. Interestingly, in contrast, our research found that CEOs view candor as a two-way street along which both CEO and employees must walk. In top dogs' eyes, employees have a reciprocal obligation to be open and honest with upper management. Certainly, as long as employers and employees see their relationship as an adversarial one, trust won't be formed quickly or easily. Mutual candor is as good a starting point for building trust as any we can recommend.

Communicating with the person at the top can be an intimidating prospect for some managers and employees, particularly if they don't know the CEO personally. Carl Karcher, founder and former CEO of Los Angeles-based Carl Karcher Enterprises, which includes the Carl's Jr. hamburger chain, tries to be sensitive to his employees' reluctance to talk to him when he's in the field. "I can see them thinking, 'I'm sitting here with Carl Karcher, the old man who started this.' It seems to faze them. I know if I ask how they're doing today, they're going to say 'fine' when they'd like to say, 'If you want to know the truth, Carl, I feel lousy,'" he says, during an interview at his corporate headquarters. "But if I give them enough opportunities, they'll usually open up and express themselves."

Even seasoned professionals can be awed by a fancy management title. Some workers just won't share their true feelings with the folks in power, fearing the worst, regardless of top management's sincerity, guarantee of confidentiality, and assurances that there'll be no repercussions. In an effort to lessen the awkwardness some employees feel about communicating with upper-level managers, Cedars Sinai Medical Center of Los Angeles has created a buffer between the top tier and the rest of the organization—two professional staffers whose principal role is to act as physician's liaison. Their job is to meet with medical staff privately in their own offices where they're more apt to say what they really think and feel, and then discretely and confidentially deliver that feedback to the top. "The physicians say a lot more and different kinds of things to the physician liaisons then they would if I were to go out myself and say, 'Tell me what you like and don't like about the hospital,'" explains Tom Priselac, CEO of Cedars Sinai. "There's a certain amount of candor that comes out when they're not talking to *the* administrator."

Candor Applies to Outside Audiences Too

Candor is crucial in communicating with people inside the organization because of their direct and tangible stake in the organization's success. Equally important is how open and forthright management is when dealing with external audiences who also care about and can influence an organization's prospects. The issues related to candor, however, are increasingly complex and filled with dangers when CEOs move outside the safety of their familiar boundaries.

Internal and external communication fulfill different needs. Depending on the audience, the issue, and the circumstances, external communication is much more apt to be perceived as partial, massaged, or even slanted. Such perceptions arise primarily because the communication objectives and concerns of a business organization and an outside audience can be very different.

Take the media, for example. Given the constantly looming fear of being misrepresented or misinterpreted by busy, deadline-oriented reporters, how open should CEOs be, knowing that even the best reporters can tell only a portion of the full story? Too much candor too soon can backfire at times. The media's prime motive—to tell a provocative story—is substantially different than that of a business executive who is most concerned with protecting his and the organization's reputation. The troubling realization that the media always have the last word has made many CEOs extremely cautious about how frank to be with reporters and editors.

"There are some things you say to your family you wouldn't say to people outside your family," Cedars Sinai's Tom Priselac believes. "When you're dealing with the external world, you have a different agenda or set of objectives. You're doing it for purposes of image development or enhancement, you're doing it for fundraising purposes, you're doing it for news reporting purposes, or you're doing it for marketing purposes."

Times-Mirror's Dick Schlosberg agrees, pointing out that the inside-outside distinction, which he also puts in a family context, can't ever be taken lightly. "I'm much more careful in talking with outsiders about the *Los Angeles Times'* performance. I make a mental note about whether this communication is inside the family or outside. I'm very open with the outside, but I'm not as open. If it's inside the family, I give more information. There are things that should stay in the family."

Although no organization can completely control what its members say to outsiders, being aware of the potential pitfalls is a critical first step. "Internally, when I talk to employees, we both pretty much say what we think," says Dr. Noel Hinners, associate deputy administrator of the National Aeronautics and Space Administration (NASA) in Washington, D.C. "But I've seen enough times when some of our people talked about things they don't like to someone outside the agency and it's come back to hurt us some way. So I think more about what I say externally. I don't want to say something that's going to have a negative impact on what we're trying to accomplish. Things you say can come back to bite."

The prospect of dealing with the media can cause any CEO to become gun shy and anxious, even for veterans like Schlosberg, who manages a media operation. "I'll be real honest. I don't like talking to reporters. It sounds funny, but I've been misquoted enough—at least I feel like I was misquoted enough—that I'm nervous about it. So, my guard goes right up when I get calls. I get very conscious. It's a heck of a thing for someone in my position to admit."

Priselac's hesitation in being candid with the press is no different. "With the media, I'm certainly on guard more than when I'm meeting with donors. When you're talking to a reporter, you have a very limited opportunity to get your message across. You don't know what the reporter's agenda is. You always run the risk of having your real message edited out."

We certainly don't want to leave the impression that the only safe way to be consistent is to avoid the media. Not only is that untrue and poor advice, it's downright impractical. The point is that regardless of who a CEO is communicating with, the principle of consistency applies—but particularly with media due to their influence on all other audiences. Organizations should consider carefully what they say when the media are within earshot. Apparently, accounting giant Ernst & Young didn't. The "Big Six" CPA firms have been sponsoring an industry-wide lobbying effort to get legislation passed to relieve CPA firms from the potential $30-billion burden of ongoing litigation expenses. Such monumental costs, argue the CPA firms, threaten the survival of the entire industry. Yet, that argument seems to lose some of its "oomph" when Ernst & Young agrees to pay $400 million to settle a number of savings and loan cases and happily proclaims publicly that the settlement won't severely impair the firm's earnings.

Using the Media: The Avon Case

Occasionally, a strategy deliberately intended to make external communication more candid and less guarded is necessary, as was the case at Avon when the cosmetics giant needed to boost its public profile. According to former CEO Hicks Waldron, Avon had been a family-owned company for many years that was used to and comfortable keeping things to itself. After it went public, Avon's continued growth became dependent on a strategy to increase its sales force. But at that time, the late 1970s, many women had begun working outside the home, thus reducing Avon's traditional pool of sales agents. As a result, the company's long-standing financial health went into cardiac arrest and the media jumped on the story. When reporters started asking questions, Avon management, not accustomed to having to explain itself, clammed up, which alienated some media. Eventually, media exposure of Avon dried up, as did the company's public presence, except for the dwindling numbers of Avon ladies still ringing doorbells.

Before Waldron became CEO of Avon in 1982, he admits that he'd never met anybody from Avon in person, at any function, anywhere. "I'd been 40 years in the business world prior to coming here. I'd met somebody from probably 80 percent of the Fortune 500 companies, somewhere in my lifetime. But I'd never met an Avon employee, not even one ringing my doorbell." And he couldn't remember having read anything about Avon either.

Waldron's communication strategy was to take Avon's story public, to use the media's credibility and mass distribution power to get certain messages directly to the general public and indirectly to employees—an approach that was a 180-degree turnabout from the company's traditional "keep your head down" practice. "We wanted to let everybody know about Avon, because everybody is a potential customer. We invited the press and the business community in. We knew we were going to get toasted on occasion, and we did. But our research showed that people feel better about a company they know about."

His strategy apparently worked. Waldron became a business celebrity and popular spokesperson, including being the subject of a book about life as a CEO by *New York Times* reporter Sonny Kleinfeld, who shadowed Waldron at work and home for several weeks. More important was Avon's financial revival toward the end of Waldron's watch, which ended in 1990 as part of a planned succession. By the end of the first quarter of 1992, Avon had emerged from red ink, reporting over $22 million in gross revenues.

Consistency of Priorities

Closely related to *how* CEOs communicate is *when* they communicate, because *when* pivotal information is shared, or held back, says much about what and who CEOs consider most important.

The timing and timeliness of a CEO's communication, particularly with employees, can make an enormous difference in a stakeholder group's acceptance or rejection of a company's message. If a group is given the inside scoop directly from the top and before it is disclosed to the public, an organization's members instantly know their position in the CEO's scheme of priorities. If, on the other hand, they are among the last to hear and then only by accident and through a third party, like the media, they'll perceive themselves as having low value and may withdraw their support of the CEO, the issue, or the organization.

Employees, more than any other public, need to know that their organizational leader will keep them fully informed, will *always* tell them the real story and will tell them *first*. "If you fail to keep employees fully informed, you're breaking a basic trust," says Robert Dockson, former chairman of California Federal Savings. Releasing information to employees in advance of its public release was one of his most important self-imposed communication obligations, says Waldron, "It really makes the employees feel that they're important and in tune with what's going on in the business."

When employees have to read about their company in the local newspaper, whether it's good news or bad, they're placed in an embarrassing position. "Their friends and family are going to ask what's going on. And if they have to say, 'I don't know,' they look silly to the person asking the question. So does management," believes Carl Sardegna, president of Blue Cross/Blue Shield of Maryland. "And it shows a lack of respect for employees."

Communicating with employees first and making certain they receive and understand the message adds an extra step to the normal information dispersal process. And, depending on the urgency of the message, that additional step can be taken through normal communication channels or by faster, more direct ways. At now defunct Builder's Emporium, for instance, when management had an important announcement it wanted sent to employees before it went to the media, phone calls were made to the general managers of each operating unit to alert them to what was coming. A written fax message followed shortly thereafter for immediate and prominent display on all employee bulletin boards. This meant that managers, tipped off as to what was going on, could discuss the matter with employees and refer them to the posted, written version of the announcement well *before* seeing it on that night's TV news or reading about it in the next morning's newspaper.

As noted already, CEOs are, by their very nature, chameleons, constantly changing colors to fit the background and situation. Such transformations can make being consistent quite difficult. But that's precisely what faces top managers as they bounce between their sometimes clashing communication roles with internal and external audiences.

Consistency of Roles

No individual better embodies an organization's cultural values than the CEO. So it should be no surprise that many organizations have capitalized on their top manager's high public profile, popularity, and personal credibility as *the* top manager by using the CEO as the organization's official spokesperson—for both internal and external audiences. For instance, much of Iacocca's fame was due to his early appearances in Chrysler television ads and in representing the company at news conferences, on Wall Street, before Congress, and at trade shows.

CEOs as Public Figures

A similar marketing strategy was adopted several years ago by Vons Grocery Company in tapping its then CEO Bill Davila, personable and articulate, to lead the company's advertising effort. Competitors were using well-known entertainment personalities—actress Shirley Jones for Ralph's Supermarkets, local personality Stephanie Edwards for Lucky (Lucky has since switched to using its CEO), and actor William Daniels from "St. Elsewhere" for Hughes Grocery—to sell their organizations, mostly by talking about price issues. With Davila making the pitch, Vons decided to counter by playing up the quality of its products and operation.

"We decided the best way to do that was to use a spokesperson who could talk up what Vons had to offer that our competitors didn't. Our concern was credibility," says Davila, Von's spokesperson since 1987. "Does it seem logical to the average homemaker that Shirley Jones goes to Ralph's every week to shop? And that she pushes the basket around? We felt there was a lack of credibility and didn't want to fall into the same trap."

Davila doesn't get paid just to represent Vons on TV and radio, like celebrity spokespersons do—he works at the company every day, his livelihood is tied directly to Vons' welfare. In essence, he *is* Vons; his stake is real and meaningful and viewers know it, which makes him more genuinely credible than a paid performer who merely reads a script. And CEOs who fulfill this role as the company's public point person are often a source of pride to employees. "The employees like the fact people are saying nice things about me. They take pride in that, they like that," says Davila. "It's a compliment to them, because it's the president of their company. And I think the employees take some comfort that I'm not making a jackass out of myself."

And, points out Bill Marriott, leader of Marriott Hotels, Resorts & Suites, when the head of a company puts his face and reputation before the public, he's sending messages to multiple stakeholders. Marriott, who starred in the company's ad campaign in early 1993 promising hotel customers "to make it happen for you," views his appearance as making a commitment on behalf of his organization. "I want our customers to know we're committed to giving them an outstanding experience," he says. "I'm putting my name on the line to make it happen. It's my personal commitment ... and it's also a message to employees. If it doesn't happen, I expect to get calls and mail."[6]

Being the CEO-spokesperson, however, can have its downsides. Especially on a CEO's private life. Historically, most CEOs were little more than faceless names that employees read about in the company newsletter and customers had never heard of. But more and more today, CEOs are visible and recognized by internal and external constituencies. When that happens, they enter life in the public fishbowl. Some CEOs thrive on it, others abhor it and never adjust to its inherent intrusions. "People come up to me in our stores and everywhere—in Munich, Germany, Acapulco, Mexico, on the beach in Hawaii, and in restaurants or bars—because they recognize me," notes Davila. "I have no more private life. I'm a public figure. It's a change of lifestyle. I'm given the same type of attention a celebrity gets. All I wanted to be able to do was communicate our points in a believable manner. And it's worked."

Projecting the Right Image: Sigoloff at Wickes

Relying on the CEO's personal charisma and reputation was also the strategy used by Builder's Emporium when the company was in serious financial trouble in the late 1980s. Research told Wickes Cos. management that in order to get people to shop in a store in which they'd had a bad experience—in other words, to give Builder's Emporium another chance—the CEO himself would personally have to lure them back.

To convince skeptical customers that Builder's Emporium was serious about making the necessary changes to win them back, the company launched an advertising campaign featuring an unsmiling and serious-looking Sandy Sigoloff. His message was, "You know I'm a tough guy and I'm going to make this store the kind of store that you want to shop in. I'm going to make it happen." The tagline was, "At Builder's Emporium, we have to please a very tough customer ... Sandy."

"He talked tough," points out Mike Sitrick, Sigoloff's then-senior vice president of communication, during an interview at company headquarters near Los Angeles. "There wasn't much to smile about. It was a tough message. It's tough competition." Sitrick credits the ads for leading the chain's turnaround. "That's not to diminish the impact of the merchandising or employees' hard work. As Sandy has said, the battle is won in the stores, by the people waiting on and servicing the customers," Sitrick adds. "But by agreeing to be the spokesperson, he was saying to the employees, 'I'm putting my name and reputation on the line for you guys. Don't let me down.' And they didn't."

There's no getting around the fact that once a CEO abandons the seclusion of the executive suite, he or she has entered the oftentimes "glitzy" business of image-building. That was a tough adjustment for Sigoloff, who neither sought nor welcomed center stage. Sigoloff, who appeared in the ads without his suit jacket, was projected as a shirtsleeve kind of manager. To some, that may have seemed orchestrated and perhaps artificial. Yet to those who know Sigoloff, the image was consistent with the Sigoloff reality. So, the picture of an informal top executive was the core of a deliberate strategy designed to show a CEO who was deeply involved in his company and meant what he said.

"We could've done Sandy's pictures in a threepiece suit, sure. But that's not who Sandy is," Sitrick says. "Sandy works in his shirtsleeves. Is showing Sandy at his desk working late, with just a desk light on, overly dramatic? Maybe. But what does it communicate? That, if necessary, he works seven days a week, 24 hours-a-day to get the job done. That the average day isn't nine to five, but 12 or 14 hours. And that he works often into the night. We didn't create an image of something that isn't true. We projected what is, the reality of the situation."

Throughout the company's ordeal and its intensive advertising campaign, Sitrick consistently positioned Sigoloff as a dignified business professional, as the company's chairman, its top executive. "We didn't have him getting out of his shower with a razor in his hand as Remington's Victor Kiam does, because Sandy's role is the guarantor—the guarantor of the product, the guarantor of the quality, the guarantor of the service, the guarantor that you're going to get your expectations met," explains Sitrick. "And so he had to look like a chairman at all times."

The principle of consistency, so vital to a CEO's credibility, demands vigilance and regular reevaluation of plans, words, and actions. The consequences of compromising one's consistency—that is, one's credibility—can be swift and severe on the CEO and the organization. A lack of consistency can make a CEO's word and integrity vulnerable to question or attack; those who appear to be hedging or speaking with forked tongue will lose their ability to be effective.

What chief executive officers say, what they don't say, how they say it, what they do, what they don't do—everything about them is observed, catalogued, analyzed, and evaluated by insiders and outsiders. But many CEOs don't realize the reach and impact of their own influence. Many are unaware of, and therefore insensitive to, the far-reaching impact of their own positive example or, as in the following case, negative example.

The Unfortunate Case of Sharp Vision Camera

This case, which spanned close to four years, is unfortunately true (although we've changed the names to the protect the guilty and the innocent) and is as relevant to business today as it was in late 1988 when it began. It was told to us by a young couple—let's call them Don and Beatrice—who lived an all-too-frequent, exasperating experience with employees whose rudeness and low regard for customers merely reflected their CEO's attitudes and actions. The case is a graphic reminder of the CEO's enormous sway, intended or otherwise, over how employees behave on-the-job, and the impression that such behavior leaves with customers and the public-at-large.

Most of us have our own horror stories about being mistreated as a customer. Don't be startled, then, if you see yourself or somebody you've met somewhere in this story. Strategically interspersed throughout the case are indented, italicized excerpts taken from a distress letter Beatrice sent to the CEO of a national camera store chain—so named Dave Sharp of Sharp Vision Camera—when her frustration reached its zenith. The letter was never acknowledged or answered by Sharp or any of his people.

Late November, Year 1. It all began when Don and Beatrice, a typical two-career couple—with two young sons and a house in the suburbs of Washington, D.C.—decided they ought to have a video camera to capture their family's many precious "Kodak" moments for the upcoming and future Halloween, Thanksgiving, and Christmas holidays. So off they went to a Sharp Vision Camera store, where they were encouraged by a friendly sales representative to buy a $1300 GE camcorder.

> *When we decided to purchase a video camera, we thought it would be better to buy from a local store which could give us support and service if we ever needed it ... We knew we could purchase the camera for about $300 less at a mail order house in New York, but decided it would be wiser to buy locally from a reputable company ...*

September, Year 2. After just 10 cassettes and two seasons of holidays, approximately 20 hours of use, some problems with the camera arose that they could neither explain nor fix. The camera's motor raced for no apparent reason, thereby involuntarily pulling the videotape out of the cassette, and the zoom stuck. So, realizing that their GE and Sharp Vision warranties had expired, Don and Beatrice returned to the flagship store to get the camcorder repaired.

They were told by a Sharp Vision employee that they would be called to pick up the camera when it was fixed or, if the estimate was over $100, they'd be called with a repair estimate. Two weeks passed without any word. When Beatrice called to find out the status of the camera, she was told curtly by a receptionist, "Don't bother to call before four weeks have passed ... we don't have any word on repairs in such a short time." Okay, let's be patient, Don and Beatrice told themselves, and let the system work.

Early December, Year 3.   Halloween and Thanksgiving passed and still nothing from Sharp Vision. After seven weeks, Beatrice phoned again. This time she was told by a rude receptionist (maybe a different one, she wasn't sure) not to call for another week since all repairs take at least six to eight weeks. Their frustration was building. No estimate, much less a repair, appeared in sight.

> *... This is when I started on one of my long hard journeys through your staff. Thirty minutes later, someone finally tells me that the head of your repair department, Ken (real name changed), will call me back. He didn't call back that day—I assume he got the message just before he was to go home for the day.*
> *The next day he didn't call. I had to call him. His reply, 'You can't expect to come into the store at 5 p.m. and get help.' I was never in the store. I was put on hold, transferred repeatedly, scolded and talked down to for about 30 minutes before I left a message for Ken, who went home before returning my call. CONFIDENCE IN SHARP VISION CAMERA IS UNBELIEVABLE AT THIS POINT.*

Mercifully, they finally received a repair estimate later that day—for $319. Beatrice gave the go-ahead, asking that the camera be returned in time for Christmas, now only a few weeks away. Although Ken and his staff were polite as the negotiations marched on, Don and Beatrice believed that "making excuses" was their strategy. She was told by Ken, in a magnanimous effort to appease her skepticism, that Sharp Vision had never spent so much time with any customer. During one of her many phone calls seeking information about the status of the camera, she asked for the top executive and was told it was David Sharp. Whenever and however she attempted to contact him, his employees shielded him. He was unreachable.

> *I asked to talk to you. I got various conflicting reasons why you couldn't come to the phone or see me when we came into the showroom or return a call. You're well protected from your customers. If this is how we rank in your organization, I guess you must feel a need to be protected.*

Mid-December, Year 3.   Don and Beatrice picked up the camera a week before Christmas. To their pleasant surprise, the repair cost was reduced by 10 percent, thus making the cost $287 for two months without a camera and lots of headaches. Two days later, they were back at Sharp Vision again—all the same problems were still there and, as Beatrice noted in her letter, "Plus we got to pay $287 to Sharp Vision Camera for this nonservice."

Not knowing what else to do, Beatrice called David Sharp's office again. She was told to call back on a different number, which brought her to the same person again. Following several time-draining transfers to various people who were unable to assist, she finally reached Mr. Sharp's secretary, who refused to put her through to him. In a touch of irony, which vividly captures the essence of the case, his secretary told Beatrice, *"Mr. Sharp doesn't talk to customers. You have to write to him."*

They were given a loaner camera for Christmas—which, of course, after they got home and turned it on, didn't work properly. They returned it immediately (fearing they'd be charged for repairs). No video record of Christmas was made. A few days later, their original camera was returned to them again, still exhibiting all the same problems, some of them even worse than before the so-called repairs.

Mid-January, Year 4. They received a call that the camera was fixed and ready for pick up—again. Predictably, when they got there and tested it in the showroom, it still didn't work right. At this point, Don and Beatrice refused to accept the camera and demanded that Sharp Vision stand behind its reputation and give them a new camcorder, preferably a different brand and model.

Mid-February, Year 4. After almost a month of arguing and negotiating, Sharp Vision ultimately caved in and agreed to exchange the GE camcorder for a new model, which, Don and Beatrice graciously point out, the company was under no obligation to do. But, they were informed, the exchange will take "a few weeks to arrange and take care of all the paper work." By this time, Don and Beatrice had few illusions that anything would be handled correctly or on time. As customers, they'd lost all faith in Sharp Vision, its CEO, its employees, its reputation, and its word.

Late February, Year 4. Don and Beatrice made the bittersweet, triumphant trip to Sharp Vision to pick up their new camera—almost four years after it all started. During this ordeal, they were never able to reach David Sharp and he never made any effort to contact or console them. Luckily, the second camera has operated without a hitch. They've never returned to any of Sharp Vision's stores for any reason and, they say, they never will, even if it means going far out of their way.

> I am so disappointed. Your staff is a mixture of some very nice people and some very stupid and rude people who have treated me, a lowly customer, like an idiot. I have been reduced to using tactics I have never used before—simply to get the most basic information from some of your people … I feel like I have to apologize to your staff for being a customer.

When all was said and done, how did the customers feel? In Don's letter to us, he summed it up: "… the most significant event was that a customer drafted a multipage letter to the head of the firm and took the time to hand-carry it to the CEO's office—and we never received a direct reply from him. Even a one-sentence letter, letting us know that our problem was being handled, would have made us feel entirely different about Sharp Vision."

Is this story unusual or atypical? We don't think so. That's a sad commentary, but unfortunately true. Is it fair to hold the CEO solely responsible for how an organization's employees behave? If not the CEO, then who? The employees? If they are merely mimicking the CEO, should they be faulted?

Should a CEO have to become involved in every customer complaint situation? Of course not. But sometimes, circumstances can become so out of control that no one but *the* person in charge can make it all right. Some CEOs, like Dave Sharp, avoid getting involved with irate patrons. Other CEOs go out of their way to communicate with and help disappointed or upset customers; some top dogs see it as a chance to salvage what would otherwise be lost customers. But the central point is that it's the CEO whose example employees will follow and customers will define as *the company*. If the top manager says customers are important, but doesn't act like they are, employees won't feel compelled to treat customers any better than their top executive does.

So what's the moral to the Sharp Vision Camera case? Consistent—or inconsistent—behavior starts and ends at the top, with the chief executive. Employees' attitudes and practices are a reflection of their CEO, who through his or her words, actions, beliefs, and priorities, specifies how the organization will relate with its stakeholders.

A Final Word

CEOs are often unaware of, and therefore insensitive to, the power of their own example and its impact on others. Whether they seek the public spotlight or not, CEOs are role models. To many impressionable would-be business leaders (especially younger ones), the CEO represents the height of success, wealth, power, fame, and influence. Being a CEO carries with it huge responsibilities, and means living under a public microscope—with one's words and actions recorded and assessed for their meaning, and their consistency.

If a company falters by appearing to act contrary to the best interests of, say, its employees, the effects on the CEO's and the organization's credibility can be swift and devastating, and not soon forgotten by those adversely affected. Even the most popular and trusted CEOs won't survive long if they consistently violate the principle of consistency; for if people can't trust what a CEO says and does from one day to the next, building lasting relationships will be little more than a pipedream.

Returning to Arlen ...

When last we saw Arlen, he seemed to be praying for some sort of divine guidance in how to rescue Royal from its emerging credibility crisis. He sought counsel from Jim Stamps, Royal's chairman and Arlen's role model and strongest backer. Stamps pledged his conditional support for his protege, making it clear, however, that Arlen had to find a way to turn the situation around quickly—or they both might be unemployed. In the course of their heart-to-heart conversation, Arlen learned about some ethically questionable management decisions Stamps had made earlier in his career when he, like Arlen now, had to weigh the so-called greater good of the company against saving his own hide.

As we rejoin Arlen, the CEO is reviewing Rick Jamieson's proposed crisis management plan—which includes a strategy that positions Arlen as Royal's primary public spokesperson, a role Arlen is fighting against playing. He is about to come face-to-face with how the CEO's communication role is really changing, and, not surprisingly, raises questions whether he's up to the challenge.

"The Game Plan— Who Says What to Whom ..."

Wednesday, October 10, 2 p.m. The phone blared, jarring Arlen from the first moment of reflection he'd stolen since yesterday. It had been 24 hours unlike any he'd experienced since becoming CEO.

He felt like he'd been pressed and pummeled by everybody, making it next to impossible to maintain his perspective on Royal's unfolding predicament. He felt more like a referee than a CEO, attempting to mediate among the subtle finger-pointing and groundless speculation of his vice presidents, Stamps, and the board. As was Arlen's way, he tried his best to remain objective, aloof, analytical, giving everybody's viewpoint equal weight. But he also knew he couldn't withhold judgment for long. Time was the one nonrenewable resource he couldn't control. And it would work against him and Royal as soon as the big news got out and the clock started ticking.

"Yes?" he said curtly into the speaker phone. His annoyance came through in that single word. But he knew that his executive secretary, Susan O'Reilly, wouldn't have interrupted him if it wasn't justified.

"Rick Jamieson just called," O'Reilly said. "He says he has to see you right now. That it can't wait." As Arlen gathered his thoughts, O'Reilly added, "It sounds urgent."

"Okay. I'll call him." Arlen hit 07, Jamieson's autodial code. Before one ring had completed, Royal's VP of corporate communication answered. "Jamieson."

Arlen couldn't resist. "So, it's always an emergency with you communication types, isn't it? What's so hot I can't get 20 minutes to myself alone on the john?"

"How'd the speech go today?" Jamieson asked, skillfully playing the dummy role.

"Fine, fine. Better than usual, I think." His elation had now worn off. Jamieson started to speak, but Arlen cut him off. "You didn't call to talk about the speech. What's up?"

"Ever since this morning, I've been thinking about what our communication strategy ought to be. So far, I've come to two conclusions. The first is that we need to put our action plan—whatever it is—into play … yesterday. And the second is that the key to the plan working is you, Arlen." Jamieson paused for a reaction that didn't come.

Arlen said, "Go on."

"Look, this is something I'd rather not get into over the phone. Just give me 10 minutes. I've got a rough plan outlined. But we've got to move fast to have a chance. This can't wait. I've got to start the ball rolling in the next hour or so."

Arlen sat up, shrugged, looked at his watch and said, "Okay, Rick, come on down."

"I'll be there in two minutes," Jamieson said as he hung up. Less than two minutes later, Jamieson walked in with a stack of papers tucked under his right arm.

"So, what's my time?" Jamieson knew when he threw out a two-minute challenge, he'd be held to it.

"A minute fifty-three," Arlen responded, not really knowing, gesturing for him to sit in the chair to the left of Arlen's desk.

"I've really wrestled with this thing. And, Arlen, in this kind of an embarrassing, impossible-to-explain situation, you, the head honcho"—he pointed at the CEO with both index fingers—"have to be the point person. You're the one person with the title, with the built-in credibility, who can explain what happened—and who just might be believed. I know you prefer the low profile, but this potentially explosive situation is anything but normal. Right now your direct and full involvement is imperative."

Jamieson got up, moved behind his chair, looked directly at Arlen and continued. "We've got to try to limit the damage to our employees' and stockholders' perceptions of management. Our employees should hear about this from us, not from the damn grapevine or some garbled news report.

"After they know, then we'll deal with everybody else, starting with the stockholders. Whether we like it or not, the media's not going to cut us any slack. So, after our workers and investors, the key target groups are the customers, media, Wall Street, suppliers, travel agents, community leaders, and so on down the list."

Jamieson returned to his seat, his tone and mannerisms growing more persuasive as he listened to his own arguments.

"But, without question, it begins and ends with our employees. If they lose faith in us and the company, we're dead. We can't run the hotels without them. So you, Arlen, have to be the one to tell them, explain what went wrong and assure them the problem's being fixed. It can't be anybody else." For the first time since starting his monologue, Jamieson stopped for a moment to take in some air, keeping his eyes trained on the CEO. Arlen was doodling furiously on his yellow legal pad.

Jamieson braced for Arlen's resistance, or at least a tough question or two. When neither came right away, he chose to assume the optimistic outcome. "Okay, glad you concur." He detected a flicker of a grin on Arlen's lips. "So Phase I will be a live, simultaneous video hookup to all properties. That way, all employees get the story *directly from you*, all at the same time. Plus doing it this way adds a sense of urgency that'll capture their attention."

Hearing Jamieson emphasize "directly from you," Arlen's thoughts turned introspective, tuning out Jamieson temporarily. He felt a bit overwhelmed with the weight now resting on his shoulders: Not only did he have to make the decisions, but he also had to be the one to persuade lots of skeptical, angry people he made the right decisions. He knew intuitively his trepidation was a conditioned reflex. He recalled a discussion he'd had with his friend Barry Lewis just prior to Arlen's appearance on the Sunday morning talk show "Business Confidential." Their conversation was about Arlen's dread of not being the one in control of situations. "CEOs have to be in control and appear poised," he'd told Lewis, deliberately staying in the impersonal third person. "But the truth is that when it comes to facing employees or the public, CEOs suffer as much fear of misspeaking or screwing up as anybody else."

Lewis prodded Arlen in a way only a close friend could. Squinting over the top of his designer reading glasses, he had asked pointedly, "Why do you keep talking about CEOs as though your points don't apply to you?"

Arlen had laughed nervously. "Sure, I'm talking about me. But I assure you I'm in good company." He often thought it was probably the public part of the job that took the greatest toll on unsuspecting top executives, and why most don't last in the job for more than five or six years.

The uncomfortable silence in the room brought him back to Jamieson. To buy more time, he asked a question of his own.

"Shouldn't the initial announcement to employees come from the general managers of each property rather than from the CEO, a CEO who many have never met and trust far less than the GM they do know?" he countered. "As you said, Rick, it's imperative that they believe our message. If they don't, everything else you're planning to do won't be worth a plug nickel."

"That may be true during typical times. But not in this case. You're the key to this plan," Jamieson argued. "When the company's future is on the line, which is how employees will view it, the information's got to come from the one person who's in a position to speak for the whole company. The managers can help explain and reinforce later. But only you can offer truly meaningful explanations, guarantees, and predictions."

Uncertain whether Arlen was raising questions for academic debate or actually preparing to resist, Jamieson stepped up his intensity. "You're the key. Only you can provide the personal assurance to convince employees and others outside Royal that the company is still in good hands and that most of management hasn't lied to them."

Jamieson considered playing a trump card—Arlen's stellar performance at the luncheon a few hours earlier—but decided against it, for now. Can you imagine the reaction if Iaccoca had had one of his lieutenants tell Chrysler's workers the bad news when some of its dealers were caught turning back odometers on demonstrators? It would've looked weak."

Arlen stood without a word, loosened the knot in his tie slightly, strolled to the window-wall and leaned against it. A moment later, he retraced his steps to behind his desk, but remained standing. He realized that by stepping into the public spotlight now, regardless of how he came across or how the situation played out, things would be different for him from now on. He could feel his professional life changing directions ever so slightly.

"Can it really make that much of a difference?" Arlen asked, raising a final objection. "It's been drilled into my head ever since business school that the best source of information for employees is their immediate supervisor. Why don't we have our managers deliver the message so our people are getting it from folks they already know personally and trust far more than they do me?"

Jamieson jumped back in without missing a beat. "Remember when the CEO of Exxon didn't go to Alaska when the Valdez ran aground and spilled all that oil? He was crucified in the press. He was the company, but he didn't show up. His absence said 'no problem' when there was a huge problem. People inside and outside interpreted that as Exxon not really caring. If you're not the one to tell employees, stockholders, and the public what's going on at Royal, how do you think your absence will be interpreted?"

Finally perceiving Arlen's resistance slackening some, Jamieson spelled out the final part of the plan before the argumentative CEO could raise any other objections. "And before anyone outside hears about it, we'd better plan a news conference for Friday. Again, you'll be the point man. By then, you'll probably be enjoying it. Face it, Arlen, CEOs are public figures—whether you like it or not."

They both fell silent, almost as if a cease-fire had been imposed. Arlen drifted to the wall that held his baseball memorabilia. He stopped in front of a photo given him by Jamieson after last year's company picnic and management-employee softball game. The managers had surprised everyone and beaten the company-sponsored employee team, named "The Royals," which had won a local league championship the week before. The photo showed the traditional post-game hand-shaking ceremony, the two teams facing in parallel lines, exchanging high-fives. Thinking back, Arlen most cherished the feeling of being "one of the guys," a member of a team rather than the guy at the top who never gets invited to play. Reality was, however, he couldn't be one of the players—his role was like nobody else's, a role that didn't allow him to escape being constantly in the line of fire.

"The CEO has no place to hide," he told himself several times. With that realization beginning to register, he turned around and, with a glint in his eye, said, "I surrender. Lead on, MacDuff."

"All right, I've outlined the full plan," Jamieson said, pleased with himself. "It's almost 2:30 now. I need approval by three so I can begin making arrangements for the national video hook-up. I've got to get my people going on this right away to have any hope of pulling it off." Jamieson handed Arlen the three-page outline.

"Okay, let me give this a quick read. Why don't you call Susan at three and she'll let you know what's what," Arlen said as he started shepherding Jamieson toward the door.

Jamieson stopped, half turned and faced Arlen, his expression more subdued now. "I hear you've become an accomplished extemporaneous speaker." Jamieson's eyes twinkled with delight at surprising Arlen, who grinned slightly and shook his head at the thought of trying to repeat his past performance. The communication VP turned to leave.

Arlen couldn't resist. "Well, you've finally got me doing your job, too," he called to Jamieson, who never turned back. The CEO shifted to O'Reilly, who was sitting at her desk, and asked her to hold all calls and interruptions until three o'clock. "And," he added, grabbing the door to his office, "no exceptions this time."

Pulling the door shut behind him, Arlen returned to his desk, picked up Jamieson's outline, marked boldly in red "Draft" and "Confidential," and began to read.

* * * * * * * * *

As he plunged into Jamieson's draft of the crisis management plan, Arlen found himself becoming immersed in the logic, details, and sequencing of the variety of activities in the multiphase program. Jamieson's ever-present sense of humor was evident even in the plan's title.

"Cooked Books" Crisis Management Recipe

- Daily 8 a.m. meeting with executive team until further notice.
- Primary spokesperson: Royster

Phase I: Internal Communication

Wednesday, Week #1

- *4 p.m. EDT* Confidential CEO e-mail to all property managers (4-star priority). Information is confidential, for managers' eyes only. Set schedule for Friday's company-wide satellite video linkup; all employees except those needed on skeleton crews to attend.

  To Do: Jamieson to draft Royster statements for manager and employee videoconferences; press conference; and employee and stockholder letters w/staff input and Royster approval. Get Royster signature on employee letter; Royster & Stamps on stockholder letter.

Thursday, Week #1

- *8-9 a.m. EDT* Executive staff meeting to discuss plan. Approval of employee & stockholder letters from Royster.
- *9 a.m.*—Print copies of Royster letters. Labels run, envelopes addressed. Letters stuffed & sorted.
- *10-11 a.m.* Royster statements & Q&A discussion.
- *2 p.m. mail pickup* Letters mailed overnight to each employee & stockholder @ home address.

- *3-3:30 p.m.* Dry run of videoconference, technical checks in studio at The Castle.

Friday, Week #1

- *8-9 a.m.* Executive staff meeting.
- *9 a.m.* Employee videoconference preparation; run-through, final technical checks in studio.
- *10-10:20 a.m.* Live pre-conference TV satellite feed for line and staff managers only. Brief statement by Royster on crisis facts and plans, explanation how employee conference will work; no interactive Q&A.

  Strategies: [1] Single out managers as a special group and enlist their help to get through crisis. [2] Staff meetings to be held @ all properties following conference, conducted by general managers and directors of human resources management. [3] Statement about handling media relations and corporate policies over next few weeks.

- *11-11:45 a.m.* Live TV satellite feed for all employees and managers. Opening statement by Royster, 10 minutes. Tape broadcast for nonattenders. Interactive for Q&A. Regional HRM staffs to hold immediate feedback sessions to gauge employee reactions. FAX written summaries of discussions to corporate headquarters by 6 p.m. EDT.

  Strategies: [1] Tell employees what is known, what isn't known, how situation is being handled and assure them they will be kept informed. [2] Stress that you want employees to know about this before it becomes public and speculation begins; also, point out that they are the key to Royal overcoming crisis, their loyalty needed now more than ever. [3] Emphasize that no blame will be assessed or major changes made until all facts are known—and that your major concern is solving the problem and making certain it never happens again.

- *6 p.m.* Postmortem evaluation of day's events with executive staff.

Week #3

- Royster, select VPs begin on-site visits to strategically chosen hotel properties. Hold all-employee meetings while at properties. Confidential meetings with top HRM people. Book local talk shows and newspaper interviews.

Week #4

- Special edition of Royal employee newsletter, interviews with Royster, Stamps, other top managers. Include photos from visits to properties.

- Royster follow-up videotape on crisis distributed to all sites. Incorporate cuts from on-air interviews, site visits.

Phase II: External Communication

Thursday afternoon, Week #1

- *10 a.m.-noon.* Notify media about press conference scheduled for Friday, 3 p.m. EDT @ The Castle. Assemble media kits, to include standard materials plus copy of Royster statement. To be handled by Jamieson's staff.
- Plan and put in place image advertising campaign, to start Week #2, in broadcast & print media. Royster to be spokesperson. Buy air time, newspaper, magazine space. To be handled by Azoulette's staff.

Friday, Week #1

- *8-9 a.m.* Dry run for Royster news conference; Jamieson and Coletto to play reporters; written brief with all possible questions and suggested responses.
- *3 p.m.* Royster news conference @ The Castle. Have available VHS tapes w/edited sound bites from employee conference; plan national distribution to media through satellite news bureaus and wire services. Ed Hines, head of forensic auditing team, present to answer questions.

Saturday, Week #1

- *10 a.m.* Conduct videotaping of Royster for ads. Location: Royster's office.

Week #2

- Initiate 3-month, progressive ad campaign. Invitation-only briefings for key Wall Street, institutional and pension fund analysts. Key speakers: Royster, Bernard (investor relations) & Stamps. Handled by Bernard's staff.

Week #3

- Conduct follow-up market research on stockholder, customer and public perceptions in response to advertisements, media coverage, etc. To be handled by outside research firm.

Arlen looked up and checked the wall clock to the right of his office door. He'd needed 20 minutes to absorb Jamieson's detailed outline. He was reminded of the detailed coordination and timing required to make a corporate-wide communication program work. Until he'd started working with Jamieson at Royal, Arlen's idea of corporate communication was pretty much deciding "here's what I want to say" and then getting a communication person to write it for him.

Arlen flipped back to the section of the plan addressing events for Friday. He reached over to the right-hand desk drawer, pulled it open and—without looking—grabbed the fluorescent highlighter pen he knew was there. Gripping the cap in his teeth, he uncapped the pen and put a squiggly line across the page between the 11 a.m. employee videoconference and 6 p.m. postmortem paragraphs. He recapped the highlighter, dropped it back into the drawer and pushed it closed.

He ripped a yellow note from the post-it pad near his phone, stuck it on the page, picked up his desk pen and began to write. "Rick: have set up 12:30 p.m. meeting w/auditor. You & Coletto should be there. Work with Joe on draft of opening statement for press conference and get it to me ASAP."

At the bottom of the last page, he added a boldly scribbled "Looking good, but ..." Reaching for his phone, he keyed in Jamieson's extension.

"Rick, Arlen. Look, about your plan. Everything looks well thought out and reasonable. Only one concern, though. You've got me going in 25 different directions all at once. Take another look at that. I know everybody wants a piece of me, but that just can't be—if I'm to do my job. I have to keep my eye on the whole store, remember?

"Let's establish some priorities. Certain things that I'll absolutely commit to doing. For instance, I'll do the two live internal broadcasts and, of course, the press conference. The others I'll do if I can. But you have a back-up ready to go in case things change."

Realizing that he'd won Arlen's tacit support, Jamieson didn't want to push his good fortune. He couldn't resist one final plea, however.

"So, who do you want for a back-up?" Jamieson asked, pretending a false air of innocence.

"How about Jim Stamps?" Arlen offered quickly. "He's the only one I can think of."

"You ask him, okay?" Jamieson countered. "But I need to know today."

"What else is new? All right," Arlen sighed. "I'll call him as soon as we finish. But, in the meantime, you work on a contingency plan."

"Now, one more thing. There's something you've slipped into the plan that ticks me off ... and you knew it would," Arlen began.

"Let me guess. Inviting a few media people to the employee videoconference." It wasn't a question. "I didn't think that would fly, but I want to explain my logic. But face-to-face, not over the phone. Withhold judgment until we can talk more."

"Talk about what?" Arlen challenged. "This isn't open for discussion."

"It has to be," protested Jamieson. "Don't jump to conclusions. We'll talk about it later. Okay?" It was almost a plea.

Arlen said nothing for a moment. When he spoke, it was in half jest. "Geez, what's next? Ask a reporter to cover our staff meetings? You're going to have to go a long way to convince me on this one."

"Thanks," replied Jamieson, relieved the issue was still alive, barely. "What time are we leaving for the ballpark tonight?" he asked, referring to the Yankees-Red Sox playoff game at Yankee Stadium.

"Rick, as out-of-character as this may sound, I don't think I ought to go, not with things the way they are around here and at home."

"You're probably right, but remember who we're scheduled to sit with?"

"Sit with? Tonight?"

"I was afraid it might've slipped your mind. Sharon Jillian, president of the Marissa Fund, that hot new mutual fund that's been buying Royal stock the past few months like it's the next Intel. Like you, she's a red hot Yankee fan and has been patiently waiting to meet you. We set this up over a week ago when it looked like this playoff game might happen. If you didn't show up now, Jillian could get mighty curious about what's going on that could keep you away. Do you want her and her gang of analysts snooping around, asking all sorts of questions?"

Arlen could see his point. Best to keep everything looking normal—for as long as possible.

"Okay, Rick, point well taken. Timing is everything. Jeffrey will have the limo out front around six," Arlen said. "Come by and get me on the way."

"I love going to games with you. I get to go in style," Jamieson laughed.

"Don't get used to it. We may both be out of jobs by next season," quipped Arlen. The two had slipped back into their normal banter.

"Maybe I should pass on the game and go see my barber so I look presentable in front of the cameras," Arlen chided.

"Nope," Jamieson objected in mock sarcasm. "We'll sacrifice this one night for good old Royal and suffer through another boring baseball game. What's a poor executive to do? Anyway, we can talk some strategy on the way to the game."

"Only if necessary. For me, baseball's a religious experience and shouldn't be interrupted with mundane matters, like business." The thought of Yankee Stadium filled to the rafters, the tension of the playoffs, the sweet smell of hot dogs and mustard, two arch-rivals scraping for every out ... boosted his spirits in a flash.

But there was no escaping, and Arlen knew it. "Some mundane," he thought.

* * * * * * * * *

"Okay, I've cleared things up with Jamieson, so let's get back on schedule," Arlen began by telling Susan O'Reilly, who had unobtrusively entered his office when she saw the light on his private line go out. "Go ahead and set up my appointments for the next couple of hours. I can see people until 5:30. Rick and I are going to leave around six for the ballpark. I'll want a little time to grab a quick shower and change."

"Coletto's already called half a dozen times. He's itching to see you. Something important concerning the SEC," Susan told him, checking her notes.

"Okay, get him over here. And make sure Gloria's here too," he said, plopping into his chair.

"She'll be glad to hear that," Susan advised. "She's called three times in the last hour."

"Sounds like you've been busy out there," cracked Arlen.

"Yeah, you've been more popular than usual today. Everybody's after you."

"Keep this under wraps for now," he said, handing her Jamieson's outline. "Make a copy. I'll give you more details as I get them."

"You know, the grapevine's already in spasms over what's going on up here. It's all I heard talked about at lunch. The big pow-wow this morning. Your VPs cancelling their appointments. The lid's on and everyone's getting worried. It can't be too long before the reporters start calling. I think that's one of the things Coletto's concerned about." Her information was given matter-of-factly, without emotion or judgment.

"Yeah, I figured it would go this way, but not quite this fast. It'll all come to light soon enough," Arlen added.

"Okay, I'll try to keep the wagons circled a little longer." O'Reilly could see in Arlen's eyes the strain he was under, and trying to hide. She started to leave the office, but his anxious expression stopped her.

"I definitely need to see Grubner ASAP, Susan," Arlen insisted, his voice rising slightly as he thought about Royal's finicky vice president of finance.

"I'll try him again right now. Funny, he's one of the few VPs who hasn't called this afternoon for an appointment," O'Reilly commented.

"I'm not surprised. He's probably trying to lay low right now." Arlen wasn't sure what Grubner's involvement in the bookkeeping scheme was, but he was determined to find out. Grubner, on the other hand, was doing his best to avoid the CEO, O'Reilly speculated, remembering ...

* * * * * * * * * *

Earlier that day, O'Reilly had tried tracking down Grubner without success. After repeated calls to his office got her nowhere, she accidentally stumbled on him when she stopped by to chat with Phyllis Benjamin, her closest friend at Royal and Mike Keller's secretary.

As O'Reilly had approached Keller's office suite, she could see all four of the phone lines on Benjamin's desk blinking wildly. Benjamin, talking much faster than usual, was expertly moving from one conversation to the next, although her mussed hair and stiff jaw gave away how frazzled she felt. Keller's office door was shut, but O'Reilly could just make out Grubner's distinctive profile through the glass panel next to the door.

Standing to the side of her friend's desk, which was strewn with scribbled telephone messages and notes Benjamin had jotted to herself, O'Reilly could hear Benjamin's end of the conversation.

"Good to hear your voice too, Mr. Lieberman," she said, straining to keep her tone energetic. "As soon as I can get in to see him, I promise I'll have him call you." Benjamin was fending off long-time Royal board member Donn Lieberman, one of the more aggressive members who wasn't used to taking "not available" for an answer.

Just then, Benjamin spotted O'Reilly standing in front of her. Winking, Benjamin waved her hand to say she'd be just a moment. A second later, she jumped up and said pleasingly into the phone, "Yes, sir. He'll call you before lunch today if I have to nail his ear to the phone. Good-bye."

As if the telephone knew of Benjamin's frustration, the one line still blinking went dark just as she reached to depress it. "Thank you," she said to the phone. "Now stay that way for five minutes, please!"

She sighed at O'Reilly. "Hi," she said, forcing a half smile. "It's been this way ever since the staff meeting broke up this morning. Something big's happening, isn't it, Susan?"

O'Reilly hesitated, not wanting to betray Arlen's confidence, but also not wanting to offend her friend. "I guess so," she said noncommittally. "But word should be breaking very soon." Her twitchy eyelids asked Benjamin not to probe further.

After a second or two, Benjamin sat down, grabbed the phone and brought it to her ear, "I'd better tell Mike to call Lieberman back before the old man has a heart attack."

O'Reilly reached out and stopped Benjamin's hand from touching the phone. "Before Mike makes that call, Phyl, tell him Arlen's waiting for him and the schedule's very tight," she said. Benjamin detected the urgency in O'Reilly's voice. She froze for a moment as she studied O'Reilly's face, and then stood up again.

Looking at Keller's appointment book, Benjamin looked puzzled. "I don't show an appointment with Arlen scheduled. And Mike didn't mention anything to me this morning."

"It just came up a little while ago. It probably just slipped his mind."

"I've been wondering what all the scurrying around and hush-hush conversations are about. But now you're beginning to alarm me, Susie," Benjamin confessed, her speech slowing as her concern rose. She broke eye contact with O'Reilly, reluctant to ask her friend for information she knew was taboo. But her emotions won out. "Can you at least tell me how big this thing is?" she queried delicately. "I'd never ask you to divulge anything really confidential, you know that. But since I'm in the middle of whatever's already in motion, I'd appreciate some idea ..."

O'Reilly empathized, yet her conscience pulled at her. She rubbed her hands together as she thought, then stepped back from Benjamin's desk and looked at Keller's closed office door. She wondered what Royal's VP of Operations was doing at that moment, and how it would affect Arlen and Royal. Her stomach did a light flip-flop.

Then, avoiding Benjamin's eyes, she heard herself say, "Okay, Phyl, from what I know, which isn't everything mind you, this thing could—and I stress *could*—shake up the company from top to bottom ... and that includes Arlen and Mike." Benjamin sat down slowly, sifting through the implications.

"Believe me," continued O'Reilly, "I wish I could say more. But it'll all be out in the open in a couple of days." Seeing the anxiety in Benjamin's eyes, O'Reilly tried to reassure her. "If it helps any, Phyl, I don't think we're likely to be affected." Then, as an afterthought, she added a touch of reality, "At least not immediately."

O'Reilly pointed at Keller's closed door. "He's suddenly pretty chummy with John."

At first, Benjamin didn't answer, still registering what she'd just heard. Then, looking up, she said, "Yeah, I suppose. This is the second time today they've been in there with the door bolted closed."

"Oh?" O'Reilly's eyes narrowed as she considered the possibilities.

Benjamin picked up the phone and tapped Keller's intercom button twice in a signal prearranged for only the most urgent business.

"Mike, Susan O'Reilly's here," she said, training her gaze on her fellow secretary-gatekeeper. "Arlen's waiting to see you and his schedule's evidently pretty tight, so you need to get down there lickety-split. You have a number of messages, but I've told them all you probably wouldn't be available until later. Donn Lieberman's called twice and insists he's got to speak to you before lunch. Should I get him on the line?"

Benjamin listened for a minute, intently following Keller's instructions. Picking up a pen, she made a quick note on her pad. "Nana Ziroli's, 12:30. Lieberman and Gross."

O'Reilly was able to read the note upside down. "Why would he be having lunch with those two?" she wondered. She figured that Royal's crisis probably wasn't Keller's top priority. As usual, though, Keller was.

"Okay, I'll set that up right away, Mike," Benjamin said obediently. She paused for some final words, then broke the connection. Keeping her finger on the disconnect button and cradling the phone against her shoulder, she looked up at O'Reilly, who was turning to leave, and said, "Tell Arlen he'll be right down."

Before O'Reilly reached the door, Benjamin asked one more question. "Can I call you at home tonight?" she asked hopefully.

"You can try, Phyl," she offered reluctantly, "but I may be here until who knows when. Just hang tight. Everything will work out. It always does."

As O'Reilly left her office, Phyllis Benjamin tapped in Donn Lieberman's phone number. The battle for the CEO title was underway.

* * * * * * * * *

"And make a note, Susan. Susan? Caught you daydreaming, did I?" Arlen spoke louder to recapture her attention. He smiled, amused, waiting for her to return from wherever her mind had taken her. She shook her head, appearing slightly embarrassed.

"Sorry. My mind drifted. What was that?"

"I said I need to talk to Ed Hines first thing in the morning." Arlen wanted the auditor's opinion about Grubner and Keller having any prior knowledge of the bogus books.

O'Reilly nodded. "I'll call him right now and set it up." Then she left.

As he wondered about what Hines had found, he heard Joe Coletto knocking.

6

Compassion—
Being Empathetic
and Responsive

The early morning rocket attack lasted only a few minutes. The "old timers," those airmen who'd been in Vietnam more than a few months, knew from the terrifying sounds that several had found targets. They could only wait for the "all clear" siren, wondering who among them hadn't made it.

One structure hit was the two-story supply building at the south end of the base, where four airmen had been working upstairs when the explosion came. Within minutes, the word began to spread—no survivors. Two men had died sitting at their desks. The other two, who'd been standing, were shredded by the rocket blast and thrown to opposite sides of the room. Floodlights were set up to illuminate the building for crews to recover the bodies. Off-duty squadron members straggled in and stared silently at the ruins, wondering why fate had inexplicably spared them this time. Rocket blasts could be heard in the distance.

Into the grizzly scene strode a lieutenant colonel in full-dress uniform: the squadron commander. Spotting one of his senior officers, he charged over and demanded loudly, "Well, how bad is it?" In a hushed voice, the major informed the commander that four airmen had been killed. The colonel barked, "What about the computer? Did they hit the damned computer?" People within earshot froze. Assured that the supply operation's main computer was still functioning, the colonel wanted to know how soon he could get into the computer room.

The story is all too true. The commanding officer's insensitivity to the emotional needs of his men that night would eventually have serious and far-reaching effects on his squadron. Unit efficiency and morale, which were never easy to maintain in Vietnam, dropped off dramatically after the incident, and remained low long after the lieutenant colonel had rotated stateside. Rumors persisted that he'd made full colonel and landed at the Pentagon. His successor had a difficult time overcoming the squad's hardened perception of commanders as cold leaders who cared only about meeting mission objectives and enhancing their own careers.

Compassion—the expression of genuine caring—may do more to cement a relationship with followers than any other quality a leader can possess. It can transform the CEO in others' eyes into a real person who isn't merely an order-giver or taskmaster to be feared or scorned, but someone with feelings and emotions not all that different from anybody else.

In this chapter, we examine compassion, a crucial dimension of leadership, from a variety of perspectives. In fact, we believe that this principle is the most fundamental of the four principles comprising the C-C-O-S model, because its impact—positive or negative—can override or undermine the influence of the other three principles. Ultimately, compassion, or the absence of it, is what generates—or destroys—people's belief in a leader.

Compassionate leaders attempt to do three fundamental things, each of which we examine in depth and illustrate through examples:

1. listen to and understand others' perceptions and expectations;

2. respond to what's heard; and

3. exhibit empathy for others' concerns and needs.

First things first, however. We start by exploring further the definition and meaning of compassion.

Defining Compassion

Of the four principles comprising our C-C-O-S model, compassion is the one most shaped by who the CEO is: his or her personality, philosophy of leadership, and personal value system. It is also the toughest of the principles for any corporate chief to *believably* demonstrate. Compassion means showing concern for and understanding others' emotional, as well as pragmatic, needs. Simply stated, genuine compassion involves relating to how others see and feel about something, and then letting them know you care about what's important to them.

From an organizational standpoint, compassion can be the most critical factor in bridging the trust gap that too often segregates senior management from employees, stockholders, and customers. This gap can severely strain a CEO's ability to communicate in meaningful ways and mold lasting relationships. It seems a curious paradox of business life that CEOs—who were, after all, imperfect human beings long before they became corporate executives—find it so difficult to show their feelings and relate to others in their work world.

Compassionate leadership embraces managing, in its most tender sense, people's emotional needs and perceptions, which for many managers is a frightening prospect. Compassionate leadership is strenuous for many CEOs, mostly because it demands more than merely being intellectually sensitive to employees' needs. The top manager must also be emotionally empathetic—in plainly visible ways—to people's feelings and needs, and be willing to respond to those feelings honestly and candidly. It's a leader's genuine responsiveness—that rare, unvarnished form of honesty, expressed openly and freely—that provides the basis for authentic trust and constructing long-term relationships.

Compassionate leadership is nothing but a pipedream if it isn't sincere. Followers might be fooled for a short time, but eventually most will see through CEOs who try to play-act the role. Top executives who think they can succeed by manufacturing an appearance of empathy are likely to learn otherwise; employees and customers, in particular, seem to possess internal radar to detect a manager's lack of conviction. And they will resent and reject those who they think tried to exploit them by turning on the sensitivity only when they wanted or needed something.

True compassion is more than being accessible or mouthing concern; it requires that the top manager consistently demonstrates a desire to understand and do something about others' anxieties and expectations. In organizational settings, this means that CEOs must maintain relatively frequent direct contact with those whose allegiance they seek, and not be shy about showing others they care about them.

Managers who aren't afraid to display their true feelings—and are believed—can overcome many other mistakes and deficiencies. Says Jean Pierre Garnier, executive VP of health-care giant SmithKline Beecham, "The most important characteristic to being a good communicator is being yourself and not trying to portray someone you're not."[1] Why? Because, fundamental to any meaningful business relationship is people connecting with people through emotions and feelings, rather than through memos and balance sheets. That's exactly the point Royal Accommodations' Rick Jamieson, the company's communication guru, is trying to impress on Arlen Royster: When he's just himself, allowing the real him to surface, he's most believable and, therefore, most effective as a corporate leader.

Much easier said than done for Arlen and many real-life CEOs, however. Business leaders must be able—and willing—to express their passions, even though many view displaying any emotion as a sign of weakness contrary to the traditional definition of a good manager. Such a perception, if it ever was valid, is no longer. This point is being reinforced in an emerging body of research on gender differences in management and leadership styles which offers an engaging new perspective on the role of compassion in management-employee relationships.

Lessons from Women Leaders

Is compassionate leadership instinctive or learned? Are certain types of managers more likely to be empathetic and exhibit compassion than other types? Are there significant differences in the way women and men approach managing and leading? These are among the queries addressed in an expanding body of work—spearheaded by management professors such as Judy Rosener of the University of California at Irvine (UCI) and Bernard Bass of the Center for Leadership Studies at SUNY-Binghamton—on women leaders and their distinctive styles of management.

The thrust of the research findings supports the notion that women managers tend to be more sensitive to human conditions than men. It's precisely this empathy, once considered a disadvantage to women in business, that will in years to come characterize the most effective managing styles, irrespective of gender. Sally Helgesen, journalist and author of *The Female Advantage—Women's Ways of Leadership*, insists that this point is important, not only because more women will attain positions of power in the near-term, but because the negotiating approach taken by women managers is vital to relating to an increasingly gender-conscious, change-driven, participation-desirous workforce.[2] Sensitivity, once thought to be a management liability, has become an asset to today's business leaders, who must continually respond to employees', customers', and stockholders' varying and oftentimes conflicting demands and expectations.

Paradoxically, despite the escalating need for empathetic corporate leadership styles exhibited more often by women managers, 98 percent of America's CEOs are men. That number, however, is very likely to change over the next decade, we believe, for two reasons: one, because it is fundamentally inequitable; and, two, because the call for responsive, caring corporate leaders able to adapt to diverse constituencies will rise dramatically.

How is it that women managers have this propensity for compassion and relating to others? Some argue that empathy is purely innate, yet the research also reveals that many women have been conditioned to *not* be confrontational or aggressive, almost from birth. Instead, they've been encouraged to listen, explain, and interact sympathetically with those around them. Thus, women's style of managing is often characterized by talking frankly with employees, sharing information rather than withholding it, including others in decision-making, and leaving their office doors open.

This profile contrasts sharply with men's prototypical way of managing, which tends to restrict contact with employees to only what's necessary to conduct business and reveal information only on a need-to-know basis. Traditionally, male managers have relied more on their sense of power to *control* people and situations, while female managers have relied more on their desire to *inspire* others to take control of their own worklives and circumstances.[3]

One potentially helpful way to view leadership styles and the role of compassion, suggests the research, is by distinguishing between transformational and transactional leaders. According to Rosener, women tend to manage in a transformational style. Broadly speaking, *transformational leaders* try to motivate workers by helping them to transform their own interests into those of the organization, and vice versa. The transformational style suggests that managers openly share information and encourage candor, traits which necessarily enhance give-and-take communication, and the enhanced ability to sniff out problems before they blossom into crises.[4]

Transactional leaders, in contrast, see employees as needing specific directions in order to perform a series of transactions to get the job done. To get them to carry out these transactions, leaders offer rewards for acceptable performance or punishment for inadequate performance. Such managers are more likely to use their status, rather than rely on reasoning or negotiation, to get others to do what they want.[5]

This difference in style is apparent in the way Grace Pastiak manages compared to her male counterparts. Most of Pastiak's subordinate managers at New York's Tel Labs, Inc., are men, many of whom admit that she manages her people differently than men in similar roles. Project Manager Duane Dhamen, referring to the male head of another division, says, "He talks to one or two key people and lets the information filter down to the ranks." In contrast, Pastiak "puts a stronger focus on the team and open communication."[6]

At H&E Hardware Stores, a chain throughout the high desert region north of Los Angeles, a woman is the best manager in the company, said Herb Stein, co-founder and CEO, during a talk at the company's headquarters in Victorville. "Her greatest ability is not being afraid to let an employee have the glory for a good deed well done. A lot of managers feel threatened by anybody under them who's capable," Stein believes.

Transformational-type leaders, not unexpectedly, rely on communication strategies that reflect a change-oriented style of managing. They use tactics that seek confirmation, create connections, establish rapport, and reinforce intimacy. Because these more indirect, "stroking" forms of managing tend to downplay rather than highlight the executive's position and expertise, managers with a transformational style are sometimes perceived, especially by transactional types, as being weak and insecure. Transformational leaders, when communicating, are apt to ask many questions in order to better understand, to clarify, or to make sure no relevant information is overlooked, a practice often (mis)labeled as proof of indecisiveness or uncertainty.

Transactional managers, suggests the research, rely on communication to achieve, to negotiate status, to protect their independence, to dominate. "Men are definitely more solution-oriented," points out Atlanta psychologist Sandra Hoffman. "When they talk, they're more interested in getting the facts right, and they see communication as a means to an end."[7] Transactional managers have a tendency to turn conversation into a lecture, since they see the person with the most information as having the higher status. They also typically neither see the value in nor give much immediate feedback to employees.[8]

Our purpose in discussing this research on gender style differences is not to make value judgments about men vs. women managers or to suggest that men aren't or can't be compassionate. We know better. Rather we see the value of this work in what it can teach us about leading and managing, irrespective of gender. The lesson here, we believe, is that each sex ought to learn (and borrow) from the other those "unnatural" elements of style they've tended to ignore or overlook.

A classic illustration of men and women learning from each other about management styles is the Arlen Royster-Joyce Hadley relationship. Arlen, long obsessed with the need to feel in control, learns much about his own management style and its limitations from conversations and debates with his VP of human resources. Due to Hadley's prodding and challenging, he eventually acknowledges the possibility that his top-down, power-oriented style restricts his understanding of Royal employees' needs, which, in turn, hinders his effectiveness as CEO. Only after this realization, which he accepts reluctantly, is Arlen able to consider altering his bureaucratic style to one more sensitive to others' wishes. Similarly, Hadley, because of her exposure to Arlen's pragmatic way of thinking, eventually comes to see that her unwavering, single-minded fixation on human concerns is not a panacea, and starts broadening her managerial perspective. Over time, both Arlen and Hadley see in the other certain style characteristics wanting in themselves, and each gradually comes to see that "one style doesn't fit all," but depends on the people and the situation.

With this emerging research providing a context for our discussion, we now return to exploring the three aspects of compassion we introduced earlier: listening to and understanding others; responding to what's heard; and exhibiting empathy.

Listening and Understanding

As we pointed out in Chap. 2, today's employees expect managers to care about them as people and respect their ideas, to willingly share information with them, and to invite them to participate in workplace decisions. Yet, for the most part, American workers view top executives as turning a deaf ear to their needs and wants.

Our review of some 20 years of management and communication research leads us to the conclusion that employees see top management as largely unaware of and insensitive to employees' concerns. That point was reinforced recently in a nationwide study conducted by the Wyatt Company, a management compensation and benefits consulting firm. Researchers reported that only four out of 10 line employees believe management shows a genuine interest in their well-being and treats them with respect and dignity.[9] Management's persistent failure to aggressively solicit feedback from workers, listen to it, and act on it was cited as a major failing by employees participating in the study. In a word, employees said that top-down communication has been employed effectively, whereas bottom-up hasn't.

Since the 1980s, myriad studies have consistently confirmed that employees' perceptions of top management—encompassing such weighty factors as trust, openness, and shared decision making—are directly linked to employees' job satisfaction and work performance. What this finding suggests is that top management, through its projected attitude and behavior, significantly influences the formation of employees' attitudes and expectations. Line workers and managers have distinctly different emotional and information needs; nevertheless, each expects an increasingly larger portion of those needs to be met by top management. CEOs who truly understand employees', customers', and stockholders' desire to be informed, recognized, and involved—and who try hard to address and meet those needs—will stand the best chance of winning their commitment.

Tom Clausen of the Bank of America understands the powerful implications of that point. "Employees aren't bystanders," he notes. "A successful manager has to believe that. To keep everyone on board, you have to keep them informed, keep them feeling that they're participating to keep them motivated." Bank of America, or any organization for that matter, isn't merely an institution comprised of assets or profits, in Clausen's view. "We're an organization of people. People are the only resource that we truly have and can count on. And the organization in the financial service industry that has the best people is the organization that's going to win. We're nothing without employees." As a result, concludes the retired chief, the CEO and senior management should view and treat employees as a top priority.

Employees want managers who not only give them the information they need, but who also empathize with their need to receive it. Accountability without compassion is divisive and destroys trust, argues Hyler Bracey, co-author of *Managing from the Heart*. "Talk to people respectfully, not about them disdainfully," he advises.[10]

That advice apparently wasn't heeded by Kellogg President Horst W. Schroeder, who in 1989 was fired by the company's chairman and CEO after only nine months at the helm. The central reason for his dismissal, according to news reports, was his derisive, autocratic style, which triggered a plunge in employee morale and prompted the premature departure of many of Kellogg's top people. One former company official portrayed the ousted executive as "demanding and abrasive, and often unwilling to listen to subordinates." An example of his harsh style was the way he publicly classified unimpressive oral presentations by managers as "a CE performance"—meaning "career-ending." His style seemed to tear at the cultural seams of an organization described as a "family company in a small midwestern town." At the time of his ouster, Schroeder had few, if any, supporters.[11]

Listening Leads to Understanding

To understand others, you first have to listen to them, closely and continuously, in order to hear their message and appreciate its meaning.

At the heart of compassionate leadership is how carefully a top manager listens to people's words *and* emotions, understands their meaning, and then responds. Some top dogs, like former university president Jewel Plummer Cobb, do realize how important it is for CEOs to listen more than they talk. "I've worked for years on improving my listening," admits Cobb. "Because when I'm talking as president of the university, I'm not a participant, I'm the president. And what the president says registers in a different way than it does for others. People hear and respond differently when it comes from the top. So I remind myself to not talk so much, to shut up and listen."

Listening can enlighten and suggest new directions, if one listens with an open mind and is willing to make changes. "You must treat everyone with dignity and respect, listening to what they have to say," insists General William Lyon, chairman and CEO of the William Lyon Company, the nation's largest home builder. Because, as Lyon has learned, sometimes you'll hear things that will make everybody's job easier and benefit the company at the same time. When Lyon was head of AirCal, he called a meeting of employees to discuss how the airline could cut costs. "A baggage handler pointed out how our practice of bumping passengers to allow [AirCal] company executives to fly went against my push for greater attention to the customer," he remembers. "That policy was dropped that night."[12]

Unfortunately, listening is too often practiced crudely and inconsistently by top-level executives, most of whom view it as merely "busy work." To be effective, true listening, however, particularly within an organizational context, needs to be more systematic and focused. In other words, listening should be purposeful, not frivolous, and targeted, not random. In so doing, listening serves as a valuable precursor to understanding others' needs, which is a prerequisite to making intelligent decisions—which describes the process used by IBM's recently-hired CEO as he sought to develop a new business plan.

When Louis Gerstner was hired by the computer behemoth in early 1993, he walked into what *Business Week* has called "the toughest management challenge in Corporate America."[13] The business giant was losing large chunks of its market share and red ink was gushing from its income statement as never before. As Gerstner, former head of RJR Nabisco, stepped into the high-profile job, the company's Wall Street critics and unhappy stockholders were already exerting pressure on him to come up with the quick fix for the company's ills. In the face of this mounting pressure, Gerstner admitted that he didn't know how best to put IBM back on track—and probably wouldn't for awhile, at least not until he got to know the organization and its people.

His initial strategy was simple: Listen carefully to IBM's employees and customers. "I've got to immerse myself in this company," he said. "I want to see as much, hear as much and feel as much as I can ... of the business of the company."[14] He listened in a variety of ways: at customary meetings with executives, during informal chats over lunch with middle managers, while touring company plants in the United States and overseas, and when visiting key customers.

Five weeks after he joined IBM, Gerstner was asked by *Fortune* how he'd been spending his time. "I've been moving all over the company, mostly listening to people," he reported. After scheduled meetings, according to the new CEO, was when the real meetings, with lots of give-and-take, took place "in the hallway, with everybody from managers to support staff people." And, he listened after office hours too. In the weeks following his selection as CEO, Gerstner's evenings were spent reviewing e-mail messages—to the tune of 200 to 250 a day—sent to him by concerned IBMers, mostly suggestions on what he ought to do, most of which he passed on to appropriate VPs with his reactions and suggestions.[15]

Listening Through Feedback

Appreciating the value of listening means knowing different approaches to listening, which, of course, will vary with objectives, groups, and circumstances. Some forms of listening are, by design, general in nature; that is, they seek surface-level information intended to paint the big organizational picture, based heavily on stakeholders' perceptions. General types of listening, such as a survey of stockholders, also can pinpoint red flags—that is, early warnings of potential problems—that may prompt management to listen more closely, like through a series of focus group interviews with a cross-section of stakeholders.

The process of listening to an organization hinges on obtaining reliable feedback. Feedback—bottom-up communication—is the flip side of two-way communication, and perhaps its most vital half. Feedback accomplishes two objectives for corporate chiefs: first, it generates information about constituencies vital to their decision making; and, second, by directly involving employees, it increases their commitment to the organization and its cause.

Unfortunately, though, many managers resent, and thus resist, what they see as the obligation to obtain feedback. For many supervisors, the idea of *needing* input from others, especially lower-level employees, is tantamount to admitting that they're not doing their job. Yet for feedback to really mean something, management has to believe in its value and create an environment that encourages others to offer candid input. No feedback system will be fully accepted as credible if the top manager—the CEO—hasn't endorsed it and is involved in it to some extent. The top manager's *Good Housekeep-*

ing stamp of approval—meaning the system is fair and even-handedly regulated, protects individuals' privacy, and is taken seriously by all management—sends the message that feedback is valued and will be considered in decisions.

How CEOs Get Feedback.   Getting feedback looks easier than it is, and requires considerable time and effort. Too many CEOs, all struggling to fill many roles, are woefully out of touch with what's on employees' and other groups' minds—mostly because they tend to insulate themselves from direct, regular contact. Survey results showed, for example, that CEOs believe in the value of employee input, yet they tend to get it through informal, limited scope and largely unreliable forms of feedback, such as casual conversations and small group meetings.

Because the feedback they get is often questionable, many chiefs must depend on staff to brief them on others' attitudes. The danger of such second-hand information is that it's apt to get filtered or distorted, or worse yet, passed on by underlings who tell the boss what he wants or ought to hear. Henry Rogers, founder of the public relations firm Rogers & Cowan, believes that "many CEOs make the mistake of living in the proverbial ivory tower. In order for a CEO to be successful," he said during an interview at his Beverly Hills, California, home, "he has to get out of the tower and meet the people, walk up and down the hall, let the people know he's there."

This image of management descending from its ivory executive suite was put in slightly different terms by Joe Torre, manager of the St. Louis Cardinals baseball team. Asked to respond to the suggestion that a baseball manager today could work from a TV booth as easily as from the dugout, Torre's retort could be a "cardinal" rule for managers everywhere: "Upstairs, you can't look in their eyes."[16]

Referring to what he calls "organized listening," SmithKline Beecham's Jean Pierre Garnier cautions CEOs and other top managers that *they* must "constantly listen to the organization and not just to direct reports, because in large corporations you're isolated from the real world."[17]

Those top executives committed to the concept of listening get their feedback in a number of different ways. We review several methods, including management-by-walking-around (MBWA), small group and townhall meetings, and more formal methods.

Management-by-Walking-Around.   MBWA, an increasingly common face-to-face informal method of communication, forces top managers to directly touch and be touched. The MBWA concept covers any management-initiated action that brings executives into informal contact with workers, such as surprise on-site visits, drop-in chats, or unscheduled "skull" sessions on special subjects. But eyeball-to-eyeball approaches aren't always practical. When time or organizational size don't permit personal contact, other media can be substituted to simulate face-to-face communication, such as telephone hotlines, videotapes, satellite teleconferencing, and electronic and/or voice mail.

Perhaps the quintessential MBWAer was the late Sam Walton, founder of Wal-Mart and Sam's Club. Walton often boasted that, up until the 1980s when his failing health slowed him down, he visited each Wal-Mart store at least once a year. With over 1700 stores, 200-plus Sam's Clubs and roughly 150 new store openings a year, even the energetic Walton soon had to resort to some alternative forms of contact, although he did so irresolutely. He always said that visiting the stores was the most important thing he did as head of the company—and, he would add, there wasn't anything he enjoyed doing more. Those visits, Walton believed, are critical to retail managers' ability to identify problems early, before they escalate into crises. He learned about the CEO's impact years ago as an apprentice clerk at a J.C. Penney store in Des Moines, Iowa. One day James Cash Penney himself dropped in for a visit and, as Walton tells it, showed how much he cared about his workers by personally teaching young Sam how to tie an attractive package "with very little twine and very little paper."[18]

Walton never forgot the lasting impression Penney's brief visit had on him. Today, Penney's legacy to Walton is being carried forward by Walton's descendants. It's hard to find Wal-Mart executives in their offices; they live on the road. A Wal-Mart regional vice president, for example, supervises between 11 to 15 district managers, who oversee 8 to 12 stores. In a typical week, a Wal-Mart VP visits 10 to 12 stores, each in a different city, thereby averaging about 200 days a year talking nose-to-nose with employees.[19]

Sadly, many employees in big organizations rarely, if ever, see or have a chance to talk to their CEOs. Some don't even know their CEO's name or what he or she looks like. Dr. Noel Hinners, associate deputy administrator of the National Aeronautics and Space Administration (NASA) in Washington, D.C., has worked for companies in which workers hardly ever saw their division director or department head. To prevent that from happening at NASA, he tries to set aside time each week to visit a building, a room, or a floor at random, just walking in unannounced to talk.

"It took a while to establish trust, for people to believe that I wasn't there spying on them," Hinners explained during an interview in his Washington office. "When people found out I wasn't digging for information with which to hit them over the head, that I really just wanted to find out what was going on, there was no problem. And after I'd walked around for a couple of months, the other managers started to walk around too."

Quite unexpectedly, one outcome of Hinners' unplanned, unpublicized visits is that NASA employees think he spends more time with them than he really does, which, Hinners points out, has generally positive effects throughout the organization. "I've had people from the lowest working level at headquarters call me. They have a problem and feel they can come to me. I wouldn't want or expect them to come to me with every problem, but it's good to have an environment where, if people really feel they must talk to me, they can."

When Harold Rudnick, then vice president of Vons Companies' grocery division, was given responsibility for the supermarket chain's service deli department, he was unfamiliar with the operation. To familiarize himself with the day-to-day trials faced by service deli employees, he initiated a somewhat unconventional form of MBWA. He assigned himself to work at a deli for several days in order to learn the business. He wore the green apron and cap, and asked both managers and line workers to treat him like any other employee, as he rotated among all the various jobs in the deli. He sliced turkey, mixed potato salad, cleaned equipment, and served customers.

As far as he knows, this was the first time a top executive at Vons had done such a thing. "Many people thought I was nuts, but it turned out to be a terrific learning experience," says Rudnick. And, to his pleasant surprise, his personal credibility was enhanced beyond anything he'd intended or could have imagined. "Seems like in a few days everybody in the company knew I'd done this," he recalls. "For months afterwards, I'd walk into one of our stores and employees would talk to me about it."

A key to integrating a "wandering manager" approach into an organization's culture is to make visits routine and nonthreatening so that an unannounced arrival "elicits only familiar greetings, not paroxysms of terror."[20] CEOs must win managers' *and* employees' trust before MBWA forms of contact will work. Trust is earned if, and only if, such efforts are genuine—and don't kid yourself, employees know the real from the imitation—and normal, not just when management is pushing a hidden agenda.

Another positive effect of an MBWA-based style is that employees perceive it as evidence that management cares about and wants to listen to them. It's recognizing people's need to be recognized that marks the face-to-face leadership style of Mary Kay Ash, CEO of highly successful Mary Kay Cosmetics. Says one of her leading salespeople: "You wouldn't just walk over to, say, John Akers. But Mary Kay calls you her daughter and looks you dead in the eye. She makes you feel you can do anything."[21] Even those employees who don't actually come into direct contact with the CEO or senior VP, but who hear about a top manager's visit from a peer will be influenced and feel as if they're participating in the feedback process, even if only vicariously.

Small Group and Townhall Meetings. A common method corporate decision makers use to gauge constituents' state of mind is formal meetings. The purpose of such meetings is to create a forum for managers and employees or other publics to share ideas and information through largely unstructured and unrestricted discussion. Two popular meeting formats are the traditional small group meeting and the townhall meeting, which is catching on these days. Similar in purpose and operation, the two formats differ most substantially by the number of those who are permitted to participate in and observe the meeting. Small group meetings, which may range in size from 5 to 100 people, are usually restricted to only those directly involved in the discussion. Townhall meetings, meanwhile, are commonly held in public settings (and may be televised) in order to allow others not at the meeting site to observe and possibly participate by asking questions via audio or video hook-ups.

Small group meetings, whether by design or coincidence, are a preferred way many CEOs elicit feedback from employees. At Pacific Bell, CEO Phil Quigley and his top officers meet with 1000 middle managers at mid-year to keep their finger tightly on the organization's pulse. "We discuss some of the key strategies of our business and get feedback on our performance to date." This performance calibration requires eight three-hour meetings at different company locations throughout California, each hosted and facilitated by the CEO.

To let Maryland Blue Cross/Blue Shield employees know that the organization had to undergo a 360-degree transformation to remain competitive, top executive Carl Sardegna used small groups to deliver the message personally to employees, and then open up discussion on their reactions. "We did nine one-hour sessions in two days with about 150 employees at a time," says Sardegna. "I would talk for about half an hour and then answer questions for the last 30 minutes."

The CEO also counted on his personal, informal network of contacts to bring him additional feedback. "I listened to my network of people who I know will tell me the truth, because they're interested in what's good for the organization. I asked them, 'What are people thinking?' From their feedback, I'm able to tell whether or not the message is getting through. Or whether the message getting through is totally off-target from employees' concerns." Sardegna's "anybody, any time" open-door policy was well-known and people used it as the new program unfolded.

Details related to setting up meetings can be the difference between a productive meeting and a waste of time. Seemingly trivial issues, like location, can make a big difference in people's willingness to join in and open up. If, for instance, the meeting is held in what's perceived by workers to be management-controlled territory, like an executive conference room, they may feel inhibited and clam up. At Avon, CEO Hicks Waldron hosted weekly coffee groups of five to seven randomly selected employees in his office atop the Avon building in midtown Manhattan. "At the beginning, some of them would come in scared to death," Waldron recalls. "Their first question was always, 'What's this all about?' Then the word got around that I wasn't a bad guy, that it was just coffee and chitchat about whatever was going on."

To counteract some employees' trepidation at receiving an invitation to a meeting in the CEO's office, Dick Schlosberg, chief of *The Los Angeles Times*, would distribute in advance of his informal lunch meetings with a cross-section of 10 to 15 employees a specific agenda of topics. It serves as a sort of ice breaker. "There was always some focal point, so the people had some sense of why they were coming," Schlosberg advises. "For instance, it might be how are the health care providers doing with our people? Are there any problems or complaints? But the discussion usually broadens. We always get into another topic or two."

Obtaining feedback from all corners of an organization can play havoc with a CEO's sleep schedule and social calendar—but it's imperative that at least some portion of *all* stakeholder segments be given an opportunity to provide top management with input. CEOs responsible for scattered operations should make sure they don't inadvertently single out, exclude, or appear to favor only certain groups. Like not visiting folks working graveyard shifts or on holidays. Insensitive scheduling of the CEO's time will long be remembered by those snubbed. At Los Angeles' Cedars-Sinai Medical Center, top management has arranged its communication activities to include all shifts, says Tom Priselac, senior VP of operations and COO. "Many nurses work 12-hour shifts, so our communication strategy is organized to reach everyone. We have a lot of recognition programs and they're deliberately scheduled to cover all shifts. Our holiday parties, for example, are held at three different times during a day." Priselac and other top managers try to attend all three, which can make for an arduous agenda during holidays.

When it comes to the public platforms available through townhall meeting formats, no chief executive has used them more frequently, or more effectively, than Bill Clinton. At a retreat held at Camp David shortly after his inauguration, President Clinton hosted a session for members of his Cabinet on how they could better connect with one another during meetings. At the president's request, the session was helped along by several outside professional "meeting facilitators."

Clinton's reliance on townhall-type meetings and summits, both live and electronic, where he solicits viewpoints from differing constituencies and encourages debate on tough issues, reveals much about his desire to come across as a compassionate leader. According to aides, the first "baby boomer" president is a shirtsleeves type of manager who readily makes surprise visits to White House offices, drops in unannounced on staff meetings and isn't likely to surround himself with a protective "palace guard." Such brands of MBWA, which some of his critics call "unpresidential," have two built-in advantages: Clinton has an opportunity to get a first-hand read on his staffers' attitudes and problems, and he's able to send the message through his presence that he's interested in them.

Clinton's populist example of going eyeball-to-eyeball with people has inspired other elected officials, including the two newly-elected senators from California. Within weeks after taking office, rookie Senators Barbara Boxer and Dianne Feinstein held seven townhall forums with over 2000 Californians from every walk of life. The meetings, which were usually held in city hall chambers filled to capacity, received positive reviews by the citizens attending, many of whom were getting their first live look at a U.S. senator. The issues raised covered the waterfront, from tax policy to endangered species, and were discussed bluntly by senators and citizens alike. Such give-and-take, two-way formats, although used by some state legislators and House members, have rarely been employed by senators, whose constituencies are state-wide and more broadly dispersed. Boxer, whose outgoing personality naturally fits well with live encounters, claims that "this is the part of my job I like best ... to me, this is what democracy is all about."[22]

The townhall approach appears to be catching on in corporate America, too; for example, Chrysler Corporation's top three executives—the chairman, president, and CFO—hold about 35 townhalls a year with 100 to 150 employees participating in each session. The "top management live" model is apparently going over well with Chrysler workers, who listed townhalls among their top five preferred sources of information in a recent company employee opinion survey.

SmithKline Beecham's Jean Pierre Garnier, affectionately known to his employees as simply "JP," is among those few top executives who select the meeting settings strategically. For instance, he uses large meetings when he wants to maximize impact and make certain his message won't be mistranslated when descending the normal layers of management. Small group meetings give him a "good feel for what's going on" because he's able to listen closely to a number of people concurrently. And he relies on one-on-one meetings to have an emotional, long-lasting effect on individuals' loyalty.[23]

More Formal Feedback Systems.   High-level managers may unconsciously over-rely on informal feedback methods, like accidental conversations, notes from colleagues, or meetings with small groups. Although such input can be useful at times, informal listening should always be a supplement to, rather than a replacement for more formal types of feedback, such as attitude surveys, focus group interviews, or content analyses. By definition and design, formal feedback systems seek—by scientifically *measuring* attitudes and behavior of targeted samples—to create a *representative*, dependable portrait of an organization, or at least a substantial portion of it.

The mechanics of upward communication systems can speak loudly about management's belief in and commitment to such systems. When feedback is sought through a standardized and acceptable process, like an organization-wide survey, the process itself, which attempts to reach all or most in a population, boosts employees' expectations that they'll be heard and their ideas taken seriously.

"Right to the Top" is a formal feedback program instituted by Alexander Trowbridge, former head of the Washington, D.C.-based National Association of Manufacturers. Employees are encouraged to write down their concerns, their curiosities, their likes and dislikes about the organization. The written comments are then sealed in an envelope, either signed or anonymously, and sent directly to the CEO, who is the only one with authority to open the envelope. "It was a way individuals could vent their anger or ask something they may not have felt comfortable asking through the chain of command," Trowbridge explains. "I received quite a few letters in the early stages of 'Right to the Top.' Now I probably get six or eight a year. We remind them that the program's there, but morale has improved and employees understand more about what's going on. They feel confident they can raise issues with their supervisors and get them resolved."

A relatively new, individualized, yet formal method, of bottom-up feedback is currently being tried at a number of major corporations, including Amoco, Cigna, and Du Pont. This approach asks employees to anonymously rate their bosses, including, in some cases, their top executives as well.[24] CEOs with the courage to institute upward appraisal systems will no doubt enhance their believability in employees' eyes by appearing more accountable and caring. In some organizations, like Union Pacific, employee feedback on front-line and mid-level managers' communication effectiveness is taken so seriously by upper management that improving communication with employees is a major factor in determining managers' salaries and bonuses.[25]

One final point about listening: There's as much added-value in the feedback *process* as there is in the feedback itself. That top managers make an effort to listen and obtain feedback is what's important; the particular methods used or information obtained, while always important, matter far less. Simply offering employees uninterrupted, unfiltered access to top management communicates an organization's commitment to bottom-up communication, notes Norm Leaper, president of the International Association of Business Communicators (IABC). And rest assured, that message doesn't escape the attention of employees and others connected to the company. "Any IABC member can pick up the phone and call me," says Leaper, a former corporate communication manager. "Sometimes what they want is mundane. But knowing they can get to me says we're committed to fulfilling member needs, which, given the business we're in, we'd better be. It's symbolic."

In actuality, symbols and policies make up employees' reality. If the symbols or policies change, so will workers' view of reality. Even if a "Right to the Top" program is used only occasionally, its very existence is a symbol of management's abiding commitment to the value of employee feedback, and comforts employees in their knowing they have entry to the top if they want it.

Responding

Listening compassionately to—and thus hearing—people's opinions and desires is terribly important. Ultimately, though, empathetic listening brings with it an obligation to respond quickly and constructively. Otherwise, those who were asked to give feedback will think their time was wasted and management either didn't really care or didn't really listen. Certainly that's true when companies conduct system-wide attitude surveys, for example. After participating in a survey, a process usually intended to identify areas needing fixing, employees' expectations will be that management will share and discuss findings with them, and that results will eventually be used to make decisions leading to making things better.

Getting stakeholders to "buy in" to the feedback process can strengthen their desire and commitment to be a part of the solution. Tracy Accardi is manager of ultrasound computer engineering at General Electric who entered the company at the lowest entry-level position. During her climb up the GE corporate ladder, she learned that if you can get people to offer suggestions and then respond without delay with reasonable decisions, they'll want to help implement the decisions. She now tries to waste no time reacting to employee ideas and recommendations, because, she says, "I realized how much a slow decision by management can hurt an organization."[26]

At times, managers may not have enough time to get input before a decision must be made. Robin Orr, national director of hospital projects for San Francisco-based Planetree, a consumer health-care organization, realizes there are moments when she can't wait for intelligence to bubble up, but has to act before things get out of hand. "Things move too fast sometimes, and decisions need to be made," she says. "You can't always bother to ask 15 people what they think."[27]

It's unrealistic to expect managers to consult with stakeholders before every decision. But when time constraints don't allow for feedback, the value of stakeholders' input isn't necessarily diminished. Managers who regularly solicit feedback will obtain, at a minimum, a general sense of a group's state-of-mind to help in decision making. Also, employees and others who believe their top managers know them and *normally* take into account their concerns before making decisions are far less apt to object to or resent managers for not consulting them during those times when feedback can't be gotten.

Contrary to what many executives believe, responding doesn't necessarily imply management is "knuckling under" or "giving in" to demands. Responding means that after listening, hearing, and, hopefully, understanding, things improve—whether it be a new policy or procedure, an improved attitude, or, short of those, an explanation why things can't or won't change. Sometimes, certain nasty decisions—like shutting down a plant, holding back on salary increases, or slashing operating budgets—can't be avoided and, no matter how they're spelled out, won't please anybody.

A good example of a no-win situation occurred when President Bill Clinton, shortly after taking office, announced a controversial middle-of-the-road policy on homosexuals serving in the military. All sides were displeased and didn't hesitate to say so—the generals, the gay community, civil rights activists, average citizens. At such times, management's obligation, in our view, is still to listen, consider the input and respond compassionately so that all parties feel that their voice matters, even if nobody gets exactly what they want.

When all is said and heard, what makes a manager a truly credible listener is what changes for the better. "The difference between success and failure of a feedback system is the interpretation of information," points out Tom Priselac,

CEO of Cedars-Sinai Medical Center. "One of my key roles is to take feedback, synthesize it, distill it and make a rational judgment about how we should allocate our limited resources to best meet the needs of the organization."

Avon's former top dog, Hicks Waldron, offers a wonderfully succinct summary of the listening-responding link: "What we say isn't as important as what's changed based on what we've heard."

Exhibiting Empathy

It's not enough that CEOs feel empathy for others; they also have to express their empathy if they expect to positively influence the organization-at-large. The principal way a corporate leader demonstrates empathy is by communicating with people about what's on *their* minds and what's important to *them*. The more direct and personal that communication, the more likely that leader and followers will be drawn together. This shouldn't be difficult for most chiefs, since they normally prefer and are most comfortable with interpersonal forms of contact. Small group and townhall meetings, discussed earlier, are examples of straightforward ways top managers communicate their messages and feelings to followers.

Expressing empathy believably involves not only CEOs' spoken and written words, but their tone and attitude as well. "What you say is often less important than the manner in which you say it, your body language, the setting, the air of confidence or the feeling behind what you say," notes Dick Schlosberg of Times-Mirror. "It's all translated and remembered far beyond your words." Vons Companies' Bill Davila agrees, "You can communicate with a look or with a gesture. Or just by showing somebody attention or interest."

Syndicated political columnist David Broder argues that Bill Clinton was elected president because of "his ability to convey emotion—the empathetic hugs ... the energy of his bus tour stops and, most notably, his almost intimate emotional bonding with the woman voter at the Richmond debate who asked the candidates how they had felt the recession personally. That was the moment I think Clinton cinched the election."[28]

Employees, customers, media, and stockholders have long memories when it comes to caring gestures by those at the top of the organization chart. Herb Stein, chairman of H&E Hardware Stores of Victorville, California, is a "street savvy" entrepreneur with a real soft spot for his several hundred employees. He sees them as his second family. "If you've ever worked for a large company, you've had people walk in a room and never acknowledge you. You don't exist in their world. I try not to do that," he explains. "I ask people about their families, which is important and not forgotten by them. And I compliment them. And while I may eventually forget what I complimented them about, they won't. It's one of the secrets of human communication, to let people know that you know they're there, and that they're valuable to the organization."

Top management has to constantly reinforce the "every person matters" slogan with actions, as New York's Tel Labs, Incorporated, did when the economic recession forced a reduction in orders for the company's products. Instead of laying off workers, notes Grace Pastiak, director of manufacturing for the company, executive management shifted to four-day weeks for everyone until business picked up.[29]

At no other time is top management's expressed empathy as crucial as during major organizational upheavals—a company restructuring, layoffs, tainted product reports. During such trying, uncertain times, employees are frightened, vulnerable, and unsure about their own and their organization's future. That's when they want—and need—unfiltered information directly from the top executive, the person in charge. The CEO represents a "stable communication focal point in all the confusion," says Carl Sardegna, president of Blue Cross/Blue Shield of Maryland. "So employees look for messages from the top, more so than they would in a stable environment." Sardegna's cogent argument—that the CEO must step up and assume the dominant communication role when employees are crippled by uncertainty—parallels VP Rick Jamieson's attempts in the last chapter to persuade a reluctant Arlen Royster of his fundamental communication responsibilities as CEO.

In the past decade, major organizational and cultural changes have become the norm as many companies struggle to adjust to deregulated markets and intensifying domestic and global competition. One company that had to manage itself through a highly unstable and fast-changing environment was AT&T, one of the largest organizations in the world. "When you have change occurring as fast as it was in our business," recounts Phil Quigley, president and CEO of Pacific Bell, based in San Francisco, "you need to keep your employees informed to lift the mystique from some of the company's major decisions. They've got to know what's happening."

What employees most want to know, says Quigley, is "How will the changes affect me and my family?" Because of Quigley and his management staff's strategy to keep employees informed about all changes touching them and the organization, Pac Bell employees held their focus on adapting to marketplace shifts and customer concerns, instead of being diverted by incomplete information springing from the rumor mill. "A better informed employee is a happier employee," Quigley emphasizes, "which means, in the long run, we're a better company."

Whether people see the CEO as compassionate, cold-hearted, or ambivalent will influence their feelings toward the organization as a whole. If the top executive is perceived as aloof or uncaring, stakeholders will mimic that perception in their thoughts and actions. The CEO's personality, management style, personal credibility, and perhaps most importantly, empathy with key constituencies can make a big difference, maybe *the* difference, to an organization's and its CEO's future. That is the point of the following case about a CEO who failed to learn the lesson of compassion.

The Sad Case of Jack Davidson

Let's call him Jack Davidson. He's a composite of two actual top executives we've observed first-hand. Each was new to the job and each ran into similar difficulties in trying to win the hearts and minds of the people in his new organization.

Davidson has just been appointed CEO of Knapp Engineering, Incorporated, an 80-person architectural and engineering consulting firm in northern Ohio. Bright and personable, the 54-year-old Davidson was recruited by Knapp's board of directors from outside, because they believed the company needed an infusion of fresh thinking and enthusiasm. He came from a highly successful management consulting firm in San Francisco, where he'd been a managing partner the past five years.

Davidson's hiring in the wake of his predecessor's untimely death received extensive publicity from the trade media, most of it applauding his polished management skills. His appointment, however, shocked many of Knapp's employees; most expected one of the firm's senior managers to take over. Employees were jittery about how the change in leadership would affect them and the company's long-term prospects. To each other, employees' reactions to Davidson's hiring went something like this: "We don't know this guy. We have no history or relationship with him. He's coming from the 'zany' west coast culture. We can't trust him, at least not yet." They took a wait-and-see attitude toward their new CEO. But they weren't going to wait long before passing judgment.

In contrast, Davidson was excited beyond words for the chance to be the head honcho and direct a corporate turnaround. He couldn't wait to get started. When interviewing for the job, Davidson talked with many Knapp managers and line workers about the organization's problems and challenges. Since then, he'd been reading everything he could get his hands on about the company's history and the state of the architectural industry. As a result, the new CEO arrived at Knapp convinced he knew how to revitalize the workforce and get the company back on firm financial footing.

First Impressions Linger

On the first Saturday after he started, Davidson hosted an all-employee family picnic at a local park. He was all smiles and charm as he introduced himself to employees and their families. Initial reactions to Davidson were cordial yet guarded. After several hours of hot dogs, socializing, and softball, he gathered everybody together for a pep talk.

"I want to thank each of you for coming today," he began enthusiastically, "and for your wonderfully warm welcome to me and my family. I can't tell you how excited I am to join you in the challenge of making Knapp Engineering the toast of the industry—once again." He didn't hear the collective gulp among those listening.

"I'm looking forward to sharing with you my expansion and restructuring plans. I think they'll put us in a strong position to expand on all fronts over the next couple of years." Davidson, warming to his own words, looked up at his audience, oblivious to the distressd looks on their faces.

"There'll always be a place in this company—and a generous paycheck—for those of you who don't mind working hard and truly committing yourselves to Knapp Engineering. To begin preparing for that expansion, I've already begun recruiting some of the stars of this industry." Employees' original curiosity was now turning into apprehension. Davidson was unfazed. "This is a social gathering, so I won't bore you with the details. But I want you to know how eager I am to hear your ideas and suggestions." Few heard Davidson's last comment; they were already worrying about what they perceived as the new CEO's veiled threats to their jobs.

Insensitivity Hurts—Everybody

So much was he enjoying the spotlight and the sensation of power that Davidson never heard employees' minds shutting down. He had shot himself in the foot, yet he didn't realize how much pain he was in. As one employee said to another on their way to their cars, "I was just starting to like him when he starts yakking about how he's going to change everything, just like that. Don't we have any say in what's going on around here? Where'd he get all this wisdom about what's best for the company in just a week's time?"

"Yeah, right, he wants to hear our ideas," snorted the other. "He just wants to see us sweat. Because if we don't, his superstars will take our places, right? I think maybe it's time to dust off the ol' resume."

From his narrow perspective, Davidson thought he was painting a picture of an exciting future, but because he didn't know the people whose loyalty he sought, he never even considered how they might react. What he said and what they heard were worlds apart. The result was that Davidson's hopes of getting employees on his side disappeared, only he didn't know it.

Time would have been Davidson's ally, if he had used it wisely. But since he wasn't willing to wait for the input he claimed he wanted, time became his enemy. Employees needed time to get to know him; time to like him; time to talk things over with him; time to share ideas with him; time to learn to trust him; time to get comfortable with his management style; and time for him to understand them.

Unfortunately, he didn't give time a chance to work for him. His unintentional insults of workers' past contributions and his excluding employees from planning and decision-making turned off the very people whose support he needed most. He'd entered their domain uninvited and before they could get a good look at him, he'd put them on the defensive.

Another *Faux Pas*

Shortly after the picnic, Davidson held a series of small group luncheon meetings with employees to, as he put it, "find out what was on their minds." A good idea for getting feedback, soliciting ideas, and building support for himself and his plans. Under typical circumstances, all those things might have happened. But since he had already poisoned the well, cynicism was running high before he said a word.

During each meeting, Davidson talked far more than he listened. He answered the few questions asked, although he had hid behind the Fifth Amendment when asked about his plans for restructuring the company and if it meant budget cuts and layoffs. To tough questions he didn't want to answer, his patronizing retorts went something like this: "Why don't we just cross that bridge when we get to it. No need to concern yourself with that right now. Let me worry about it. That's what they pay me for."

In each session, he asked employees for their thoughts on what Knapp's future direction ought to be, always assuring them their input was "indispensably important" to *his*—never our—decisions. Not once did he take notes during the meetings. Many admitted later that they'd attended the meetings because they thought it mandatory since Davidson was, after all, *the* CEO. Employees' perceptions of Davidson remained mixed. The meetings seemed to buy him a little time to try to redeem himself, but only enough that he couldn't afford to waste any of it.

But again he misused his limited time. In the months that followed, Knapp Engineering employees saw little of Jack Davidson. He hardly communicated with employees, leaving it to each lower-level manager's discretion. He traveled frequently, sometimes for a week or two at a time, presumably to meet with present and potential clients, and—according to company scuttlebutt—to interview the superstars he was trying to lure to Knapp. He met occasionally with senior managers behind closed doors, presumably to "formulate company objectives" but it usually ended up being "Jack on Jack." He'd swear these executives to secrecy, telling them that "the time isn't right to trust workers with such sensitive information."

Periodically, he invited a hand-picked group of managers and their wives to dinner at his home where he'd expound at length on his "bold new ideas" and "recruiting adventures." While all this was going on, he was quietly developing plans to reconfigure and reposition the company, based on his "revision" of the future.

Actions Speak Loudest

At first, several departments were restructured and a few employees were given pink slips or, in a few cases, replaced by people from the outside. "Streamlined for greater efficiency" was the euphemism Davidson used in memos announcing these so-called adjustments. Such misleading jargon became symbolic of the black humor passing among Knapp employees. A common question was: "Who's going to be 'streamlined' out of here this week?"

Davidson hired a number of so-called superstars, tagged "Davidson's Disciples," at salaries above the company's maximum pay scales and usually with abnormal incentives, like an extra week's paid vacation—which Davidson told them they could use as time off or redeem for cash. These side deals, financed out of Davidson's private slush fund, were kept hush-hush; he knew these "sweetheart" arrangements wouldn't be viewed favorably, yet he kept doing them.

Employees' resentment of his behavior and suspicions about his motives escalated. The once-friendly and open atmosphere of Knapp Engineering was fast evaporating. Employees became noticeably close-mouthed and guarded, even with their peers, as one-time friends were having to choose between pro- and anti-Davidson factions.

During Davidson's first year as CEO, employee productivity plummeted and turnover climbed dramatically as the brightest people bolted. Sales stayed flat. For each new client brought in, two existing ones bailed out. Davidson's ambitious growth objectives continually had to be pared back as the disappointments mounted. Communication between the CEO and employees was sporadic and awkward. Contact consisted mostly of his stuffy, stilted memos announcing a decision he'd made or another outsider he'd hired. Employees lost all confidence in Davidson; they stonewalled him at every opportunity.

Davidson and those he'd hired were blacklisted when it came to social gatherings. The rumor mill, ripe with stories about "Jack the Ripper" and his secret plans, became, for many workers, their major source of information. Throughout the architectural industry, the word was out that Knapp Engineering was a sinking ship.

The Final Straw

Matters came to a head 10 months into Davidson's tenure. A number of senior managers, all veterans who predated Davidson's arrival, met in secret to consider a "no confidence" vote. That had never been done in the company's 63-year history.

After four hours reviewing Davidson's misguided, disruptive management style and the damage it had done to the company, most top managers were convinced he had to go before the company was destroyed beyond repair. A few feared that skewering their own CEO would, once it became public, shine an embarrassing spotlight on Knapp management's inability to solve its own problems. In the end, though, the group catalogued in writing its rationale for firing Davidson, and sent it to the board along with a recommendation he be replaced by one of Knapp's current senior managers.

At first, the board tabled the group's recommendation. Its members met with Davidson and tried to persuade him to adjust his "bull-in-a-China-shop" leadership style in hopes that employees might, once again, open their minds and give him another chance. Unfortunately, it was a case of too little, too late. Distrust was very high, and had been allowed to fester for too long. Fate had finally caught up with Davidson.

Less than a year after the hoopla surrounding his appointment, the board, realizing the futility of trying to "teach an old top dog new tricks," forced Davidson out—gladly buying out the remaining two years of his three-year contract. In the news release announcing his "resignation," Davidson's departure was loosely worded as his personal decision to "pursue other professional opportunities." But the people of Knapp Engineering knew better, as did Jack Davidson, who to this day refuses to accept the simple truth that he destroyed his own dream, because he never learned the meaning of compassion.

A Final Word

Today's workers "universally expect their leaders to know the business, be fair and honest, be consistent, be understanding, be open-minded, and be able to motivate, communicate and delegate," says Robert Grandford Wright of Pepperdine University.[30] Unfortunately, employees' expectations and their perceptions of reality don't match. For years, most have said repeatedly they think top management is unaware of and insensitive to their concerns and feelings.

What that means is employees don't think management cares about them or their problems. And they're saying that top managers ought to be more ears and less mouth. Such skeptical, mistrusting views can erect invisible and impenetrable walls between workers and managers. Compassion—listening to and understanding what's important to others, responding appropriately and expressing empathy—is the most common missing ingredient in effective CEO-leadership. Ironically, it's also the most essential.

With many workplace and marketplace changes already in motion and others projected in the future, some business scholars are predicting that the core societal values dominating our world of tomorrow will grow out of the concept of cooperation, not competition. Therefore, the next generation of senior managers will need to be increasingly participatory, equitable, nurturing, and consensus-building. Simply put, the successful top managers of tomorrow will appreciate the crucial role compassion and empathy play in corporate leadership.

Returning to Arlen ...

In Chap. 5, Arlen argued unsuccessfully against his serving as Royal's public spokesperson as outlined in Rick Jamieson's crisis management plan. His long-standing fear of reporters, TV cameras, and public speaking has caused him many sleepless nights thinking about being at the media's mercy. But, in truth, he knew he was the most logical one—the only one—to be the company's voice when the company is fighting for its life. He reluctantly accepted his fate as Royal's chief communication officer (CCO)—for the time being, anyway.

And while he was busy reviewing Royal's crisis plan, Susan O'Reilly accidentally learned that a mutiny was being hatched by Mike Keller, VP of operations, and comptroller John Grubner. As we rejoin Arlen, the pressure on him is mounting to address Royal's predicament and his worsening problems on the homefront.

"CEOs Don't Have to Be Schizophrenics— But It Helps"

Wednesday, October 10, 3:30 p.m. Joe Coletto had just left Arlen's office. The feisty attorney had done most of the talking, except for Arlen's occasional questions and requests for clarification of Coletto's cumbersome legalese. By the time Coletto completed his treatise on "how to properly announce that we screwed up without admitting any fault," as he delicately put it, both men were drained from thinking about the worst case possibilities Coletto profiled.

Consistent with his training, Coletto was inclined to over-analyze situations, exhaustively reviewing every potential negative outcome. But despite his sometimes harsh way of phrasing things, Coletto knew the law's fine points and pitfalls thoroughly, plus he possessed a sixth sense for danger, a reliable early warning system Arlen had come to respect.

"Look, Arlen," Coletto had pressed with bulging eyes and a wig-wagging index finger, "Royal's good name will be flapping in the wind the minute you tell the world our books were funny for several years—no matter how nicely you say it. The only thing that'll matter to most stockholders is how it's gonna affect their dividend checks. Some of the bigger ones will probably file class action suits before the close of business that day.

"The big pension funds may bail out of our stock, which'll beat the hell out of its value in the short-run. Say as little as necessary and for heaven's sake don't say anything that even hints you might've had any prior knowledge of any improprieties. One innocent slip of the tongue and Royal—not to mention you and the rest of us with fiduciary responsibility—could get hung out to dry by the SEC or a few angry stockholders. It's gonna be messy, no matter how you slice it."

Arlen was especially intrigued with Coletto's detailed description of a recent SEC action which held a company's top executives—the chairman, CEO, and CFO—directly accountable for what the regulatory agency called their "lack of diligence" in detecting and rectifying employees' illicit activities. In that case, which involved a major Wall Street brokerage house and one of its junk bond masters who trampled over scores of securities regulations, all three managers were banned for life from serving in the same jobs with any securities firm and from holding any supervisory position for three years. The agency's rationale, Coletto lectured Arlen, was that the top managers failed to "reasonably supervise" employees under their charge.

Trying to cut through the legal mumbo-jumbo, the articulate New York-bred attorney put the point in perspective for the CEO, "You're now expected to sniff out the problem before it becomes a problem, because, if you don't, then you'll be the one with the problem." A CEO's dual obligations, Coletto tutored, are: first, spot the red flags of illegal activities, and, second, report the problem and then take appropriate, corrective actions. Arlen expressed utter amazement that the SEC could get away with dictating such a wholly unrealistic obligation on top executives, who, he argued angrily, "can't be expected to be guardian angels looking over the shoulders of literally hundreds or thousands of employees spread all over the place."

"Arlen, what you're saying is true and reasonable, under most circum-stances. The problem is the SEC has to lay blame, the ultimate responsibility, at somebody's feet—so the agency looks like it's doing its job of policing and punishing. Let's not jump to any hard-and-fast conclusions yet, particularly since this is based on only a single case. The implications aren't all that clear yet," Coletto cautioned a worried-looking Arlen, "but," he added with a touch of trepidation, "this may throw open the door for government to come down hard on a CEO for not detecting and correcting legal misbehavior by employees. This shifts the rules of the game considerably. And you can bet the SEC is on the lookout for more cases to make its point."

Coletto's candid warnings had seized Arlen's attention. There was no getting around Royal's long-term legal obligations and the fact that settlements were going to be expensive, he outlined, trying to prepare Arlen. "Expect an instant barrage of lawsuits and the nuisance publicity that come with them," warned the cautious lawyer.

Deep in his gut, Arlen knew that, even considering Coletto's sound advice, if Royal was to escape the public speculation and finger-pointing, he had to divert attention away from the controversial liability issues and onto management's ability to fix the problem. He thought about presenting the "cooked books" snafu as more of a cultural aberration than a chronic disorder. If he could somehow accomplish that, he told himself, then maybe he could minimize the damage to Royal's credibility.

But just how to pull off the miracle had Arlen's head gyrating as an emotionally drained Coletto gathered his papers strewn across the conference table and departed. The perplexed CEO drifted back to his desk, where he unconsciously shuffled the same mound of incoming correspondence for the third time, his mind darting elsewhere.

"Everybody seems to be telling me what to say, how to say it, listen to this, listen to that," Arlen thought. Jamieson. Coletto. Andrea ... Andrea. Their troubling telephone conversation earlier that day still gnawed at his ego ... and one thing Andrea had said kept returning to him, eating at his conscience ... "Arlen, you've lost touch with your son."

In the middle of an already nasty day, as he was trying to sort out Royal's predicament, they'd somehow gotten into an argument about Arlen's deteriorating relationship with his son, Glenn. And, as usual, Arlen resented her bringing it up—and now of all times.

Arlen and Andrea's recurring argument was over Arlen's objections to Glenn's decision to pursue a master's degree in marine biology instead of business. From the moment Glenn decided on sea life over corporate life, Arlen, hurt and angry at being rejected, kept demanding that Glenn explain how he planned to make a living "studying how fish mate."

Andrea believed their son was simply following his heart, while Arlen was convinced that Glenn often used their rocky relationship to rationalize his decisions, which usually were whatever Arlen opposed. It had been that way for at least 10 years. When Glenn was nine, Arlen signed him up for Little League, a typical proud father wanting to teach his boy about America's game. Of course, Glenn's playing baseball was as much for Arlen as it was for Glenn. After only four games, however, Glenn told his father he was giving up the game, because, he said, "It's boring and I don't like the other kids laughing at me when I strike out or drop the ball." Not even Arlen's promise to come home early to practice with him could change his mind. Glenn never played baseball again. And Arlen somehow felt cheated out of one of his fatherly rights.

About the time Glenn dumped baseball, Arlen's career began taking off and a furious travel schedule kept him away from home much of the time, which drove a wedge between father and son that widened over time. As their alienation escalated, Glenn, who could read his father's moods like a book, relished provoking Arlen's anger. And so the harder Arlen pushed against marine biology, the harder Glenn held to it.

When it came to Glenn and just about anything, Arlen's patience was on a short leash. Even just talking about his relationship with Glenn, he would see red in a flash, as he had that morning in his argument with Andrea. Now, regretting his insensitive behavior, he replayed their exchange in his head. "Try talking to Glenn, Arlen," Andrea had urged, practically begging him. "Really talking to him. Listen to his heart, not just his words. He can't always say to you what he feels. He thinks you'll misread his meaning."

"I'm the ogre as usual, right Andrea? I'm not sure it matters what I say any more. To him or to you. Whatever I say or however I say it, it's always wrong or hurtful," Arlen complained, beginning to feel sorry for himself.

"No, my dear, you're not the ogre," she disagreed gently, trying hard not to sound patronizing. "You're the father. You're suppose to be the mature one. You're head of a huge corporation, for God's sake. You've got to be the role model." Then she paused, hoping her message might penetrate his thick skull.

"Will you call him today?" she asked, her tone taking on the tender edge of a plea.

"Today? You must be kidding, with all the crap coming down around me here. As soon as I clean up this mess, I'll call him, I promise you. But, quite honestly, Andy, I don't know how much good it will do." Growing nervous and fidgety now, Arlen jabbed the speaker phone button, moved behind his desk chair, and tightly gripped the head rest with both hands.

Expecting her to scold him, Andrea surprised him. "Were you always as practical as you are now, Arlen?" she queried, pulling him in a different direction. "Didn't you ever do something simply because it felt right—without worrying about what others thought?" He said nothing. "Did you do everything *your* father wanted you to do?"

Her questions disarmed him momentarily. He knew what she was trying to do, but he didn't know how to counter, or maybe just didn't want to. It infuriated him that she often knew his private thoughts better than he did. He knew he couldn't deal with any more unanswerable questions right now.

"Come on, Andy. I'm just not sure he and I can relate to each other at the moment—and I don't want to make things any worse."

Her tone remained compassionate. "But that's just it, Arlen my dear. I don't know how or when it happened, but somewhere along the way you lost the ability to put yourself in your son's shoes and see the world as he does. Can't you remember what it was like to be driven by your dreams?"

Arlen's thoughts were rushing in all directions at once now, ripping at his conscience. "Maybe I have ... maybe I have," he said uncertainly, unable to think of anything else to say.

His relationship with Glenn had gradually evolved into a misguided game of "one upmanship," he thought, instantly realizing how similar it was to the game he'd played during his climb to the top of the Royal corporate ladder.

"Please, Arlen, think hard about this." Andrea was trying to reach the inner him. "I know you've got your hands full right now with Royal's problems, but they can't be more important than Glenn's welfare, can they?" she goaded. "This is important ... to Glenn ... to you ... and to me."

The reference to herself clutched at his emotions, just as she had intended it to. Arlen sat back down, perched his elbows on the desk, closed his eyes, and clasped his hands in front of his face. "I know," he whispered weakly. "I know."

"You've got to love your son for who he is. He's not you. And you're wrong to expect him to be." Her voice broke slightly.

"Andy, let me ...," he started, before she abruptly cut him off, her voice controlled again, except for a slight tremble. "So what if he doesn't love baseball? So what if he's not dying to jump on the corporate merry-go-round? So what if he's not a perfect duplicate of you?" She swallowed so hard Arlen heard it.

"Why didn't you follow in your father's footsteps?" She knew the answer, but wanted him to say it aloud. Arlen's father, Ben, approaching 80 now and retired, had spent his entire adult life as the sole owner of a corner candy store in the busy Flatbush section of Brooklyn. He still lived in the same two-story house next to the store that had been home to Arlen and his younger brother and older sister. Ben was easy-going and uninspired, content with the six-block square that was his world. His hopes for his children, who he doted on, however, barely extended beyond high school and the family candy store. Ben's limited view of what his children's futures could be held down Arlen's brother and sister from realizing their potential, but not him. He used his father's lack of ambition as the impetus to stoke his own drive and dreams.

"Well, why didn't you follow in your father's footsteps?" Andrea asked again, this time more forcefully.

"You know the answer as well as I do," Arlen replied lethargically. "But I ..."

"There are no buts in this case." Her voice snapped out her frustration. "Don't do to your son what you'd never allow anybody else to do to him ... or to you."

Her persistence was starting to wear him down. He slumped in his chair and rubbed his eyes methodically, seeking some form of spiritual clarity. Pangs of guilt assaulted him. He knew Andrea was right about much of what she'd said. He loved his son, he kept telling himself, yet he couldn't figure out why he had so much trouble expressing that love in ways that didn't drive him further away.

He was about to speak when her voice was in his ear again. "Have you nothing to say? Arlen, please talk to me," she pleaded.

Several seconds passed before Arlen returned. "I'm thinking ... and wondering, that's all. I'll call Glenn later today." He sounded sincere, though a bit tentative.

Somewhat startled by his sudden shift in tone, Andrea jumped at the opening. "That sounds like a super idea. I think he's planning to be in his apartment most of the day studying, so you ought to be able ..."

Just then, a penetrating, low-pitched buzz cut off Arlen's daydreaming. He popped the button on his speaker phone. "Yes, Susan?"

"It's a Megan Walters on the line. She says you're expecting her call. She wouldn't tell me what it's about, but insisted you'd want to speak to her. Is she right?"

"Yep. I'll take it." He stared blankly at the blinking line several moments before grabbing the receiver.

* * * * * * * * *

"Hi, Megan, wondered when I'd hear from you again." Arlen used his best "Mr. Royster, CEO" voice. Megan Walters was president of a highly regarded executive search firm—Walters, Stephens & Joseph—specializing in top-level executive management positions, particularly CEOs and COOs.

Her voice was ringing with excitement. "Hi, Arlen. Sorry, I've been out of touch for a few days. I was away on a business trip, checking things out in Dallas and Chicago."

He had worked with Walters in the past to fill several VP slots. She had the charm skills to get in the front door, and the nose to sniff out hidden potential from wordy resumes and 10-minute phone chats. Articulate, well-connected and persistent in a nonirritating way, Walters, who pronounced her first name with a long "e" and instantly corrected anyone who mispronounced it, had approached Arlen four weeks earlier on behalf of Mahoney Inns & Resorts, an old-line hotel chain and Royal's major competitor. Mahoney Inns, which had recently repurchased two million shares of its stock to extinguish persistent rumors of takeover attempts, was secretly on the prowl for a new CEO. The company needed a top executive who could lead it in the development of a new line of upscale executive suites in North America and launch a long-awaited expansion into major cities in Europe and South America.

Bruce Mahoney, the company's 85-year-old founder and dean of America's hotel industry, had been the company's only CEO and chairman until two years ago. At that time, he partially retired, maintaining his chairman title, while bowing to family pressures to keep corporate control in the hands of a Mahoney by appointing his marginally competent grandson, Fred, as acting CEO. To the elder Mahoney that meant, as he explained to Walters, "giving Fred just enough rope to hang himself and threaten the family's asset base so that I can remove him without objections before he does any serious damage to my company."

Apparently, Mahoney's plan was working, Walters had explained to Arlen during their initial conversation, because, although "this is very hush-hush," she said, "Bruce told me that Fred's out, although Fred doesn't know it yet. He wants you, Arlen. He likes your experience, your professional manner, your tenacious bottom-line orientation, and, most of all, he's thrilled that your last name *isn't* Mahoney."

Arlen's curiosity got the better of him. "Why would Mahoney, whom I'd met socially a few times at hotel industry dinners and conferences, single me out?" he wondered. Intrigued to know the answer, Arlen agreed to meet privately with Mahoney, away from roving and speculative eyes.

A week ago Monday, Arlen and Mahoney dined for three hours at the elder statesman's penthouse apartment atop the 63-story Mahoney Towers Office Complex near the United Nations building on the east side of Manhattan. When Arlen stepped off the chairman's private elevator, the prime rib buffet, which Mahoney had somehow learned was Arlen's favorite, was beautifully laid out, and the two men dined alone, save for one unobtrusive waiter. Their conversation meandered among sports, current events, and the troubles of the hotel industry. Not until dessert did Mahoney broach the topic that had brought them together. After several minutes of preliminaries about their general views of the future, Mahoney cut to the chase.

"What really turns you on about being a business person, Arlen?" he asked, his deep bass voice defying his frail posture.

"Helping companies discover their true potential," Arlen said without a moment's hesitation, peering into Mahoney's lively blue eyes, which contrasted with his milky white hair, still thick and plentiful.

"What's the key to good managing, in your view?" Mahoney probed deftly, politely.

"Never getting caught with your pants down," Arlen shot back glibly. He then reconsidered. "Let me rephrase that. Knowing your industry, your organization, and your people so well that nothing could ever surprise you." Arlen hadn't thought much about his definition of managing before Mahoney's question; today, four weeks later, thinking back on his impromptu answer, he felt like a soothsayer.

Walters' eagerness was still evident. "I am sorry for the delay in getting back to you ... but I think it was worth the wait." She paused, allowing his curiosity to build. "I don't know what you said to Mahoney, Arlen, but he loved you. If you're agreeable, he wants to begin talking contract."

He never expected something to happen this fast—and this easily. The ego boost couldn't have come at a better time. He instantly began weighing his options.

"That's great to hear, Megan. I really enjoyed getting to know him a little better. He's quite a guy. A very shrewd businessman, I suspect." Then to lighten the mood, he added, "Although I have to wonder about his jumping to a conclusion about someone's character and competence after just two hours."

Walters picked up instantly on Arlen's meaning. "Oh, don't worry about Bruce. He's as sharp as he ever was. And don't let his fatherly manner fool you either. He does his homework and he always has good reasons for everything he does."

"I'm sure. Believe me, I'm honored to even be considered as his successor. But I'll be honest with you, Megan, I can't pursue this right now. Some new problems have cropped up here that demand my full attention. And that's probably gonna be true for the next few weeks." He stopped, not wanting to give away any more.

"Nothing too serious, I hope," she replied, the air rushing out of her balloon. She was furiously trying to read between the lines. "Arlen, is this your way of politely blowing this off?" Walters was never one to beat around the bush, Arlen remembered.

"Not at all. I'm definitely interested, based on what little I know. But priorities are such right now that I can't divert my concentration from my responsibilities to Royal and its concerns. That's all I can tell you right now. I'm sure Bruce would expect nothing less of me if I were working for him."

"I see," she said slowly, even though she didn't know what to make of his nebulous explanation.

Arlen's thoughts were racing in circles. Would he need another job soon? Was his tenure at Royal—not to mention his ability to be effective as a CEO—about to come to an end? Could he leave his mentor, Jim Stamps, at a time like this? Was staying at Royal the best thing for him? For his family? Should he get out before he's thrown out and his market value plunges?

He repositioned his torso, leaned forward, and squeezed the phone closer to his ear. "Please pass on to Bruce, Megan, that if he feels he needs to move forward right now, I completely understand and wish him the best."

"I don't think that'll be necessary," she said reassuringly. "How about if I get back to you in 10 days or so and see how things are going?" she asked gingerly, trying not to let her disappointment show.

"Sounds good. I'll talk to you then, Megan. Take care." He replaced the phone in its cradle, removed his glasses and massaged his temples. "First things first," he mumbled under his breath.

A quick glance at his watch told him time wouldn't wait. He stood up, stretched, moved to the doorway adjoining O'Reilly's suite, arched his head around the doorjamb so she could see only his face and asked, "Susan, what does the schedule look like?"

O'Reilly jumped at the sound of Arlen's unexpected voice. She looked up to see his haggard face. "Sorry, didn't mean to sneak up on you," he apologized.

"Boy, you look terrible, Arlen. Why don't you take a break? I can hold off the hordes for an hour or so."

He flashed a big smile and winked, as if to say, "Don't worry. Everything's under control."

She hoped they were, but somehow doubted it.

* * * * * * * * * *

Down the hall and around the corner from Arlen's office, Mike Keller and John Grubner were huddled in Keller's office, the door locked and phone calls on hiatus, set to begin their third secretive tete-a-tete of the day.

"Now, let's make sure we understand each other," Keller lectured coldly, his hand pumping up and down in front of Grubner's face. "I'll be meeting with Lieberman and Gross in the next day or two to lock up their support and start them calling other board members. How soon can you get in touch with Ray? Monday will be here before you can say ... 'Adios, Arlen Royster.'"

Robert Ray, Jr. was a member of Royals' board and a senior partner in Ohle & Orville Associates, a highly successful real estate and insurance firm based in Boston. Ray and Grubner became acquainted several years back when they served together on Royal's benefits and compensation committee, and discovered they shared many of the same interests, particularly long-distance running. Grubner had persuaded Ray to join him in several senior mini-marathons held in the New York area. Their custom was to conclude the runs with an expensive bottle of French wine, paid for by the one with the slowest time.

"He's on the west coast," Grubner reported sheepishly, "but I'm tracking him down now."

"Find him, whatever it takes," Keller commanded, leering at the nervous accountant. "We've got to know where he stands on Arlen and get to him before Arlen's people do. We need him on our side. Think about the consequences if he's not with us, John. I mean, you're the perfect scapegoat for this so-called financial reporting scheme. Nobody's really gonna believe that the CFO didn't know anything about this. Besides, even if you didn't know, they'll say you should've. If the axe does fall in our direction because we didn't have the votes, your head will be the first one on the chopping block. You know Arlen's doing everything he can to make sure it isn't gonna be his. Do whatever it takes to find Ray ASAP and don't stop until you do."

In Keller's emerging plan, Ray was the crucial member of his anti-Royster coalition. He knew that Grubner was the key to locking up Ray, and he thought he had the key to locking up Grubner. Unbeknownst to most of Grubner's colleagues, Keller knew the quiet CFO hungered for the title and power he felt he'd always been denied.

"I'm not convinced trying to talk to Bob before the board meeting will do any good, Mike. He might resent it and then be more apt to turn against us." Grubner got up and walked around the meeting table. He stopped on the opposite side, stuffed his hands in his pockets, and shivered as if an Arctic blast had just blown through the room.

Keller, suppressing his irritation with Grubner's doubting-Thomas attitude, stood and walked directly in front of the thin CFO. "You know, John," he began, revealing a patronizing grin, "I've been starting to think about some of the things I might do when I become CEO ... like ... well, like needing an executive vice president, for example ... someone who would report directly to me and ... and handle only the most sensitive and important projects for the company." Keller was improvising, but effectively playing to Grubner's weak spot.

When Keller said "executive VP," Grubner's eyes widened for just an instant, a reflex caught by Keller's keen eye. Keller inched closer to Grubner, subconsciously trying to close the psychological gap between them.

The notion of an executive vice president, an heir apparent to the CEO, had on several occasions been proposed to Arlen by different members of his executive staff. "You really could use some help, Arlen," Bob Azoulette urged last year when the subject came up during a top management retreat. "That's no reflection on you, Arlen, but the CEO job has mushroomed in so many ways that one person can't be expected to adequately handle it anymore." True to form, Arlen rejected the idea out of hand, afraid that admitting he needed help would be seen as a sign of weakness. Yet, among some on his staff, the lure of such a position lingered in their fantasies, Grubner's included.

"How would you feel about being Royal's first-ever executive VP?" Keller asked, touching Grubner's bony forearm, his eyes trained on his face. "I think that could be a smart move for both of us. Nobody knows this company like we do."

Grubner subtly pulled back from Keller and returned to his chair at the conference table, trying to imagine himself with the XVP title. "Would you be willing to put that in writing, Mike?" He stared coldly at Keller, who, after a moment, looked away, wondering if Grubner was serious.

Before Keller could say anything, the phone rang. He moved quickly to his desk, spoke for a moment and then put the receiver down. "Royster wants to see me again," he said, annoyed. Keller returned to the meeting area and was met by a suddenly more confident-looking Grubner.

"That's certainly an interesting proposition," Grubner admitted coyly. "I wonder if you really mean it, Mike, or whether you're simply baiting me." Keller smiled at him as if to say, "It's all yours, if you play it my way."

"Come on, John, you know me better than that. This stuff's too important and time is too short to play games. I'm as serious as I can be—and I want you as executive VP when we finally get rid of Royster." Grubner stared hard into Keller's unwavering eyes searching for a flicker of sensitivity. The CFO's wistful expression told Keller that, despite Grubner's expressed skepticism, his craving for what he didn't have but wanted was stronger than all other pulls.

Grubner knew unequivocally that the price for an XVP title would be delivering Ray to Keller. When Grubner thought about his future at Royal if Arlen remained in power, he knew his days were numbered. His options were limited. His only legitimate hope, as shaky as it was, was to join forces with Keller, whose forcefulness Grubner admired but whose underhandedness he distrusted. But if they won the power struggle, Grubner told himself, he'd become Royal's first executive VP. That prospect blinded him to all the danger signs he would otherwise detect.

Grubner walked shoulder-to-shoulder with Keller to the door, the two appearing to outsiders as close, trusting buddies. They stopped a few feet from the door. "Ray's vital to making this whole thing happen, John. Don't let me down," Keller said without emotion, offering his hand. Grubner shook it firmly and nodded his understanding. Then he left. As the door shut behind him, Keller, pleased with himself, believed he now had control over Grubner's disguised ambition.

"Power," Keller ruminated silently, savoring the very sound of the word. "The power of power itself. Its temptation can be irresistible, even to those who claim no interest in it. And its pull can make people do things they never before imagined—and would be embarrassed to admit later."

Then Keller realized he could use the same promise of the executive VP job to entice others to join his cause. Of the five VPs besides Grubner, only Azoulette and Bernard might be susceptible, Keller calculated quickly. Azoulette had come to Royal three years ago, ostensibly to be the orchestrator of Arlen's ambitious plan to take Royal international on a grand scale. But not long after he arrived, growth plans had to be scrapped indefinitely when the world economy stalled. Azoulette understood the realities involved, but was frustrated nonetheless. He wanted—needed, was more accurate—a bigger challenge. Although Azoulette wasn't one of Keller's biggest fans, Keller figured he could seduce Azoulette to join him if he could convince the marketing VP that the move overseas would come sooner under a Keller-led regime.

As he entered the hallway leading to Arlen's office, Keller's thoughts switched to Gloria Bernard, Royal's most junior VP, both in tenure and age. Keller knew the risks in approaching her, but he thought it worth the gamble, given the potential payoff. He thought his strongest approach would be talking to her about his inner fear that a tainted Arlen would destroy Royal's good name on Wall Street. The lure for Bernard, Keller thought, would be the opportunity to reestablish Royal's badly tarnished reputation and make a name for herself among the elite of the "Street" around which her world revolved.

If he could nail down her support, Keller fathomed, he'd considerably strengthen his pull with other board members. The more chinks I can put in Arlen's armor, Keller reasoned, the more vulnerable he becomes. He'd pursue Azoulette and Bernard later. In the meantime, Arlen was waiting.

Picking up his pace, he soon entered the CEO's outer office and greeted Susan O'Reilly with a congeniality that camouflaged his deep-rooted disdain for Royal's "temporary" leader.

7

Organization— Integrating Strategies and Tactics

Alexander Trowbridge had agonized over the decision. And once he'd made it, he agonized over how to best tell those affected. The only things he knew for sure was that *he* had to be the one to deliver the bad news and that how he organized and presented his message would determine whether it was accepted or rejected. The memorandum from him to all employees, titled "NAM Staff and Budget Reductions FY '88," began: "This is undoubtedly the most difficult memo I have had to write since becoming the National Association of Manufacturers' President almost eight years ago."

The three page, single-spaced memo explained frankly and in vivid detail the rationale for and implications of his decision to cut 25 staff jobs and $1 million from the trade group's budget. "I couldn't delegate this—it was too important," says the former Secretary of Commerce under Lyndon Johnson. "People's jobs and lives were being affected. It had to come from me. That's what being a leader means." At the time, NAM, like most of its 13,000 member companies, had been hit broadside by the unfolding economic recession. Trowbridge knew that NAM employees were running scared about the future, closely watching top management's every word and action for any sign of hope or, short of that, fair play.

That's why before Trowbridge composed the memo, he consulted his senior staff on employees' and members' likely reactions to the decision. As Trowbridge tells it, his staff realized that their credibility would be on trial and that they couldn't afford to be seen as insensitive to the harsh realities of the crisis. The memo outlined management's decision to eliminate the NAM executive car and to freeze the salaries of the executive vice president and two senior vice presidents the following year, and of Trowbridge's personal decision to cut his own salary by 10 percent. "These moves were more symbolic than substantive and probably didn't make anybody affected by the layoffs feel any better," he admits. "But we wanted them to know we understood and would take a little of the hit, too. I think it helped our credibility by not trying to 'blow smoke' or fool anybody. When you do, it just comes back to haunt you."

Trowbridge, a naturally compassionate man, lost much sleep thinking about how to structure and present his sobering message. He knew that demonstrating his personal concern was important, but it wasn't sufficient; how he arranged the news and orchestrated its delivery could be the decisive difference. Besides the memorandum, he considered a number of other methods, such as hosting a large meeting or personally visiting departments hit hardest by the layoffs. Ultimately, he concluded that, more than anything, he needed to safeguard against his message and its rationale being misinterpreted or distorted. He didn't want to risk someone else putting their own spin on the message. To control the message and its initial presentation, he placed his thoughts and words on paper—thereby creating a fixed and permanent record—and thus assured sending the same message to everybody simultaneously.

The Trowbridge/NAM scenario illustrates the principle of organization (as well as compassion) in action—and highlights several features comprising the "O" in the C-C-O-S model, among them the intricacies of selecting media and linking CEO communication to organizational goals. This chapter focuses on the strategic and tactical factors influencing how top managers ought to organize and practice their communication role. After further describing organization, we discuss its component parts in some depth. After that, we take an inside look at how CEO Tom Clausen led the rescue of Bank of America and how his hand-picked successor, Richard Rosenberg, whose management style contrasts substantially with Clausen's, is shepherding the financial giant through a mega-merger.

Aspects of Organization

The principle of organization embraces the core strategic and tactical aspects of CEO communication. Organization is crucial to effective CEO communication because it assures that the CEO's activities are aligned with the organization's mission and coordinated with other managers' communication efforts. In operational terms, organization helps ensure that how a CEO communicates with employees fits within a company's culture and traditions.

Organization is a highly complex and practical principle. It involves the CEO in creating an appropriate message, merging the message into the organization's overall communication plan, and correlating that plan with other managers' communication activities. The CEO's communication efforts should never be in conflict with or detached from the corporation's mission or what other managers are saying and doing. And, the CEO must recognize his or her responsibility for making sure that *all* communication—particularly communication aimed at multiple levels of an organizaion—is bound together through a *cohesive, systemwide* strategy understood by all.

Organizing the communication process is vital because no CEO can hope to, or should want to, operate as an independent agent, especially in a multisite company. The job of assuring ongoing communication with employees and other key stakeholders is simply too big for one individual or even one tier of management. Inside any organization, regardless of its size or type of business, communication between managers and employees never stops. It may be positive or negative, but it's constant. Given that fact, overworked CEOs need managers up and down the organization chart to serve as local agents for them, acting to implement and reinforce the universal communication plan. As influential as the CEO's voice may be, it is only one voice—a voice that will soon fade without a strong supporting chorus behind it.

Whether an organization's communication strategy bubbles to the top or flows downward, it must incorporate those at the top to have any chance of catching on systemwide. Allstate Insurance's Donald Craib, who has since assumed the top slot at TWA, realized this when he launched a structural overhaul of the company in 1982. The CEO recognized that the key to remaining competitive was bolstering manager and employee productivity rates. This meant decentralizing a centrally-controlled and operated company.

The strategic plan that eventually emerged attempted from the outset "to involve management at every level and in every operating department," Craib explains. The vehicle for obtaining this involvement was the tight link between Allstate's communication plan, which involved Craib as the major player, and its companywide strategic change plan. "We placed more emphasis than ever on communication throughout the company—not as a gesture, but as a management tool in support of our growth objectives," notes the CEO.[1]

In broad terms, the principle of organization comprises three distinct, but closely related, functions:

1. *Designing* CEO communication that augments overall organizational and communication objectives,

2. *Integrating* the CEO's internal communication role with other managers' communication responsibilities and efforts, and

3. *Choosing* appropriate media for delivering the CEO's messages.

Designing Communication That "Fits"

CEO communication strategy and tactics should grow out of and conform to an organization's natural structure and to employees' expectations. If the top manager's efforts don't fit into an organization's cultural climate, then communication everywhere in the organization is likely to be off-target. To design an organizational structure that fits, several factors are important:

1. Crafting an organizational structure that encourages systemwide communication.
2. Enticing the CEO to participate in major communication decisions.
3. Constructing a sharply-focused CEO communication plan.
4. Establishing a productive counseling relationship between the CEO and top communication professionals.

"Structuring" Communication

Through their decisions and management styles, CEOs create, intentionally or otherwise, the psychological and physical structures that shape the nature of information flow and relationships. The pliability of that structure will either encourage or discourage communication among employees and managers across organizational levels and within organizational units. The CEO's influence on the company's communication climate radiates from the top manager's decisions on a number of fundamental management issues, including the nature of reporting relationships, reliance on the chain of command, arrangement of office and meeting space, and use of new communication technologies, such as electronic mail and real-time management information systems.

In a government or military organization like the Navy Department, for example, which is heavily bureaucratic and separates members based on rank and title, routine communication will be slow and deliberate, tightly channeled from level to level, and relatively constrained in tone. In contrast, in a less rigid and more dynamic organizational environment, like a high-technology firm such as Apple Computer, communication will occur frequently and openly in a variety of settings, moving in multiple directions simultaneously, and involving employees from different levels and different divisions with little regard for formal title or rank.

Every company has within it perceived and real barricades and gatekeepers that may either restrict or expedite the CEO's and other managers' communication efforts. Viewpoints vary over the ideal role a CEO should play in influencing the contour of the organizational structure. Some say the CEO should set the overall corporate strategy and then leave it to front-line managers to put together the appropriate design. Others say the CEO should pick an organizational framework that fits his or her philosophy of managing. Whatever the CEO's obligation, the essential point is this: CEOs are the primary architects of organizational structure, which by implication makes them the architects of the communication structure as well.

The precise nature of those structures will ease or hinder the process of integrating management communication up, down, and across the organization. For integration to occur, the CEO must be committed to making it happen, as well as persuading and holding managers who might otherwise resist participating in the integration process accountable. All too frequently, managers may want to nix structural alterations that open paths of communication, because they fear that by sharing information or decision making with employees they'll weaken their own positions and authority.

Despite some managers' reluctance to accept the new order, more and more CEOs are beginning to dismantle tightly-bound, communication-strangling hierarchical structures. Replacing the multilayered pyramids are flatter, more flexible, open, "high involvement" organizational designs—designs more receptive to new ideas and information, more nimble in making decisions and acting on them, and more responsive to feedback from employees, customers, and the marketplace. These reconfigured structures tend to be free-flowing, interactive communication systems—a core ingredient to manager-employee team efforts.

An illustration of one company that's been undergoing such a metamorphosis for about 10 years now is General Electric, a multibillion dollar, 300,000 employee operation. Under the direction of Chairman and CEO Jack Welch, who took charge in 1981, the giant conglomerate has been successfully struggling with the slow, lengthy, and sometimes painful process of restructuring. Fortified by continual retraining of many GE managers, Welch has created a textbook case for the "big company operating small": divisions operate independently yet share resources; decision-making authority has been pushed to the rank-and-file as part of a new emphasis on teamwork, which is expected and rewarded; and structural change is being accompanied by cultural change.

Leading the charge and the cheers is the highly visible and outspoken Welch, whose face seems to appear on the cover of leading business publications almost as often as Lee Iacocca's or Ross Perot's. The centerpiece of his change strategy is reshaping the GE manager from one who relies on power to one who relies on persuasion. "We've got to take out the boss element," notes Welch. "We're going to win on our ideas, not by whips and chains."[2]

Fueling the structural "flattening" of organizations is the need to make them more fluid—that is, to remove obstacles that constrict the movement of information and ideas among employees, thereby increasing workers' autonomy as well as their perceived and actual control over their worklives. As corporate bureaucracies are compressed, headquarter staffs and layers of field management—especially middle managers—are squeezed out, resulting in a redefined notion of "span of control" for those managers who remain. Whereas the rule of thumb used to be that span of control meant five or six units or employees reporting to a manager, today, with the accent on self-managing and horizontal designs, there don't seem to be any hard-and-fast rules. It's no longer unusual, for example, for a senior executive to directly oversee 10 or 15 different departments or divisions. And what many managements are learning the hard way is that you can't manage 15 the same way you manage five.

With these shifts in decision-making authority to nonmanagement employees comes a new kind of manager-employee relationship, one demanding more sharing of information and depending on mutual trust. Such adjustments don't come easily for many managers and they almost never happen quickly. They require lots of convincing and reassuring, mostly by the CEO, as well as on-the-job training on ways to adapt the old, rigid, "telling" styles of unidirectional communication to the new, more flexible, "listening" styles of multidirectional communication.

Employee autonomy does not lessen the need for integration of functions and people—quite the contrary, the need increases. The integration process will not work without frequent communication between managers and employees who need to work together to make the new system operate. No longer obligated by formal reporting relationships to share information and collaborate, managers in decentralized structures need to realize that open, give-and-take communication is fundamental to fostering teamwork and building employee commitment.

More than anyone else, the CEO turns on or off the spigot of an organization's communication pipelines, which is a powerful form of indirect control over an organization. Ralph Larsen, CEO of Johnson & Johnson's Interventional Systems Company, describes his role as that of an "orchestra leader." Referring to the structural overhaul he guided his organization through as the 1990s began, he attempted to give his members inspiration and direction, while simultaneously making sure they had the freedom to express themselves as individuals.[3]

Turning on the communication spigot may be indirect. Sandy Sigoloff, former CEO of Wickes Companies, insists on answering his own office phone—a seemingly trivial gesture, but one that sends a powerful message throughout the company that cumbersome bureaucracy is not welcome and that managers should be easily accessible to their employees. Or it may be as direct as Managing Director Scott Kohno moving his "walled-in" corner office into the middle of an unwalled work floor in the Los Angeles-based design firm he heads. He took this unconventional step to remotivate his 30 employees. Although some were skeptical at first, he soon found his contact with staff was "100 times more frequent," which helped "move the company 10 times faster." The continuous contact reenergized employees, who then devoted less time to trying to hide problems and more to solving them.[4]

CEO Involvement in Decision Making

In an ideal world, those responsible for executing decisions will always be directly involved in formulating those decisions. Unfortunately, the real world doesn't always work that way, especially when it comes to CEOs and their expanding communication role. Until quite recently, most CEOs isolated themselves from communication planning, preferring to delegate that mundane task to underlings in personnel or public relations. But to assure that CEO communication strategies are aligned with the organization's mission and communication plan, CEOs must be active participants in the discussions and debates behind formation of organization-wide communication strategies.

The advantages of involvement are numerous. For one thing, the top dog's involvement leads to his or her buy-in and personal commitment, and ultimately to an embracing of the CCO role. For another, nobody in an organization possesses the CEO's understanding of the company's direction, capabilities, and potential. That insight alone can make the difference between a fuzzy and a sharply focused strategy. There's simply no substitute for the CEO's unique vision of the future, intuition, knowledge of the company and key players, sensitivity to organizational politics, and an ability to engender emotional commitment. Furthermore, if others in an organization, particularly lower-level managers, see the leader personally involved in a program, they'll automatically attach more credence to it and want to jump on the bandwagon.

A number of CEOs interviewed for this book were adamant in their belief that the top executive can't remain aloof from communication planning. That's the best way, they argue, to make sure things are done as they should be. One such CEO is Bill Davila, former president of Vons, the largest grocery chain in southern California. Several years ago, Vons' board and advertising agency approached Davila about serving as the company's spokesperson in its TV and print advertising campaigns. Articulate and outgoing, he was a natural choice.

Davila knew that other companies, including grocery trend-setters such as Pathmark, were using top executives successfully in similar roles. But he hesitated, expressing concern about placing himself in a position of carrying the company's reputation on his shoulders—and he worried about the potential of jeopardizing Vons' credibility if an ad in which he appeared was ever found to be offensive or untruthful. With some reluctance, he finally agreed, only on the condition that every bit of information included in ads was absolutely accurate and that he would never be portrayed as a "pitchman or used car salesman," as he put it.

To ensure that these conditions would be met, Davila assigned himself responsibility for approving all ads. "I was involved in setting the tone of the ads and we assigned the manager of advertising the job of acting as the 'guardian' of the president, if you will, to make sure I wasn't hurting Vons or myself," explains Davila, who recently retired as CEO, but remains as Vons' spokesperson and a member of the board. "Our research has shown that I come across as believable, honest, and informative," he notes. "As long as that's the case, I'll continue to be the spokesperson for Vons as long as the company wants me."

CEO involvement is not, however, a panacea; it has its limits. There are some top managers, like Norm Leaper, a one-time corporate communication manager who is now president of the International Association of Business Communicators (IABC), who have the urge to be too involved in planning and execution. He openly admits that he'd like to see every piece of paper before it leaves IABC headquarters "to make sure it's concise and to the point, and doesn't beat around the bush"—even though he realizes how impractical that is. He chooses when and how to be involved very deliberately.

Similarly, Phil Quigley of Pacific Bell would like to review all messages going to his 50,000 plus employees before they're released—not so much to proofread, but to make sure employees' feelings have been adequately considered. The president and CEO, who's been with AT&T since 1967, says, "I go over every word before I send the message. I try to be sensitive to the people on the receiving end. When you're communicating directly with employees, you can't afford to make a mistake, to leave an answerable question unanswered. Every word is critical—you can accidentally send the wrong message by using inappropriate verbiage."

Quigley tries to be sensitive to how workers are likely to react to a message and to the person delivering it. Ultimately, CEOs can't escape responsibility for the tone and content of all companywide communication, no matter whose name happens to be attached to it. When employees or stockholders are upset, they'll come looking for the person in charge. And when they do, that person had better know what's going on and be ready to explain. That's precisely why top managers today can't afford to remain segregated from the strategy-formulation and planning processes—if they expect communication strategies to be on target, reflecting appropriate organizational priorities and nuances.

Turning Planning into a "Plan"

Once the planning decisions have been made, the various strategies supporting them should be woven together into a single, cohesive communication plan. Like any effective plan, a communication plan specifies details, such as schedule, deployment of human and capital resources, budget, and management responsibilities. Frequently, the vice president of corporate communication or public relations—who is probably the CEO's personal advisor on communication matters—draws the primary responsibility for developing the plan and supervising its implementation. That way the CEO's special leadership role isn't likely to be overlooked or underestimated as the plan is formed.

It's precisely this sort of participatory planning process which can ensure that the plan will reflect and support the organization's goals. Before the plan itself becomes corporate gospel, a draft ought to be shared with those managers who will be most involved in and responsible for its execution. Since they hold a personal stake in the outcome, their feedback may be the best guarantee that all parties' interests, most notably the CEO's, will be incorporated into the overall plan.

Current reality, however, is often far from the ideal. We know of very few companies that have developed distinct and dedicated CEO communication plans. Most company communication plans aren't that specific about individual roles and responsibilities of particular top-level executives. Decisions about how and when to use the CEO as the company's CCO are frequently made on an ad hoc basis, which can make for CEO communication that is disconnected and unpredictable. One company that has seen the value of creating stand-alone CEO communication plans is Avon Products.

Hicks Waldron, CEO of Avon from 1984 to 1989, brought to the company an open communication philosophy that marked his stewardship. "I've come to realize that the business of communicating is not just communicating *about* business," he says. "It's communicating to *improve* business. And a substantial part of that job belongs to top management."[5] So seriously did Waldron take this responsibility that he insisted that a *top management* communication plan be prepared and revised annually, and that he and his top management team be involved in casting its strategic direction. In fact, the plan only becomes a plan, emphasizes Waldron, "when I sign off on it. Then it's a plan."

Such strident language reveals Waldron's ardent belief in purposeful, planned communication, and in directly involving the CEO in forming the plan. This was the strategy underlying his leadership of Avon's successful restructuring in the mid-1980s, as the company attempted to adapt its products and distribution system to women's shifting roles from the home-front to the workplace. Waldron assigns much of the credit for Avon's successful turnaround to the plan: "We couldn't have come nearly so far or so fast without a strategic plan that included a solid, forceful communication program."[6]

Avon's first communication plan for top management consisted of four pages of spread sheets, covering a three year time period, which designated the CEO's and chairman's proportional share of the responsibility for communicating with key stakeholder groups. The plan was organized by internal and external stakeholders—such as domestic and foreign security analysts, employees by division, and national and international press. In certain instances, even the target media were specified, such as an employee newsletter or a public speech.

To illustrate how it works, the plan for 1991 indicated that the CEO would assume 60 percent of the responsibility for interviews with local print media; for 1992, as the CEO's priorities shifted elsewhere based on the company's overall strategic plan, the chairman of the board would take on 70 percent of that duty. Regardless of how many adjustments might eventually be made in the plan, the Avon example points up the advantages of, first, anticipating the CEO's and other top managers' varying communication and leadership roles and responsibilities across situations and circumstances; and second, thoughtfully planning when and how to effectively deploy top managers in carrying out the plan.

Counseling the CEO

Behind most strong CEO-leaders, we found, is usually a counselor, a trusted comrade and expert who guides, cajoles, assists, challenges, and educates the top dog on communication and human relations issues. In fact, that's exactly the role communication VP Rick Jamieson is playing for CEO Arlen Royster. Although Arlen often bristles at his counselor's advice, because it puts the CEO in situations he finds uncomfortable, he seems to begrudgingly appreciate the fact he needs such help.

We can't stress enough the importance of CEOs having advisors who understand communication, leadership, and the organization's priorities and culture. But even all that isn't enough. The best counselors also can—and do—identify the CEO's strengths and weaknesses, and aren't afraid to give blunt and candid advice, even if it means puncturing the CEO's ego or pointing out faults. Indeed, top dogs typically criticize their staff public relations advisors for not being candid enough with them, according to a 1993 survey of The Omega Group's Chief Executives Council.[7]

Those CEOs interviewed who hold close working relationships with their top communication professional appeared most likely to understand the CEO's communication role and how it fits into overall communication strategy. The counselor, generally a vice president of public relations or corporate communication who has known the CEO for many years, usually has prime responsibility for devising and executing the company's strategic communication plan. Also, that individual needs to have an in-depth knowledge of communication, public opinion and human behavior, experience as a communication practitioner, and a thorough familiarity with the CEO's managerial and communication style and capabilities. Regrettably, only about half the CEO-respondents in national surveys completed for this book reported that their top-ranked communication practitioner reports directly to them.

Most CEOs need a communication alter-ego, a personal devil's advocate, more than they realize. Rarely are communication-related decisions black and white; they almost always encompass a host of interrelated and overlapping issues and possibilities, most of them gray. Consequently, CEOs, whether they admit it or not, subconsciously crave advisors who aren't hesitant about openly, yet discretely, challenging their decisions or pressing them to consider alternative points of view.

From the counselor's side, this relationship can be both the best and worst of times. Being the CEO's advisor has the advantage of placing the counselor at the CEO's elbow and near the center of decision making. At the same time, the advisor faces the disadvantage of playing a precarious, ever-shifting role fraught with built-in discomforts and hidden dangers. At any moment, a counselor may be transformed into the top dog's psychologist, conscience, battering ram or critic, especially when it comes to matters related to company reputation and relationships with stakeholder groups. Trusting CEO-counselor associations take time to mature. But once trust is established between CEO and advisor, the counselor's role becomes two-fold: first, to exploit and magnify the CEO's and the organization's strengths; and second, to minimize exposure of the CEO's and organization's weaknesses.

At times, professional counselors must be the messengers of news CEOs may not want to hear, such as "you're weak fielding questions from the media and need more training." The best counselors offer advice even if it means being brutally honest about the CEO's foibles or blind spots. At other times, counselors may double as teachers, coaching CEOs before they appear at a press conference or make a videotape for employees, for example. In the end, the nature of this relationship depends on what the CEO, far more than the counselor, allows it to become. But if CEO and counselor can agree on what they're trying to accomplish and have faith in each other, they're likely to operate as one mind.

That's precisely the kind of relationship Ron Rhody enjoyed with his CEO, Tom Clausen, at the Bank of America (explored later in this chapter). Clausen hardly ever refused a Rhody request, because, says Clausen, "If Ron felt my involvement was needed, then I knew it was important I do it. I always trusted his judgment." Rhody, a widely respected communication manager, earned that trust by understanding the top manager's special position, and by not misusing or wasting Clausen's time or stretching his communication capabilities past their natural limits.

Sometimes, counselors, who have healthy egos, too, may believe so completely in the efficacy of their position that their recommendations can become more like edicts. There are moments when that's exactly what's needed. When Sandy Sigoloff, former CEO of Wickes Cos., was exploring ways to save a dying, bankrupt company, his Senior Vice President of Communications, Mike Sitrick, recommended after considerable research and in no uncertain terms that Sigoloff be the company's spokesperson in the advertising campaign intended to rescue the organization from the jaws of its creditors. Says Sitrick: "Our research clearly showed that the company's reputation was linked to Sandy's reputation—and that if he put his reputation on the line, we had a chance to bring back customers and retain employees."

Typical of most media-shy CEOs, Sigoloff balked at Sitrick's suggestion, not wanting to get within 10 feet of a live TV camera. But Sitrick, firmly convinced that Sigoloff was the firm's strongest asset and last hope, persisted unrelentingly until finally a nervous, doubting Sigoloff agreed to do one TV advertisement as an experiment. The ad featured Sigoloff, sincere and articulate, standing in front of a company store, surrounded by a band of excited employees. It opened with him saying, "I'm Sandy Sigoloff, and I'm the toughest retailer in America." After delivering the message about cost and value, he closed with, "If you don't like it when you get home, we'll take it back." Then the camera panned back to the employee group, which shouted in unison, "We got the message, Mr. Sigoloff!"

Within weeks, that maiden commercial, the first in a series, pushed up sales at Wickes Furniture by 43 percent. Sigoloff figured it had to be a fluke, but even he finally had to admit that "something was working" when the year ended with all revenue indicators well above the prior year. "Those ads saved us. People believed in Sandy," says Sitrick. But what really convinced the tough retailer that he'd made a difference, especially to employees, was an incident just after the company emerged from Chapter 11. Sigoloff, dressed in jeans and a sport shirt, was shopping in one of the company's hardware stores on a Sunday morning. A young clerk spotted him from across the floor, ran over, hugged him, and blurted out, "Sandy, we really did it! Just like you said we would."

Integrating the CEO's Communication Role

As crucial as the CEO's role is to an organization's management communication effort, it's only one of many roles that must be played effectively if the overall communication program is to be successful. CEOs can't do it alone. Managers at every level have built-in supporting and reinforcing roles to play. Without coordination between CEO and all other managers, employees are likely to receive inconsistent and confusing messages. So essential are managers' augmenting roles that we believe all managers should be held directly accountable for the quality of their communication with employees and those to whom they report.

Attempting to maintain relationships with employees scattered around the country or the world demands ongoing and regular participation by local managers who need to see themselves as part of the CEO's field "sales force." "If you stop at yourself, it'll never happen," says Carl Sardegna, president since 1985 of Blue Cross/Blue Shield of Maryland, based near Baltimore.

How top managers translate a communication plan into action—through their tone, word choice, and timing—determines how other managers define their communication obligations. Although the CEO's and other managers' roles differ, as they should, Vons' Davila points out that the varying roles still must reinforce one another: "It's not that I'm trying to delegate away the day-to-day communication with workers. I'm just being realistic. Lower-level managers see them more than I do, as they should. I want employees to have as much confidence in their supervisors' leadership as they do in mine."

Managers don't always know or understand their role—beyond turning a profit. Sometimes, their supporting roles must be spelled out to them—either in their job description or by the CEO's example. If a CEO fails to make expectations clear, managers may tune out and turn off—a lesson Tom Priselac, president and chief executive officer of Los Angeles' Cedars-Sinai Medical Center, learned the hard way. Several years ago, when he was COO and filled with high hopes of improving organizational performance, he implemented a new communication program across the expansive medical facility that had him making unscheduled visits and holding unplanned meetings with cross-sections of executive and employee groups from various working units throughout the organization.

Priselac's hope was to "raise the collective performance of the whole organization." The CEO says he wasn't trying to find out what people were doing wrong or attempting to identify weak performing middle managers. Rather, he wanted to learn how he could better support them and show them that he cared. In fact, he sees the middle managers' role as "critical because they're the initial screen. By the time things get to me, something's already wrong somewhere in the system. If they don't play their communication role accurately, the organization suffers dramatically."

But the new program, which didn't single out middle managers per se, was never explained to them by Priselac or any other top manager. And the response was predictable, Priselac realizes in retrospect: "They [middle managers] found the approach very, very threatening. They saw me and the top administration cutting them out of their vital role." Over time, some of the middle managers' initial fears faded as they came to better understand the purpose of the program and why they weren't a part of it. But the initial uncertainty they felt about their jobs lingered for some time.

Choosing the "Right" Media

On a tactical level, the principle of organization means fitting CEO messages to the right (that is, most appropriate) medium or media. What a CEO intends to communicate—however important the message—won't come across if the context surrounding the communication is inappropriate or distracting. The right, or most effective, medium enhances both delivery and receipt of a message; the wrong medium hampers or prevents both. People react as much to the medium as they do to the message itself or to the source of the message. That, of course, was social researcher Marshall McLuhan's major conclusion following his studies of TV's effects on society, which he summed up in his now famous line: The medium *is* the message.

Poorly chosen media can also interfere with target audiences' understanding of a message. To some managers, the medium doesn't seem important enough to worry about. After all, they ask, "If I like a particular medium or can easily gain access to one, what's the difference how the message is delivered—just as long as it's delivered?" Throughout the 1930s, '40s, and '50s, the so-called "magic bullet theory" prevailed, which said the message was all-important and little else mattered. During the past 30 years, however, new research has debunked that theory. The medium can make a big difference, sometimes *the* difference to those on the receiving end. The message should be matched with a target audience's media habits and preferences, not selected arbitrarily, because the sender likes or is most comfortable with a certain medium, like TV or private chats.

Each medium has its own special attributes and limitations that best fit certain scenarios. A number of factors sway, to varying degrees, media decisions, including these five:

1. *Speed of transmission.* If it needs to be there tomorrow, a monthly newsletter won't do.

2. *Cost and cost-effectiveness.* $5 per video per employee is expensive, yes, until you consider the cost of employee turnover that it might help prevent.

3. *Need for and ease in obtaining feedback.* Getting instant reaction to a speech isn't very likely if you ask for it through a questionnaire to be returned by mail.

4. *Complexity of message.* Trying to explain the company's position on proposed tax legislation to employees through voice mail may leave them wanting.

5. *Need to control message content, timing, and context.* If you don't want the message changed or tampered with, buy advertising space or create a direct mail brochure rather than relying on unpredictable coverage by mass media.

"Formal" and "Informal" Media

CEOs use common sense, instinct, and/or personal preference to select how they'll communicate, according to our data. While common sense and instinct shouldn't be ignored, relying solely on such subjective criteria fails to take into account the inherent properties and characteristics—pro and con—offered by each medium. It's often at this juncture that CEOs are likely to need counsel from those who should know the subtle strengths and weaknesses of using various media.

One useful distinction made by professional communicators is between formal and informal media. *Formal media* are routine, impersonal, simple, and information-driven—such as letters, memos, or newsletter articles. *Informal media* tend to be nonroutine, personalized, complex, and interactive—such as casual conversations, meetings, or unscheduled walking tours.

Some management researchers have studied how effectively business executives are able to combine a medium's "richness," or information-carrying capacity, with a message's "routineness," or ease in being understood.[8] *Rich media* are interpersonal and interactive (that is, informal); *lean media* are impersonal and static (that is, formal). A face-to-face meeting between a CEO and an employee would be an example of a rich medium; a flyer announcing a free nutrition seminar pinned to a bulletin board would be a lean medium. Messages can vary from the routine, such as a memo requesting a copy of a report, to the nonroutine, such as a candid, no-holds-barred discussion about the implications of a potential merger. The challenge facing executives is to match routine messages with lean media and nonroutine messages with rich media. Such decisions can determine a manager's effectiveness; for instance, research has shown that high performing executives do a better job of combining messages and media than do low performing executives.

There may be instances when the line between formal and informal media becomes so faint that it's practically invisible. Take the case of Carl Karcher, founder of Carl's Jr., and his public battle with the company's new board of directors over control of the board itself and the organization's future direction. As news bits about the complicated internal struggle seeped out, the parties increasingly used the press, especially local newspapers, as a vehicle to make their cases to confused stockholders and employees. At one point, for instance, Karcher sent a so-called internal written memo to all employees telling his side of the controversy.

Somehow, sections of the memo were quoted word-for-word in the next morning's newspaper stories. Obviously, the memo, considered a formal and internal medium, had been used in untraditional ways that transformed it into an informal and external medium. Although supposedly written to employees only, by allowing the memo to "mysteriously" fall into the media's hands, Karcher essentially recast the nature and purpose of the medium by extending its reach beyond company walls and giving it the aura of an inside, confidential glimpse of his true thoughts and feelings. How media are used in particular circumstances can affect how we define their purpose and view their attributes as vehicles of communication.

Many of the CEOs interviewed for this book, like Maryland Blue Cross/Blue Shield's Carl Sardegna, rely on their own rules of thumb that parallel, in some respects, the media selection criteria just outlined. For instance, Sardegna's approach consists of three basic tenets: (1) basic, noncontroversial information should be sent through formal or nonpersonal media, like a memo or "canned" videotape; (2) the more personally relevant and timely messages ought to be delivered by face-to-face means, like a live speech or a meeting; and (3) the more complex, negative, or stressful the message to employees, the greater the need for the CEO or another top-level player to be the main communication source.

When the topic is personal or highly sensitive, it's best to look people straight in the eye and close the physical distance, insists Bank of America's former CEO,

Tom Clausen. "If you have to scold somebody, bring them in and talk to them across your desk," he suggests. "If you're delivering good news, then come out from behind your desk and sit next to them, not at a table." Being formal at informal gatherings can create an uncomfortable, counterproductive atmosphere—as Clausen learned at the first group session he attended after he left Bank of America to become president of the World Bank.

"I walked into the room the new kid on the block—and everybody was sitting there hidden behind name plates stuck in front of them," he recalls distastefully. "I was put at one of the conference tables. A very cool, uninviting approach. It was tough getting a read on anybody. In contrast, at our B of A senior management retreat, we all sat in a circle, visible to everybody else, so we could see who was wiggling their toes and who was giggling. Body language doesn't lie."

Perhaps the height of misfitting a nonroutine message with a lean, formal medium was the widely reported way the Detroit Tigers baseball club informed its then-General Manager, Bo Schembechler, one-time football coaching great at the University of Michigan, that he'd been fired: by faxed letter.

CEOs' Media of Choice

The Pincus surveys and interviews conducted for this project discovered that CEOs are partial to the most direct or interpersonal media, such as meetings, conversations, speeches, telephone calls, and MBWA (management-by-walking-around). David Price, founder and CEO of American Golf Corp., a major builder and manager of public golf courses, looks at formal media as having the capacity to sometimes hurt communication. He believes that standard types of communication cannot only be a waste of time, but can pinch off opportunities for more personal contact. "We have all these memos flashing around," he says. "When I see a memo, I go to the author and say, 'Very nice memo, very well written. But next time, just get up, go across the hall and tell the guy.'"

As managers rise through corporate hierarchies, they no doubt are forced to become increasingly persuasive in one-on-one and small group settings. Then later as CEOs, their thinking may be something like this: "If it worked to get me here, then it ought to work to keep me here." We don't agree. We believe that CEOs have overemphasized face-to-face types of communication to the extent that they've overlooked or avoided using forms of mass media, like video, when such media are most suitable. The upshot of mismatched media and messages is inefficient use of a CEO's precious time and less than optimal communication.

As new media technologies have multiplied, so too have the media options and applications. Most situations are best handled with a mix of media—one medium playing the primary role and other media the back-up roles. This way, those in the target group who may miss the message through one medium may still get it through another one; even better, they may get the message several times. Or media may be used in a predetermined sequence, with the nature of each medium's role shifting at each stage of a campaign. For example, a CEO may rely on mass media, maybe a videotaped message or a bylined article in an internal newsletter, to announce a new overtime policy being considered by management. Then to explain the policy's implications in greater detail, answer employees' questions and collect feedback on employees' reactions, the CEO and/or other managers might choose to use more interactive media, such as focus group interviews or small group meetings.

Pacific Bell's Quigley describes each medium's role as a leg in a relay race. "I do as much of the communication as I possibly can, and then it becomes a kind of a relay process, passing the message down and supplementing it through videotapes or even voice mail." Some, like Vons' Davila, employ particular media for managers and particular media for employees, depending on the objective and circumstances. "When we've developed our five-year business plan, which we update annually," he explains, "we (top management) meet with our store managers and share with them our visions and what the plan represents. Then we adapt the same thing on videotape and send it out to the stores for all our employees."

Some organizational media are more conspicuous than others. Certain unorthodox, although easily accessible and influential, media operate outside traditional channels and, because they can't easily be controlled or diverted, may at times frustrate management. The most prevalent of these unconventional media is the so-called grapevine.

The "Grapevine": Invisible But Powerful

The most natural avenue of communication in any organization is the infamous grapevine, which is both adored and feared. Often regarded by top managers as a useless and troublesome "rumor mill" or "gossip dump," in reality, the grapevine can be a powerful ally to management's organizational communication system. Embedded within the grapevine is an underworld of alliances, coalitions, and power relationships that can exert potent influence throughout a company, if shrewdly and selectively tapped.

In the absence of timely, believable information from top management, employees will immediately turn to the grapevine to fill the void. When management forsakes its communication responsibility, the grapevine may become employees' major source of information, or perhaps misinformation, and thus sabotage management's leadership position. When left uncontrolled, grapevines can spread information which is rarely accurate or complete, instantly and wildly up, down, and across an organization.

For years, organizational research has reported that employees believe they get far too much information from the grapevine—and far too little from top-level management. This suggests that the rumor mill has been allowed to flourish, largely unchecked, because top management has been delinquent in developing mutually satisfying relationships with employees. Contrary to legend, the grapevine can, if intelligently harnessed, be made to work for rather than against management. To minimize the destructive aspects of the grapevine requires an understanding of the pros and cons of all media, and how best to deploy them.

In the Bank of America case just ahead, you'll see how one company nullified the potential negative effects of an out-of-control grapevine by inviting 150 influential employees to a special meeting *prior* to a big announcement to all employees and asked for their help in accurately spreading the message to other workers.

Sandy Sigoloff sees much of his direct contact with employees as part of an effort to counteract the grapevine, which he calls "the most insidious thing in a company." That belief motivated the former Wickes Cos. CEO to "do everything I can in written and verbal communication" to counteract rumors. When he assigned himself to the field during the early days of the Wickes turnaround effort, he spent time talking to employees before he talked to managers, because "If you don't, the grapevine wins."

He points out that if a CEO visits a VP or store manager and doesn't talk to employees, employees will suspect something big is about to happen and will speculate about it in the halls and behind management's back. When he visited field operations, Sigoloff made sure he met face-to-face with employees, usually as part of what came to be called a "Bagel Pause." Without any formal agenda and with lots of cookies or bagels available, all employees were invited to hear the CEO tell them what was happening, followed by them telling the CEO what they thought. "It was a great way to sense their mood," says Sigoloff. "When I thought the grapevine was competing with me, I always went to direct talks with our people before things got out of hand."

Employees hold the controls to the grapevine, and can turn them on or off whenever they feel the need. There are times when a CEO tries everything to keep things under tight wraps, but somehow, inexplicably, the word gets out through the speedy grapevine and moves at the speed of light. On other, more rare occasions, the grapevine can actually work to the CEO's benefit.

That's what happened to Air Force General Bruce Holloway, former commander of the Strategic Air Command, one Christmas Eve when many of his people had to work through the night in underground missile silos. The general decided to pay a short visit to a two-person Minuteman missile crew in North Dakota, insisting there be no publicity. Within days, the word of his unscheduled visit had spread like wildfire and apparently touched a receptive chord with the troops—because Holloway was bombarded with invitations from crews all over the country wanting him to visit them next.[9] Friend or foe, the grapevine is ever-present.

CEOs' Discomfort with Electronic Media

Even though this is the age of electronics, of instant transmission, of television, most CEOs are not at all comfortable with electronic media. Certainly, Arlen Royster's persistent efforts to avoid being Royal Accommodations' public voice are typical of most CEOs. Paradoxically, CEOs as a group have been mysteriously slow to incorporate new technologies into their daily work routines, so much so that many have even resisted bringing personal computers into their offices. But that may be starting to change, as more CEOs are becoming aware of the multiple benefits available to them through their companies' on-line computer systems. Pacific Bell's Phil Quigley, for example, uses his company's voice mail system to instantaneously communicate with his 28,000 managers "who can literally pick up their phones, dial their access codes, and then for 3 to 5 minutes, I'm talking with them. Then, if they want to respond, they just do it in reverse."

One particular medium is so unsettling to CEOs that, according to reliable rumor, many will do just about anything, including forfeiting their annual bonuses, to avoid it. That medium is video, with its hot spotlights and ogling red eye. Ironically, even though many CEOs fear video, employees—many of whom grew up with television and are comfortable with it—prefer getting much of their information through the "tube."

Especially in large organizations, video is an invaluable tool for reaching the mass of employees directly, simultaneously, and cost-effectively. CEOs themselves predicted during interviews for this book that their reliance on new communication technologies—like videoconferencing, voice mail, and computerized faxes—will grow considerably in the future. Some findings suggest that this trend may already be underway. For instance, Pincus' surveys found that CEOs of big organizations (10,000 or more employees) use mass media significantly more frequently than their counterparts at smaller organizations.

CEOs of large, multilocation organizations who tend to depend too much on face-to-face forms of communication will invariably miss reaching key segments of their stakeholder audiences. Examples abound of top executives who've learned how to make the most of the video medium. One is oil giant Atlantic Richfield's Lodrick Cook, who uses the monthly internal TV show "PrimeTime" to "personally" talk with and listen to employees throughout the company. In one in-house studio are Cook and a small group of employees; in a second studio at another site, say Dallas or Anchorage, is another group of employees. For two hours, Cook leads a candid and freewheeling dialogue about anything employees want to bring up. A day or two later, edited videotape versions of the session are distributed company-wide.[10]

Another example of a top manager turning on to video is John McDonnell, chairman of McDonnell Douglas. In 1989, as times were turning sour for the jumbo aerospace firm, McDonnell launched "90 Days," a takeoff on CBS' "60 Minutes." The quarterly video show was geared to meeting the information needs of the company's then 140,000 workers around the country. Intended to improve faltering communication between upper management and worried employees, McDonnell saw the video cassette, at a cost of three to four dollars apiece, as a cost-effective way to candidly address issues that were troubling workers.[11]

The challenge facing the new chief communication officer is to become more adept at understanding and using a range of mass and interpersonal media. Top managers can hardly expect that the demand for them to use video technologies—internally and externally—will lessen in the future. As with any new technology, the more they use it, the more comfortable they'll become and the better they'll get at personalizing a seemingly impersonal medium. Once that happens, CEOs will more fully appreciate the medium's many applications and potential impact, as well as its intrinsic ability to, in effect, simulate eyeball-to-eyeball communication through the TV screen. Wrote a CEO of a large midwestern industrial firm who participated in one of the surveys: "A greater emphasis on technology has made timeliness possible. Through the video medium, I've been able to take a greater personal role in communicating with employees."

Organization in Action: The Case of Bank of America

Focusing on each individual aspect of organization, as we did, is the first step in understanding the complexities and nuances comprising this multiheaded principle. The next step is to figure out how these various aspects relate to one another and how they play out in a business setting. In the Bank of America case, many of the dimensions of organization come to life.

The B of A example includes two CEOs with very different styles, hundreds of millions of dollars of red ink, one of the most remarkable turnarounds in business history, a merger that created the second largest bank in the United States—and a communication rescue plan, which heavily involved the CEO and the top public relations professional, that worked. Like many business stories, this one begins with a problem, a very big problem.

The Situation

By 1986, after a series of bleak years, the Bank of America, the largest and one of the most respected banking organizations in the world, was facing bankruptcy. The bank reported deficits of mammoth proportions, including over $6.5 billion in loan losses. Corporate customers were jumping ship in droves, closing accounts at the rate of 1000 a month. And, as the bank's financial position eroded further, cross-state rival First Interstate Bancorp launched a takeover campaign in hopes of capturing B of A's many sites and its customers at firesale prices.

In some respects, B of A's financially deteriorating situation was puzzling. To outsiders, it may have seemed as though the banking titan had gone from ecstasy to agony practically overnight. Just five years earlier, the company was enjoying lots of black ink and the future never looked brighter. At least, that's how things appeared. But a number of changes were underway that eventually brought the once mighty Bank of America close to financial ruin. For example, one change that hit B of A between the eyes was its large foreign loan portfolio and an increasing number of countries which couldn't meet interest payments. In addition, there was a changing of the guard at the top—exit one CEO, enter another.

The CEOs.   In 1981, A.W. (Alden Winship) "Tom" Clausen, the 58-year-old, tough-minded banker who headed the company for 11 gainful years, retired after 32 years with the company and left for Washington, D.C., to take over the leadership of The World Bank. Taking Clausen's place was his hand-picked successor, 42-year-old Samuel Armacost. Within a year, profits nosedived $200 million. Over the years that followed, things went from bad to worse to calamity as the bank's losses mounted and its reputation tumbled. Then in late 1986, the Board of Directors decided a change at the top was needed and turned to the only person it believed employees, stockholders, and customers respected enough to follow through the dark days ahead and who could make the tough decisions necessary to save the bank: Tom Clausen. Clausen agreed to leave the World Bank and return to his old stomping ground atop the now shaky Bank of America headquarters building in San Francisco—and try to pull off what most observers considered the impossible.

The news of Clausen's return, although heralded by most employees, was received with skepticism by some in the financial community. Critics argued that it was Clausen's fixation with short-term profits, fueled by overly aggressive lending policies and inadequate investment in new technologies, which had propelled B of A into its fiscal morass.

The Turnaround

With desperate times calling for desperate measures, Clausen immediately formed a restructuring team, which included Ron Rhody, then senior vice president of communications and external relations, to assess B of A's plight. It didn't take long before he announced the inevitable conclusion: What the bank needed to do to regain its liquidity was to sell off many of its international operations, bolster retailing efforts in California and chop the payroll by 25,000 people (a 30-percent reduction). Our focus in the next few pages, based largely on interviews with Clausen and Rhody, will be on how Clausen's communication strategies effectively guided the bank through massive layoffs and plummeting employee morale.

One of Clausen's first moves was to establish a senior management council, composed of himself and all the bank's executive and senior vice presidents. He expected the council to collectively create the objectives and strategies that would guide the company over the rocky road ahead. In his mind, this management body was not "puffery"; he wanted ideas and input from those who knew the company best. This participative management approach, which wasn't necessarily a Clausen trademark during his early days, marked his style throughout the turnaround period. "I've always appreciated collegiality," says the CEO. "I'm for putting issues on the table and talking about them together. I want to listen to what others have to say, rather than me spouting off and telling them it's ultimately my decision."

While Clausen sought consensus most of the time, the final decisions were his and nobody else's—for among his attributes the bank's board believed it needed during this crisis was his decisiveness. Nonetheless, maintains Rhody, the two-time CEO worked hard encouraging members of the council to share their differing viewpoints and engage in no-holds-barred debate. But after the dust had cleared and a decision was finally hammered out, "Tom expected people to lock arms," Rhody points out. Looking back, Clausen is satisfied with how the council worked. "It was a team effort," he says. "Sharing and understanding the objectives, setting the strategies and priorities, keeping a watchful eye focused on the objectives—these all contributed to our turnaround."

Clausen's management style is difficult to classify; it seems to meander between democratic and autocratic. The autocratic label may be a remnant of the past. During an hour-long interview, Clausen came across as a staunch supporter of consensus-building and shared communication between management and workers. Always portrayed by the media as a stiff-necked, insensitive tyrant who ran the company with an iron fist, Clausen denied ever being an authoritarian manager and explains why he thinks he's often perceived as a Jekyll and Hyde. "When I say I'm not autocratic, that doesn't mean I don't have and express strong views," he admits. "I'm a perfectionist and I like it right—and I like it right the first time. I have high standards which I don't apologize for."

Rhody, who served as Clausen's media and communication counselor during his second stint as CEO, adds, "Tom never suffered fools easily. He was always hard on himself and others, and expected people to be prepared—and when they weren't, he came down hard on them. And that includes the media." Rhody tells the story of his prematurely terminating an interview between Clausen and a business reporter, because the reporter hadn't done his homework and was asking only boilerplate questions. Clausen's annoyance surfaced quickly and after the two "danced around in circles for awhile," Rhody pulled the plug before the reporter had finished. To no one's surprise, the result was a negative story.

Clausen may be one of those leaders whose public and private personalities aren't aligned, or maybe they just come across differently to different audiences. Regardless of how outsiders depict or view Clausen, Rhody argues, he has a "real feeling for people and those who know him see him that way." Rhody shares an anecdote he believes reveals the private Clausen. At the time of the interview, Clausen was about to have knee surgery to repair an old football injury made worse when, following an earthquake, he walked down 40 flights of stairs accompanied by a group of employees who refused to evacuate the building unless the CEO, who was resisting, came with them. That night, one of the employees who wasn't able to get home was a guest in the CEO's home.

The Communication Plan

The top priority of B of A's communication program wasn't winning over the media; it was winning back the trust and respect of "BankAmericans," the employees. Clausen believed passionately that without employees' support, survival would be impossible. The strategy guiding the plan was amazingly simple and direct: Tell employees exactly what the problem is, what has to be done to solve it, and how they can help. Then, and only then, Clausen reasoned, would they buy-in and commit themselves to the company for the long haul. This core strategy—which positioned Clausen as the principal communicator with both internal and external audiences—was then incorporated into the company's business plan, thus boosting the status of communication and assuring it a prominent place in all managers' plans.

From the moment of Clausen's return, he was frank with employees, customers, stockholders, and media about the seriousness of the situation the bank faced. "Being candid and honest and direct is the only way," he explains. "You'll get far better results and your chances of being misunderstood are less." The CEO's message to employees was that the bank was overstaffed, period. And to eliminate that problem, staff had to be reduced to bring expenses back in line. No punches were pulled. "Employees are smarter and more realistic than we often give them credit for. They understood," Clausen says.

The cornerstone of the plan was to use Clausen and his two vice chairmen as the key sources of communication in an effort to rebuild management's and the company's waning credibility. Rhody believed that Clausen's dignified and somewhat formal personal style, if not misperceived as cool or aloof, was just what the doctor ordered for B of A's shell-shocked and wary employees. In fact, the communication plan incorporated separate substrategies, that positioned the CEO and vice chairmen as spokesperson-leader on certain issues with certain publics. The plan's details were very specific concerning such issues as treatment of messages, type of media, and each top managers' assignments.

Clausen, for example, was designated as the major speaker on the issue of the company's changing structure.

The communication plan outlined, in nitty-gritty particulars, all the major communication opportunities anticipated over a 24-month period, including the occasion, purpose, target audience, message, medium, source (such as Clausen or the vice president of human resources), and the staff public relations professional responsible for coordinating the activity. Members of the senior management council then took the plan to the managers reporting to them and discussed with them the implications to their units. In turn, those managers did the same with their staff and soon the process was repeated at each level of the organization.

To implement the two-year plan, Rhody projected using a wide range of communication techniques, each carefully chosen to maximize impact: face-to-face talks, small group meetings, speeches to large groups, employee publications, and videotapes, as well as the organization's informal communication network, the grapevine. Rhody and Clausen recognized the speed and power of the grapevine to help spread their message, so rather than avoid or circumvent it, they used it to their advantage. Each year, for instance, about 150 employees throughout the company identified as good communicators (that is, opinion leaders) were personally invited by Clausen to attend his "state of the bank" speech.

After the speech and reception following it, these employees were asked by Clausen to help by sharing with other employees management's message, taking special care to make sure everyone got the *same* message. Another way Clausen distributed his messages informally was through his Chairman's Luncheons. These periodic lunch-time chats between the top manager and 20 or so randomly selected employees had no particular agenda other than sharing thoughts and ideas—although, if things went well, Clausen's and Rhody's hope was that employees attending would bring back to their units answers to common questions and positive impressions of the CEO and the future of Bank of America.

External visibility was not a high priority during the early stages of the plan, but, says Rhody, it was always an important consideration. To make sure that Clausen's time was not diverted from his top priority of employees, Rhody and Clausen imposed limits on Clausen's communication activities with outside groups and carefully selected those platforms. For instance, they limited his major public speeches to five a year. And constraints were placed on his exposure to the media. Even though Clausen received more than 200 requests a year for interviews, the braintrust decided he would grant no more than 8 to 12 interviews, with those interviews meticulously selected with the plan's central strategies in mind.

The Changing of the Guard—Again.   In May, 1990, four years after "unretiring" from Bank of America, Clausen retired again (he's now a company director). The remarkable turnaround he began engineering in 1986 had reached its zenith by 1990 as the company reported record net income for the third consecutive year and billion dollar-plus earnings for the second year in a row—a feat never before accomplished in U.S. banking history.

And as he did before, Clausen abdicated the CEO throne by anointing his personal choice to be the new king of B of A: Richard Rosenberg, a marketing wizard with an undergraduate degree in journalism who was lured away from Wells Fargo Bank in 1987 by Clausen to assist with B of A's restructuring effort. Some believe that Clausen's bait in hooking Rosenberg was the promise of the CEO title when Clausen called it quits for the second time. Rosenberg was an interesting choice by Clausen. If the conservative Clausen had sought a successor more opposite him in personality, style and background, he couldn't have found a better one than the outgoing Dick Rosenberg. But, then again, Tom Clausen has always had an uncanny ability to size up a problem and figure out what—and who—was needed to solve it. His choice of Rosenberg may reflect a realization that the B of A of tomorrow will require a brand of leadership quite different than his own.

Contrasting Communication Styles

The Clausen-Rosenberg comparison is an enlightening example of how two different CEOs, each committed to identical organizational goals, can approach and organize their communication roles differently, yet each be successful. Of course, each CEO served in different times, demanding perhaps different approaches. After Clausen's return, he managed the company during a time of imminent crisis; Rosenberg took over during a time of unprecedented prosperity. Today, Bank of America is thriving and expanding, and is completing the process of merging with Security Pacific Bank to form a new BankAmerica Corporation, the second largest bank in the United States.

When asked to compare the Clausen and Rosenberg communication styles, Rhody is reluctant to do so because of his close working relationship with and personal regard for each man. Yet, the differences in their approaches and styles are so striking, not even he can resist. "Clausen was the quarterback, while Rosenberg is the coach," he compares. "Employees respected Clausen very much. They feel genuine affection for Rosenberg."

These distinctions may best be explained by looking at each manager's fundamental perspective on employee communication. Under Clausen's watch, there was so much trauma in the organization as problems mounted that the focus was on getting information to management and employees as directly and quickly as possible. But under Rosenberg's leadership, employee communication is approached "in greater depth," says Rhody, by relying much more on employee attitude surveys to identify issues of concern to workers so proactive communication strategies can be built and executed.

Moreover, Rosenberg, blessed with natural charisma, insists on frequently attending employee functions, including those in branch offices, something Clausen did only on special occasions. Clausen made these appearances relatively frequently and whenever asked, but usually only after it was suggested by others he do so. Rosenberg has made it a point to press all managers to get more involved in employee activities. To demonstrate his seriousness, all members of his management council receive each month a printout of scheduled employee-oriented events and are expected to attend at least one of them.

Style differences emerge in strategies as well as tactics. Take, for example, the annual Bank of America Founder's Day festivities, a celebration of the company's cultural values. In Clausen's final year as CEO, his preference was for a very low-key, dignified approach—wearing typical business attire, he visited a branch or two, and made a few prepared, relatively statesmanlike remarks, normally to employees and long-time customers assembled for the occasion. In contrast, Rosenberg's first year as CEO saw a big employee picnic at the "Great America" theme park. And Rosenberg, dressed casually, entered the picnic on a motor boat from across a lake. He was then presented with a special "chairman's" jacket by the employees, which he never took off as he adeptly worked the crowd throughout the afternoon.

Rosenberg's self-confidence as a communicator surfaces, according to Rhody, in the company's revised set of CEO communication strategies and tactics. "We use Dick more aggressively and frequently. He doesn't resist working with the media," says Rhody, a former broadcaster himself who recently left the bank to start his own consulting venture. "Intuitively, he's an excellent communicator, whether it be on an interpersonal or a mass level. He believes that the quintessential management skill is communication, and his buying into this notion is critical to our success."

Armed with a journalism degree and experience in public relations with Wells Fargo, Rosenberg should be an easy sell when Rhody pitches a communication strategy, right? Not really, says the senior VP. For a CEO, Rosenberg's unusually in-depth knowledge of the communication process and tactics often cause him to question options presented to him, which can trigger lively discussions before decisions are finalized.

A Final Word

The concept of organization is far more complex than it first appears, as the Bank of America case illustrates. The essence of this multifaceted principle is the merger and alignment of company and CEO objectives, CEO and lower-level managerial roles, and CEO messages and media. Simply put, organization, as we've defined it from the CEO's perspective, means deploying CEO communication strategies that meld with an organization's culture and add value to the organization's efforts to build healthy relationships with stakeholders inside and outside the organizations.

Central to the notion of organization is CEO involvement in decisions about the nature of a company's overall communication plan. The CEO's input to and active participation in strategy formulation discussions—that is, incorporating his or her unique understanding of the organization's needs and direction—are crucial to developing on-target communication strategies.

Returning to Arlen ...

In the last chapter, the beleaguered CEO of Royal Accommodations was under heavy fire on both home and career fronts, struggling to detach himself from his past and begin discovering his future—an uncertain future he sees filled with unclear options. On the homefront, he couldn't seem to convince his wife, Andrea, that he was doing the best he could to patch up his shaky relationship with his estranged son, Glenn, who bitterly resents his father's single-minded objection to Glenn's decision to pursue a nonbusiness career path. On the workfront, Arlen's ego was turning somersaults, flattered by Bruce Mahoney's offer to take over the leadership of Mahoney Inns & Resorts and flattened by the Mike Keller-initiated move to knock him out of his CEO chair at Royal.

In the next chapter, Arlen tries to temporarily escape from Royal and his personal troubles by shifting venues from the executive suite to the ballpark, but it doesn't take him long to realize there's simply no escaping.

"When the Going Gets Tough, the Tough ... Go to Yankee Stadium"

Wednesday, October 10, 6:40 p.m.   The stretch limo inched up 59th Street, slowed by the crush of early evening commuter traffic. Jeffrey Andrews, Arlen's chauffeur and part-time security specialist for Royal's VIPs, was calm and controlled behind the wheel no matter how distracting the other honking, impatient drivers were.

Arlen hit the remote to lower the smokey, one-way window dividing the driver's seat from the passenger compartment. "What's our estimated time to the stadium tonight, Jeff?"

His eyes fixed on the traffic in front of him, Andrews said, "Maybe 30 minutes. Once we make the Triboro Bridge, I'll make up a little time. You'll be there for the first hot dog, Mr. Royster. Count on it." Andrews' eyes shifted to the rearview mirror in time to catch Arlen's embarrassed grin. He knew his boss' silly superstition about not biting into the obligatory hot dog until the first pitch was thrown.

"Great," said Arlen. Raising the window, he fell back and eyed the limo's lush interior. Trimmed in Royal's official colors, maroon and white, the compartment had a full wet bar, a nine-inch color TV, a cellular phone, and a small fold-away desk. Consistent with Arlen's personality, the limo was functional without being gaudy. Arlen had always been slightly bemused by the bullet-proof glass Andrews had insisted be installed. After all, he'd argued, the limo was frequently pressed into service for shuttling VIPs from Royal's flagship property, the Castle on Central Park, to local airports and other meeting sites.

Arlen turned to Jamieson who was in the left seat. "The dogs and beers are on you tonight, buddy. And don't try to weasel out of it," he barked sarcastically.

Holding up his hands in mock surrender, Jamieson acquiesced. "Hey, no problem. It'll be my pleasure buying for the unhappy loser."

Arlen had changed into casual slacks and a solid blue Yankees polo shirt. Jamieson had removed his tie and replaced his suit jacket with a pullover blue-and-red Red Sox cardigan. Normally, prior to such an important game, this odd couple would be trading quips and barbs, savoring the chance to escape from their pressure-packed business lives and be wild-eyed, screaming kids again, exhorting their fantasy heroes to victory. Today, however, their enthusiasm was missing; their expressions appeared sullen and distracted, their minds flooded with "to do" lists and strategy possibilities.

"This game couldn't have fallen on a worse day," Arlen observed sourly, his anxiety surfacing. The limo was slowly weaving through dense traffic on FDR Drive, a heavily travelled thoroughfare running parallel to the Harlem River.

"I suppose you're right, but after everything that's happened today, I could sure use a little fun. It'll be good to take our minds off our problems for a few hours. But ... I hate to think how much worse you'll feel at about 10 tonight when your Yanks have finally gotten their fannies whipped," Jamieson kidded. "Just promise me you won't take out your disappointment on me, okay?"

"Keep dreaming, Rick." Arlen's words sounded hollow, unemotional; he looked vacantly past his companion. His mind was bouncing among his many problems; he intuitively steered the conversation back to Royal and the dilemma of the moment.

"You said you wanted to talk about a few things," reminded Arlen. "Let's do it before we get to the ballpark so we can concentrate on the game and convincing Sharon Jillian that Royal is still the best buy in town for her mutual fund. Anyway, I don't plan to be civil to you once the game starts."

"Here's what I've sketched out for your on-air bit with the managers and employees. I'll finish the script before the noon briefing tomorrow. But I need your input first." Jamieson pulled out several sheets of computer-printed text strewn with cross-outs and rewrite suggestions. On the other knee, he balanced his legal pad, ready to scribble additional notes.

Arlen sat back in the cushy bucket seat, folded his arms and crossed his ankles. Gazing out the side window, he absently watched the city creep past, a blur of sooty, brick tenement buildings and filthy, litter-strewn streets. His attention was caught by a yellow Checker cab sliding past the limo. The cabdriver was engaged in a heated conversation with his passenger, both oblivious to the worsening bumper-to-bumper congestion. For the briefest moment, Arlen imagined himself as the cabbie, who at the end of his shift, returned his cab to somebody else's garage and went home, his mind free until the next scheduled shift. Before he could think about it more, he forced his attention back to Jamieson's request.

"There are three major issues, as I see it," reported Arlen, swiveling his head in Jamieson's direction. "One, employees, stockholders, and customers have got to know what's going on, how it happened, and how we think it affects them.

"Two, what are the short- and long-term repercussions to the company likely to be? And what are we, meaning top management, doing to solve the problem?

"And three, after we tell the employees and managers on Thursday, can we trust them not to blab to anyone, especially the media bloodhounds, before the scheduled press conference? And how should we deal with the inside information issue?"

Before Jamieson could respond, the phone on the console in front of Arlen buzzed. He reached for it reflexively, but then pulled back his hand, realizing that recent events had programmed him to expect the worst. As he lifted the receiver, his jaw muscles tensed.

"Royster," he said guardedly.

* * * * * * * * * *

"Hi, honey, it's me." Hearing Andrea's voice sent a pang of guilt slicing into Arlen's gut.

"Oh, Andy, hi. Didn't expect to hear from you," he said without thinking, but quickly added, "... but I'm glad you called. If you can't see it, I'm waving a white flag above my head. Can we declare a truce?" He wished now he'd made the call to her, as he'd said he would.

"A truce it is. I'm glad I caught you before the game starts, Mr. CEO."

"What's up?" he pressed impatiently.

"I wanted to know what Glenn had to say," she inquired diplomatically, referring to Arlen's conciliatory promise earlier that day to call their 22-year-old son and try to patch things up.

The question touched a raw nerve in Arlen, who hadn't yet called Glenn and resented getting caught in his own mistake. "Why couldn't she wait until I got home tonight?" he thought, irritated with her thoughtlessness. Andrea was frequently Arlen's unwelcome conscience, forcing him to look honestly at himself when he preferred to look away. By not waiting, however, she was applying subtle pressure that rarely failed to trigger his guilt—and his wrath.

After years of feeling as if he was on trial for not understanding his son, Arlen had begun to fight back in self-defense. He told Andrea on several occasions that she and Glenn hadn't made much of an effort to understand him and how he felt.

"What the hell do you want from me?" he screamed during a recent blow-up. "You all reap the benefits of my success. It's given you a first-class lifestyle. But it didn't happen without sacrifices ... my sacrifices." Guilt usually kicked in, but not before the words had cleared his mouth, and he usually ended up apologizing later.

Arlen knew his family didn't understand why he couldn't turn on and off his roles as husband, father, and CEO on demand. Sometimes he wished he could compartmentalize his personal and professional lives. While he decided what to say to Andrea, he thought again about his dual roles and how they so often collided. "How do I balance my son's needs for an attentive father with Royal employees' needs for a savior who'll protect their jobs?" he asked himself in frustration.

Deep down, he knew his trepidation about communicating with both Glenn and his employees was irrational, illogical. He sometimes felt like he'd been born with emotional blinders on. Ironically, though, he had no trouble communicating with his daughter, Janet. He'd never figured out why it worked so easily with her and not at all with Glenn.

He knew his son needed him and Arlen wanted to be there for him, but he also knew he'd do just about anything to avoid the arguments and heartache that came with trying. At that moment, he couldn't be certain whether he'd really forgotten to call Glenn or if he'd purposely buried himself in his work so he could rationalize not making the call. Work had always been his best excuse for avoiding people and responsibilities. "When push comes to shove," Arlen thought, "I'm wedged between a rock and a hard place, and I can't break loose no matter what I do."

Retreating from his private thoughts, Arlen spoke quietly into the phone. "Since I hung up with you this morning, Andy, it's been a constant parade of people and problems. I just didn't have time to call. I'm sorry," Arlen told her. "I'll call him when I get home tonight or first thing in the morning. Okay?"

She allowed several seconds to pass in silence. When she spoke, her tone was cool. "I guess that'll have to do, won't it?" She knew that trying to reason with him now would be a wasted effort.

"You did call Janet, didn't you?" Andrea pressed on. "Or at least have Susan send her some expensive flowers with a card from you?" Andrea's sarcasm cut into Arlen's psyche with the sharpness of a surgeon's scalpel. This was his wife's not-so-subtle way of testing him—again. He'd been caught for the second time that day. Arlen always meant well, Andrea knew, but to her, that rationale had worn thin years ago. The last time he'd thrown that excuse at her, her retort had hit him squarely between the eyes.

"Meaning well doesn't get it done, Arlen," she harped. "Doing well is the only thing that counts. Isn't that what you tell your managers at Royal?" He'd mumbled something pointless and trite, clearly stung by the truth of his own inconsistent behavior and his failure to adjust it.

Now, with no excuses handy, he resorted to a white lie rather than admit his failures and start the whole discussion all over again. The words fell too easily from his mouth. "I was saving that call for later. In fact, I was going to call her from the limo before we went into the stadium. That way, given the time difference, I knew she'd already be at work at the radio station. I'll call as soon as I hang up."

The irony was lost on Arlen: he'd gladly take time to call Janet, but conjure up any excuse not to call Glenn. It didn't escape Andrea. "Are you sure you have the time now?"

"Certainly," Arlen replied quickly, sincerely, ignoring her cynicism. "This is no ordinary occasion. It's not every day my little girl turns 21."

"Well, I'll let you go then. See you around midnight," she said, wondering if things would ever change.

Arlen hit the disconnect button and looked at Jamieson, speaking as he dialed Janet's work number from memory.

"Sorry, Rick," he said. "This'll only take a minute."

"God, I can't believe it, Arlen. Janet's 21? Tell her I'm gonna have a beer in her honor tonight. I still have those pictures of her in braces and pigtails at the company picnic when she must've been about 16 or so. Geez, with her face and brain, she's bound to be the next Diane Sawyer."

Janet was a senior in broadcast journalism at the University of Southern California, Arlen's MBA alma mater. Her heart was set on a career in TV news. Energetic and ambitious like her father, she worked part-time at a Los Angeles radio station writing news copy and doing some occasional on-air announcing. Arlen indulged her. He felt he understood her since she was always receptive to his suggestions, unlike her brother, whose knee-jerk resistance to his father's counsel was as predictable as Arlen's irate response.

Several minutes passed before the radio station's receptionist tracked down Janet. Arlen's conversation with her was, as always, comfortable and free-flowing. Jamieson, a captive eavesdropper, was struck by Arlen's sudden transformation from stiff businessman to easy-going father as soon as he heard Janet's voice. For the first time all day, the Royal chief executive smiled a real smile and relaxed momentarily as he chatted with his daughter.

Listening, Jamieson felt a touch of envy of Arlen. He believed that the barrier dividing Arlen and Glenn was their own doing, caused by their individual brands of pig-headedness. In contrast, Jamieson's separation from his 13-year-old son was beyond his or his son's control. His ex-wife, who had custody, lived in Dallas, which created a physical distance resented by both father and son.

After about 10 minutes, Arlen was forced to end his conversation with Janet, who had to finish taping an ad. He chided her about being so professional and wrapped up in her work that she couldn't take time off to talk to her old man. "I guess I'm just a chip off the old block, Pop," she laughed. He wished her happy birthday one more time and, like many fathers do even after their children are grown and gone, reminded her about drinking and driving and the company she kept. Janet told him that there was little chance of her doing much drinking or driving since she'd be at the station until 10 and had a mid-term exam tomorrow. They would have to wait for the weekend, she told him. They said their good-byes and closed with "I love you."

* * * * * * * * * *

The intercom buzzed and Andrews reported that Yankee Stadium was 15 minutes away. Arlen nodded. Jamieson picked up his notes, knowing that he'd have Arlen's attention for only a few more minutes.

"Okay, back to business," Jamieson started.

Arlen broke in. "Wait a minute. What were the three issues again? Gimme the *Reader's Digest* version, Rick."

"Right. Let's see. One, what happened, how it happened, and what's being done about it. Two, the effects of the situation on employees. And three, the potential problem of inside information being leaked." Jamieson didn't give Arlen a chance to respond.

"In the interest of time, let me just lay out what I think you'll need to cover on each point. I'll whip it into script form later tonight and we'll review it tomorrow morning."

"Okay, shoot," Arlen said, relieved that Jamieson was taking the initiative. All he had to do was give feedback. He was more tired than he'd realized, which made him again wonder whether trekking to Yankee Stadium was such a good idea. Talking to Janet had invigorated him, although the potency of his exhilaration was short-lived. Arlen dropped back heavily into his seat and closed his eyes, concentrating on Jamieson's continuing monologue.

The communication VP's delivery was hurried and curt, stressing conclusions, not the rationale behind them. "With the managers, the thrust of your remarks should be on their need to counsel employees to understand what the crisis is all about and how best to get through it. We'll probably preface that with a quick summary of what's happened and what we think it means to Royal's future.

"You'll ask the managers to be patient in trying to understand workers' anxiety. Emphasize that employees will need a steady flow of information from them, as well as a compassionate ear. Then you'll remind them that things will probably get worse before they get better, while also reassuring them that this too, like all bad times, shall pass—and with their help and cooperation, it'll pass that much quicker and easier."

Seeing Arlen's eyes still closed and his head nodding slightly, suggesting he understood or agreed, although Jamieson wasn't sure which, he went on.

"With the employees, you'll lay out what's happened as far as we can tell, what we're considering doing to correct the problem and stress like crazy that senior management is in control of the situation. Emphasize that steps are being taken to find out all we can about the problem so we—be sure to say we, by the way—can solve it.

"And you'll personally commit to keeping them informed every step of the way, and that you and their line managers will answer all questions candidly and honestly—even if the answers aren't ones they want to hear or you want to give them. You can preview your intention to visit a handful of properties in coming weeks, although we may not have the list finalized by then. And you'll tell them about the press conference that afternoon and the ad campaign which they'll be hearing more about on Friday."

"Sounds fine, Rick. Logical. Comprehensive. So far so good," Arlen said placidly, his eyes sliding open. "Keep going." His body had relaxed somewhat from the lulling motion of the smooth-riding, sound-proof limo.

Jamieson perused his notes again before proceeding. "Next are the anticipated effects on employees and on the organization. Here, I think you need to be excruciatingly clear and direct about how damaging misreported financial results can be to a company's legal position, bottom-line, and reputation, yet, in so doing, make sure they understand that this isn't the end of the world or the end of Royal, and, most importantly, that it isn't the end of their jobs. I'm assuming, of course, that that's the case. If it isn't, then we'll have to put it differently.

"One of the things Joyce Hadley is hounding me about is telling our people what we're going do with the managers who've been caught finagling with the books. She's concerned about the message we'll be sending to employees on how the company views—and punishes—this kind of behavior." Jamieson stopped to study the CEO, whose expression remained noncommittal.

Hearing the word "punish," Arlen leaned forward, clasping his hands tightly together and wiggling his fingers. "I'm not sure about that one right now," he said, the sound of a warning in his inflection. "We most likely won't have the auditors' final report until after the teleconferences and the press conference on Friday. For the time being, just write a general statement about being committed to doing everything necessary to correct the problem, blah, blah, and prevent it from ever happening again, blah, blah. And, Rick, just so you know, I do mean *everything* necessary ... no matter what it takes."

Arlen leaned back again, uncertainty written across his face, and peered out at the river, appearing unusually still and empty this night. The streetlights along FDR Drive had begun to take hold as a soothing amber dusk descended upon the city. He could see the Triboro Bridge rising in the distance, growing larger by the minute.

"Joyce says, and I think she makes a good argument," Jamieson continued, "that if there's been no outright theft or embezzlement, the company ought to be lenient on the guilty managers—particularly those who didn't actually profit from their ... their indiscretions. On the other hand, those who lined their pockets ought to be fired and prosecuted so people get the message that this kind of stuff won't be tolerated here."

"Well, I can appreciate where she's coming from," Arlen interjected. "But this is an issue with lots of sides and angles. I won't be able to decide anything until I have more information and a little time to think. It's got all sorts of legal and ethical implications attached that I have to weigh. You can be sure that whatever decisions are made, many of the troops won't be happy. Just write the general statement for now, Rick. Let's see if more information surfaces before I have to go before the cameras."

"But people will want—and expect—to know more than the generalities," Jamieson warned, unwilling to back away. "The managers. The employees. Remember, the videoconferences will be interactive sessions. The questions will be tough, I'm sure. The media will go for the jugular, as will many of our employees. You're going to get questions like, 'So who are you firing, Mr. Royster?' and 'Why didn't you know about this long before now, Mr. Royster?'" Jamieson's voice had turned squeaky and sarcastic, his gestures pronounced, as he took on the probing persona of a jaded reporter. Arlen raised an eyebrow and smiled faintly at Jamieson, amused by his theatrics, knowing they had a serious point.

Seeing Arlen's receptivity, Jamieson bored in. "And 'What about you, Mr. Royster? Are you going to resign?'" he asked, his play-acting voice trailing off. Arlen's eyes, suddenly alert and wide open, showed that Jamieson had hit a nerve. "Arlen, you're not even thinking about ... about resigning, are you?" His eyes narrowed on his boss, who spoke softly into the window.

"Remember what Keller said at the staff meeting about the pressure I put on him ... you ... the others ... all of you?"

"Forget Keller. He's a jerk," Jamieson snapped back, louder than he'd intended.

"He's right, though, at least as far as my shouldering much of the responsibility for all this," Arlen countered, his arms extending outward in a sweeping motion, before turning back to Jamieson. "I can't stop thinking about what he said."

"You can't be serious about resigning." Jamieson's tone was incredulous.

"If that's what it'll take to rescue Royal, I'd do it in a minute," he explained, his conviction indisputable. "I mean, how do you define, and then assign, responsibility in a situation like this? I'm certainly not free of blame, am I? If we were in Japan, there'd be no question about my resigning."

"So you think bailing out is the answer? Leaving Royal without a leader? Come on, Arlen. I can't believe the 'never say die' Arlen Royster I know would ever do that," Jamieson said pointedly, throwing himself back against the limo's rear seat and angling away from Arlen's gaze.

"I've got to ask myself: When does pushing people under the guise of motivating them for the company's good go too far? Did I press them so hard that they felt justified in fabricating their financials in order to keep their jobs and not get their people fired ... even though they knew it was wrong?"

Inclining toward Jamieson, the top dog pressed the point. "Okay, Rick, time for some brutal honesty. Tell me, how often do you feel pressured by my ... my obsession, I guess ... with making Royal the best? How much extra time do you put in because I'm constantly pushing you? And how often have you pushed your people to work extra hours or weekends, because you're trying to please me—and they're trying to please you?"

Arlen's eyes, jumping wildly moments ago, were under control again. He studied his hands before posing his final question. "Who's responsible ..." He looked at Jamieson coldly. "... the pusher or the pushee or do they share the blame equally?" It was intended as a rhetorical question, yet the obvious implications directly touched Royal's predicament as well as Arlen's personal quandary. "No matter how I break it down ... I can't escape the fact that I'm as much to blame as anybody, regardless of your and others' attempts to convince me otherwise."

Jamieson had no comeback. He preferred not to think about the specter he'd raised. He stared out the window, oblivious to the bridge abutment looming before him as the limo moved onto the Triboro's span. Arlen rubbed his eyes vigorously with his fists, probably trying to erase the disagreeable picture of himself he'd just painted. As a reflex, he then switched topics.

"What about the possibility of disgruntled employees leaking information to the press, to the media, to competitors and to who knows who else—after the internal broadcasts? How do we make sure that doesn't happen?"

"That could be tricky and, legally speaking, pretty risky. Let me think about that one," Jamieson said, doodling on his legal pad. "My gut tells me that the managers will keep the information to themselves. Of course, if I'm wrong about that, we could be inviting big-time trouble. Whether hourly employees would keep it under their hats is another question. Coletto says we're already in hot water up to our eyeballs with the SEC, anyway. He says we should avoid taking any unnecessary risks, which, of course, he defines as saying just about anything. Hell, that's what I'd expect a lawyer to say," Jamieson added for good measure, knocking Joe Coletto, Royal's head legal counsel, but then adding apologetically, "But when it comes to the insider trading issue, I can see his point—up to a point, that is."

"Well, then, maybe we ought to brief the managers and employees at the same time to reduce the likelihood of a leak," Arlen speculated, playing devil's advocate.

"The last thing we need is the SEC coming down on us for something else. If that happened, our reputation wouldn't be worth a used subway token. Just think about it: here we are already caught red-handed cooking our books, and then, when we supposedly try to fix the problem, we get caught again for violating insider trading regulations. If there was any doubt about self-destructing, that'd ice it, without question."

"Remember, Arlen, we've already sent e-mail messages to the managers alerting them about the scheduled broadcasts," Jamieson reminded, aggravated that Arlen was considering changing the rules of the game after he'd already signed off on them.

"We have to be upfront with our managers or we're dead in the water with no hope of resuscitation," Jamieson rebutted, trying to reposition his argument to notify the managers first.

"It's just smart communication strategy. We need this group to help hold employees together. If they're told early—directly from you—what's going on and how important their roles are, they're gonna feel important and that you trust them. That'll help motivate them to hang with us through the rough weeks coming up and ...'"

"Dammit, Rick," Arlen snapped angrily, "unlike you, I don't have the luxury of concerning myself with *only* the communication aspects of issues. Things are more complicated than that, and you ought to know that by now."

The CEO looked at his communication VP and noticed a slight flush above his collar. Already regretting his outburst, Arlen retreated, realizing he was about to shoot the messenger, a messenger he had faith in and respected.

Softening, Arlen tried to placate. "Look, Rick, I know you're doing your best. But we can't afford to shoot ourselves in the foot because we didn't consider all contingencies before we acted. We've got to be completely certain about our legal exposure before we say or do anything. We're already easy bait as it is. We don't have the freedom to say everything we'd like to say without opening ourselves to legal challenges we might not be able to defend against. I know you know that, Rick. Sometimes, though, I think you conveniently forget it. Your point, however, is duly noted."

Jamieson knew that a second legal setback would be Royal's kiss of death. He could understand Arlen's cautious nature in this instance, even though he disagreed with it.

"Look, there's no guarantee the whole story won't be on CNN ten minutes after we tell our employees," Arlen said, reaching for a cufflink that wasn't there. "You'd better have your people ready at a moment's notice so we don't get caught with our pants down ... again," he added, somewhat grimly. "I think this is one of the riskiest parts of the plan. But," he continued, raising his hand to postpone Jamieson's rebuttal, "I just don't see any other choice." Jamieson nodded, content again to listen.

"Which brings us to your thought about inviting certain media people to observe the manager and employee broadcasts," Arlen kept going, more strident now. "That's even riskier. In fact, I think it might be like putting a loaded gun to our heads. Sure, maybe we'd appear to the media and some outsiders like we're not trying to hide anything, as you point out. But, in our employees' eyes, sharing such important and sensitive news with them and the media *simultaneously* would be an insult, and just might kill their remaining trust in us. And with media there, any hope of a candid discussion about what's on employees' minds would vanish as well. So let's keep out any media until the scheduled press conference, shall we?"

As Arlen was concluding his instructions, the limo pulled into the reserved parking area adjacent to Yankee Stadium. The ear-shattering rumble of the elevated subway running alongside the ballpark cut off further conversation. Andrews hopped out, crossed in front of the towncar and pulled open the right rear passenger door. As Arlen swiveled to get out, Jamieson thought about defending his position that media attendance adds an air of legitimacy, but immediately thought better of it. He couldn't deny that Arlen made some valid points, but what really stopped him was how forceful Arlen sounded. Jamieson knew this wasn't an argument he could—or maybe should—win.

"Okay, Arlen, you win that one," Jamieson said to the CEO's back as he flipped his legs out of the car. "But tonight, it's my turn to win, so get prepared to be a gracious loser."

Arlen stood up and turned around to face Jamieson as he slid out of the limo. Grinning, he poked at Jamieson's ego, trying to change the mood, "The best good losers I know, Rick, are Red Sox fans, because they've had so much on-the-job training." Jamieson feigned a hurt expression as Arlen lightly jabbed him in the chest, while waves of excited fans streamed passed them toward the stadium gates.

"Your day is coming—and I have a feeling it's tonight. Let's go meet Sharon Jillian, hear more about her wonderful mutual fund and start you eating your humble pie." With that, Arlen put on his worn Yankee baseball cap and threw a salute at Jamieson, who screwed up his face. Turning to Andrews, who had just closed the passenger door, Arlen said, "I've got my beeper, Jeff, so you can get me if need be. Stay close to the car phone—and root for the home team. That's an order!"

Tired and hassled, weighted down by problems that seemed unsolvable, Arlen Royster looked up at the towering concrete facade of one of the world's great stadiums of competition. The sight of this imposing, man-made structure infused him with a feeling of hope. His doubts were suddenly gone; he was glad he'd come. For the next few hours anyway, he welcomed exchanging the disturbing perplexities of business and life for the pleasing complexities of the baseball diamond. Through that exchange, he hoped to find some of the perspective he needed to prevail.

As Andrews glanced back at his passengers, they had already disappeared into the noisy, swelling crowd.

8

Selectivity— Maximizing the CEO's Impact

When John Lucas was appointed head coach of the San Antonio Spurs basketball team only 20 games into the 1993 season, he had little to lose. Things were going from bad to worse. In what was supposed to be a banner season for the Spurs under Jerry Tarkanian of University of Nevada at Las Vegas fame, the team opened with a disappointing 9-11 record. Worse yet, the players were losing faith in themselves. This lack of confidence is what most alarmed team owner Red McCombs.

His remedy, based more on a hunch than prescribed business thinking, was to fire the proven Tarkanian and swallow his three-year contract, in favor of a 39-year-old recovering drug addict who had practically no prior coaching experience. In the inexperienced Lucas, a one-time All-American at the University of Maryland and 14-year NBA veteran, McCombs sensed a powerful presence and robust leadership potential. Fortunately for McCombs and the Spurs fans, they didn't have to wait long for the gamble to pay off. Over the next 25 games, the Spurs won 22 in convincing style and the players again started thinking of themselves as winners.

The catalyst to the turnaround was Lucas' free-wheeling management style, evidence of which surfaced during the first timeout of Lucas' first game. Instead of huddling with the team near the bench and passing out instructions, as every other coach does, Lucas instead told one of his players, bewildered veteran

Vinnie Del Negro, to handle the timeout and the new coach walked to midcourt and eyed the crowd.

During a timeout later in the game, he told point guard Avery Johnson, a castoff from several other teams, to diagram a play for the squad while Lucas listened along with the team. "I almost choked on my water," Johnson recalls. "Luke's" philosophy of delegating management responsibilities to players hasn't been limited to only timeouts; players also run portions of practices, give post-game talks, assess fines on teammates for unteam-like behavior, and even have a say in some personnel decisions.

The rookie coach, who scuttled his own chance for NBA superstardom because he couldn't stay off drugs and alcohol, claims that all he's doing is "treating the guys the way I wanted to be treated."[1] In actuality, though, Lucas did more than that: He selectively limited his management role and transferred a portion of it to his players-employees, which, contrary to conventional management logic, made the enterprise more effective and bolstered his leadership position. Whatever he did and whatever you call it, it worked. The Spurs went on to finish the regular season with a 49-33 record and advanced to the second round of the playoffs before the team's season ended.

By strategically removing himself from handling some of the typical upper management duties, a move most top managers would resist for fear of forfeiting control, Lucas enhanced his personal impact by adding value to those times he does select to play the more traditional CEO role. The young coach intuitively recognized that top managers who try to do all the managing themselves, and thus cut off other managers and line employees from participating in the managing process, dilute their own impact by diminishing the perceived importance of their role in workers' eyes.

Most CEOs err not in communicating too much, but too little and, in many instances, too late. Whether CEOs overplay or underplay their communication role, messages from the top that are poorly designed, ill-timed, or mismanaged violate the principle of selectivity, the S and last piece of our C-C-O-S model of CEO communication.

Walking the wobbly tightrope of selectivity is a risk every CEO must take, over and over again; it comes with the job. Those who can keep their balance will thrive. Those who stumble may never get another chance, because so much is at stake. A wrong move can spell disaster for the CEO and the organization. CEOs should never step onto the unsteady public highwire before they've carefully considered each move and the audience's likely response.

In this chapter, we look at some of the tangled issues CEOs must unravel in selecting when, how, and how much to communicate. After further probing the meaning of selectivity, we examine the following aspects of this multipart principle:

1. *timing* the CEO's and other managers' communication activities to achieve maximum impact;

2. the *amount of time* CEOs should devote from their agendas to directly communicating with employees and other constituencies; and

3. the CEO's crucial *leadership role* during times of organizational crisis.

To help illustrate these points, we examine situations at a number of major organizations, (IBM, Exxon, Bethlehem Steel, and Scandinavian Airlines System), to see how a few CEOs have used and/or abused the principle of selectivity. First we take a closer look at what selectivity is all about.

Defining Selectivity

The principle of selectivity is based on a fundamental maxim: Less is sometimes more. Applying that notion to organizational life, selectivity implies that CEOs ought to choose their communication spots strategically; that is, the CEO's communication role should be a discerning one, selectively deployed to maximize its impact on the organization and its people, while guarding against usurping or interfering with other managers' communication roles and relationships with employees, customers, and others.

The heart of the challenge is discovering the elusive dividing line between too much and too little communication, and then timing the communication so it's neither too early nor too late. Clearly, there are times when the CEO—and *only* the CEO—should be the principal voice, the messenger, just as there are times when the CEO ought to back away and let others lead the way.

Think of selectivity this way: The CEO's communication moments ought to be chosen so that, to paraphrase an E.F. Hutton ad, "when the CEO speaks, stakeholders listen." The principle is universal: Too much of anything waters down its effect, whether it's listening to the same song over and over, eating the same food for lunch every day, or hearing the same speaker week after week.

CEOs who communicate too often—which isn't a common problem—run the risk of diminishing the potency and uniqueness of the CEO's singular role. One of the reasons the Queen of England's public appearances are so eagerly awaited and so highly attended by her subjects and media is because her appearances are intermittent, usually reserved for special occasions of national concerns. Precisely timed, targeted, and regulated communication by the head of an organization is "value-added" in employees' minds, because of its special significance, its rarity, and its anticipation. If Christmas or Thanksgiving were celebrated every month instead of once a year, they wouldn't be nearly as coveted.

Under normal circumstances, for example, CEO communication with employees should be recurrent, yet irregular and unpredictable. If something can be consistently inconsistent, then that's what a CEO's communication role ought to be. That is, frequent enough not to be forgotten or appear patronizing or obligatory, yet not so frequent that the CEO's role is taken for granted. A top executive's communication should have an air of intrigue or anticipation to it so that when the CEO does grab the lead role, ears perk up and eyes open wide.

The reality of a CEO's hectic and cluttered life makes *direct* and *continual* communication with employees or any other group impractical, if not impossible. So, when it does occur, it should be memorable. Bruce Burtch, president of The William Bentley Agency in San Francisco and a former employee at several multinational corporations, remembers how he felt when the guy at the top spoke to him: "If the CEO said to me face-to-face, 'I believe this is the direction we ought to follow and I need your help,' I believed it—because that sort of contact doesn't happen very often in a big company. He doesn't usually want to go around his lieutenants."

Our point is that CEOs ought to communicate more than they do, but not too much more. If that sounds a bit like a contradiction in terms, it probably is. The key is not found in the amount of communication, but in the quality and tightness of focus. That makes for some tough decision making by the CEO, to be sure. And the first decision is often when to speak out and when to remain quiet.

Timing: How Often and When to Communicate

Some professionals, particularly obstetricians and bomb squad specialists, believe that "timing is everything." *How often* and *when* something takes place can augment or diminish its impact on an intended audience. Timing is an issue affecting CEO communication decisions on two levels. On one level is CEOs' concern with selecting only the highest impact issues and events on which to assume leadership. On another level is CEOs' concern with not overcommunicating or mistiming communication so that middle and front-line managers, who maintain day-to-day and first-hand contact with employees and customers, aren't overlooked or undermined, and thereby weakened in their roles. The less obvious result of a CEO usurping another manager's position, even unintentionally, is that employees' expectations of the CEO's direct and ongoing involvement in routine affairs will elevate quickly. The dangers of such rising expectations are obvious, particularly given the continually pressing demands on CEOs' time.

CEO Means "Important"!

In surveys of *Fortune* 500 CEOs for this book, top managers reported that they believe their communication activities have a significant and positive influence on employees. That's good. But those CEOs, as well as the other 25 interviewed, also realize that too much of a good thing can become a not so good thing.

That's why CEOs need to selectively pick their communication spots so that employees won't view the top manager's contact as "ho-hum"—"Oh, it's just good ol' Harry again, saying the same stuff he did last week." Top-level executives must find the precarious balance point between employees' desire for more communication from top management and CEOs' desire not to overplay their role as chief communicator.

When something is *really* important to employees, customers, stockholders, or any major stakeholder group, the CEO should be the originator of communication—to announce, explain, answer initial questions, and lead the charge. Then, depending on the nature and life cycle of the issue, the CEO may continue as the primary communicator until a turning point is reached and the CEO's and other managers' roles shift accordingly. For example, Dick Schlosberg, CEO of *The Los Angeles Times* and executive vice president for The Times-Mirror Co., relies on his own intuitive criteria for deciding when he or another manager should be the principal communicator.

"The number one factor is strategic importance or level of urgency," he says. "As you go down the scale of less urgent and less important, the CEO should look for opportunities to have others take the communication leadership role." Furthermore, Schlosberg thinks the "CEO should get there pretty quickly" whenever "things impact people's lives." He remembers a time when a rumor that the company was going to be taken over was spreading through the *Times* headquarters building in Los Angeles. "People were getting very upset," he recalls. "So that's when I click in and clarify things."

By the same token, a leader's effectiveness can be damaged if employees see him personally committing time to communicating on what most consider unimportant matters, believes Tom Priselac, chief executive officer at Cedars-Sinai Medical Center in Los Angeles. "The work force in health care is, by and large, highly educated. They expect [a CEO to] mind the store and address the important organizational issues," he says. "You have to keep a certain balance in order [for the CEO's communication] to be valued. It does depend on the setting, the people and the nature of the business. Hospitals are highly social organizations so *what* I say is almost as important as people knowing *who* I am. If employees' only contact with me was through written communication, I wouldn't have a tenth of the impact I do by relying on more personal types of contact. But every setting is different."

When the Issue Makes the Difference

"Significant" was a word frequently used by CEOs interviewed to describe the situations and circumstances when they feel compelled to assume a communication leadership role. Of course, each head of an organization will add his or her own twist to the meaning of "significant."

Emerging from our analysis of survey findings was the revelation that CEOs see themselves as the appropriate level of management to assume the lead communication role only on certain issues that can affect the entire organization. CEOs indicated, based more on a sixth sense than any objective criteria, that they do discriminate among levels of management as to which level is best suited to take charge on particular kinds of issues. Such choices—which often swing on how important a matter is, time or timing pressures and personal preferences—are never clear-cut or easy; they're judgment calls.

In most CEOs' minds, however, the major distinguishing factor is how much an issue can directly, or indirectly, impact a stakeholder group. As that potential influence increases in scope in the CEO's judgment, so does the need for a senior-level manager, possibly the CEO or a designated VP, to serve as leader. For the issues that can make or break an organization, the chief must seize the point position.

The National Association of Manufacturers' past president, Alexander Trowbridge, says that when a "significant change affects 5, 10, 15 people, the president has got to be not only the person who makes the decision, but the one who announces it and discusses the rationale. You can't delegate that kind of thing." He notes three events and occasions he considers truly significant:

1. If an employee receives a major award, "I should make the announcement because that enhances the value of the award to the employee and the organization."
2. If it's a letter to Congress on a macro-issue, Trowbridge signs it, but "if it's more limited to a technical area of a specific piece of legislation, I'd prefer the vice president in charge of that policy area to sign it."
3. The top manager signs or takes prime responsibility for all policy-driven communication with the organization's board of directors.

Some top executives, such as Bill Davila of grocery giant Vons Companies, has not yet found the slippery middle ground between over-communicating and under-communicating. Most chiefs would like employees to instantly equate the CEO's personal participation with issues of vital importance. "When I communicate with our stores," explains Davila, "I want them to think, 'He's got something important to say, otherwise he'd be sending out a bulletin or a memo.'"

Yet, having said that, Davila, whose face and voice are seen and heard daily on Vons' TV and radio ads in southern California, immediately points out how careful he is to keep his role in check. "I don't want it to appear that I *only* communicate with our people when the issue is big time. And I don't want to become *so* familiar to them so that when I do have something important, it won't receive their attention. I'd love to write to [employees] every week, maybe have a page in the operations bulletin to talk about things I think we should be doing for our customers. But that's probably the role of the supervisors, the store managers, the district managers, the vice presidents—they're the ones with the hands-on, day-to-day contact with employees."

Limiting the CEO's Role

For certain topics and in certain circumstances, the CEO's role should not be the dominant one *indefinitely*; it ought to be viewed as a short-term assignment. Once a new issue or program begins to be absorbed into an organization's culture and the need to sell it slackens, the CEO's initial, aggressive cheerleading role should gradually fade and become more intermittent, as other managers, acting as extensions of the top executive, move in.

There may be times when the CEO's visible presence is absolutely crucial. One such time is during the start-up phase of a new program or campaign, when employee commitment hasn't yet crystallized, but is essential. To gain workers' support, the CEO should play an aggressive advocacy role until employees begin to buy in. Then when acceptance begins to grab hold, the CEO should gradually pull back and assume more of a reminding or reinforcing role as other managers take over the prime responsibility for direct contact.

Research has shown that CEOs see their communication role as "quick hit" in nature. Many characterize it this way: Wave the flag, sell the message, paint the vision, build excitement, point the way, and then step aside and allow the everyday managers to take over. Most top managers acknowledge that their role, however crucial, is limited by design and practical constraints, and must be differentiated from supervisory managers at all levels.

To illustrate, after introducing a topic or initiating a campaign, chief executives should allow other managers to fill in details, answer questions, refer people to proper information sources, and continually augment the CEO's central message. But even after the baton is passed, the CEO still has a job to do—at every appropriate occasion, the CEO repeats and drives home the overriding message, explaining why it is the key to the organization's future and assessing the organization's progress, or lack of it, in approaching its goal.

If the top manager has created the right sort of communication climate and recruited the right kind of middle and upper-level managers, notes Bob Dockson, one-time chairman of California Federal Bank, then the CEO is, in effect, implicitly communicating with employees on an ongoing basis. "The top person creates an atmosphere, a culture, by employees seeing him in the hallway, talking with him in the elevator, just by them knowing that he's working for their benefit," he notes. "I don't think employees feel the need for the CEO to communicate directly with them all the time—like through speeches or memos—because if he's done his job of communicating through others, he's really communicating with them all the time. As long as they know that Bob Dockson's here and that they can call him on the phone at 6:30 a.m. and get him, then I've done it right."

Think of the CEO's role like that of the pace car at the Indianapolis 500: Set the direction and tempo, kick things off, and then retreat into the background while those closer to the action try to maintain the pace. Vons' Davila likens his role to that of a head football coach. "A football team has receivers, running backs, linebackers, and linemen," he says. "A head football coach doesn't get involved with each of these groups every day. Most of the time, when he communicates, it's with his assistant coaches, who actually call the plays on the field and then communicate what's happening back to the head coach who may then provide new directions. After the game, the coach talks to his players about their roles, trying to motivate and unify them. A CEO operates an organization's lines of communication with employees similarly."

Never Enough Time

Closely related to the issue of timing is time itself—that is, how much time a CEO ought to personally devote to communicating with employees and other constituencies. Since most CEOs argue that there isn't enough time for anything, we'd expect them to say that about handling their communication role. And indeed, they do appear to be frustrated over their inability to put more time into communicating.

As we discussed briefly in Chap. 4, *Fortune* 500 CEOs reported in two national surveys that they currently devote about 15 to 18 percent of their time to direct, formal communication with employees, which they admit isn't sufficient. CEOs say they are already committing—actually, "stealing" was a word frequently used—more time for internal communication than their predecessors did and about 3 to 5 percent more than they did a year or two before. What's more, they indicate that if they could, they'd put in around 23 percent of their working time to communication. Most complain that there are just too many other demands competing for their time, a common lament of most senior executives.

With time shortages a permanent condition in top managers' work lives, perhaps the focus ought to be less on the number of minutes CEOs give to communication and more on how those minutes are used. Sometimes the correct amount of time is obvious; at other times, particularly during normal periods when the CEO's role tends to be irregular, the decision of how much is enough isn't always obvious.

When Time Itself Counts Most

When circumstances are unclear and the stakes high, the organization's designated leader must step forward and take control, regardless of the time commitment required. That's what Jan Carlzon of Scandinavian Airlines System (SAS) did when his company drifted off course. When he became CEO of SAS in 1980, the company was facing a $20-million loss after 30 years of modest profitability. The airline's expenses had been pruned back with no improvement to the bottom-line. Employees were losing faith in management and in the future. In his effort to turn things around, Carlzon unveiled a daring new marketing plan designed to lure high-spending business travelers. The plan was filled with risks, however, as it required an additional $45-million investment in new equipment and an annual increase in operating expenses of $12 million, mostly for programs designed to enhance employees' customer service skills.

Carlzon's rallying cry was that every employee had to redefine his or her job in customer service terms and assume personal responsibility for satisfying the customer. Central to implementing the aggressive strategy, he knew, was gaining the emotional commitment of SAS' 20,000 employees. To do that, Carlzon assumed primary responsibility for spreading the word, because he "couldn't risk the message becoming distorted as it worked its way through the company."[2] In fact, communicating with employees became his top priority. During the first year of the new plan, Carlzon estimates he "spent exactly half of my working hours 'out in the field' talking to SAS people." In the end, employees heard and believed his message, and the company increased earnings by $80 million in the first year alone.

How a CEO disburses his or her time over a day or a week will ebb and flow based on a number of different factors, including the CEO's personal preferences. But far more relevant to time-driven decisions is evaluating the state of the organization's climate (such as problems, evolving issues), particularly key stakeholder groups' perceptions of the organization. Such an analysis should push to the surface useful information suggesting what the CEO's role ought to be. One of the most reliable ways to assess an organization's mood is through ongoing employee attitude research (such as surveys and focus group interviews). Data-based feedback on company-wide problems and possible solutions can help CEOs select the most appropriate communication strategy, which in turn should determine what the CEO's time commitment should be.

Because a CEO's time is always in short supply, a CEO's communication activities must be selectively allocated. As a rare commodity, time must be apportioned with discriminating precision, frequently requiring CEOs to make hard choices that are neither easy nor fair, but probably traumatic. There's simply never enough time, argues Times-Mirror's Dick Schlosberg. "The pragmatic realities of operating a business this size has resulted in my devoting less time to my role as a communicator and leader of the company," he admits. "I don't get around as much as I should. I delegate it to first-line supervisors and senior managers more than I want to. I'm disappointed I can't do more because we underestimate employees' need for 'touching' top management."

Pacific Bell's Phil Quigley sees the CEO's role as limited, if for no other reason than the physical impossibility of being in more than one place at a time. "The CEO is the chief communicator of the company's strategic vision, of the values of the culture, and the conveyor of bad as well as good news. In a large company such as ours, I need a lot of help doing that because it's just impossible for me to get out before employee groups as often as I'd like."

To Jim Verney, former head of Winchell's Donut House, time restrictions have forced him to think carefully about his time with employees and try to make certain that not a minute of it is wasted or nonproductive. He eschews the quantity approach, preferring to emphasize the quality of the time he spends with employees, even though he realizes he's trading off visiting more stores and seeing more people. "Sure, we have to apologize to those who want to see us but can't," he points out. "But people know when we visit a store, we really look through the operation. If the regional or district manager is there, either of them will take over the store while I sit down with the manager and counter people over coffee and a donut and talk about the business. Sometimes it's a small group and sometimes it's one-on-one."

Occasionally, top dogs may feel compelled to make time for communicating just because it feels right. Bank of America's Tom Clausen recalls just such a time. At one point when the bank was beginning to emerge from hard times, Clausen pledged to give each B of A employee 10 shares of stock a year later if the company kept improving. At the time of his announcement, he received an anonymous letter that said, as Clausen recalls, "There you go again. Promises, promises, promises. Mañana, mañana, mañana. Nothing for us *today.*"

So, when the joyful time arrived to tell employees of their 10 new shares of stock, Clausen wanted that announcement all for himself. "I suppose any manager could've announced the issuing of the stock," he admits now. "But there's the ego of the chairman that sometimes gets in the way—particularly when I'm the one who made the promise." With obvious self-satisfaction, he recalls that after the stock rewards were distributed, he received another anonymous letter that simply said, "Well, you remembered."

There are times when the top executive must step in and assume the leadership role temporarily, because lower-level managers aren't doing it or aren't doing it well. "I retake the major communication role when I feel there's a need to assist," explains one-time Vons' CEO Davila, who oversaw managers of supermarkets throughout California and Nevada. "When I sense things aren't happening the way they should, and that comes from experience, I'll get involved. But I try not to tell people how they should do things. They're the experts in their areas—and they're the ones who've got to communicate with and give directions to their people ..."

When the *#&*! Hits the Fan:
Only the CEO Will Do

There are certain times in CEOs' worklives when they select when and how to play their communication role. There are other times, however, when CEOs are selected without having much say in the matter—like when an organization's future is placed in jeopardy. At no time is it more imperative for CEOs to intensify their communication leadership role than when a major crisis hits, a situation that threatens key constituencies' confidence in top management. That's when strong, visible leadership from the titular head is no longer optional, but mandatory.

During unsettling, uncertain times when a company's public exposure is greatest, CEOs' natural inclinations are to delegate the public communication role to more communication-savvy underlings, as Arlen Royster attempted to do to his corporate communication VP, Rick Jamieson. But as Jamieson vociferously and correctly counter-argued, when things appear the bleakest, only the person at the top will do, much as families turn to their patriarch or matriarch for guidance and reassurance when tragedy strikes.

This need for bold, steadying leadership is especially essential during the early, breaking stages of a crisis when employees' and stockholders' fears are greatest. That's when the news usually isn't good and the situation usually isn't clear. It's also when the people who stand to lose the most want and need to hear from the person at the top—the only person who knows all that's going on and who they trust (hopefully!) to protect their best interests. Maryland Blue Cross/Blue Shield's Carl Sardegna, who guided his organization through a tumultuous cultural transformation, puts this point into perspective: "During normal times, if the message is simple and positive, the CEO doesn't have to worry about it too much. You can let the managers do most of the message giving and reinforcing. But if [the company's] in a crisis situation, [the CEO has] to assume most of the communication role."

Whether the crisis is a corporate takeover, a tainted product, a structural overhaul, a labor strike, or a consumer boycott, employees' immediate "stressed-out" reaction is to turn inward to their personal crisis. When this happens, preoccupied workers' primary concern is not how the organization is being affected, but how they and their families will be affected. Productivity rates will tumble and employees will ignore regular communication from management as they turn to underground sources (the rumor mill) for information. Worried workers will offer a tin ear to company concerns unless they can be convinced by management—and usually only the CEO will do—that it's in their best personal interest to listen.

When a crisis begins to unfold, and things are unclear and changing from minute to minute, employees need emotional reassurance from their "leader-father/mother" figure that things are or soon will be under control and all is being done to protect their livelihood. A now infamous example of a clumsy attempt to offer emotional reassurance occurred just minutes after the assassination attempt on President Ronald Reagan, during those panicky moments when the President's physical condition and fate were still unclear. Then-national security advisor General Alexander Haig, who was at the White House at the time, off-handedly told a national TV audience that he "was in charge" and that the situation was under control. Politically, Haig was later admonished and subsequently apologized for ostensibly overstepping his authority. Nevertheless, his instinctive reaction to reassure a frightened and baffled nation is hard to fault. And despite the subsequent criticisms lodged against Haig for his presumptuousness, his words probably allayed many worried Americans' fears that the government was without leadership or that the unthinkable might be happening.

When the CEO Is Needed
Front and Center

When a crisis descends on an organization and stakeholders' apprehensions rise, the CEO must instantly transform himself or herself into the CCO and assume a visible and vocal posture, relying on candor and sensitivity to hold things together until balance can be restored. During these times, business— and communication—as usual is no longer possible or appropriate. Approaches and strategies must be adapted to employees, stockholders, customers, suppliers, and others who are suddenly frightened, bewildered, and wondering how their lives will be adversely changed.

While every top executive has had to tackle tough problems at one time or another, some CEOs have learned the lessons of crisis communication management better than others. When the first Tylenol tampering crisis struck in the early 1980s, then-CEO James Burke, who had received specialized media training a year earlier, seemed to be everywhere at once—on the nightly news, on TV talk shows, in front of employees, meeting with the crisis management team—explaining what Johnson & Johnson knew and didn't know, what it was doing to fix the problem, how it would honor its commitments to customers, and so on. Despite the tragic deaths that triggered J&J's crisis, Burke's calm, articulate, reassuring public style was a key factor in preserving consumers' and employees' confidence so that the company was able to reintroduce Tylenol a year later in tamper-resistant packages and eventually recapture its lost market share.

A CEO's behavior during a crisis, when all eyes are trained on a leader's every word and decision, can have immediate and long-term effects on a company's prospects and others' perceptions of a CEO-as-leader. A number of business observers have credited Exxon CEO Lawrence Rawl with spearheading a bold reconfiguration of the oil company's bloated bureaucracy and antiquated corporate culture. Labeled as "tough and folksy" by *Business Week*, Rawl has at times appeared to be tough when he should have been folksy. That mismatch has damaged employees' and outsiders' views of Exxon and its top management. For example, when he launched the internal restructuring of Exxon, employee morale plunged, because management didn't sufficiently explain to employees the implications of coming changes. Not one to get personally involved in communication matters if he could avoid it, Rawl "appeared on videotape for the *first* time in his career in a 'rap session' with three other Exxon executives" who were trying to comfort anxious employees.[3]

Rawl's communication choices were also the butt of criticism during the early days of the Exxon Valdez oil spill in Alaska, the worst-ever environmental catastrophe of its kind. Rawl selected not to go to the disaster site until weeks following the spill, long after he'd been blasted by media and other stakeholders for his—and therefore, Exxon's by implication—detached attitude toward the wildlife destroyed or threatened by the renegade oil. The CEO's absence from the scene, while the world watched animals die, portrayed Exxon as unfeeling and uncaring. If the truth be known, Rawl is at heart an ardent environmentalist whose questionable decision to stay away and communicate through less visible channels caused him to be branded by portions of the public as someone his family and friends would say he isn't.

A colleague of ours who used to be manager of public relations for a large consumer products company told us a story about his CEO that demonstrates how a top executive's poorly chosen and inappropriately timed words can literally paralyze an organization. This CEO had for years roundly boasted about his commitment to being a champion of employee rights and open communication. When the time came, as it has for so many companies these days, that he was forced to institute mass layoffs, his beliefs were tested and he didn't measure up.

His memo announcing the layoffs was carelessly worded and failed to follow his public relations counselor's advice. In the memo, the CEO tried to comfort employees by telling them that *only* "nonessential" jobs would be eliminated, and indicated that layoffs would occur from September through the following April. To add insult to injury, the CEO, in effect, told already distressed, out-of-work employees that they weren't important to the organization. And, because layoffs were stretched out over eight months instead of getting the bad news over with all at once, employees who remained were wracked by uncertainty and fear for the better part of a year. As a result, our associate reports that "no work got done while everybody waited for the next shoe to drop."

The principle of selectivity offers CEOs two fundamental choices in any situation: Choose to play the communication leadership role or choose not to play it. That sounds simpler than it really is. Whichever choice they make, if it's the wrong one, the consequences can affect their employees and organization for years to come. When the situation is dynamic and volatile, many nervous and tentative top managers, such as fictional Arlen Royster, prefer the low profile approach. Stay out of harm's way, play it safe and things will take care of themselves, they reason. These CEOs think that since they have little, if any, solid information about the situation, it's best not to say anything until they do. Unfortunately, that won't stop the media.

Ostrich-like top managers may justify their silence by telling themselves that it will buy them time to get all the information they need so they can be completely candid. Or maybe they believe that too much public discussion will expose their future plans prematurely, thus limiting their strategic options. Some managers might not want to risk appearing uninformed or inept in front of employees, customers, or stockholders, because they're unable to answer all questions. Sometimes, however, saying nothing—known as *strategic silence*—can send the loudest message of all. The decision *not* to communicate during a crisis, however, can cause the very effects on employees CEOs are trying to deter.

The notion of strategic silence is rarely, if ever, justifiable, in our opinion. But that's never more true than during times of stressful change. The risks attached to saying nothing in the false hope people will somehow find enlightenment elsewhere are simply too high. Lack of communication and information from the top inevitably creates a vacuum in the organization—a vacuum likely to be filled with speculation, innuendo, and misinformation. Just what a leader doesn't want.

When such voids develop, CEOs are automatically pushed into a reactive posture, which eventually forces them into trying to appease people who are already upset and who distrust top management. The prospects of winning back folks who've been lost aren't good. In contrast, CEOs who embrace their leadership role when tough times arise and who are proactively involved from the outset, will have a far better chance of shepherding their organizations to safety. That proactive approach was tested by CEO Walter Williams in his quest to save the once powerful steelmaker Bethlehem Steel Company.

The CEO Enters the Fray: Saving Bethlehem Steel

Walter Williams, a civil engineer by trade and a conservative manager by choice, doesn't instantly appear to be a strong candidate to practice hands-on, give-and-take communication with employees. But appearances and stereotypes can be misleading. Especially when the top executive is facing the dismal prospect of his corporation's extinction. From desperation often comes innovation. In this case, before Walter Williams tried innovating, he did some listening first.

In 1986, the newly appointed chairman and CEO of Bethlehem Steel, who started his career as a management trainee with the venerable steelmaker 34 years earlier, walked into a situation considered by most industry observers as beyond repair. A world-wide recession—along with growing competitive pressure from low cost, high-quality imported Japanese steel—had devastated Bethlehem's market position and prospects. Its stock price was at $4 a share, an all-time low. Customers were on the verge of cutting and running, because of inferior quality and tardy deliveries. The company had chopped 39,000 jobs over three years. Many small-town mills had been shut down. Employees were upset, scared, and threatening to strike.

The CEO Had to Be the One

When Williams created "Operation Bootstrap," a comprehensive plan to rebuild the crumbling company, he believed its success hinged on his ability to reenergize Bethlehem employees. "In tough times, the CEO and his senior managers have to do everything possible to overcome all those things which negatively impact morale and dampen employees' desire to participate and be part of the team," he explains.

"I don't think somebody who hasn't gone through this realizes how bad it can be on a person's spirits. In the last two years, my number one job has been communicating with employees—from managers and salaried employees to union members—to help them understand what needs to be done and encouraging them to do it."

Williams immediately took off for the field, visiting upwards of 50 customers and every steel mill and sales office each year, never passing up a chance to repeat his message of the need for quality improvement. He challenged employees and customers in eyeball-to-eyeball meetings to ask him the tough questions so that the dialogue would be real and meaningful, not the usual eyewash. Said a union official at Bethlehem's plant in Burns Harbor, Indiana: "Williams comes out of his ivory tower and gets his feet dirty walking the plant."[4]

Shortly thereafter, he initiated a quarterly video program so he could report regularly to employees on the company's performance. He persuaded jittery bankers to stick with the company for the bumpy ride ahead. He convinced labor and management to form joint teams and visit customers so they could recommend ways to boost the quality of Bethlehem's products.

Keeping His Ear to the Ground

Looking back now, Williams believes that one of the most important things he did was to listen, really listen, to employees' concerns and feelings. Indeed, his decision—better yet, his selection—to be a receiver rather than a sender of information is a good example of how two or more principles of the C-C-O-S model may work together and overlap (selectivity and compassion).

"If you're in management and really want to involve employees, the real communication is listening," says Williams. He recalls an instance shortly after becoming CEO when he became involved in a rough-and-tumble United Steel Workers labor contract negotiation in Pittsburgh. Those tough, adversarial negotiations had always been handled by Bethlehem's VP of labor or industrial relations. But with the state of affairs deteriorating rapidly, Williams asked the union leadership if he could speak to union members directly and "let them know how serious things were." He was told to come. No Bethlehem top manager had ever asked to enter the lion's den before, much less possessed the audacity to actually show up.

There's No Escaping if You're the CEO

In retrospect, this move to place himself directly in the line of fire of the organization's most disenchanted constituency may have been the turning point in the crisis. His tone was serious as he described the situation and what happened: "There were 100 people in the room, including all the key union officials from around the country. No other Bethlehem executives were there except our labor relations guy. It was a closed meeting. I gave my talk for half an hour and then, after pushing me for answers to their questions, they really unloaded on me. For four hours, I just stood there and took it. I know I didn't convince too many people to switch their position, but I allowed them to get it off their chests and see who I am."

After Williams absorbed union members' most bitter criticisms and pent up anger, the air slowly began to clear and communication again seemed possible. He adds, quite proudly, "We then entered negotiations and set-tled" matters, including obtaining some necessary concessions that had been labeled nonnegotiable.

As much time as he put into communicating with employees and customers, he admits that "it wasn't enough, not as much as I should do, but I'll always go out of my way to do it if it's needed." At the heart of it all, insists Williams, is that employees have "to see the dedication, the commitment by top management to including workers in the process." He tried hard to practice what he preached.

That's why when the company had to close the Lackawanna plant—the site where he'd started his Bethlehem career—three days after Christmas, Williams went there himself to meet with management, the union leadership, community leaders, and the media to try to ease the trauma. "I couldn't let something that major be passed off to someone down the line, like a plant manager," he says. "The people of that community deserved upper management. So I returned to where I'd started my career. I knew those people. I couldn't let somebody else do it—I had an obligation."

Deep in his gut, Williams knew how vital his hands-on participation was if Bethlehem Steel was to win back employees' lost belief in upper management.

Unfortunately, not all or even most CEOs are blessed with such natural instincts. That's why it's essential that top managers understand the true meaning of the principle of selectivity and how to artfully regulate their communication leadership role.

A Final Word

Selectivity is a principle designed to preserve CEOs' unique influence on employees and other key groups by strategically deploying the CEO-as-CCO for high-impact occasions, events, or issues. In essence, by intentionally limiting the CEO's communication role, the top executive enhances his or her effectiveness and places the responsibility for the lion's share of routine and day-to-day communication where it rightfully belongs: with middle and front-line managers. Selectivity represents a tightly focused laserbeam approach to CEO leadership, as opposed to the shotgun approach. Shotgun CEOs communicate often and broadly—probably too often and too broadly—hoping something, anything, might hit the target. In contrast, the laser CEO, primarily concerned with maximizing impact on an organization, communicates selectively by aiming only at specific targets at specific times.

Returning to Arlen ...

When last seen, Arlen and Rick Jamieson were making their way into a jam-packed Yankee Stadium for the Yankee-Red Sox playoff game. During the bumper-to-bumper limo ride from midtown Manhattan to the Bronx, the two pressured executives reviewed and debated plans for Royal's public admission that its financial records have been phony for the last few years. They went over how Arlen ought to handle some of the embarrassing and tricky questions he'll be asked by Royal employees and reporters after he makes the announcement two days from now.

Surfacing during his talk with Jamieson and an unexpected telephone conversation with his wife Andrea was Arlen's recurring sense of guilt—guilt over his indirect role in triggering the corporate crisis and guilt over his inability to reestablish a meaningful relationship with his son.

As the next chapter opens, Arlen is being pursued by Karen-Elaine Marshak, a provocative and clever *Journal* reporter who simply won't take no for an answer.

"I Have Seen
the Enemy—
and It Is Me ..."

Friday, October 12, 4:30 p.m. Susan O'Reilly looked up at the elegantly dressed woman who'd stationed herself squarely in front of her desk. As was the executive secretary's habit, she made an instantaneous eyeball appraisal. O'Reilly had learned after years in status-obsessed corporate America that one's title and position, as well as appearance and demeanor, were critically important to climbing up—or being passed on—the proverbial organizational ladder.

The woman standing before her, O'Reilly noted, was slender, wide-eyed, with shiny, shoulder-length reddish hair. Her finely-tailored, taupe suit was perfectly accented by a bright orange and brown scarf wrapped loosely around her neck. The woman's eager, artificial smile, and jumpy hand movements gave O'Reilly the feeling that this wasn't someone easily put off.

"Can I help you?" she asked in her best professional manner.

The woman extended a business card held at the ready. It read: "Karen-Elaine Marshak, business reporter, *The Wall Street Journal.*" O'Reilly was a bit surprised, but camouflaged it; a reporter wouldn't have been her first guess.

"Is Mr. Royster in? I just have a couple of quick follow-up questions. Won't take but a minute," Marshak promised glibly, knowing that no interview ever took just a minute.

O'Reilly stood so she could meet Marshak at eye level. "Mr. Royster's time, as you can imagine, is very tight these days, Ms. Marshak, is it? Perhaps Mr. Jamieson, our vice president of corporate communication, could spare a few mintues. I'd be happy to call and see if he's available."

Marshak shook her head, her imitation smile melting away.

"Or you can leave your card," O'Reilly patronized, "and I'll check with Mr. Royster as soon as he gets back ... though it may be a week or so before he'll be able to fit you in."

"So he's not in?" asked Marshak, angling herself to catch a peek into Arlen's office. The sneaky but effective move irritated O'Reilly, who was rarely, if ever, outmaneuvered on her own turf. The secretary-guard dog took silent delight in Marshak's disappointed expression when she saw an empty office. The resourceful reporter immediately began considering alternative approaches.

"Okay, thanks anyway," she said, ignoring O'Reilly's sudden move to pull the CEO's office door closed. "A gatekeeper who takes her role seriously," Marshak thought.

Turning around to face the elevators, she said with sweet insincerity, glancing down at O'Reilly's nameplate, "You won't forget to tell him I stopped by, will you Ms. ... uh ... Ms. O'Reilly?" As the carefully chosen words sputtered out, she pointed to the business card still in O'Reilly's hand. O'Reilly, miffed at the inference, took the comment as a directive. The secretary's intuition was telling her that Marshak was trouble for Royal—and for Arlen.

* * * * * * * *

Friday, October 12, 5:15 p.m. The upbeat mood of a half hour earlier had turned pensive, almost somber as the fivesome—Hadley, Jamieson, Coletto, Azoulette, and Bernard—sat around the horshoe-shaped wooden booth at the back of O'Brien's Irish Pub. A popular watering hole among Royal's executive staff, O'Brien's was at once a fine restaurant and a traditional Irish pub, complete with a row of dart boards, wooden tables and chairs, shamrock art, and an assortment of ales and beers from around the world.

Mentally spent, the group sat quietly, each reflecting privately on what had just happened. At the conclusion of the press conference where Arlen publicly disclosed Royal's misreported financial results, Joyce Hadley had suggested they all could use a thumbs-up drink before returning to Royal's HQ for the scheduled 6 p.m. post-mortem review of the day's events. They'd decided to walk the six blocks from Royal's Castle Hotel, site of the media event, rather than grab a cab. As they strolled along the city's swarming streets, the fall weather was turning colder by the minute as dark, threatening clouds approached. But their temporary high didn't last very long, not with the uncertainty of their futures weighing on their minds.

Rick Jamieson sat at the center of the table's curve. To his left was Hadley, head of human resources. Marketing VP Bob Azoulette claimed the outside position, stretching his long leg into the aisle, exposing a red-and-gold Argyle sock. Opposite Azoulette was legal beagle Joe Coletto, who had backed his pudgy torso next to Gloria Bernard, VP of investor relations, who was scrunched between him and Jamieson.

"How cozy," noted an exhausted-looking Bernard, surveying her colleagues' equally worn faces. She folded her hands and waited—for what she didn't know. Coletto picked up a bar napkin and absently wiped the damp table. Azoulette dropped his head back and closed his eyes.

"Okay, guys, I give up, is this a funeral or a celebration? In Ireland, it's sometimes tough to tell one from the other, I know ...," quipped Hadley, trying to prick the group's gloomy disposition. "Hey, I know you're all tired, but let's not assume the worst case until we have to, shall we? You all look like you've been to Armageddon and back. We're hanging in there pretty good, I think."

"Joyce, you're right, I suppose. The reality is," said Coletto matter-of-factly, "this thing isn't close to being over. It's just getting underway."

They all knew Coletto was right, but probably would've preferred leaving the thought unspoken for now. Their futures hinged on how Royal's employees and stockholders ultimately responded to Arlen's performance at that morning's two closed-circuit teleconferences, one for employees and one for managers, and the press conference that followed in early afternoon. Until the feedback began drifting in tomorrow, they could do little except wait, which kept them on edge and feeling philosophical.

No one spoke again for several minutes, except to place their drink orders. Finally, Bernard couldn't stand it any longer. "I thought Arlen was great today. I've never seen him as articulate and forceful," she observed. "Yet, he seemed to come across as sensitive, and very caring."

"Yeah, a real Bill Clinton," cracked Azoulette, smiling slyly.

The employee broadcast—a one-way video, two-way audio satellite hook-up—reached many of Royal's 63,000 workers throughout the company. The hour-long session had been a lively, no-holds-barred Q & A session between Arlen and some of the company's most outspoken employee-critics. As Jamieson and Hadley had warned, the questions came in all forms and from all directions, ranging from the minutely specific ("Will this affect my hours next week?") to the more introspective ("How much market share do you expect Royal to lose in the short- and long-term?").

Arlen had opened the broadcast with a meticulously planned, yet extemporaneously delivered explanation of the "problem," as he put it. In uncommonly candid terms, he described what he knew about the situation, what steps he was considering to correct the problem, and how he thought Royal and its employees would be affected. Then, for about half an hour, he fielded questions, his composure never wavering, even in the face of some angry outbursts. He closed the broadcast with a plea for employees' support, asking them to trust him and his staff to follow the right and fair road.

"The next few weeks may be among the toughest in Royal's history," Arlen had warned, staring solemnly into the camera's uncaring lens. "But we'll weather this storm as we have all others. And after we do, we'll emerge stronger and wiser than before. To do that, though, I need your help and your loyalty to stay the course with me. Friends, if you believe in this company, its people and our future together—as I do—then fasten your seat belts and get ready for what's likely to be a bumpy ride for awhile. I'll do everything in my power to smooth it out as soon as possible."

Then, unable to help himself, he had ad libbed a promise without really knowing whether he could deliver, "We'll all be smiling again by year's end." Later, when Jamieson called him on his hasty prediction, he simply said, "I believe it."

The broadcasts had gone about as well as they could've under the circumstances, most around the table agreed, although to varying degrees. Almost before Arlen had signed off, several members of Hadley's staff began making random phone calls to managers throughout the hotel system to check on employees' reactions. Early sketchy feedback showed that employees were impressed with Arlen's sincerity and openness; nevertheless, most said they didn't really understand this "cooked books" thing, but were worried about how much damage it could do to Royal's reputation. Most workers were, as one assistant manager delicately phrased it, "cautiously hopeful." A senior catering manager in Miami seemed to capture how many Royal workers felt: "My people aren't all that clear on what this stuff is all about, but Mr. Royster's comments made them damn well see the company's in hot water and Royal's reputation will take a beating on Wall Street and in the media."

"There were some pretty dumb questions Arlen handled with a straight face," Azoulette interjected, shaking his head.

"What'd you expect, Bob? Most employees were still in a state of shock about what this misreporting stuff means," Hadley said, her natural defense of employees surfacing.

"Like that dishwasher in Chicago who asked if he'd have to give back his raise?" goaded Azoulette.

"What about the bellman from LA who wanted to know who's responsible and if those 'idiot managers'--I think that's what he said—have been fired or thrown in jail yet?" prodded Coletto, pointing at Azoulette, who was nibbling on a swizzle stick. "That wasn't such a dumb question. And, fortunately, Arlen didn't treat it that way."

"The managers' videoconference had me worried," Hadley admitted. "I figured Keller might try to do something to make Arlen look bad. It must've been Mike who planted those leading questions that came up in the employee session. Like the guy from Seattle, I think it was, who asked him how long he'd actually known about the 'fraud!' That seemed to put Arlen on the defensive and make him appear culpable and incompetent."

"Speaking of Keller," cut in Azoulette, "where'd he and Grubner go? I noticed they didn't stay around for the press conference." Mike Keller and John Grubner had quietly left The Castle near the end of the managers' tele-meeting and hadn't been heard from since.

"I'm sure they had more pressing obligations," Jamieson said acidly, washing down his comment with a slug of beer.

Of the two broadcasts, the managers' teleconference had brought the more vocal and vehement reactions. Several managers expressed their distaste and resentment at being tainted by association with the guilty managers, demanding to know what Arlen planned to do to the "scoundrels" caught participating in the illegal scheme.

Arlen had purposely danced around the issue of punishment of the few "bad apples," pointing out several times that he still didn't know the whole story. He explained that this sort of complicated scheme isn't usually the work of one or even a handful of people, and he needed to know for sure if the crimes were more the result of misguided noble intentions or greed.

He'd chosen medical-oriented terms to describe the problem, characterizing it as a "disease, a perverted way of thinking" that needed to be "surgically removed from Royal's culture before it spread any further." Through it all, his own feelings of guilt never peeked through. Several irate managers bulldozed him into addressing the issue of responsibility, which he faced head-on, admitting regretfully, "Ultimately, I must accept the blame for not seeing the cancer growing soon enough."

He told workers that one area already under review was the management bonus system, which he thought might be tied too closely to short-term profit targets. Another move being planned, Arlen disclosed, was developing a Code of Ethical Conduct which all Royal employees, regardless of title or rank, would be required to sign annually. And he indicated there would be more frequent and in-depth audits of inventories and record-keeping practices at all Royal properties.

"The press was surprisingly tame, I thought," noted Bernard, switching focus to the press conference.

"That was the master plan," grinned Jamieson, a little boastfully. "We wanted to control and preempt the media's usual negative slant." Then, after a moment's thought, he added, "At least for the time being."

Arlen started the press conference in typical fashion by reading a brief opening statement, finalized by Jamieson early that morning. The statement itself hadn't come easily. It was hammered out by Jamieson and Coletto during several loud deliberations. Coletto, the consummate conservative attorney, held to the position that Arlen's prepared remarks shouldn't contain any admission of wrongdoing or any hint that Royal was ready to accept liability "that could be used against us" in a class action lawsuit.

On the opposite side of the issue was Jamieson, waving the First Amendment at Coletto as he argued for openness "beyond what the law requires," charging that "saying nothing just to avoid legal hassles" created an "impression of guilt or, at a minimum, that we've got something juicy to hide." He contended that Royal needed to be proactive, even though the company was clearly in a reactive, defensive position.

Although Coletto was never completely convinced, he eventually conceded that taking an "out front" position did have "some" merit. Their endless wrangling over the legal implications of divulging too little or too much information failed to convince Arlen one way or the other. So he ended up compromising, admitting nothing while carefully selecting nonspecific language designed to paint Royal as the concerned, responsive organization he believed it was. For instance, he talked of his commitment to correct the "unfortunate and regrettable irregularities" in Royal's financial statements caused by misguided managers' indiscretions. He told the media about the employee and manager teleconferences held earlier that day, and assured reporters that Jamieson's staff would have video clips and hard copy excerpts for those who wanted them. Finally, in an unplanned comment, Arlen swore his personal commitment to "making all necessary adjustments in our internal system that may have contributed to this troublesome situation."

The Q&A following Arlen's canned remarks—the verbal war of words and nerves when reporters try to get the CEO to say what he doesn't want to say—most worried Jamieson. In several practice sessions, he and Coletto had grilled Arlen with a series of tough, mortifying questions in the shotgun, accusatory style of Mike Wallace and Sam Donaldson. Preparation helped, Jamieson knew, but media confrontations, particularly when reporters suspected a businessperson of hiding something, were filled with potential land mines set to explode with any innocent slip of the tongue. And one such unforseen mine had almost blown up in Arlen's face.

The Wall Street Journal's Karen-Elaine Marshak had asked a seemingly harmless question about the scope of the misreporting problem at Royal, which Arlen answered directly and completely, closing with a polite referral to the company's news release. Then, without warning or prelude, she dropped a bombshell on him.

"Mr. Royster, isn't it true that there's a mutiny underway at Royal, orchestrated by disgruntled members of your staff committed to pushing you out?" she had asked pointedly, knowing she'd just stolen the show. All eyes snapped to attention, first in her direction, then to Arlen for his response.

The CEO appeared flustered and overtaken by surprise at first. As he groped for words, he tried to buy a little time. "Uh ... What was the question, Ms. Marshak? ... Why would you ask something so totally absurd?"

"That's a question, not an answer," she pressed. "It's a simple question, Mr. Royster. Are you the target of a mutiny attempt by several members of your staff?"

"No, I'm not," he said curtly, more a reflex than a considered response. Peering straight at her, he wondered what she really knew and where it had come from. "Who's your source for this groundless conjecture, Ms. Marshak?"

"A most reliable one, I can assure you, Mr. Royster. If I wasn't sure of that, I wouldn't be asking." Marshak smiled sweetly, content to wait for Arlen's next move, determined not to be drawn into a public debate with him before she knew more.

"There's nothing to it." He managed to say the words with enough artificial conviction in his voice that he almost sounded like he believed it. The band of reporters again looked at Marshak, who remained calm and patient. Most who knew her well assumed she was preparing to continue verbal combat with a helpless foe she'd surely demolish.

Arlen's brain shifted into neutral, uncertain of what to say or not say, fearing all options. Wishing he were anywhere else and anyone else, he awaited her next salvo by sifting among a menu of truths, half-truths, fabrications, and fibs flashing before him. He was helpless at that moment, and he knew it.

But rather than demand an answer, which she knew was her reporter's privilege, she decided to break off pursuit, inexplicably. Marshak, to everyone's surprise, had backed away, a move very unlike her. When she didn't repeat the question, the flabbergasted band of reporters inched closer to her, several trying to steal a look at her notes.

When Marshak didn't follow-up, Arlen wasted no time trying to shift subjects, but the other reporters would have nothing of it. They pelted him with biting questions about the alleged mutiny, while he steadfastly refused to comment on such a "ridiculous supposition." And, of course, the more intently he refused, the more belligerent they became. Marshak slipped to the back of the room, watching Arlen closely.

"I wish he'd thrown that question about a conspiracy to us," said Hadley.

"How could he, Joyce?" perked up Jamieson. "He's the CEO, for Pete's sake. He'd look like a jerk if he tried sidestepping the question any more than he did." Jamieson's intuition told him that if Marshak had chosen to force the issue, Arlen might've been in big trouble. But for some strange reason, she hadn't and that troubled Jamieson even more. Yet he knew that by her merely asking the question, Pandora's box had sprung open and would remain so indefinitely. Jamieson also deduced that Marshak's question must have originated from an inside tip—somebody who wanted to make Arlen look bad and put him in harm's way. "That damn S.O.B Keller," an angry Jamieson conjured.

Jamieson's recall of his anger passed in a few seconds. He then returned his focus to the ongoing discussion with his fellow VPs.

"All in all," Azoulette was wrapping up, sipping on his Lowenbrau, "I think Arlen came through in one piece, so we're still afloat for the time being, anyway. He managed to come off as sincere and compassionate. Even if he did look pretty flustered when the mutiny thing came tumbling out of left field."

"A testament to his handler," bellowed Coletto, looking toward Jamieson. "A toast to Rick Jamieson, Arlen's alter-ego." Jamieson put his hands up in protest, embarrassed by the unwanted attention coming his way.

"Considering what it took to get him to agree to be the front man, I salute you, Rick," added Hadley, lifting her Rusty Nail triumphantly toward Jamieson.

"Look, all we did was the strategic work. Arlen carried the day by himself," Jamieson insisted, shifting uncomfortably. "Let's drink to the CEO. To Arlen." All glasses rose in unison. If only they'd known how sweaty-palmed nervous Arlen had been throughout the day, Jamieson thought to himself.

Paraphrasing former Supreme Court Justice Thurgood Marshall's assessment of himself, Jamieson concluded his toast. "Arlen may not be the most natural public speaker in the world, but today he did the best he could with what he had."

"Here, here," they each added.

Hadley glanced at her watch, which read 5:50, leaving them only ten minutes before the official post-mortem review back at the office.

"Oops, time to go." She pushed Azoulette out of the booth, dragging Jamieson by the right arm. Coletto helped Bernard out the other side. "It's almost six and you know Arlen'll be there right on time wondering where we are. We'd better get hopping."

* * * * * * * * *

Friday, October 12, 5:30 p.m.   While Arlen's staff VPs were having drinks and picking apart his public performance, Marshak was standing outside the Royal Accommodations headquarters building. Motionless and disturbed by her failure on the thirtieth floor, she looked up and recognized Arlen's chauffeur, Jeffrey Andrews, leaning against the stretch limo she'd seen Arlen enter a few days before. She froze for a second, looking thoughtfully back at the building and then again at the limo. Arlen must be somewhere nearby, she realized. She rummaged in her bag, found a small spray bottle of perfume, spritzed some on her neck and behind her ears, slipped it back into her bag, and moved toward the car.

"Hi. You're Mr. Royster's driver, aren't you?" she asked matter-of-factly, moving close enough to Andrews so he'd pick up her scent, which he did. "I saw you the other day at The Castle, after Mr. Royster's speech. I'm Karen-Elaine Marshak."

"Oh yeah, I remember. The *Journal* reporter," Andrews grinned, studying this cocky, appealing woman who he thought had caught Arlen's eye.

"Look," she lied, consulting imaginary notes, "Susan O'Reilly sent me down here to find you, because she said you'd know where Mr. Royster was. I really need to ask him a few questions. Is he still in the building or has he gone somewhere else?"

Andrews pushed himself off the limo and took a half step toward Marshak, closing the distance between them to a few inches.

"No, she didn't, Miss," Andrews answered with a cold stare. "Susan O'Reilly wouldn't do that." He searched Marshak's face for a sign of embarrassment. "So what's the game? What're you really after?"

Marshak stood her ground, playing along. "Go ahead, call her. I'll wait."

The two remained face-to-face for several seconds, neither one moving or blinking. Andrews thought he saw a flash of anxiety pass before Marshak's eyes. He opened the limo door and grabbed the car phone.

Before he could key in the number, Marshak put a hand on his arm. "Wait," she said indecisively with a quick, nervous smile, avoiding his eyes. He stopped and turned back toward her. "Okay, you win," she admitted softly. Andrews replaced the phone and looked at her, expecting an explanation.

"Arlen and I hit it off pretty well the other day so I've been following the Royal situation pretty closely since then. I unloaded some pretty heavy information on him at the press conference a little while ago. I'm pretty sure he'd want to discuss it with me." Then, licking her lips, she said, "I just need a couple of minutes with him. Can you help me out?"

"Sorry, Miss Marshak. I can't do that." Andrews folded his arms and glanced down the street to his right toward Central Park, hoping his boss might instantly appear and take him off the spot.

Marshak stepped closer, her penetrating fragrance engaging him. "Just tell me where he is ... because if you don't, when I do find him, which I assure you I will, I'll tell him it was you who gave him away," she pressured, brushing his chest with the spiral end of her notepad.

Andrews laughed, amused by Marshak's pointless threat. "You don't give up easily, do you, lady? Anything for the inside story, right? Even intimidating a lowly chauffeur."

Marshak rolled her eyes, her expression turning innocent. Andrews paused and looked once again toward the park, his mind spinning, not sure what to do. Should he steer this pretty, pushy reporter, who just might have information Arlen wanted or needed, toward his boss or should he keep her far away from him?

Ten minutes earlier, a preoccupied and troubled Arlen Royster had told Andrews he needed some time to decompress after the press conference, which had just ended. He wanted a few minutes alone in his personal oasis, Central Park.

As Arlen had started for the Park, Andrews offered to pick up a sandwich for his boss. "Nah. Go get something for yourself and bring me the tab, Jeff. I'll grab a hot dog or a pretzel if I get hungry," Arlen called back. "See you in about 45 minutes. Just need to sort a few things out." Loosening his tie and breaking into a trot, Arlen quickly disappeared on one of the many winding concrete paths that criss-cross the tree-lined urban preserve.

"I wouldn't normally do this, lady, but I think for some strange reason he might actually want to talk to you," Andrews said, pointing directly across 59th Street. "He's somewhere in the park, but I'm not sure where," he continued, at once regretting his indiscretion. Then, shaking his head and frowning, he added under his breath, "Because he said he wanted to be alone."

Marshak didn't hear Andrews' last words. She was already dodging traffic, waving cars and taxis off with her notepad, knowing she had only minutes to find Arlen and get him to open up. Entering the park at a slow jog, she hadn't gone 25 yards when she spotted him, sitting alone on a park bench, his listless eyes transfixed on the horizon. His tie was off, and his suit jacket was draped over the back of the bench. Next to him was a steaming hot dog, untouched. A can of diet Coke glittered in the late afternoon sun as it played peek-a-boo from behind the darkening storm clouds.

He was oblivious to everything except his own thoughts, searching among them for an answer, a sign, an omen. He looked dejected, like a schoolboy who'd been expelled for something he didn't do. The slump of his body exposed a man exhausted, physically and mentally, journeying deep within his soul.

In his mind, Arlen hated the uncertainty of not knowing how people inside and outside Royal would ultimately judge his leadership. And his frustration was made worse by his indecisiveness about his own future, an issue separate from how the Royal situation would play out. What's more, he couldn't stop thinking about the auditor's report he'd received earlier in the day. Major accounting "irregularities"—the accountant's euphemism for fraud—had now been found at eight of the 11 Midwest properties. Plus, he couldn't escape the nagging dilemma of what to do about the managers who'd been playing the funny numbers game: fire them, prosecute them, reassign them or ... maybe secretly thank them for waking him from his own dream world.

With these thoughts all colliding, the one that gnawed at him most was Keller's accusation that he, Arlen, was really to blame for the managers' misbehavior, that his obsession with profit margins had pushed otherwise hard-working, loyal managers to rationalize immoral and illegal acts. Although he despised Keller for saying it and for using it against him, Arlen couldn't deny that the accusation had merit, maybe more than he was willing to admit. It stabbed mercilessly at his conscience.

Keller and Grubner had been unusually subdued and distracted at staff meetings the past two days. "Coconspirators against me," Arlen thought, feeling dejected and angry concurrently. But, he comforted himself, now at least he knew how they planned to come at him. It would be at an emergency board meeting set for Monday afternoon, called at the insistence of two board members, Donn Leiberman and Marcia Gross, both long-time Keller supporters. The meeting was certain to be filled with plenty of political fireworks and power brokering—and, Arlen realized, would determine his future, at Royal and perhaps beyond.

He wasn't sure whether he cared one way or the other.

* * * * * * * * * *

Marshak stood perfectly still for several seconds, studying Arlen Burch Royster. She was acutely conscious of the tranquility surrounding her, a sharp contrast to the cacophony of shrill car horns, screeching brakes, and shouting voices just a few yards beyond the park's shrub-lined borders. A swirling wind whisked a seemingly endless parade of brittle, multicolored leaves across the park's expansive grounds.

Feeling a bit like a voyeur peeking into a person's soul, Marshak saw a man at war with himself, not the same energetic, confident CEO she'd met and been attracted to a few days before. Standing there, looking upon Arlen, who appeared troubled and vulnerable, Marshak, the reporter, clashed with Marshak, the woman; she didn't know whether to leave or try to offer comfort.

But her reporter's instinct wouldn't allow her to go without trying to check out "the story." A few seconds later, she was just a few feet away from the wood-slatted green bench on which Arlen sat. He was still unaware of her. She waited, not sure what to do next.

"So, how's life for the naked emperor in the glass office?" she blurted out nervously, her words running together. At first, she wasn't sure he heard her. No movement, not even a blink of recognition.

Then, ever so slowly, his head pivoted toward her, a strained grin appearing, "You do seem to show up in the strangest places and at the strangest times. Not just a coincidence, I'm sure."

"May I join you?" she asked politely. He gestured for her to sit, which she did, instinctively reaching in her handbag for her pen and notepad.

"I won't even ask how you found me. A reporter's instinct, right? So, to what do I owe the pleasure of this unscheduled visit? No doubt, something to do with that mutiny question you sandbagged me with?"

He wasn't angry, more contemplative. He turned toward her, pleased by the sight of her eager face, but unaware of his need for the compassion—as well as the flattery—she seemed willing to provide.

She studied him closely, wondering what tact to take with this man who she couldn't easily classify. A moment later, she flipped closed her notepad, dropped it in her purse and tossed the bag under the bench.

"I had to ask, I hope you understand that." Her eyes never left him, although his drifted toward the lake. Then, automatically trying to improve her position, she added a bit sheepishly, "I could've pushed you harder, but ..."

"That's true, I suppose. But what I can't figure out is why you backed off." He looked at her quizzically, incredulously.

She became annoyed, her eyes hardening. "Let's just say it didn't feel right to me and leave it at that for now, shall we?" She was switching directions quickly and emphatically, and Arlen didn't know why. But he decided to leave it alone; if she wanted to tell him more, she would.

"So, tell me, how are you doing, Arlen? You wanna talk about anything? Just person-to-person—off the record, of course. I'm a pretty good listener."

Arlen was puzzled by her sudden display of compassion. He couldn't help but wonder if it wasn't a ploy. He snorted, his businessman's cynicism returning. "Rick Jamieson has preached to me for years *never* to talk off-the-record to a reporter. He says there's really no such thing. How can I be sure you don't have a tape recorder running right now?" He kicked at her pocketbook.

"You wanna frisk me?" She looked straight at him, raising her arms. Her reaction, which seemed genuine, surprised Arlen, who wanted to believe she was there for more than a story, yet his businessman's antenna warned him to question her motives. The thought of frisking her, however, was not unappealling to him. He was being drawn to her and he wasn't sure he wanted to resist. Was she really reaching out to him? Did he want her to? Or was he reaching out to her?

"I didn't mean to question your integrity—or your sincerity," he said firmly. "But, we haven't known each other very long so I'm not sure how you operate. The tape recorder crack was a cheap shot. Sorry."

Now it was her turn to evaluate his honesty. Partially accepting it at face value, her mouth spread into a delicate smile. "I know I'm not always easy to figure out. It's an occupational hazard, I guess. Most business people don't think reporters have any scruples ... or personal feelings."

Arlen peeked at his watch. It was time to head back to the office. "I have a meeting with my staff right about now ... unfortunately," he said, disappointed.

"Look," she said seriously, "the real reason I wanted to talk to you was to explain about the mutiny question. This morning I got several calls from sources claiming to be highly placed Royal insiders who wanted me to know that ... that ... one of them used very graphic language ... how was it phrased ..."

She reached into her bag for her notepad, flipping through about half the pages before she found it. "That Humpty Dumpty's about to fall off his wall and break into a million pieces. That's where the question came from. After I did some checking on my own, I felt secure enough to ask the question in order to make it part of the public record and to make sure you took it—and me—seriously. You ducked it quite adeptly, by the way."

"Calls from who, dammit?" Arlen bored in impatiently, wanting her to tell him more. "And how many calls did you say you got, exactly?"

"I didn't say and I won't. You know I can't reveal my sources after I promise anonymity," she countered, growing more uncomfortable now.

"Can't or won't?" She looked away. "But you do know who these callers are, don't you? Are they living, breathing people or just voices from the great beyond?"

"Oh, they're real all right. Real enough to be in a position to know what they're talking about. That I checked before anything else. Look, Arlen, I can understand your anxiety, but I can't give you the details I know you want. I don't have any specifics, except ..." Marshak bit her nails, trying to decide whether to say any more. She was distressed with herself for allowing this man she hardly knew to penetrate the psychological partition separating her professional and private selves. The words kept flowing.

"I was told that your speech last week on corporate leadership was a crock—although the language the caller used was considerably more colorful—because you wouldn't know leadership from scuba diving. That is, other than knowing how to lead Royal into oblivion. I was urged to dig into the curious fact that Royal has consistently turned a profit during a down period when the rest of the hotel industry hasn't seen black ink in over a year. How could I ignore that?

"The hint given me was that Royal's financial health was just an illusion you'd created through manipulation and deception. You were characterized as somebody who'd sell out his mother if it meant an extra dollar of profit—the caller's words, not mine."

Arlen clenched his teeth, too angry to speak. "He has no scruples, that ...," he fumed silently, now certain one of the callers had to have been Keller or Grubner, or their designees. "A preview of things to come from Keller & Company," he thought, grateful for the warning. By trying to air Royal's dirty laundry in public, for strictly political gain, they had violated an unwritten law of corporate life: unequivocal allegiance to boss, company, and colleagues, in that order. Breaking that law meant burning one's bridges, forever. In a bizarre sort of way, Arlen admired their daring, their willingness—or was it foolishness?—to risk career and reputation for what they wanted most. He wondered if he could ever take such a risk.

A staccato of angry car horns blared in the background, registering commuters' impatience with New York City's rush-hour parade. Neither Arlen nor Marshak heard the noise; they heard only the troubling questions and answers rumbling through their heads. She continued the game of cat-and-mouse.

"So, who's out to get you, Arlen? What does all this have to do with Royal's misreporting problems? Why not tell me what I already suspect and which is bound to come out soon anyway? You've got my word that I'll write it just as you tell it."

Arlen reminded himself of the potential dangers of biting on Marshak's loaded questions. He thought about their respective, oftentimes conflicting, roles: she wanting to tell the so-called inside story; he wanting to keep the inside story inside. He snickered at himself for forgetting, even for a moment, why Marshak, first and last a reporter, was there. Although he was enjoying her interest in him beyond the story, and the way it made him feel, he knew what really motivated her, and what he had to do.

"Nice try, Karen-Elaine. But commenting on speculation isn't my style. It merely gives conjecture a legitimacy it doesn't deserve and may inadvertently lead people to false conclusions. Now, you wouldn't want to be a party to such a thing, would you?"

His sarcasm irritated her, but she let it pass. She examined him carefully, her exasperation surfacing in a frown, realizing she wasn't going to get what she'd come for.

Unaccustomed to walking away empty-handed, Marshak retreated, her thoughts already conjuring how she could win next time. She asked pleasantly, tactfully, "I can see this isn't a good time for you. Can I call you for an appointment? I'll be writing a feature story on Royal's 'cooked books' dilemma and how you handled it. Maybe by next week we'll be able to talk ... less cryptically."

"Well, I don't know if that's such a good idea ... I'm not sure ... maybe we could try again after the dust settles," said Arlen, relieved her interrogation was over and surprised at his own delight at the thought of seeing her again. "Why don't you check back with my secretary next week to see how crowded my calendar is. No promises, but I'll try."

Arlen remained on the park bench, watching Marshak scurry away, not once looking back at him, he mused. Her interest in his problems and general well-being, however genuine or well-acted it might've been, had nevertheless flattered and invigorated him. Before she showed up, he'd felt alone, weak and vulnerable, a victim of uncontrollable forces. But their pointed verbal exchange had stirred his self-confidence as a man and refocused his perspective as a businessman.

He stood up, and after dumping the uneaten hot dog and unopened soda can into a trash bin, headed back to Royal headquarters—and reality.

* * * * * * * * *

Friday, October 12, 6:10 p.m. Rather than start the meeting on time, Jamieson watched his associates, scattered throughout the corporate conference room, chatting casually, their mood upbeat again. Glancing at his watch, he knew if Arlen had been there, he wouldn't have waited for anyone, regardless of their importance to the discussion or position in the company. But Jamieson never claimed to possess either the maniacal drive or the need for control his boss did.

"So, where is the man of the hour?" Azoulette asked, slumped comfortably in a cushy, high-backed leather chair adjacent to Jamieson.

The communication VP shrugged. "He'll be here," he flipped back. Unthinking, he plopped down in Arlen's favorite spot at the end of the conference table, nearest the door. "Something important must have come up."

All there thought they understood the pressure Arlen had been living with the past few days, but they couldn't really know. And, there was no let up in sight yet. Meetings like this one—group dissections of top-level managers' public performances—had been hatched by Jamieson early in Arlen's tenure as CEO. As CEO, Arlen knew he'd be the favorite target of such scrutiny, and although he didn't relish the prospect, he recognized its value.

The door behind Jamieson burst open. Conversations stopped in mid-sentence. Jamieson swiveled around to face Arlen, who appeared more relaxed than he had a right to under the circumstances. Jamieson started to get up, but was waved back down by the CEO.

"No, stay where you are, Rick. This is your party," Arlen instructed, swinging Jamieson's chair around so he faced the table and the others. Arlen's left hand was hidden behind his back.

"Sorry I'm late," he continued, nodding at the other VPs. "I had to stop by my office to pick up something," he grinned mischievously. Bringing his hand out from behind his back, he held a deep-blue baseball hat with the distinctive white interlaced Yankee logo on the front. He jammed it onto Jamieson's head, surprising him so that his eyes sprung wide as he grabbed for his head.

"It's a very special hat," Arlen smiled broadly, "made just for hapless Red Sox fans, like Rick." The CEO drifted to the opposite end of the table and sat down next to Bernard. He leaned forward, anticipating Jamieson's reaction. The VP pulled the cap off, turned it around so he could see it, and chuckled at what he saw. Across the back in inch-high, Red Sox blood-red script letters was stitched "The Curse of the Bambino," a reference to Boston's inability—or bad luck, as Sox fans believed—to win a pennant in the 70 years since Boston sold Babe Ruth to the Yankees.

All eyes were on Arlen, wondering what was next. His unusual presentation had caught them off guard. "Just a small memento for Rick from Wednesday night's unforgettable game," Arlen explained. The Red Sox had lost again, as usual, 4-3, despite a three-run ninth inning that ended with Boston runners standing on every base.

"You were a pretty good sport the other night, Rick ... but, then again, you've had more than your share of experience learning to lose gracefully," derided Arlen. "Maybe next year, eh?" Arlen laughed softly, enjoying the moment.

"So, where are we?" the CEO asked, switching to serious in a flash, looking to be brought up to speed.

"We were just getting going," Jamieson fibbed, slipping the baseball cap back on his head defiantly. "I'd like to keep this short, since we're all bushed and have full agendas tomorrow. Joyce, before we look at highlights of the videotapes of the teleconferences, what's the current feedback on reactions to Arlen's presentations today?"

Hadley launched into her answer, but Arlen's attention had already started wandering through an itinerary of topics he knew he couldn't sidestep ... Keller and Grubner's assault on his job ... Glenn's wayward career ... Marshak's pretty face ... Andrea's lofty expectations of him ... the Mahoney offer ... Marshak again ...

He felt pulled in too many different directions at once, trying unsuccessfully to be different Arlens to different people. At that moment, he felt like nobody he recognized.

PART 4

Where Are We Going? A Look to the Future

9

The Future: Seeking a New Breed of Top Dog

Sometimes, if you look closely at events unfolding today, you can catch glimpses of tomorrow.

In 1988, when the California Angels brought up young outfielder Dante Bichette from the minor leagues, he had a "can't miss" label plastered on his chest. Tall and rangy, powerfully built, and blessed with a rifle arm, much was expected of him. Maybe too much. But less than three years later, the potential star was traded to the Milwaukee Brewers for an aging star who wouldn't last through the next season.

Something had gone terribly wrong—but neither the Angels nor Bichette knew what. Was it just a case of another "hot shot" upstart not living up to his potential? Or was it a case of management not giving him enough time or the right kind of coaching? Or was it something more?

To hear Angels management tell it, Bichette's problem wasn't his God-given physical talent, but his lackadaisical attitude and lukewarm dedication to team and game. As you'd expect, Bichette disagrees vehemently with his former club, arguing that the Angels never really understood him and didn't give him the help he needed to develop.

Although Bichette hasn't reached the superstar status originally predicted, he's become a solid major leaguer, hitting around .300 for the Brewers (and now with the expansion Colorado Rockies). There seems little question that the key to his transformation was rediscovering his drive, his motivation. The difference, according to Brewers manager Phil Garner, is that Milwaukee management tried to figure out what makes Dante tick before they passed judgment on him. "Dante was one of the most misunderstood players around," says Garner, a former player himself. "I'd heard he was on the moody side; you never knew what he was thinking. I don't think anybody understood him or knew him. He's very, very sensitive. A lot of people probably didn't know his feelings or sensitivities were hurt, and he withdrew. They took that as rebellion."[1]

Garner's relationship-building approach to managing—that is, adjusting to employees' diverse values and lifestyles, rather than treating everybody the same way—offers a glance at the sorts of capabilities tomorrow's managers will be expected to possess, regardless of the type of organization or industry. The days of managing, and leading, by edict and rule books are fast becoming taboo. Those in positions of authority must tread lightly with their authority or face revolution. The biggest demand will be for relationship-makers, for that's what leadership is all about. Tomorrow's business leaders will be those managers who aren't squeamish about leaving the executive suite, communicating directly with skeptical or angry groups who expect more than may be reasonable, and then hammering out compromises.

Illustrations of such alliance-creating behavior are becoming more prevalent as the trend takes hold. An example that graphically makes this point involves the recently appointed Chancellor of the University of California at Irvine, Laurel Wilkening, and her handling of a student protest on campus. Following the not-guilty verdicts of police officers in the first Rodney King trial in April, 1992, students assaulted UCI's administration building, smashing windows and doors, demanding to speak to top executives about racism on campus.

The university president was out of town, but Wilkening, then next in line, was there. Rather than wait for instructions or attempt to negotiate through emissaries or written notes, she responded directly and openly. The planetary scientist-turned-executive waded into the crowd, and when she couldn't be heard, shed her heels and hopped onto the table that the protesting students had been using as a battering ram. After a few minutes of intense give-and-take, students calmed down enough so that Wilkening and leaders of the protest moved to the foyer of the administration building to discuss matters in a far less confrontational setting.[2]

Another example of a top executive who seems to appreciate the value of relationships to organizational effectiveness is C. Michael Armstrong, a long-time IBM senior executive who became CEO of Hughes Aircraft in mid-1992. As an outsider whose unpopular central task was to restructure, the company, Armstrong was viewed with trepidation by many of Hughes' executives. Even before he accepted the job, Armstrong spent eight days studying the company's seven top managers to determine if he thought he could work with them and they with him, and whether they could develop a "mutual respect," as Armstrong phrased it.

Once convinced of the managers' talents and receptivity, he took the position, gathered the executive team together to discuss plans for restructuring and gave each of them a week to decide if they were in or out. His bluntness and expression of respect for them apparently worked; all stayed and all committed themselves to the reorganization—and profits are now way up.[3]

Make no mistake about it, managing human behavior is far less concrete and predictable than managing tangible assets, like production lines and balance sheets. However, in years to come, the difference between success and failure of leader-managers will increasingly be determined by their ability—or inability— to make sense of the fickle human condition: to relate, to construct coalitions, to build teams, to negotiate, to inspire commitment. And those who can't will be tossed out—or, far more likely, won't get a crack at the top job in the first place. But those would-be leaders who master the vagaries of the "mortal" side of management can write their own tickets to the top.

Returning to the C-C-O-S Model

In the preceding four chapters, we laid out in detail each of the four principles of our C-C-O-S model of CEO communication: consistency, compassion, organization, and selectivity. The model is intended to provide business executives with a useful and usable set of guidelines for strengthening their communication effectiveness and, consequently, their leadership effectiveness. As is true with any general set of guidelines, each principle is important by itself and serves a distinct purpose in the overall model, yet the true power of the model is realized only when all four principles work together simultaneously.

Our central point to CEOs and aspiring top managers is that they must master all four principles, separately and as an integrated whole, to become effective corporate leaders. Not easy to do, but the ideal, the goal, nevertheless.

As we peer ahead and attempt to visualize the CEO of 10 or 20 years from now, we think the two principles most lacking will be compassion and selectivity. That's not to say that consistency and organization are any less important or don't play instrumental roles in the model's relationship-construction process. Not at all. It's just that the notions of consistency and organization are, we believe, better understood by CEOs and already somewhat assimilated into their thinking and actions.

Compassion and selectivity, on the other hand, are concepts not yet fully appreciated or accepted by many contemporary CEOs, and therefore are more apt to be underused, misinterpreted, or misapplied by future chiefs. In time, these principles will become part of top management's everyday vernacular, we hope. But it'll take some more time. In this brief peek at the emerging profile of the next generation CEO, our observations will primarily center on aspects of compassion and selectivity.

More precisely, in this final chapter, we dust off our crystal ball and attempt to bring into focus some of the adjustments we believe top dogs of the twenty-first century will need to make to be effective leaders. Our recommendations will encompass several areas. We begin by looking at the CEO's evolving relationship-building role and how it will change the ways top executives think, act, communicate, and solve problems. Next, we focus on an area that can transform the way future leaders define their role: America's MBA programs, and how their curricula need to change to better prepare today's entry-level managers for tomorrow's leadership challenges. Finally, we explore how CEOs are modifying the way they work, including what the CEO office of the future is likely to look like.

Redefining the CEO's Role

Sometimes, if you detect changes before they happen, you can help shape them instead of just reacting to them.

Tomorrow's CEOs will not look, sound, or behave like today's top executives, who likewise bear little resemblance to yesterday's chiefs. Sweeping changes within the workplace and to the people in it never cease. Unavoidably, business executives also must continually redefine their management role and style in order to adapt to these changes. That fact will never change.

Unlike their predecessors, whose bent was hoarding information and controlling people, the next generation corporate leader will share data and negotiate compromises—not because it's faddish to do so, but because it adds value to their organizations. At General Electric, for example, a major factor in executives' performance reviews is managers' ability to relate effectively to others. CEO Jack Welch explains in *Control Your Destiny or Somebody Else Will* that GE is now "breeding a new generation of leaders distinguished by their ability to elicit cooperation from others."[4] Fast emerging is a new view of management—one reflecting a fundamental shift in the labor-management relationship where confrontation and manipulation are being replaced by collaboration and mediation.

Harvard's Rosabeth Moss Kanter calls the changes steering this new paradigm the "new managerial work," which, she argues, is a "reinventing" of the management profession so that it will depend less on hierarchy and designated authority and more on participative management to energize workers.[5] This reborn prototypical manager will rely on personal dynamics—communication and persuasive skills—to motivate employees, not on status, title, or the power of position.

Andy Grove, CEO of computer-maker Intel, has dramatically redefined the modern-day manager's role in a way that captures the growing emphasis on communication and information sharing. His vision reflects the way tomorrow's managers will rely on the inherent power of the communication process to draw people together to share information to get the job done—in the short- and long-term. He sees managers performing three primary functions, which he defines as: (1) securing necessary information through communication; (2) making decisions based on information obtained through communication; and (3) modeling the communication process so all employees can secure information they need to do their jobs and understand the organization.

What Kanter and Grove are describing in not so many words is the kind of CEO-CCO leader we've advocated throughout the book: someone who, along with the usual business acumen, has the human relations capabilities to, for example, present and defend an organization's public position, manage its reputation, inspire constituents' loyalty, and assemble coalitions of stakeholders. In other words, to act as a leader. The emphasis will no longer solely be on the CEO to make the decisions and leave the rest to others. CEOs will be expected to take a hand in creating an organizational climate that encourages others to participate in the decision-making process with upper management and then lead the implementation of those jointly made decisions.

Top dogs of the late 1990s will make decisions having more to do with people-to-people issues than with technology or product issues. Already some progressive CEOs, such as Colgate-Palmolive's Reuben Mark, are recognizing this trend, as well as how slippery and perplexing human relations issues can be. Mark predicts that the next 10 years "will have little to do with whether to build a plant or not build a plant, but with issues like who do you promote, who do you give authority to, who do you trust and don't trust ..."[6]

What Will Future CEOs "Look" Like?

The twenty-first century model CEO will think, analyze problems, and act in ways wholly different compared to the highly bureaucratic late twentieth-century model. These changes, driven by stakeholders' shifting expectations of top management's role in organizational life, are reshaping the profile of the ideal chief executive officer. Following is a sketch of some of the ways CEOs of the future are likely to operate differently than their forerunners.

An expanded understanding of the role of compassion, so essential to developing relationships with any group, will exemplify future CEOs. The call that will grow increasingly louder in upcoming years will be for executives who are genuinely sensitive and empathetic to human foibles, and who believe in and practice a participatory style of managing. As discussed in Chap. 6 on compassion, recent research on women's leadership styles suggests that the so-called transformational style of leadership, common in many female executives, offers a useful profile of a relationship-driven manager. This style, characterized by an ability to motivate others by transforming their self-interests into the organization's interests, offers corporate America a blueprint for breeding tomorrow's best executives, irrespective of gender. Transformational managers, are, according to the data, flexible, strong communicators, comfortable working in teams, and know how to downplay ego and power.[7] These very attributes define, in large measure, the kind of CEO—sensitive to the need for creating alliances inside and outside the organization—we see as the archetype in the decades ahead.

Being able to forge relationships, while critically important, isn't enough. As boards and stockholders become brutally aware of the ferocious competition their companies face domestically and globally, they are expecting—no, demanding—more and more from the people charged with protecting their investments. Lester Korn, chairman of executive search firm Korn/Ferry, proposes the sort of CEO profile he thinks most boards want: "They want someone with successful general management experience, a strong profit-and-loss record, the capability of dealing with people, and an orientation toward marketing, finance and communication."[8]

Putting that point in slightly different terms is Jean-Pierre Garnier, executive vice president of SmithKline Beecham, an international pharmaceutical company based in Philadelphia. As CEOs are compelled to increase their visibility, particularly with outside constituencies, as seems inevitable, Garnier sees top executives forsaking some of their administrative obligations through delegation and outsourcing, while placing substantially more emphasis on building long-term alliances with essential audiences.

As the 1990s began, *Fortune* writer Brian Dumaine asked recently-appointed CEOs to identify the major challenges they see ahead. He discovered that top executives at that time held dramatically different outlooks and skills than the more "narrowly focused marketing or restructuring specialist" CEO of the 1970s and 1980s. They saw CEOs as having their own vision—and being able to articulate it. The new leader must "take a broad view" and "love to explore the new." Corporate leaders of the future must be skillful negotiators and capable of managing people and projects without having full control of them. And they must be sympathetic to employees' and customers' concerns, and "will know how to give away authority rather than give orders."[9]

Findings remarkably similar to Dumaine's showed up in a more recent study of almost 200 CEOs of U.S. organizations who were asked to share their biggest challenges. Conducted by Stephen Harper of the University of North Carolina at Wilmington, the study uncovered that the most critical and personally rewarding challenges facing chief executives have to do with people. Activities like "making sure the human side of the enterprise works at all levels," "attracting, training, and stimulating workers," and "managing and motivating people" were identified as a CEO's major concerns for the future, regardless of the size of the CEO's organization.[10]

The picture forming is of a top executive corps needing strengths not considered imperative in leaders past. The best of the bunch will be those who are persuasive communicators, employee- and consumer-oriented, creative thinkers, and expect a lot of themselves and their employees. In essence, the new CEO will more closely resemble a human resources specialist—in personality and skill capabilities—than an operations or financial wizard.

What Will Future CEOs "Think" Like?

Sometimes, if you understand how people's minds work, you can better understand why they act as they do.

Thus far, we've talked about CEOs' likely behavior as managers and leaders. Central to understanding how executives act is understanding how they think, analyze information, and try to solve problems. A person's behavior and thinking patterns are inherently connected and reveal much about the person's philosophy and priorities. Just as changes in the business environment are requiring top managers to adapt their leadership styles, so too are changes in communication technology and information availability forcing adjustments in executives' cognitive patterns. Faced with marketplaces literally exploding with information, much of it conflicting and partial, chief executives must be able to manage ambiguous situations and sift through large amounts of information quickly. Such talents will be essential to CEOs of the future, who will have to deal with change on a full-time basis.

Today's top managers are often overloaded with an endless flow of complex and technical information. How quickly and expertly they can absorb and analyze the oftentimes confusing intelligence crossing their desks will reveal much about them as decision makers. That's why tomorrow's chief executive will have to think "multidirectionally," argues psychologist Siegfried Streufert of Penn State University's College of Medicine. He says that future executives will be expected to process conflicting information from multiple sources speedily and concurrently, allowing them to "employ much more complex strategies" and be open to alternative possibilities.[11]

Managers using this type of systems thinking, explains Harvard's Dan Isenberg, will be better equipped to detect underlying patterns amidst chaos and thus focus quickly on the heart of a problem. To do this, managers will need a high tolerance for vagueness and, unlike the typical contemporary manager, welcome the unexpected as a powerful source for generating creative solutions. What's more, Isenberg emphasizes, future managers will place enormous importance on gathering intelligence before they draw conclusions, forcing them to "spend more time with people getting their input than in the actual decision-making process."[12]

Corporate leaders who can think and handle information in a complex, ambiguous atmosphere are more apt to display a compassionate management style than those who can't. Streufert and fellow psychologist Robert Sternberg discovered that the complex thinker appears to also possess another attribute essential to being a strong CEO: *empathy.* "Let's say the CEO learns that a subordinate got very upset over a company decision," says Streufert, comparing multidimensional and unidimensional thinking. "The unidimensional thinker says, 'That jerk had no reason to become upset. We did the right thing.' The unidimensional thinker has only one way of seeing things. But the multidimensional thinker says, 'Let me look at it from his point of view. I can see why he got upset. Let me do something for him and try to resolve the problem. It will be better for my company if I do.'"[13] Sounds very much like a relationship-builder, doesn't it?

The manager of tomorrow will operate in a marketplace where the frenzied pace of change never lets up; where people speak different languages and represent different cultural heritages; where the quality of information is crucial; and where employees' and customers' home and worklives are driven by their values and self-interests. To operate in such a dynamic and information-rich environment, CEOs will have to abandon the conventional linear ways of thinking and decision making in favor of more flexible ways that can accommodate ambiguity and clashing information.

Our point about CEOs becoming managers of relationships is not meant to suggest that tomorrow's CEO candidates won't also need the requisite general management experience. They will. What will be different, however, is that financial and administrative skills will be considered standard necessities, but no longer the compelling factors in hiring. It will be those candidates who *also* have the communication and relationship-enhancing attributes who will win and keep the top jobs. Those who don't have both may never even be invited to interview for the job.

Influencing the Selection Process

The isolated executive suite is no longer the safe haven it once was for CEOs who typically would sell their souls to the devil to avoid public exposure. But times have changed. Today, under constant fire from activist stakeholder groups and boards, CEOs' lives have grown more precarious, particularly for those unable to reach accommodation with groups that wield considerable influence on an organization's hiring and firing decisions.

Examples abound of top dogs who have abruptly been shown the door, because they alienated a key constituency. Many big-name corporate players—Eli Lilly, Giddings & Lewis, American Express, Sunbeam-Oster, and General Motors, to name just a few—have in recent years lost or sent packing a CEO, because he couldn't resolve a nagging conflict with the board, a major stockholder, employees, a chairman, or some other stakeholder. And, in peering ahead, it doesn't look as though it will get any easier for top dogs to stay out of the executive doghouse.

With the job changing in emphasis and style, and CEOs coming under increasing public scrutiny, we predict that it won't be long before candidates with proven relationship-building credentials will have the inside track to the top slots. Put more directly, tomorrow's corporate pilots will have to be strong communicators in addition to being strong administrators or they probably won't be selected for the job.

In the past, CEOs with human relations skills were seen as a luxury; in the future, they will be considered a necessity. Perhaps the wave of the future is already perceptible at pharmaceutical house SmithKline Beecham, where, said Executive VP Jean-Pierre Garnier during a telephone interview, "Leadership and communication skills are key criteria for promotion by managers in our change-driven culture." Most telling, however, is his prediction that executives not having the requisite communication capabilities "will be able to go only so far in this company."

Winchell's Jim Verney, still in his 40s but a CEO for several years, owes his rapid rise to his communication capabilities, which he believes set him apart from other managers. "I've always tried to make myself one of the best communicators in my organization because I thought it would propel me forward faster than others," says the current corporate leader of the Lone Star Steakhouse & Saloon chain. "Very simply, I'm a CEO today and not still in some lower position because of my ability to communicate my thoughts and ideas, and gain the trust of the many different people I work with."

Los Angeles Times' Dick Schlosberg emphasizes how crucial a manager's personal communication abilities are to being promoted and getting ahead in the Times-Mirror organization and that without such expertise, the future isn't too rosy. "Certainly the ability to get along with and to communicate with groups of employees is viewed as part and parcel to being successful here," he says. "One of our real key executives—one of the most brilliant people we've seen in a long time—has a particular flaw. He rubs everybody the wrong way. It's essentially a knockout punch. How can I give someone like that more responsibility when he doesn't know how to get along with other people?"

Maybe the key phrase is "doesn't know how." In years to come, CEO contenders uncomfortable with the vagaries of human relations issues will be disqualified by boards of directors responsible for picking CEOs. Top managers who can't or don't learn how to handle their communication role skillfully and learn it early in their careers will be committing professional suicide. Learning about the human dimensions of managing should begin where most managers begin preparing for their business careers—in America's MBA programs. Unfortunately, most MBA curricula haven't kept pace with the marketplace changes influencing how future managers will be expected to manage and relate to people.

MBA Programs:
Lagging Behind the Times

Sometimes, if you know a person's background and training, you can better grasp his or her virtues—and flaws.

How ironic it is. The very programs charged with preparing America's future corporate leaders to manage change have thus far failed to adapt their own priorities to adequately prepare would-be managers for the changing role awaiting them. As things stand today, those few CEOs whose strong suit is human resources management acquired that capability in spite of their MBA training. The problem is widespread and serious, and unless corrected soon will significantly weaken the quality of the next generation's pool of top management talent.

The problem is that graduates of most MBA programs lack the minimum human relations, communication, and leadership skills necessary to become effective corporate chiefs. Former *Los Angeles Times* business columnist John Lawrence concisely defined the predicament: "The problem with most managers, even in this era of the ubiquitous B-school, is that too often they come to the job without much preparation ... MBAs generally come to management armed more with money skills than people skills, a problem that cries out for changes in the courses they are offered and required to take."[14]

A few years ago, the first systematic study of management education in three decades sparked intense debate over what subjects B-schools should be emphasizing. Sponsored by the American Assembly of Collegiate Schools of Business, the study, which included more than 500 interviews with business faculty and corporate executives, concluded that business schools' curricula are outdated and that administrators need to seriously reassess and enhance how they teach the *human side* of management.[15] For instance, the study's researchers noted that many curricula investigated lacked a sufficient emphasis on such subjects as leadership, communication, people skills, and strategy formulation. Unfortunately, they concluded, business schools' efforts to develop students' human relations capabilities have not kept pace with efforts to develop their quantitative and analytical skills.

Communication Education Seen as Unimportant

In general, most MBA programs have thus far mismanaged themselves by resisting or being inexcusably slow in assimilating communication issues and techniques into their curricula. In a nationwide study of over 50 MBA program directors, Pincus and Rayfield found that 70 percent require *no* communication-related courses and about a third don't even recommend one. Even more disturbing is the fact that three out of four don't include communication strategy topics or basic communication skills training into any conventional MBA courses. And when it comes to human relations-related areas like marketing, sales, leadership, and organizational behavior, 60 percent of the program directors said they don't require students to take even one such course.

Why this almost total absence of communication education? Simply put, most MBA faculty and administrators don't consider communication-related subjects important to MBA education. On a 10-point scale of importance, with

10 being "very important," B-school administrators rated communication at 5.3, a lukewarm endorsement at best. Many programs incorrectly assume that incoming students either already have technical communication skills or that they'll learn them in their regular MBA classes.

Even among those programs that do include any communication requirements, the emphasis tends to be solely on technical communication skills for the individual. For instance, in Pincus and Rayfield's research, among MBA programs incorporating at least one communication course—required or elective—the strongest accent is on oral and written skills, such as writing letters and memos, and making presentations. Fundamental skills training is certainly needed and important, but it simply isn't enough.

This typical weakness in MBA curricula has not escaped the attention of some of the leaders of the business schools themselves—the deans. The University of Michigan's Noel Tichy pulls no punches when he calls business education in America "a disaster" and argues that it "needs a radical transformation."[16] "We've got to make fundamental changes" in curricula and course contents, insists Russell Palmer, former dean of Penn's Wharton Business School. Up to now, he says, "We've been tinkering."[17]

Thus far, the most common response to solving the problem is to install basic communication skills preparation. That's encouraging, but not sufficient. Skills training assists the would-be manager in micro-level situations, when he or she communicates on an interpersonal level. What B-school students also need, but hardly ever get, is exposure to macro-level communication strategy issues, like persuasion, negotiation tactics, audience analysis, business-media dynamics, crisis management, and issues monitoring. By not exposing MBA students to strategy-driven communication topics, two problems arise: First, aspiring managers probably won't understand why it is essential and how to integrate organization-wide communication strategies into organizational plans; and second, these would-be CEOs may view communication and human relations concerns as unimportant, and thus ignore them when making decisions.

Richard West, former dean of the Dartmouth Business School, believes that prospective business managers need to become more aware of how to react to substantive communication problems. "With increasing frequency, business firms are recognizing that communicating with their various publics calls for more than merely writing and speaking," he said. "Our management communication education should be not only committed to improving students' skills, but also to making them more sophisticated about the overall process of communicating."[18]

Some Changes Are Underway

Fortunately, the news isn't all bad. Some positive developments are underway and there are encouraging signs that others will be coming soon. A few examples illustrate the point. The University of Chicago now offers a leadership and negotiation course. Harvard, Dartmouth, NYU, and Penn expose MBA students to media relations and crisis communication topics. Yale offers an elective course featuring crisis and public policy management issues. Of the 10 first-year required courses in Georgetown University's curriculum, only 4 focus on traditional functional subjects such as accounting and marketing; the other 6 are skewed toward topics like communication, organizational behavior, and internationalism.

Penn State University, following a program redesign, requires all MBA students to take a year-long course in communication. The University of Denver's recently overhauled program compels students to take courses in ethics, communication, negotiations, logic and reasoning, and international management trends.[19] And one of the most intriguing potential trends may be at the University of Richmond, which offers an undergraduate degree in, of all things, leadership studies, from its Jepson School of Leadership Studies.[20]

Such improvements are good to see and bode well for the future. However, they are token changes at best and fall far short of what's needed to bring MBA curricula into line with the realities of today's marketplace. Perhaps one reason B-school programs vary so widely in curricular priorities is the absence of any universal guidelines. In an effort to fill that void, we offer two guidelines which, if followed, would bring greater balance to MBA training. The first recommendation is that all MBA programs should require every student to take at least one course in fundamental business communication skills *and* one in communication strategies. This is the essential first step to making MBA education more responsive to its major customers, who are echoing this call. For instance, in a 1990 survey conducted by the University of Pittsburgh, corporate recruiters from big companies cited communication as the single most important criterion in selecting MBAs.[21]

A skills course might include writing memoranda, letters, business plans, and performance appraisals; conducting and giving interviews; managing meetings; and preparing and giving business/sales presentations. A strategy course, in contrast, ought to stress organizational relationships; communication and leadership; public relations; mass media; public opinion; issues management; audience analysis; persuasion and negotiation strategies; and crisis management.

A promising prototype for a dual skills-strategy requirement is already in place at Emory University in Atlanta. All entering MBA students are required to take "Communication for Managers," which concentrates on (1) general skills training in presentations; (2) writing and interpersonal communication; and (3) small groups. During the second semester, students choose a specialized skills course in one of those three areas. Many prefer to specialize in public speaking, says Dr. Sherron Kenton, senior lecturer in communications, who teaches many of the courses. And in addition, an elective case-method course in "Communication Strategies" (e.g., Tylenol, Mobil) is available the third semester. Subjects explored are persuasion strategies, audience analysis, media selection, delivering bad news, and ethics in advertising and public relations.[22]

A second guideline we recommend is that all MBA faculty be *strongly* encouraged to integrate communication issues and assignments into their courses. By holding students accountable for communication in *all* their class assignments (such as writing, organization, oral presentation), they'll eventually come to view communication concerns as inseparable from business concerns. This would also give students continuous feedback on their total performance as up-and-coming business executives.

Impressions of the components comprising effective management and leadership during the MBA experience will influence upstart executives' outlooks and decisions for years to come. Unfortunately, most MBA curricula—traditionally heavy in finance, operations, and marketing—have up to now largely excluded communication and human relations topics from their curricula. A few B-schools under mounting pressure to improve the quality of their graduates, such as Harvard, Penn, and Dartmouth, are reassessing their curricula. Hopefully, those reviews will result in revised curricula that emphasize communication and HRM training far more than they do today.

In the meantime, as the business community waits for directors of MBA programs to restructure their programs for the long-term, much of corporate America is increasingly relying on customized and university-based executive education programs to keep its best management troops current and growing. To feed this voracious need in the near-term, a corporate training cottage industry has sprung up as a way "to use education and training to shake up bureaucracies and give meaning to today's managerial buzzwords and missions."[23]

Under the best of circumstances, MBA programs can accomplish only so much in building future corporate leaders. At times, executive education is viewed as replacing weak or deficient university education; at most other times, it's seen as a necessary supplement. Both pre- and post-MBA training/education are needed and need to work in tandem to prepare aspiring top managers for the multiplicity of demands they will face when they reach the top.

Up to now, we've been focusing on the CEO's changing leadership role and our belief that top executives must develop styles that incorporate the notion of compassion. Shifting gears slightly, we now want to look at some new and different ways that the CEO's job will be organized and practiced—which touches aspects of the principle of selectivity.

A New Wrinkle:
The *"Office* of the CEO"

Sometimes, if you study what people do and how they do it, you can discover what's really important to them.

The job of chief executive officer has expanded dramatically in its complexity and in the diversity of demands on the position itself and the person in it. The

CEO must be not only a jack of all trades, but a master of each. Top dogs must play many different subroles in the part of CEO—accountant, lawyer, lobbyist, economist, spokesperson, mediator, psychologist, soothsayer, and so on. No doubt each minirole makes the job exciting and stimulating, if not frustrating and perplexing at times. It seems that everybody wants a piece—an increasingly larger piece—of the CEO's time and attention. Stakeholders want to hear from and have access to the top banana. Everything about being a top executive is more complicated than it used to be—from the nature of the problems to be solved to the number of stakeholders to be soothed.

The job is fast becoming too much, too big for one person. Overworked CEOs must increasingly rely on a cadre of assistants and vice presidents to get the job done, which some argue is diluting the actual power of the position. CEOs are "less powerful today than they were 10 or 15 years ago," because "their task is much bigger," writes *Business Week's* John Byrne. "It's one thing to manage a single operation well. It's another thing to decide that you're no longer in a certain business, to change, cut back, deal with foreign competition. The agenda has been greatly expanded ..."[24] What this trend means is that CEOs will have to constantly reevaluate priorities to figure out how best to use their and others' talents and waking hours to get the job done. In other words, the principle of selectivity will increasingly guide their thinking.

With the job demands swelling and stakeholders pressing CEOs to share decision-making power with them, some companies are experimenting with new and different ways to organize the top manager function. As single discipline CEOs march toward obscurity and are replaced by multifunctional, multicultural, multicontinent top managers, a mild movement is afoot to split up the CEO's expansive job among two or more senior-level executives. In late 1993, when Ford's Alexander Trotman became the first top executive in the company's history to assume the titles of chairman, chief executive, and president, he came under heavy criticism by those who questioned whether one person, no matter how energetic and competent, could do justice to all three positions.

As the call for new, proliferated arrangements of power and responsibility at the top rises, so too do the expectations by those involved. Delegating minor responsibilities or projects to underlings can alleviate the burden on those in the top slots only so much and those standing in the wings will wait for the title and power only so long. Some top managers handling a portion of the CEO job don't believe they have sufficient authority needed in many situations and, over time, expect to be given at least a reasonable chunk of the top manager's title and compensation.

Reorganizing the Job

Just because CEOs are under pressure to do more in less time doesn't relieve them of getting it all done. How they do that is the question. Indeed, it may be precisely because CEOs, boards, and stockholders realize the value of the CEO's leadership role, and the time and talent required to fill the role, that a trend is emerging that would break up the job and spread its pieces among several senior-level executives. In some cases, one executive—perhaps the best known or most senior, or maybe the most adept at communicating—will draw the primary responsibility for relationship-building with certain key stakeholder groups.

Although quite controversial, this notion of shared leadership is already being tried in different forms by a number of companies, among them Motorola, AT&T, Corning, General Electric, Apple, Chrysler, Time Warner, Texas Instruments, and Hewlett-Packard. In the future, a lone chief executive may be harder to find, particularly at large, multilocale organizations. Momentum is building for swifter decisions by already over-burdened CEOs. To streamline decision making, the number of firms that will create "offices of the president" or "offices of the chief executive" will rise substantially over the decade, we predict.

These "office" arrangements usually blend two to six top officers into a team led by the chairman or primary CEO. Harvard researcher Richard Vancil found that the number of American organizations trying this tag-team type of leadership tripled between the 1960s and mid-1980s, from 8 to 24 percent.[25] Companies using "offices of the CEO" are driven by different reasons: Some seek to control executive power, while others want to cultivate it.

A frequent concern voiced about these approaches is leadership stability; that is, whether spreading around executive authority creates a perception, however mistaken, that nobody is in charge or able to make decisions. When computer giant Hewlett-Packard sought to streamline itself to dig its way out of a late 1990 profit slump, the top job was split between president and CEO John Young and COO Dean Morton. When asked whether this move reflected any lessening of his responsibilities as CEO, Young shot back, "Quite the contrary," pointing out that it allowed him to get "more involved in operations."[26]

In some cases, however, dividing up the top job among several insiders or between insiders and an outsider is done for a different reason: to insert a checks and balances system on what some believe is CEOs' relatively unrestricted executive power. Spurred by ongoing public debate over top executives' ballooning compensation, a number of boards and activist shareholder consortiums have called for or instituted inside-outside splits in order to keep better tabs on executive performance.

A notable example of this configuration is Sears, Roebuck & Co., the retailing and financial services company. In mid-1992, shareholder advocates, led by the New York City Employees' Retirement System, introduced a resolution calling for the company chairman to be from the outside so as to avoid any "appearance of a conflict of interest." The proposal raised the question of whether one person holding the titles of chairman, president, and CEO—as does Sears' Edward Brennan—could objectively evaluate his or her own performance.[27]

Another worry over split-leadership is the unstable situation and reduced speed in decision making when several individuals share executive authority. Doesn't an organization need one person who's clearly empowered to make the final decision and at whose desk the buck ultimately stops? Donald Hambrick, director of the Executive Leadership Research Center at Columbia University, sees a potential problem of people turning off to an organization if they can't pinpoint a person they can call the leader. "A company needs a CEO, a figurehead," he observes. "Even though we don't want our executives to be dominating, we still like them to tower."[28]

Obviously, whenever power is shared, split up, fragmented, divided, whatever the term, such arrangements will succeed only if the individual executives involved possess collegial, team-oriented styles, prefer frank, two-sided communication, and one person is vested with ultimate responsibility for the office. Corning Glass Works' six-person CEO office is referred to within the company as the "six-pack." Composed of the chairman, three group VPs, and the heads of research and finance, the arrangement works well due to members' informal styles, which generally trigger open discussions of alternatives before the group collectively decides on a course of action.[29]

Certainly another advantage of having an office of multiple CEO types trained and ready to assume the position surfaces during times of executive transition, as was the case in late 1993 when Chairman George Fisher resigned from Motorola and moved to the top slot at Kodak. Industry observers didn't worry much about a leadership void as power was reshuffled, because of the company's three-person "office of the chief executive." The COO, Gary Tooker, was immediately appointed interim chief and Motorola's stock price hardly moved. Some concerns were expressed, however, over the inevitable competition—the winning and losing mentality endemic in ambitious executives—among the various would-be chiefs.[30]

Creating a CEO office in which power is proportioned among several senior executives should catch on in bigger ways in the future. Such shared power formations appeal, in part, because the top dog's job has become bigger and broader, and more unwieldy. But far more importantly is companies' desire to stress teamwork and democratic decision making at every level, and because such designs theoretically allow the best qualified executive to be selected as CEO in an appropriately selective way.

A word of caution about allocating an organization's leadership. Every organization, regardless of its size or market niche, needs a talking, breathing human being who is visible to inside and outside constituencies as the leader of the organization, who definitively speaks on its behalf and answers for its actions. Unless *one* person is responsible for that role, the organization will face a difficult task maintaining a clear, consistent voice. We believe this point is crucial, because an organization's true power rests not on how many senior managers are at the top or how they're arranged or what titles they have, but on how effectively they can work together to maintain healthy relationships with employees, customers, media, stockholders, and other vital publics.

A Final Word

Sometimes, if you keep your eye on the horizon, you can arrive there ahead of your competition.

In summary, the CEO of the future will look, think, communicate, and act in some completely different ways than those who hold the top jobs today. The next generation of top dogs will need to be not only solid administrators and wise financial managers, but most importantly agile builders of relationships with stakeholders on whose support their organizations depend. Top managers who don't have these human relations and communication skills will face a steep uphill climb to reach success—and worse yet, may never get a shot at proving themselves in the CEO jobs.

A key to preparing these future leaders for the changing demands of CEO stewardship is overhauling the curricula in MBA programs, America's management finishing schools, to include communication and human relations training. While some MBA programs are beginning to adapt in small ways, much still has to change in approach and emphasis if these essential training grounds are to adequately prepare future executives for the changing role of a business leader.

And as the nature of the CEO's responsibilities change in scope and accent, and grow in volume and complexity, fundamental structural changes in the job will become more common. A rising number of boards of directors see the CEO job as too big for one person to handle; others believe that too much power is concentrated in a single executive. To address these concerns, some boards have created an "office of the CEO," an arrangement where the job's broad array of duties are split up among several senior executives. This trend, consistent with the call for teamwork and power sharing heard throughout the workplace, will spread into more executive suites in the years to come.

Returning to Arlen ...

In the last chapter, Arlen's public leadership performance was reviewed informally over drinks by several members of his executive staff. The CEO was given passing marks for holding things together and exhibiting a few flashes of brilliance, and a cautious vote of confidence by his most supportive staffers. Meanwhile, Arlen had escaped to the serenity of Central Park to consider his future, only to be found and confronted by alluring *Journal* reporter Karen-Elaine Marshak, who revealed to him, without naming any names, that a Royal insider was the source for her eye-popping question at the press conference about the internal plot to overthrow him.

In the next chapter and epilogue that immediately follows it, the Arlen Royster story reaches its climax as the troubled CEO faces down Royal's board of directors, comes to terms with Keller, attempts a reconciliation with his son, and finally makes a long-awaited decision about his own future.

"Every (Top) Dog Has His Day ..."

Monday, October 15, 7:30 a.m. As he entered Sol's Executive Deli on 57th St., a sullen Arlen Royster spotted shirt-sleeved Barry Lewis facing him from the worn leather booth near the back of the noisy restaurant. The CEO had called his closest friend and confidant the night before and asked him to meet for breakfast at their usual spot, situated midway between their offices.

Arlen slid into the opposite side of the booth, his stress instantly apparent to Lewis. In front of Lewis was a half-drunk glass of pulpy orange juice, two halves of an onion bagel, and a cup of soft cream cheese. Awaiting Arlen was a steamy plate of eggs, lox, and onions, a sesame bagel oozing with butter, and black coffee.

"Are you kidding with all this food?" he groused, holding his nose and pushing it away in disgust. He reached for the thick-handled coffee mug and took a long, slow sip.

"My, aren't we the happy CEO this morning?" Lewis shot back, pushing the business section of that morning's *New York Times* toward Arlen. The headline plastered across an article at the bottom of page one read, "Royal's King Target of Overthrow Plot."

"Any truth to this garbage?" Lewis asked, his bushy eyebrows rising. Arlen grunted his annoyance and without a word, folded the newspaper and dropped it out of sight onto the booth next to him. He swigged his coffee as he watched his friend intently trying to read his mood. Arlen was content to simply collect his thoughts. Such muted lapses were accepted between these friends who'd shared three decades of life's vagaries. But after a time, Lewis became impatient.

"Look, Arlen, as much as I'd love to sit here looking into your bloodshot eyes," Lewis badgered, "some of us have important things to do. So, unless you're ready to sign a book contract with my firm telling the world the inside story of Royal's power struggle, I'm out of here." The publishing company Lewis headed handled business trade books, including several best selling "tell-all" autobiographies of well-known business and political figures, including a few notable ousted executives from *Fortune* 100 companies.

This certainly wasn't the first time the garrulous Lewis had to drag information out of a solemn Arlen. He'd been Arlen's personal sounding board and pseudo-psychologist since their undergraduate days together at the University of Virginia. Lewis possessed a knack for putting into words the questions Arlen was struggling to verbalize. When Arlen called Lewis last night, that's what he hand in mind; he knew his friend's crossexamination would help him piece together the disconnected emotions and bits of information gyrating in his head. Several more seconds passed before Arlen finally entered the discussion.

"Barry, the showdown's about to come and I'm just not sure how I want it to end." Frustration was embedded in his voice; he was searching futilely for the right words. Lewis rubbed his eyes while he waited for more.

"Uh ... well ... a couple of days ago, fixing this mess at Royal was the most important thing in my life. This morning though ... I'm not so sure." Arlen left the unfinished thought suspended, shook his head and drained his coffee mug, looking around for a refill. He stared at Lewis and mumbled under his breath, "Maybe I should just bail out now."

Lewis, who'd expected as much, countered instantly. "Hey, pal, you can't mean that, not after all you've done in the last 72 hours to hold Royal together. Must be fatigue talking. Or maybe stupidity. Didn't you tell me on the phone Saturday how well the videoconferences went? And the press conference came off as well as it could've under the circumstances, right?"

Strain etched across his face, Arlen picked up the crispy bagel and nervously began pulling off small pieces and arranging them in a circle. The only other time Lewis could remember seeing Arlen this distraught was many years ago when he was contemplating marriage. His decision then—to marry Andrea—was filled with the same sort of uncertainty and confusion he was wrestling with today. Back then, thought Lewis, he made the right decision. Feeling his friend's personal agony, Lewis was struck by an unavoidable irony. To those on the outside looking in, Arlen had it all: success, wealth, power, control of his destiny. Yet here he was, practically paralyzed by self-doubts, guilt, and indecision.

"Barry, I just don't see my job, my career, or even Royal the same way any more," Arlen answered softly, haltingly, slowly shaking his head.

"Are we really talking about Royal here?" Lewis probed carefully, knowing he was entering sensitive territory. "Or are we talking about Arlen the CEO? Or Arlen the husband and father? Or Arlen the human being?"

Without a word, Arlen lifted a neatly folded sheet of paper from the inside pocket of his suit jacket and slid it across the table. Lewis opened it, spotted the Royal letterhead and quickly scanned the single paragraph above Arlen's uniquely illegible signature.

His eyes snapped to attention, clasping on Arlen. "What the hell is this?" he demanded angrily, waving the paper at Arlen. "Are you serious? It's dated today."

Arlen stared back stone-faced, amused by his friend's reaction. "Pretty obvious, isn't it? It's my resignation," Arlen said without any emotion, a wisp of a smile beginning at the corner of his mouth. He plopped one of the bagel pieces into his mouth and started chewing. Outside, an ambulance rushed by, its siren blaring an alarm for all those in the vicinity.

"Yeah, I can read. I just can't believe you're really serious about it," growled Lewis. Now he understood what this impromptu meeting was all about. Leaning forward, Lewis' words started to come in a rush, unorganized.

"C'mon, Arlen, you've never run away from unfinished business before. Why would you start now? This Royal thing isn't that big a deal. It too will pass. Dammit, Arlen, be honest with me, and yourself ... what's the truth here? Are you afraid the board might not support you? Or is your real fear that you think Keller's right about you being to blame for all of Royal's problems?" Lewis paused, looking for any reaction from Arlen. But the CEO just kept playing with his untouched food.

Then came the fundamental question Arlen had tried his best to avoid. "Or are you just tired of being a CEO?"

"Yes."

"Yes what?"

"Yes to all of the above," Arlen said, his expression softening, a hint of relief appearing in his strained eyes.

Just then, the conversation was interrupted by the loud, blue-haired waitress who'd taken the breakfast order from Lewis. "More coffee, sweetie?" she brayed in a raspy, high-pitched twang. "Whatsa matter with the food, hon?" she asked Arlen, who didn't hear her. "You don't wanna hurt the cook's feelings, do ya?" Before either man could answer, she filled both cups to overflowing before disappearing through the swinging doors to the kitchen.

Lewis, now spooning out his coffee, backed off momentarily, trying to assess if Arlen was serious about resigning or just being fashionably melodramatic. So he switched directions.

"Okay, let's back up a second. What'd you mean when you said you don't see things the same way any more?" He flipped the resignation toward Arlen and sat back expectantly.

"Barry, you know the CEO can't escape responsibility for anything. I've thought all weekend about my role, about my obligations, about what the right move is."

"Really, Mr. CEO? And after only a few hours of thinking, you, of course, know exactly what the 'right' thing is."

"There's no getting away from the fact I created, be it directly or indirectly, the environment that made those managers feel like they had no choice but to juggle the books," Arlen said hesitantly, honestly. "And I'm not the only one who thinks so. I didn't see it coming and I should've. I didn't catch it soon enough and I should've. I sent the wrong message to my people and never realized it." He took a slow, full breath. "The bottom-line is I'm responsible."

"Don't give yourself so much credit. Nobody's that good. You can't tell me they had no choice; they sure as hell did. Look, accepting your share of responsibility, to whatever extent is fair and appropriate, is one thing—which, by the way, hasn't been determined yet. Resigning, though, is something else."

The publishing executive lowered his elbows onto the greasy table, taking aim at Arlen. "When you learned about what some of your managers had done, you took immediate action to fix things, didn't you? You did everything you could, didn't you? Tell me, who could've done more? Stamps? The board? Keller? Hell, from what you've told me, that bastard did all he could to encourage the false reporting scheme. Arlen, don't be so hard on yourself—unless you're gonna do the same to all those who share the responsibility with you."

Arlen looked subdued as he thought about Lewis' entreaties. Not realizing it, he had separated the lox and onions into separate piles on his plate, still unable to take a bite.

"You've taken steps to get things back on track," Lewis pushed on. "You've told the world about the bad boys, the bad numbers and made a public promise you'll fix everything. If you walk out now, Arlen, you'll not only be forfeiting your position to Keller, but you'll be admitting to the world that the job's too tough for you." Stung by his friend's bluntness, Arlen bristled at the thought.

"And if you do resign, you do know the first thing Keller'll do, don't you?" Arlen looked up. "Before you can say 'Did I do the right thing?' he'll dismantle the organization you've spent years building and recreate the

Royal culture in his own perverted image." To drive home his point, Lewis added, "Doesn't sound like the Arlen Burch Royster I know." Now Lewis waited for Arlen.

He peered hard and long at his friend and fellow CEO, wondering. "Barry, I know what you're trying to do and I appreciate it. But I've just been lucky these past few days I haven't shot myself in the foot—or somewhere else," he said sincerely. "You know and I know, I'm not the world's greatest public speaker, and, Lord knows, I'm a mass of nerves in front of a TV camera. I keep waiting for the bubble to burst. I feel like a pinball—no control of how I'm bounced around. I suspect the other shoe will drop this afternoon at the board meeting." Resignation dominated his voice. He licked his lips several times.

"So, after thinking about this for days now, I think the board should be free to decide what's best for the company without worrying about the political fallout of who's to blame for this ... this crisis. If I resign, it'll have that freedom."

"Very noble, indeed, you martyr you. And how thoughtful of you to make things so easy for the board. And, of course, your good buddy Keller. He'll no doubt be forever in your debt for rolling over without so much as a peep. Does Andrea know about this yet?" asked Lewis, pointing to the letterhead which still lay open on the table.

"Not yet."

"You were going to tell her before you gave it to Stamps, weren't you?" It was a statement, not a question.

"Andrea would say what she always says—it's my call, she trusts my judgment, and she's with me."

"I wonder if she'd say that in this case, Arlen—with the stakes so high. Tell me, how d'you think you'll feel about yourself tomorrow morning if you throw in the towel today?"

"Probably very relieved," Arlen popped back insincerely, looking away.

"And after the relief?" pressed Lewis.

"I dunno." He waited, for what he wasn't sure. "Maybe I'll take the Mahoney offer and go play this ridiculous game in another schoolyard," he said distressed, immediately turning to Lewis for a reaction. Nothing.

"That's still an option?" Lewis asked.

Arlen nodded. He explained that Megan Walters, Mahoney's hired headhunter, reached him on his car phone that morning to remind him that the offer was still open. "Walters and Mahoney were wondering, after seeing the *Times* story, if my timetable for making a decision had changed," he related, grinning. "She told me that if Royal's dumb enough to let me get away over something like this, Bruce Mahoney isn't."

Arlen's bruised ego had been comforted by the call, he told his friend.

"I told her I hadn't yet had a chance to think about the future because I'm just too overwhelmed with the present," continued Arlen, anxiously rubbing his silver-plated cufflink. "I promised I'd be in touch soon." He considered his pledge a moment.

"She kept telling me she understood my situation," he went on, "but still kept trying to get me to commit one way or the other. I don't know why, but she said my profile in the industry had soared considerably the past few days. A strange thing to say, I thought."

Now Lewis broke in. "Not really. It's funny how the business world works for folks at the top. Sometimes you get dumped on at your current company and suddenly your name's in the news and your value everywhere else skyrockets. That's one of the many ironies of life in the executive suite."

"Well," Arlen went on, "I told her again that if Mahoney couldn't wait, I understood. But she said he didn't wanna talk to anyone else till I made a decision."

Arlen shrugged and then leaned back, his vitality ebbing again. "I told her I needed at least a month."

Lewis said nothing; he was concentrating on trying to read Arlen's jumbled brain waves.

"So, if I turn in my resignation and it's not accepted, I'm still at Royal. If it is accepted, I suppose I join Mahoney. Sounds like a win-win proposition, right?" asked Arlen rhetorically, unsurely.

Lewis snorted. "Mahoney baloney," he chided. "It'll look like you're running away from a situation you couldn't handle or didn't want to face. The Mahoney decision is a separate issue. Maybe it is the best thing for you. Who knows? But before you make that decision, take care of business—the unfinished business—at Royal. I know you, Arlen. It'll eat at your insides for the rest of your life if you leave now. You're not a quick fix or easy way out kinda guy. Is that what you're turning into?"

Arlen started to say something, but Lewis ignored him.

"I want you to promise me you'll think more about this before you do something really dumb. A deal?" Lewis extended his hand.

Smiling, Arlen reached across the table and grabbed the outstretched hand of friendship. Then he refolded the resignation and slid it back into his coat pocket.

"Have I ever refused you anything, Barry? I'll think about it. I guess there's always time for stupidity later." Arlen tapped his breast pocket, which held a key to his future. "I guess we'll all know more by the end of the day."

Lewis slid out of the booth, picked up his suit coat and put it on. Arlen stood, grabbing the check without looking at it. Reaching into his pocket, he peeled off a twenty and left it.

"Well, I guess it's the last inning again for you, Arlen ol' boy," Lewis said. Baseball metaphors were a ritual with them. The "last inning" reference was Lewis' subtle way of chastising Arlen for the many years he'd unfairly blamed himself for supposedly single-handedly blowing the University of Virginia's chance to play in the college world series when he disobeyed his coach's orders.

As they headed for the door, Lewis gripped Arlen's arm and squeezed tightly. "This time, just make sure it's a pitch you really want to hit."

                    * * * * * * * * *

Monday, October 15, 2 p.m.   Arlen was motionless, eyeing the blank legal pad before him, the words of sabotage he'd just heard washing over him like acid rain.

"Therefore, in the best interests of Royal Accommodations and its stockholders, whose faith in management's integrity and leadership has been reprehensibly compromised, I urge this board to dismiss Arlen Royster and appoint Michael Keller as Royal's new CEO, both effective immediately."

Long-time board member Donn Lieberman's eloquent 10-minute oration had held the rapt attention of the eight other members of Royal's board of directors as he shrewdly and persuasively laid out the case for dumping Arlen. Not until this moment had he uttered Arlen's name or placed the blame directly at his feet. As the fallout of Lieberman's proposal was silently considered by the people who held Royal's future in their grasp, Arlen tuned out.

"There it is," he thought, relieved, "the not-so-hidden agenda is finally out in the open." There was a time he would've reacted maliciously to Lieberman's attacks and tactics. Now, he felt indifference.

His conversation with Barry Lewis that morning had nudged him to review his roles as CEO, as husband, as father. As a result, he couldn't ever remember feeling as confused and unsure of himself. He couldn't seem to separate what was best for him from what was best for Royal.

Jim Stamps had prearranged with Arlen that he, Stamps, would take the initiative at this meeting, a game plan designed to thwart the anticipated all-out assault on Arlen by Keller's backers. Still, Arlen couldn't help but admire Keller's and his sponsors' resourcefulness in engineering a *coup d'etat* attempt in less than a week. Lieberman and Marcia Gross were both solidly in Keller's corner. They had enlisted enough support to force an emergency board meeting; not even Jim Stamps, a master at boardroom maneuvers, could prevent it.

The tunnel-like but spacious boardroom adjoined the chairman's suite and was centrally anchored by a marble-topped, cherrywood conference table surrounded by 12 thick-leather chairs. Unlike the executive staff conference room's glass wall on one side, the board room's four walls were without windows; they were trimmed with framed copies of Royal's annual report covers over the past 20 years. Arlen always felt claustrophobic sitting in this room. He missed the way the sight of Central Park beckoned his mind to wander from corporate matters.

The maligned CEO looked from Lieberman to Gross and then to senior board member Robert Ray, whose influence on other board members was legendary. When the Royal scandal first broke, Ray was vacationing on the Oregon coast and, as Arlen learned later, had been tracked down by John Grubner, Keller's silent coconspirator and Royal's vice president of finance. Somehow, Grubner, who'd become buddy-buddy with Ray over the years, had convinced the insurance industry mogul that Royal's future was in jeopardy and his presence at the board showdown was mandatory. Ray initially voiced skepticism at Grubner's argument that Arlen should be dumped in favor of Keller. He assured Grubner he'd listen with an open mind when they got together, but, that for the time being, he would remain neutral.

Despite Ray's noncommittal response, Grubner had persuaded himself of the self-fulfilling prophecy that Ray wouldn't forsake him and would eventually back Keller. So the nervous CFO reported back to Keller that Ray was, as he put it, "just about in our corner." When Keller heard the fabricated good news, he roared with delight, lauding Grubner for his sharp salesmanship, which sent the financial expert's imagination spinning with fantasies of his life at the top.

Lieberman, one of only two board members predating Stamps' reign as chairman, and Gross were long-time critics of Stamps and therefore, by association, of Arlen, who they viewed as Stamps' unwelcome clone. Lieberman, smooth in style and refined in appearance, was a self-made multimillionaire who headed Lieberman Clothiers, a nationwide chain of mall-based upscale mens' clothing stores.

The brash, feisty Gross founded her own advertising firm, Gross & Chipman, in the early 1970s, after she was mysteriously fired by one of Madison Avenue's largest agencies. Within six months of start-up, Gross' fledgling firm had landed several jumbo accounts and Gross herself quickly achieved celebrity as one of the first successful women CEOs in the male-dominated advertising industry.

Of the nine-member board, Arlen and Stamps calculated that Lieberman, Gross, and Ray would oppose Arlen. Stamps, Ted D'Adamo, and Marilyn Rhondell would probably side with him. Riley Gretta and Kenneth Jaynes were uncommitted, and didn't seem to be leaning in either direction. Although a board member, Arlen wouldn't be able to cast a vote on his own fate.

Lieberman had opened the meeting with a flare. "By now, you're all brutally aware of Royal's sadly serious predicament," he began in his sonorous baritone, holding up Saturday's *Newsday* with its bold, front page headline, "Royal Financial Data Manipulated, CEO Admits." Lieberman's angular, evenly tanned, wrinkle-free face was sharply framed by thick, wavy grey hair. As always, his fingernails were freshly manicured and his $2000, hand-tailored British suit sent the unmistakable message that Donn Lieberman was a player of substance in corporate America. Intelligent and cunning, he always carefully pondered his political cards before playing them. It was almost impossible to best him in verbal combat, blessed as he was with a vocabulary William Buckley would envy.

"I've searched deep within my soul about this matter," he said with conviction. He spoke deliberately, enunciating each word, his gestures timed perfectly with his words and inflection. "And I've come to the inescapable conclusion, the painful conclusion really, as have several others on this board, that Royal needs new leadership now if it's to survive this crisis. You each know how it works: If faith is lost in management, faith will soon be lost in everything else. We'll be blacklisted on Wall Street. Guests will go to other hotels. Employees will stop trusting us and run to our competitors. We'll become the joke of the industry. The litany of exigent possibilities is long and depressing."

Lieberman looked around the table, holding his gaze on Arlen, shifting it gradually to Stamps, and back again to Arlen. The top dog's stomach growled repeatedly. "He is a smooth devil, and he knows not to tip his hand too soon," admired Arlen.

"This company has been rocked to its foundation by these embarrass-ing—no, humiliating—public revelations," lectured Lieberman, waving the *Newsday* above his head, warming to his task. "It'll be years before we're able to find safe cover from this thunder cloud we're now under—all because of inept and unresponsive leadership. The sooner we change that leadership, the sooner we can start moving forward again."

Each adjective was purposely drawn out to punctuate his disgust, each intended to further indict Arlen. "Stockholders will surely sue us. And I wouldn't blame them. If I weren't on the board, I'd sue Royal for the careless way its management safeguarded my investment. Make no mistake, friends, the SEC will now be our copilot, following our every move like a hungry hawk.

"The bottom-line is this: we've got to show our stockholders, guests, and employees we're still in control. There have to be some changes, visible changes at the top, to reassure them."

Before an agitated Stamps could break in and try to regain command of the meeting, Lieberman bulldozed ahead.

"And before anyone accuses me of being part of a witch hunt, let me assure you, none of this is personal." Lieberman faced Arlen with both hands extended in a "forgive me" gesture. Arlen refused to meet his eyes; in his lap and out of sight, he was fingering the smooth edges of his oval-shaped cufflinks.

Lieberman swiveled his chair toward Arlen, pointing his index finger at him. "It's strictly business. Royal business. I'm convinced, as are others at this table," Lieberman went on, approaching the climax, "that the CEO—you, Arlen—created, through your insistence on wholly unrealistic expec-tations, the internal pressures that, over time, built up and finally exploded in a scheme of deceit that will haunt this company for years to come. These maverick managers, irrespective of their motivations, are your responsibil-ity, Mr. Royster, nobody else's. You are where the buck stops. You, Arlen, are the one this board must hold accountable."

Then, after patronizing Arlen for his past accomplishments, Lieberman concluded his oral offensive by calling for Arlen's immediate firing and Keller's promotion. When Lieberman stopped, Stamps, the consummate diplomat and political chessplayer, jumped back in.

"Before we start replacing anybody, let's make damn sure we know why we're doing it," he said in a preachy tone, "and that we've considered every option before we make a decision we might all regret."

The overweight chairman, trying his best to appear nonplussed, surveyed the anxious faces in front of him. "About one thing I'm absolutely certain. We have a damn fine CEO in Arlen Royster." He glanced at Arlen, who was watching Stamps intently. "And I'm not ready to arbitrarily sacrifice him simply to do something, however wrong or ill-advised it might be."

Stamps anticipated Lieberman's attack and thought he was prepared. The chairman had convinced Arlen, who hadn't resisted much, to say nothing until, and only if, specific issues about culpability and damage repair arose. The wily Stamps didn't want any uncommitted board members to be turned off by a Royster vs. Keller debate before the larger issues had been explored. Stamps thought he could control the agenda and thus steer the discussion to topics favoring Arlen. But the plan wasn't working as he'd expected. Already, Lieberman's lengthy monologue had slipped through Stamps' net.

Then Stamps posed a rhetorical question. "Arlen's recognized and accepted as Royal's leader. How would it look to our major stakeholders if he was fired now, just when his leadership is needed most?"

"It'll look like we're getting rid of the problem," cracked Marcia Gross cynically in her high-pitched squeal.

"I didn't know we'd concluded that Arlen was the root of Royal's problem," piped up Riley Gretta, a rough-and-tumble retired airline CEO who loved playing devil's advocate.

"Who else would it be?" rejoined Jaynes, head of Chelsea & Nickels, a venerable Wall Street brokerage firm, and newest member of the Royal board. He looked at the CEO. "Let's face it, Arlen, we can't fire all the managers, can we? Who else can we hold responsible?"

Without thinking and contrary to Stamps' strategy, Arlen spoke, unable to hold his tongue any longer. "Who else, indeed? Our preliminary investigation showed that ..."

Stamps cut him off sharply, trying to stick to the plan. "Arlen, please. If we start talking about blame, there's plenty to go around. It's not time to point fingers at any one yet."

Stamps didn't want Arlen broadsided again by Lieberman. Arlen, a little flustered by Stamps' unusual abruptness, withdrew.

"Jim, nobody's pointing fingers," rebutted Lieberman, seizing the floor again. "But we have to deal with this calamity honestly and realistically. We'd be remiss as a board if we didn't evaluate our options. All our options. As distasteful as it may be for you to accept the idea of making a change at the top right now ... and we all know how you feel about Arlen, Jim ... present circumstances demand we take whatever action will correct the problem."

Stamps opened his mouth to answer, but Gross was too quick for him. "And fortunately for us, we have someone in the company right now who's more than qualified for the job and who, I might add, probably should've been appointed years ago."

Gross, a shrewd negotiator with an acerbic tongue, relished boardroom politics. She liked Keller's hunger for power, but especially his willingness to use it. Over several three-drink lunches, he had proved to her how much he worshipped the same no-nonsense style of management which had served her so well in getting to the top. But her support of him didn't necessarily extend to trusting him.

As she admitted to Lieberman after their lunch with Keller last week, "Deep down, he may be a stinker, but he's our stinker." Last year, during the board's routine appraisal of Arlen's job performance, she'd casually suggested that Keller was ready for the CEO job. Almost before the words had left her mouth, Stamps quashed her suggestion. Ever since, she'd been waiting for a rematch.

"I have to agree with Donn," Gross continued, touching Lieberman's arm. "It was Arlen who misled, or miscommunicated to, our managers about what was expected of them. And then he didn't keep his ear close enough to the ground and never heard the trouble brewing. I'm not sure how many ways he screwed up, but does it really matter now? Maybe his actions, or inactions, were unintentional. Call it what you will—poor judgment, a bottom-line fixation, weak communication, too little too late, whatever. The inescapable fact is that he screwed up big time and we can't afford to have it happen again. He's got to be replaced."

Satisfied that she'd raised a few eyebrows, Gross leaned back, raising her coffee cup to her lips, all the while concentrating on Arlen's blank face. Stamps wasted no time trying to recapture the momentum, wanting to shift directions before Gross' comments had a chance to take hold.

"There's just no point in spinning our wheels looking for a sacrificial lamb. Instead, we should take a step back and look at the implications. Donn said he was worried about how this mess will affect Royal and its people. That's what we should be talking about, not who did what to who." Stamps slowed down, pleased to be temporarily back in control.

"If you look at matters objectively," he urged, peering at Gross and Lieberman, a thin line of perspiration appearing on his upper lip, "any discussion about changing CEOs is premature ... extremely premature. To force such a change without solid justification would, in my opinion, not only be bad business, but would make a bad situation even worse."

To reinforce his points and further build the case for Arlen, Stamps described the faxed messages and phone calls made to his office over the past 48 hours from Royal employees praising Arlen's performance during the broadcasts. He then reported on the Human Resources Management Department's phone survey of employees conducted over the weekend that revealed workers' continuing faith in upper management, despite considerable skepticism. Even some stories in the media, noted the chairman, praised the company for its candid and straightforward approach to handling the messy situation.

Like a locomotive gathering steam, Stamps' pace kept building. He reminded the board that since the crisis began, an outside research firm had been conducting opinion polls of some of Royal's key stakeholders: preferred customers, convention groups already booked at Royal properties, and stockholders. Preliminary data showed the damage to Royal's credibility wasn't as bad as had been feared. He acknowledged that Royal's stock had lost 12 percent of its value, dropping three points to 22 immediately after the press conference on Friday, but was holding steady since this morning. Stamps explained that Gloria Bernard was already working on the few Wall Street analysts who sounded like they might withdraw their "buy" recommendation to their prime clients. Several institutional investors had called Stamps to tell him they'd "wait and see" before deciding whether to pull out of Royal stock.

"Three cheers for the finger in the dike approach," Robert Ray interrupted, ridicule oozing from him. Senior partner in a Boston-based commercial insurance venture, Ohle & Orville Associates, the sinewy, physically fit septuagenarian had a knack for getting at the nub of issues, no matter how complex they seemed. "But that's not enough, Jim. This is a perceptual problem as much as anything. We need someone at the helm who's in no way perceived as being connected with this ... well, this scandal."

Lieberman, Gross, and Ray started talking at the same time. Jaynes tried to ask a question without success. Riley Gretta and Marilyn Rhondell, seated across from Arlen, leaned forward like Siamese twins and began chattering at him simultaneously. Stamps was overpowered by the cacophony of individual discussions. Soon, Arlen turned to Stamps and said just loud enough to be heard, "Jim, I want to say something."

Stamps immediately shook his head "no," but Arlen wouldn't be put off again. He was sitting erect now, his eyes flashing determination. He mouthed intently, "It's time."

* * * * * * * * *

Arlen stood, rapping his pen against a partially-filled water glass. "Excuse me. Can I say something, please?" Those nearest him stopped and looked up. He rapped the glass again, this time more loudly. "Can I please have your attention. I think maybe I can make this easier for everybody."

The conversations ceased and eight pairs of curious eyes swung to the CEO, who appeared unruffled and more sure of himself than he had since the meeting started. He remained standing, pushing back his chair so he could move around.

A mild form of paralysis had restrained Arlen the past few days. He'd been listless and unmotivated, very much unlike him. But as he listened to Lieberman, Gross, and company level stinging criticisms at him, his spirit had begun to reawaken. His mind, turning circles like a kaleidoscope, was in the process of rearranging self-doubts and uncertainties into a mosaic of understanding. Ultimately, he thought with renewed hope, only he could—and should—determine his future.

He started slowly, softly. "The issue isn't Arlen Royster or Mike Keller. It isn't even about the cooked books or who's responsible for them. It's about what's best for Royal's employees, stockholders, and guests, whose trust we desperately need and who very much want to trust us. The real—and only—issue you ought to be addressing today is one of leadership … that is, the kind of leadership you think Royal needs to survive today and prosper tomorrow." His voice, growing louder and more confident with each sentence, was measured and controlled. No one stirred.

He reached into his coat pocket and laid his resignation on the table in front of Stamps. Before the chairman could pick it up, Arlen explained. "That's my resignation," he said matter-of-factly, putting his hand on Stamps' shoulder. "You're all off the hook. No obligation to me. You've got a clean slate."

He looked down at the chairman and said in a half whisper, "Sorry I didn't talk to you about this before, Jim, but there wasn't time—and I wasn't sure until right now." Stamps gulped, trying to fathom Arlen's next move.

"I'd never stand in the way of what's best for Royal. The power politics being played here nauseate me and are counterproductive to solving our problems. The slick posturing underway will create a major rift within the board—a rift that could injure Royal's chance at a future. My resignation should make it easier for you to decide the 'what' before you decide the 'who.'"

The board was transfixed. Stamps hadn't picked up the resignation, perhaps afraid that touching it would make it come true. Lieberman and Gross exchanged perplexed looks, each wondering, "What's he trying to pull?" Arlen's self-assurance flourished as he talked. He moved away from his chair and drifted behind Lieberman, who didn't budge.

"First, figure out what's best for Royal and its employees, customers, and stockholders. After you've done that, then pick the person who you think can best make the 'what' happen," he charged the board. He returned to his chair, neatly rearranging his coffee cup, water glass, and notepad into a geometric pattern. It was clear he had more to say, so nobody said a word.

"I've been thinking about little else since last Wednesday when I got confirmation about the 'creative bookkeeping' going on at some of our Midwest properties." His gaze remained on the items in front of him, which he continued to shuffle in search of a mythical symmetry.

Barry was right about needing to face the real issues, he thought. But he was wrong about the resignation representing his "bailing out." It was, however, a calculated risk, Arlen knew. If the board voted him to stay, he would interpret it as an endorsement of his leadership and vision. If he was voted out, he'd read it as a signal that he didn't have the support he and Stamps thought he did, meaning it was time to move on. Either way, the confrontation with Keller and company was probably inevitable, and he'd just as soon get it over with. However it came out, he reminded himself, at least he'd know soon where he stood.

"This board meeting isn't really about me or the bookkeeping dilemma," he concluded, his eyes glaring at Lieberman, who stared back. "It's about a carefully conceived plan to run me out and install Keller. Everything else is just a diversion."

He interlaced his 10 fingers as if he were about to pray. Unaccountably, he felt tranquil as his precious sense of perspective began returning. The top executive looked up confidently, throwing a reassuring smile at Stamps.

"Recently, with the help of some friends who forced me to take a hard look at myself, I realized I'm at a professional crossroad. And," he paused briefly, his emotions stirring, "a personal crossroads. And those two roads must intersect more than they have in the past. I'm seeing things differently."

He was no longer worried about revealing something that could aid the Lieberman-Gross conspiracy.

"I know it probably disappoints some of you that I'm not going to defend myself or plead for my job. But that just won't happen. Quite frankly, I'm not so sure I still want Royal. And if Royal isn't sure it wants me, then maybe that's for the best. Could be that this bookkeeping mess is merely leading us to paths that were inevitable. I'm not sure."

His revelations caught Lieberman off-guard. He scribbled a note, folded it and slipped it to Gross, seated to his right. After a quick glance at it, she nodded, whispered something back and returned to Arlen.

"But, folks, you now have to decide who's best equipped to lead Royal to the promised land—me, Mike Keller, or somebody else. Not who you like best. And, you have to make that decision right now, today!"

Arlen turned toward Stamps, who appeared mesmerized, his eyes narrowed in worry.

"Because after today, I'm no longer available." He started to stand, the room drenched in silence, when he was stopped.

"What would it take for you to stay, Arlen?" interjected the plump, slow-talking Marilyn Rhondell, CEO of Atlanta-based Tigresse Publishing, specialists in designing and producing corporate annual reports.

"Just one thing, really, Marilyn. A vote that convinces me I have this board's full support. Without that, I'd be looking over my shoulder constantly and you'd be constantly questioning my decisions. That's no good, for either of us. I don't want to feel like I'm always one mistake away from getting canned. That's no way to manage. You—and I —deserve better than that."

Arlen picked up his Mont Blanc pen and slid it into his inside coat pocket, where his resignation had been. Lifting his blank notepad, he stood up and pushed his chair under the table.

"I'll get out of here now so nobody will feel inhibited to speak their minds." He winked naughtily at Lieberman and Gross, who glowered back, daggers in their eyes.

"Not that that's been much of a problem today," he added tartly, too softly for most to pick up.

He moved to the door, and as he was about to close it, turned around and said nonchalantly, "Call me if anything comes up I should know about."

* * * * * * * * *

After Arlen left, Jaynes proposed a 10-minute bathroom break. But Stamps overruled, unwilling to give the Lieberman-Gross coalition a chance to lobby other board members or lose the moment created by Arlen's fait accompli.

Throughout Arlen's monologue, Stamps wasn't able to get an accurate read of the uncommitted board members. And now he wasn't certain if Arlen's rogue maneuver would help win the day or explode in their faces. But he felt he had no choice but to follow his protege's lead and hope he could pull it off. To shift strategies now would confuse matters even more, he reasoned.

When Stamps looked up, he saw Gross and Lieberman whispering furiously to one another, each animated and gesturing profusely. When they turned to face the others, their expressions were deadly serious.

"Enough of this Custer's last stand stuff," injected Gross sourly. "Let's get back to reality before ..."

Wham! Startled, Gross' body jumped, instantly turning toward the source of the outburst. Jim Stamps met her astonished look, his hand still wrapped in a white-knuckled fist smashed against the table.

"Marcia, I beg your pardon, but the chair hasn't recognized you," he interrupted, "and won't until I've finished what I have to say." Gross stared at him in disbelief, but said no more, the anger beaming from her narrowed eyes. Lieberman sat motionless, speechless. Stamps looked around the table at each person, passively reexerting his control.

"If a change in leadership is the issue this board insists on confronting," baited the chairman, "maybe we should throw out the entire corporate staff and start all over. A few people, some of them in this room, are willing to use this misreporting thing as an excuse to further their own duplicitous purposes. I can't allow that to happen. Not only because it stinks, but because I think a majority of this board appreciates Arlen's leadership ability and potential."

Then, slipping off his suit jacket and loosening his tie, Stamps subtly shifted focus.

"I'd always rather have a CEO who people believe in and who can relate to them, rather than one who's major attribute is playing dirty politics," he snarled, scrutinizing Lieberman, Gross, and Ray in rapid succession.

"Arlen may have made some mistakes. Hell, he's the first to admit that. But which one of us here hasn't made similar or worse mistakes in our careers? Let's not forget the value of Royal's stock before Arlen became the chief and what it is now. He's made an enormous difference to this company ... and he's just coming into his prime as a CEO. As my grandmother used to say, don't throw out the slow-to-ripen fruit before it's had a chance to ripen, because it's always the sweetest."

Stamps rose and began methodically circling the room, his voice booming. "Arlen didn't see some things coming he probably should've. None of us did," he said pointedly, stretching out the words. "His mistake isn't unusual for CEOs of far-flung operations like Royal's. You can't be everywhere at once and you can't see everything that's going on. But is his mistake so flagrant, so inexcusable, that you really want to lose him ..."

He stopped abruptly, grabbing his suspenders while he gathered in the faces following him. "... just to show the outside world we're willing to do something, anything, even if it isn't justified? Think about it. If we act too quickly or too impetuously, we may be viewed as a board that's running scared because it doesn't know what to do. How's it gonna look? Instead of waiting to make sure we do the right thing, we panic and dump the guy at the top for no good reason. That's the easy way out, and may not solve anything. In the long run, if we do that, we'll probably lose a helluva lot more than Arlen."

Sweat was trickling down both of Stamps' cheeks; he was out of breath. He leaned back and gestured grandly, signaling he was done. Ray was the first to respond, preempting Gross.

"A point well taken, Jim. But there's more to it than that. If this were an internal problem only, we might be able to keep things hush-hush and not concern ourselves with what outsiders think. But since everything's already out in the open and Royal looks like a public disgrace, the company's credibility, its reputation, is at stake and needs fixing without delay. We can't afford to ignore that fact.

"We can't just stick our heads in the sand and hope everything'll blow over as we twiddle our thumbs. We've got a sacred responsibility, not to mention a fiduciary one, to control the damage, financial and otherwise, and do whatever's necessary to fix things. Including, if we believe it wise, throwing out the CEO." Ray had made his final choice, Stamps noted, which suddenly made him feel shakier about the upcoming vote.

Stamps figured that by now he should've been able to win over the uncommitted members: Gretta, Jaynes, and D'Adamo. That's where the vote would be won or lost. But he couldn't tell where they stood; each had been suspiciously quiet thus far. That worried him. He starting wondering how uncommitted they really were. He could see that singing Arlen's praises and playing up the "big picture" scenario weren't going to be enough—a good defensive strategy, perhaps, but now it was time to grab the offensive. That meant showing those still undecided why Keller wasn't acceptable as CEO. Generally, Stamps preferred to unleash his charm and gentle arm-twisting, a lethal combination, in private tete-a-tetes rather than in public forums. But there wasn't time for friendly phone calls or leisurely lunch chats now.

He leaned his trunk hard against the conference table. "Since this seems to be coming down to a question of Arlen Royster or Mike Keller," the hoary chairman began slowly, referring to notes inside a manila folder, "there's something else we need to consider if we're going to be completely candid and fair." Stamps stopped just long enough to realize how much he enjoyed political duels when the stakes were high.

Leiberman leaned in, eyeing Stamps closely. He had learned long ago that when Jim Stamps dropped into his laconic "good ol' boy" routine, something was simmering in that cunning mind of his.

"Replacing Arlen with Mike Keller would be a tragic error. Let me tell you why. I have here a copy of a preliminary report from the forensic auditor Arlen hired weeks ago to investigate rumors of 'funny' bookkeeping at some Royal properties."

Stamps pulled the 10-page report from a file folder and spun it across the table in Lieberman and Gross' direction. It stopped near Gross, who grabbed it and began scanning.

Stamps' voice was steady and unemotional, trying his best not to sound accusatory or judgmental. "As you'll see on page three, Marcia, the auditor found out—proved unequivocally, to be precise—that Mike not only knew about the fraudulent books before Arlen, but that once he learned about it, he didn't lift a finger to fix it and never even told Arlen about it. Indeed, it appears that Keller did everything he could to cover-up the situation from his CEO—and, although, the proof is still thin here, it's conceivable he may've been a party to the scheme from the outset."

The floodgates opened instantly. Ted D'Adamo, who'd been doodling, looked up, shocked. Ken Jaynes, in the middle of taking a drink of water, choked softly. "Are you kidding?" whispered Gretta in disbelief, "I'll be damned."

Ray stared frostily at Stamps, wondering why the shrewd chairman had held his trump card—*the* trump card—back this long. Lieberman and Gross, the blood gradually draining from their complexions, avoided eye contact with anyone; they were thinking how they could counterattack.

"What about it, Donn? Marcia? Is this stuff true? Did you know anything about this?" The interrogator was Rhondell, who threw the questions at them. Lieberman pounced back, but not at Rhondell.

"They always say the best defense is a good offense, Jim," Leiberman said flippantly, smiling artificially in an attempt to repudiate Stamps' claims, "even if it is based on questionable evidence and some auditor's fertile imagination."

"That's a nonanswer," Jaynes challenged.

Stamps cut in, saving Leiberman from further challenge. "When Keller 'discovered' what was going on," he continued, his cynical bent increasing, "he grabbed the opportunity for his own power play. He concealed it from Arlen, so he could later use it against him by deceiving us and, thus, worm his way into the CEO chair." He glanced at the empty seat Arlen had vacated a few minutes earlier.

Stamps slapped the table, driving toward his finale. "As far as I'm concerned, when he did that, he betrayed this board's trust."

Ted D'Adamo, owner of D'Adamo's Den, one of New York City's finest restaurants, spoke first. "Since I must assume, Jim, you wouldn't make so serious an accusation if you didn't have irrefutable evidence, out of curiosity, why didn't Arlen tell us about this?"

"Because he's feeling more than his fair share of guilt, Ted. More than he should, I think. He can't divorce himself from feeling responsible for Keller's and everybody else's actions." D'Adamo nodded. Before Stamps could say another word, he was cut off.

"Jim, thanks for making our case for us." The taunting voice was Leiberman's, who now realized he probably couldn't defend Keller's complicity, but he might still bring down Arlen and save face.

"It doesn't matter what Keller did or didn't do. The fact is, Arlen's poor judgment created the profit-monger atmosphere that pushed Keller and the other managers to do anything to please him. It was a form of entrapment. And for that, Arlen's responsible. Only Arlen. And he's your boy, Jim."

The dapper Lieberman pivoted toward Stamps, who looked worn and disheveled. "So, tell us, Mr. Chairman, is your resignation in your pocket?" He scowled intensely at Stamps before slithering back down in his chair.

Stamps shook his head vigorously. "I'm here for the long haul, Donn—so don't get your hopes up," he said curtly. "I believe in this company above any individual. And Arlen knows I feel that way. He does too, as he just proved." He pointed at Arlen's resignation, still resting on the table. Lieberman anxiously straightened his silk paisley tie and eyed Gross, who was biting her lower lip.

"I think we've talked this issue to death," said Rhondell with a sigh. "Arlen asked for a vote. Let's give it to him, shall we?"

* * * * * * * * *

Monday, October 15, 3:30 p.m.   Arlen walked briskly into Keller's office. Phyllis Benjamin, Keller's secretary, wasn't at her desk. She'd been lured to the company cafeteria by Susan O'Reilly. He wanted no interference or witnesses to this conversation.

The door to Keller's office was open. Arlen strode in and waited. Keller was on the phone, listening intently, at first unaware of his unscheduled visitor. Arlen plopped down in one of the four steel-framed chairs facing

Keller's spacious desk. The CEO sat back and waited for Keller to say good-bye.

"Hello, Mike," said Arlen.

"Arlen," responded Keller, trying to hide his surprise at the intrusion.

"Was that Leiberman? Or Gross?"

"Uh, no. It was just ... What brings you here?" he asked tentatively.

"You mean you haven't heard yet? That's a first." The CEO allowed Keller to consider his meaning. In a moment, the operations VP's face turned ashen.

"It was a damn good try, Mike. In some respects, I admire your moxey. Even though a lot of what you did was unethical and immoral, you weren't afraid to roll the dice. But you let your greed and power fixation get the better of you. The game's over now. You're out. And so is Grubner. I wanted to tell you myself."

To Arlen's surprise, a small smile burst out on Keller's long, angular face. He nodded, almost like he expected it.

"Only you would find your demise amusing, Mike. Your choices are to resign today or be fired. Let me know within the hour." He stood up and turned to leave when he heard Keller's jittery voice.

"I'm not sure I believe you. This was a done deal. I'm in the right, Arlen, you blew it," Keller said, rising from his seat, his face damp from nerves. He approached the tired, triumphant CEO. "You're as much to blame as I am," he insisted.

"Up to a point, you're right," Arlen agreed, facing Keller, who backed away a step. "But that's old news. When I found out about the problem, I tried to fix it. You tried to use it for yourself ... and against me and the company. You're damn smart, Mike. You just let the wrong motives sway your judgment. Resign or be fired, it's up to you."

Again, Arlen did an about-face and again was stopped by Keller's caustic sounds. "I don't think I will resign, Arlen," he said smugly, refusing to accept defeat. "And I don't think you have enough board support to get away with firing me. I know I've got at least three of them in my pocket. Think I'll call Donn Lieberman and talk it over with him."

This time, Keller turned his back on Arlen and walked back to his desk. He had no way of knowing he'd just fired his final, futile salvo.

"Go right ahead," Arlen said, trailing him to his desk where he grabbed the phone receiver and held it out. "But prepare yourself first, Mike. The vote was 7 to 1."

Keller, his eyes bulging in astonishment, sank into the chair Arlen had been sitting in. He murmured, "Seven to one? Can't be." A second later, he blurted, "Those S.O.B.'s betrayed me." Arlen looked down at Keller's slumping body, struck by the irony of his disappointment.

Lieberman, Keller's strongest backer, would tell Keller an hour later that Grubner had overestimated Robert Ray's loyalty and that Marcia Gross, who abhorred being associated with a loser, had abandoned ship at the last minute.

Arlen was just outside the office door when Keller, still clinging to an evaporated hope, called out self-righteously, "You still don't win, Royster. I always plan ahead. I've got a big, golden parachute about to open for me." Keller moved toward Arlen, his face sweaty now and his hands trembling slightly.

"I spoke this morning with an old B-school buddy of mine who's a VP at Mahoney Inns & Resorts. He told me he's heard through the grapevine that old man Mahoney has been talking to a hot CEO prospect who's gonna spearhead a big expansion plan, and my friend's sure they could use someone with my experience. In fact, he's probably talking to Mahoney about me right now."

"Really, Mike. Mahoney Inns? That's fascinating," quipped Arlen cynically, grinning for reasons Keller couldn't figure. "I wouldn't start counting my chickens just yet if I were you."

"Why not?"

"Why not? Think about it, Mike. You're a smart guy." Arlen couldn't hold back a small, vindictive smile, the mental pictures irresistible.

Keller scowled at Arlen, who had already spun around and was walking away. Suddenly, remembering something, Arlen stopped and wheeled back around. His eyes had turned somber, his voice hard and unforgiving.

"Oh, Mike, one more thing. Let's keep this between us guys. Fight any urges you have to unburden yourself to anyone outside of Royal." Keller stared back blankly.

Arlen wanted no misunderstanding. "Let me put it this way, Keller. If you or Grubner say so much as 'how do you do' to the media about what's gone on here at Royal, I'll personally make sure that you ... well, why don't I just leave it to your imagination."

The CEO placed in memory the former VP's horrified expression and walked out, satisfied.

Epilogue: "All's Well That Ends Well ... for Now, Anyway"

Saturday, November 28, 7 p.m., Six Weeks Later. Everyone had arrived on time and in a festive mood. The Royster home in the Roslyn Heights section of Long Island was the setting for a Thanksgiving celebration of select Royal faithful and guests. The sprawling, red brick house, built in the 1960s, had a comfortable, lived-in feel to it, even for its unusually large size. Tonight, the split-level dwelling was alive with energy and bright holiday colors, and warmed by a crackling fire in the spacious living room.

Roaming the house on each level were tuxedoed waiters and waitresses busily hawking assorted hot finger foods and serving up everything from Jack Daniels to Manischewitz. Andrea Royster's guest list showed that close to 70 people were there. Absent, of course, were Mike Keller and John Grubner, the departed mutineers who'd cleaned out their desks and slipped out unobtrusively the day after the now-famous board meeting at which Arlen was reanointed king of Royal Accommodations.

Everyone knew that this gathering was, in point of fact, a celebration of survival—Arlen's and Royal's. In Arlen's mind, it was a long-overdue celebration he'd earned several times over. So tonight, absent his usual reserve, Arlen was in rare form. Holding court in the center of the crowded living room, he lifted a glimmering glass of champagne above his head and called out loudly, "Friends, may I have your attention for just a moment, please. I'd like to propose a toast."

In a few seconds, conversations progressively ceased as people began drifting toward Arlen, huddling around him. As the circle formed, Andrea gently nudged her way in, balancing a silver tray topped with overflowing glasses of champagne. "Make way for this devilishly expensive bubbly," she chirped, joining Arlen at the center of the circle.

Hands sprung from all directions, grabbing for the dry Dom Perignon 1964, a case given to Arlen by Jim Stamps following Arlen's gutsy performance before the board. In seconds, the tray was empty and attention returned to Arlen who was still hoisting his glass in a Statue of Liberty pose. He was clearly feeling no pain, having begun his private celebration several hours before the first guests arrived. He knew he didn't have full control of his emotions, but he didn't care. Not tonight.

"I've been waiting for this moment for six weeks now...," he began haltingly, a trace of nostalgia crossing his glazed eyes. Gone was his usual serious expression and three-piece suit. Today, he was relaxed in both manner and dress. His hand gestures, usually the byproduct of nerves, were tonight natural and spontaneous. He sported a bulky checkered wool sweater, charcoal grey slacks, and Oxford penny-loafers. His hair was neatly trimmed and he smelled of expensive cologne.

"Is it really only six weeks since my ... or should I say our ... world was turned upside down? It feels more like a lifetime," he said, grinning widely while lowering his glass to chin level.

"Imagine how we feel," piped up Rick Jamieson from the far corner where the ceiling-high brick fireplace sizzled loudly, casting a warm, orange glow over the room and the people in it. "I think we all deserve 25-percent raises, at least—or a month's paid vacation."

Jamieson's quick, dry wit never failed to help Arlen avoid taking himself too seriously. On this occasion, the communication VP had also provided the night's juiciest gossip by arriving arm-in-arm with Susan O'Reilly, Arlen's bright and attractive secretary. Jamieson and O'Reilly had flirted for years, which most staffers discounted as harmless banter. Tonight, though, whispered speculation was running hot and sassy. O'Reilly had never before parted from her iron-clad policy of never mixing business and pleasure. When Arlen opened his front door and saw the two of them standing there together, silly smiles and slightly embarrassed looks on their faces, he couldn't hide his surprise and did an involuntary double-take. But he didn't say a word. He told Andrea later that picturing them as an "honest to goodness" couple sent his imagination soaring.

"Here, here," shouted attorney Joe Coletto from behind Arlen, stepping toward the ring of people surrounding the delighted CEO. Colletto's friendly, dark eyes darted among the Royal executive staff present: Jamieson, Gloria Bernard, Joyce Hadley, Susan O'Reilly, Jim Stamps, and Bob Azoulette, who'd flown in that morning from London where he'd been negotiating a deal to open Royal's first European hotel. Each responded in turn, laughing all the while, with a "here, here" in military roll-call fashion.

As the laughter faded, they all turned back to Arlen. "I don't know how to adequately say thank you to each of you except to tell you I've never meant anything more," he said, his voice husky with sentiment, his eyes glistening.

"Without you," he started again, punctuating each phrase, "... without your loyalty, without your smarts, without your belief in our mission, without your willingness to push yourselves to the brink of physical exhaustion, Royal Accommodations wouldn't be this year's comeback kid and the talk of Wall Street today."

The month-and-a-half since Arlen had reclaimed his position as top dog had been an emotional roller coaster with occasional dips, but a surprising number of crests. After reversing directions following the near-disaster, Arlen and Royal had used his heightened public posture as a springboard to generate a new momentum among Royal's jittery employees, most of whom were still looking over their shoulders. The Royal board's vote of confidence in its CEO, although not without its critics, looked now to have been a stroke of genius. Royal was bouncing back with a vengeance and its public reputation, while still somewhat tattered, was holding steady as Arlen had begun initiating a series of major internal changes.

Hotel guests apparently hadn't been deterred for too long; Royal's occupancy rate, after dropping almost 20 percent in the weeks following the press conference, was back to its precrisis level. Even those investment analysts who tracked Royal regularly—usually among the first to run for cover at the first sign of trouble—were pleased and surprised at how well the company had been able to weather the storm. Royal stock had lost value for a little while after the bad news came out, but it didn't seem to be suffering any long-term damage. And with a reopened eye to the future, the "new-look" board, minus Gross and Lieberman who'd resigned the day after Keller's demise, unanimously approved Arlen's and Azoulette's long-awaited plan to enter the potentially lucrative overseas markets.

Fortunately, employee turnover hadn't become the massive problem Joyce Hadley had feared; some Royal folk cleaned up their resumes and put out feelers to competitors, but few actually left. Morale was down but not out, according to the latest attitude survey. That wasn't unexpected, Arlen told his executive staff, given the widely varying reactions to the CEO's decision to reassign without penalty or demotion most of the book-juggling managers who chose to stay—if, and only if, they agreed to pay back bonuses earned by their deception and make public apologies to Royal's employees and stockholders. Several resigned rather than admit they'd done anything wrong. The company was still being investigated by the SEC, whose chairman had told Jim Stamps privately that Royal's cooperation and openness would eventually work in the company's favor, although she didn't say how.

Through it all, Arlen kept thinking about his career and his life, and how he wanted them to intersect rather than run in parallel lines. Every couple of weeks, almost like clockwork, Arlen got a telephone call from executive recruiter Megan Walters pressing him for a decision on the Mahoney offer. Each time, he gave her the same response: Royal still has to come first. But his time had just about run out. When they spoke two days ago, he told Walters he'd call her the following Monday morning with his answer. If only he knew how to answer, he thought to himself as he'd hung up.

Arlen opened his eyes and looked around the circle, a pleasing expression covering his face.

"I give thanks to you all," he said with feeling, lifting his champagne glass above his head again. "Please join me in this toast of thanks for the two most valuable possessions we have in life ... family and friends."

With that, he reached for Andrea's hand before sipping the tangy wine. The warmth of her hand in his made him recall the talk he'd had with Glenn several hours earlier, a talk that may have opened a long-clogged line of communication. What no one at the party except Andrea knew was that Arlen's ebullience—and his unusually heavy drinking—was due more to his hopeful feelings about his son than to his professional survival. He couldn't remember the last time he and Glenn had stopped arguing long enough to really listen to one another. Too long, he knew.

Everyone drank in unison, quickly draining their glasses.

"And God bless us all," Jamieson mocked. "Are you going to stand there blocking the fireplace, Arlen," he joked, "or get out of the way so we can properly smash these champagne glasses?" O'Reilly, who hadn't left his side since they'd arrived, dug her elbow into his ribs.

"Don't you dare, Rick," Andrea scolded, pointing a finger at Jamieson. "That's Waterford crystal in your hand and a wedding gift."

"I still have the floor, don't I?" Arlen snarled, pretending to be irritated. "Have you forgotten who the top dog is around here?"

Coletto, amused at Arlen's reference to himself as top dog, looked at Azoulette and silently mouthed, "Top dog?"

"As I was about to say, before the floor was pulled out from under me ..." He smiled at himself as he wobbled slightly, his light-headedness slowing his speech. "I have an important announcement that'll be made officially on Monday, but I wanna preview it here." Silence—and curiousity—quickly filled the room.

He stopped for a moment to gather his thoughts. "One of the things I've learned these past couple of months—or maybe I'd just forgotten it,

I'm not sure which—is the enormous power of the human spirit. The inner soul of a company can't be found on the P&L statement; it's in the hearts and souls of its people. Sure, the numbers have to be there or not much else can happen. But until this mess ... this ... what should I call it? ... this crisis of human values I suppose, I don't think I really understood how relationships can make or break a company. Maybe I knew it intellectually, maybe I didn't. But not until everything hit the fan back in October did this concept really start to mean something to me. And I won't soon forget it."

"Here, here," murmured Hadley under her breath so only her husband could hear.

"As a result of my ... my revelations from this experience, I've decided to appoint an executive vice president, effective immediately," Arlen said, savoring the suspense he was creating. "The CEO's responsibility for creating good relations with all constituencies is too important and too demanding to be left to one person—especially when that one person is me." He chuckled at himself, as others joined in.

During the frenzied weeks that followed Royal's public admission of its misreported financial results, Arlen's frustration with his own lack of productivity, despite working 18 hours a day, had intensified. That's when he started rethinking the idea of an executive VP. He wanted someone who would complement his own brand of thinking and style, meaning a person who was a risk-taker, adaptable, didn't need or want much supervision, whose judgment he trusted, and, maybe above all, who was a natural left-brainer. He'd made his choice two weeks ago. He made the offer in private and it was immediately accepted. Until today, he hadn't told anyone else at Royal.

"Royal's new executive vice president is ..." Arlen was really enjoying himself now. "A drum roll, if you please, maestro," he teased as groans were heard, "... is ... Joyce Hadley."

* * * * * * * * * *

It was after 2 a.m. when Arlen and Andrea finally crawled into bed, fatigued but elated over how well the evening had gone. By midnight, all had departed, happy, semi-sober and with full bellies. Yet despite the lateness of the hour, neither Arlen nor Andrea were ready for sleep.

As Andrea snuggled close to Arlen, he put his arm around her and both stared skyward in the darkened room. After a moment, she asked him what he was thinking about.

"You know me so well, Andy, you tell me."

"Okay, Mr. Top Dog," she said sarcastically, "I will, if you promise not to bite or growl." She poked him. "Glenn, right?"

"You should've been a psychic. Who else?" Actually, although Glenn had been on his mind all day, at that moment he'd been thinking of his interview the previous day with Karen-Elaine Marshak of *The Wall Street Journal* about his handling of Royal's "creative bookkeeping caper," as she'd indelicately described it.

For weeks now, Arlen had been dodging reporters' strident requests for interviews, leaving a chagrined Rick Jamieson and his staff to make excuses. At the time that the interview requests were pouring in, he had neither the time nor the patience to answer questions. But with the passage of time, his emotional wounds started to heal and his sense of balance, his need for control, gradually returned. It was only then that he consented to the Marshak interview—his final appointment before the four-day Thanksgiving weekend. Their 70 minutes together had been all business, her attempting to discover the "real" Arlen Royster and the "inside" dope behind Royal's near-demise and comeback, while each of them carefully avoided the risky repartee of their previous encounters.

"What about Glenn?" Andrea prodded again.

"I can't figure that kid out," Arlen sighed. "But I'm trying. I'm just not sure how."

"Well, that's a new tune for you. It's been ages since you tried to see the real Glenn."

"Yeah, you're probably right. Today was strange. Not strange mysterious. Strange unexpected. But encouraging, I think, very encouraging."

"You never did tell me what you both said."

"I don't know if it was so much what we said, but how we said it. Both, I guess. The usual tension, the awkwardness, our quick tempers—they were all missing today. I'm not sure why. But it sure felt good."

It was the son, not the father, who had made the initial move. Early that afternoon, a few hours before the dinner party, a nervous Glenn, home from the University of Miami for the holiday weekend, had showed up unannounced in Arlen's private office, plunked himself down in one of the guest chairs and pushed open a long-closed door by saying, "Dad, you got a minute? I think it's time we had a talk." Arlen hesitated as he thought back.

Andrea nudged him and asked again, "So what did you two talk about? Next season's pennant race?"

"Believe it or not, we actually talked about his future and my future, and our expectations of ourselves and each other. It just may've broken the ice," he reflected hopefully. "Or at least started it thawing."

He held her tightly, burying his nose in her sweet-smelling, velvety hair. "I think maybe it did." She couldn't see the tears forming in the corners of his eyes.

Once they'd started talking, it was Arlen who tried to reach his son. "How do you feel about marine biology as a career now that you've been at it for a year or so?"

"Well," Glenn hesitated, pleased to be asked but wondering about his father's usual hidden agenda, "I really love it, even more than I thought I would. There's a magnificent, mysterious, fascinating world under the sea. There's so much to learn from marine life, if we study it properly. It's like I've finally found myself, Dad. It was the right decision for me, I'm sure of that."

Arlen was touched by the gentle yet self-assured look on Glenn's soft-featured, handsome face as he talked about himself. He suddenly saw a son he didn't know, had never really known. Having convinced himself long ago that nobody but he knew what was best for Glenn, including Glenn, Arlen realized now how wrong he'd been. But, on this day, Arlen thought he might've finally heard his son's heart. And in that moment, he saw not a confused, spiteful son, but a mature young man who knew himself better than his father ever could.

"Maybe it is the right decision. Just maybe it is." Arlen bowed his head as he spoke. "I've always wanted the best for you, Glenn ... at least my version of 'the best.' To me, that means living your life according to a prescribed set of principles. But I suppose those principles change, and don't have to be exactly the same ... for a father and son to coexist in peace."

"Is that you talking, Dad?" Glenn, bracing for the standard merry-go-round of disagreements, stared at Arlen, doubt written across his face. "No sermon about the ever-lasting importance of money and prestige and power? Or about how I'm throwing away my potential on a frivolous career?"

Arlen moved out from behind his rolltop desk and sat down in the chair next to Glenn. "I don't know what to tell you, son," he admitted honestly, trying to lighten the mood. "Maybe I'm getting to be a softy in my golden years. I'm a lot more willing to listen to the other guy's viewpoint than I used to be. Hell, after the last couple of months, I'd better be. Living through traumatic times can do that to a person—even a hard-nose type like me. I'm seeing lots of things differently these days, Glenn."

They sat quietly together for a short time, neither one sure what to say or do next, but afraid of losing the moment. Finally, Arlen erased the silence. "Look, I've never really believed I had all the answers, even though I know I sometimes act like I do. I guess it's no secret who you got your stubborn streak from, is it? Maybe it's time we each did more listening than talking. Sound like a fair deal?"

"Sounds like a deal too good to pass up. I accept." They hugged each other hard, trying to make up for years of lost time, both father and son sharing a love that had never really been lost, only misplaced.

* * * * * * * * * *

Andrea rolled gently onto Arlen's shoulder and threw her right leg over his, cuddling as closely as she could under their bulky goosedown comforter. Arlen, growing drowsier but still feeling the effects of the mental high, reached around and began stroking her hair.

"What were you and Jamieson doing in the library for so long?" Andrea asked, pulling him back from the edge of sleep. He'd taken Jamieson into the library to tell him about the Hadley appointment moments before his announcement.

"Professional courtesy, that's all, Andy," he mumbled.

"Does he know that Mahoney's trying to steal you away?" Andrea asked.

"It wouldn't surprise me. You know how tough it is to keep a secret in this industry. But Rick hasn't asked or hinted that he knows."

"I suppose your time's about to run out," Andrea reminded him. "Still undecided?"

"I was until this afternoon," he said, wide awake again. "Now I know what to do." Saying the words aloud for the first time seemed to unburden him of months of anxiety. He closed his eyes, trying to picture Walters' and Mahoney's faces when he told them after all this time.

Andrea waited. "Well?" She waited a little longer. "Arlen, don't play games! This is too important, to both of us. What's it gonna be ...?"

"It's a secret," he joked, rolling away and flipping on the lamp next to the bed.

Andrea sat up, grabbed her pillow with both hands and whacked his head. Laughing, he commandeered the pillow and tossed it on the floor, out of her reach. He pulled her next to him and whispered in her ear.

She pulled away and propped herself up on her elbow, looking at her husband with genuine surprise. "Really? I guess I'm a little surprised."

"What was it that finally helped you make up your mind?"

"I think it was something Glenn said ... something about his having to be true to himself, no matter how much it cost him."

"That's our son," said Andrea, retrieving her pillow and crawling back under the covers. "He's a pretty smart kid, isn't he?"

"Yeah. Smarter than his old man, that's for sure."

"Oh, I don't know about that," she said tenderly, slipping her hand into his. "I think it's in his genes." They stayed silent and still for several moments, visualizing the future and the mysteries it held.

Then, very faintly, Andrea muttered, "Sounds like a good decision to me. Glad it won't be keeping you up nights any more."

After reviewing the twists and turns that had brought him to this moment, drowsiness began overtaking him. Andrea had already drifted off, her rhythmic breathing the only sound in the room.

Feeling himself being drawn into unconsciousness, Arlen Burch Royster, CEO and top dog, heard a voice inside his head—he wasn't sure whose it was—whisper, "Time to step into the batter's box again and ... "

He reached over, turned out the light and welcomed sleep.

Endnotes

Chapter 1

1. Joshi, Pradnya. "Fantasizing on the Job." *Los Angeles Times*, August 11, 1993, D1, D3.
2. Nelson-Horchler, Joani. "What's Your Boss Worth?" *Washington Post*, August 5, 1990, D3.
3. Crystal, Graef S. "Too Many Make-Any-Excuse CEOs." *Fortune*, July 21, 1986, pp. 116-117.
4. Bennis, Warren. *Why Leaders Can't Lead*. San Francisco: Jossey-Bass, 1989, p. 65.
5. "The Changing Role of the CEO." *Business Week*. October 23, 1987, pp. 13-28.
6. Rose, Frank. "A New Age for Business?" *Fortune*, October 8, 1990, pp. 155-164.
7. "The New Corporate Elite." *Business Week*, January 21, 1985, pp. 62-81.
8. Farnham, Alan. "The Trust Gap." *Fortune*, December 4, 1989, pp. 56-78.
9. Pincus, J. David, Rayfield, Robert E., Cozzens, Michael D. "The Chief Executive Officer's Internal Communication Role: A Program of Benchmark Research." *Public Relations Research Annual*, Vol. 3, 1991, pp. 1-35.
10. Shapiro, Irving. "Management Communication: The View from Inside." *California Management Review*, Vol. 27, No. 1, 1984, pp. 157-172.
11. Excerpt from speech by Roger Smith in "Our Top People Need Help." *Communication World*, June/July, 1985, p. 63.
12. Horton, Thomas. *"What Works for Me": 16 CEOs Talk About Their Careers and Commitments*. New York: Random House, 1986.
13. McGoon, Cliff, "A Look In ...." *Communication World*, April, 1990, p. 1.
14. "The New CEO." *Business Week*, 1990 Special Bonus Issue, October 19, 1990, pp. 22-37.
15. Drucker, Peter. "The Mystery of the Business Leader." *The Wall Street Journal*, September 29, 1987, p. 28.

Chapter 2

1. "In the Words of Gorbachev." *Los Angeles Times*, January 16, 1990, A6.
2. Kalb, Laura and Hugick, Larry. "The American Worker: How We Feel About Our Jobs." The Public Perspective by The Roper Center for Public Opinion Research, September-October, 1990, p. 21.

3. Salwen, Kevin. "To Some Small Firms, Idea of Cooperating With Labor is Foreign." *The Wall Street Journal*, July 27, 1993, A1.

4. O'Boyle, Thomas F. "Fear and Stress in the Office Take Toll." *The Wall Street Journal*, November 6, 1990, B1, B11.

5. Shellenbarger, Sue. "Work-Force Study Finds Loyalty Is Weak, Divisions of Race and Gender Are Deep." *The Wall Street Journal*, September 3, 1993, B1, B5.

6. Anderson, Harry, "Employers Waking Up to Child-Care Crisis." *Los Angeles Times*, October 16, 1990, D1, D13.

7. In Sing, Bill, "Corporate Child-Care Efforts Inching Along." *Los Angeles Times*, October 14, 1990, D3.

8. Silverstein, Stuart and Maier, Andrea. "Major Child, Elder Care Effort Planned." *Los Angeles Times*, July 10, 1992, D1, D4.

9. Shellenbarger, Sue. "Work-Family Programs Change J&J's Culture. *The Wall Street Journal*, April 28, 1993, B1.

10. Baker, Bob. "A New American Workplace Will Evolve Slowly in the 1990s." *Los Angeles Times*, January 7, 1990, D4.

11. Kanter, Rosabeth Moss. "The New Managerial Work." *Harvard Business Review*, November-December, 1989, pp. 85-92.

12. Stewart, Thomas A. "Managing: Do You Push Your People Too Hard?" *Fortune*, October 22, 1990, pp. 121-128.

13. Dumaine, Brian. "Who Needs A Boss?" *Fortune*, May 7, 1990, pp. 52-60.

14. "Self-Managing Work Teams." *The Maryland Workplace*, Vol. 12, No. 2, 1990, pp. 3-5.

15. Dumaine, pp. 52-60.

16. Ibid.

17. Granelli, James S. "Workers Borrow Against Retirement Fund, Buy 62% of Kirkhill." *Los Angeles Times*, October 5, 1989, Sec. IV, 5.

18. "ESOPs: Are They Good For You?" *Business Week*, May 15, 1989, pp. 116-123.

19. "ESOPs Allow Participation in Decision-Making Which Turns Attitudes Into Positive Behavior." *pr reporter*, October 27, 1986, p. 3.

20. "ESOPs: Are They Good For You?" *Business Week*, May 15, 1989, pp. 116-123.

21. Ibid.

22. Kirkpatrick, David. "How the Workers Run Avis Better." *Fortune*, December 5, 1988, pp. 103-114.

23. DePree, Max. *Leadership is an Art*. New York: Bantam Doubleday Dell Publishing, 1989, p. 25.

24. Ibid.

Chapter 3

1. Kotter, John. *A Force For Change: How Leadership Differs from Management*. New York: The Free Press, 1990.

2. Zaleznik, Abraham. *The Managerial Mystique*. New York: Harper & Row, 1989.

3. Steiner, George. *The New CEO*. New York: MacMillan Publishing, 1983.

4. "The Changing Role of the CEO." *Business Week*, October 23, 1987, pp. 13-28.

5. In Labich, Kenneth, "The Seven Keys to Business Leadership." *Fortune*, October 24, 1988, pp. 58-66.

6. Kets de Vries, Manfred. *Prisoners of Leadership*. New York: John Wiley & Sons, 1989.

7. Kotter, John. *A Force for Change: How Leadership Differs from Management*. New York: The Free Press, 1990.

8. Ruch, Richard and Goodman, Ronald. *Image at the Top: Crisis & Renaissance in Corporate Leadership*. New York: The Free Press, 1983.

9. In a conversation with Warren Bennis by Joe Flower, "The Chasm Between Management and Leadership." *Healthcare Forum Journal*, July-August, 1990, pp. 58-62.

10. Kotter, John P. "What Leaders Really Do." *Harvard Business Review*, May-June, 1990, pp. 103-111.

11. Kotter, John P. *A Force for Change: How Leadership Differs from Management*. New York: The Free Press, 1990.

12. Bennis, Warren and Nanus, Burt. *Leaders: The Strategies for Taking Charge*. San Francisco: Jossey-Bass, 1985.

13. Labich, pp. 58-66.

14. Zaleznik, 1989.

15. Kotter, John. "What Leaders Really Do." *Harvard Business Review*, May-June, 1990, pp. 103-111.

16. Labich, pp. 58-66.

17. DePree, Max. *Leadership is an Art*. New York: Bantam Doubleday Dell Publishing, 1989.

18. Jonas, Harry S., Fry, Ronald E., and Srivastva, Suresh. "The Office of the CEO: Understanding the Executive Experience." Academy of Management *EXECUTIVE*, Vol. 4, No. 3, 1990, pp. 36-47.

19. Bennis, Warren and Nanus, Burt.

20. Stalk, George, Evans, Philip, and Shulman, Lawrence E. "Competing on Capabilities: The New Rules of Corporate Strategy." *Harvard Business Review*, March-April, 1992, pp. 57-69.

21. Walton, Sam. "Sam Walton in His Own Words." *Fortune*, June 29, 1992, pp. 97-106.

22. Kouzes, James and Posner, Barry. *The Leadership Challenge*. San Francisco: Jossey-Bass, 1990.

23. Ibid.

24. Labich, pp. 58-66.

25. Bennis, Warren. *Why Leaders Can't Lead*. San Francisco: Jossey-Bass, 1989.

26. Conger, Jay A. "Leadership: The Art of Empowering Others." The Academy of Management *EXECUTIVE*, Vol. 3, No. 1, 1989, pp. 17-24.

27. Wyden, Peter H. "Tough Image May Belie Another Side of Iacocca." *Los Angeles Times*, October 4, 1987, Sec. IV, 3, 26.

28. Lee, Patrick. "Iacocca Back in the Spotlight, But It's Just Not the Same." Los Angeles Times, May 18, 1990, D1, D14.

29. "More on Iacocca: When CEO Becomes Public Personage Can Be Risky If It Goes Too Far." *pr reporter*, November 3, 1986, p. 3.

30. Iacocca, Lee. *Iacocca*. New York: Bantam Books, 1984.

31. Ruch, Richard and Goodman, Ronald.

32. Ibid.

Chapter 4

1. Foster, Chris. "Torre Finds Managing Is Easier the Second Time Around." *Los Angeles Times*, July 12, 1992, C12.

2. Farnham, Alan. "The Trust Gap." *Fortune*, December 4, 1989, pp. 56-78.

3. Pincus, J. David. "How CEOS View Their Communication Roles." *Communication World*, December, 1987, pp. 19-22.

4. Pincus, J. David, Rayfield, Robert E., and Cozzens, Michael D. "The Chief Executive Officer's Internal Communication Role: A Benchmark Program of Research." *Public Relations Research Annual*, Larissa A. Grunig and James E. Grunig, co-editors, Chapter 1, Volume 3, 1991, pp. 1-35.

5. O'Brian, Bridget. "Guests at These Hotels Can Go Right to the Top." Tracking Travel section, *The Wall Street Journal*, July 10, 1992, B1.

Chapter 5

1. Direct quotations from the "Dateline" broadcast of December 22, 1992, were taken from a transcript of the show.

2. Weintraub, Daniel M. "News Analysis: Governor Stumbles On Budget Challenge." *Los Angeles Times*, April 3, 1992, A3.

3. Davis, Bill. "IBM, Fiesta Bowl Team Up." *Tempe Daily News Tribune*, December 22, 1992, A1, A4.

4. Norwood, Robyn. "Hockey Violence Puts Eisner in the Hot Seat." *Los Angeles Times*, September 26, 1993, A1, A16.

5. Richter, Paul. "Clinton Denies Charges He's 'Gone Hollywood.'" *Los Angeles Times*, May 28, 1993, A1, A31.

6. Fisher, Christy. "Marriott chief gets personal in ads." *Advertising Age*, March 15, 1993, p. 12.

Chapter 6

1. Gordon, Gloria. "A CEO who communicates = A CEO who builds trust." *Communications World*, June/July, 1993, pp. 17-20.

2. Summers, Diane. "Another battle of the sexes—Do women or men make better bosses? New research into management styles. *Financial Times*, February 3, 1993, p. 16.

3. "How to keep women managers on the corporate ladder." *Business Week*, September 2, 1991, p. 64.

4. Rosener, Judy B. "Ways women lead." *Harvard Business Review*, November-December, 1990, pp. 122+.

5. Summers, p. 16.

6. Holusha, John. "Grace Pastiak's Web of Inclusion." *The New York Times*, May 5, 1991, Sec. 3, p. 1.

7. O'Brian, Don. "The communication gap." *Atlanta Journal/Constitution*, July 27, 1992, B1, B4.

8. Ibid.

9. "Soliciting feedback, listening to it and acting on it is still a key organizational problem despite TQM and rhetoric to the contrary." *pr reporter*, January 13, 1992, Vol. 35, No. 12, p. 1.

10. Cole, Jesse. "Managing from the heart." *Sky*, April 1992, p. 20.

11. Gibson, Richard. "Personal 'chemistry' abruptly ended rise of Kellogg president." *The Wall Street Journal*, November 28, 1989, A1, A8.

12. "CEOs speak about leadership." *USC Business*, Summer, 1992, p. 10.

13. "I'm going to let the problems come to me." *Business Week*, April 12, 1993, pp. 32-33.

14. Ibid.

15. Kirkpatrick, David. "Lou Gerstner's First 30 Days." *Fortune*, May 31, 1993, pp. 57-58.

16. "Sports Briefings." *Los Angeles Times*, August 15, 1990, C2.

17. Gordon, pp. 17-20.

18. Huey, John. "Cover Story: America's Most Successful Merchant." *Fortune*, September 23, 1992, pp. 46-48, 50-54, 58-59.

19. Saporito, Bill. "A week aboard the Wal-Mart express." *Fortune*, August 24, 1992, p. 84.

20. Kiechell, Walter III. "How to escape the echo chamber." *Fortune*, June 18, 1990, pp. 129-130.

21. Farnham, Alan. "Mary Kay's Lessons in Leadership." *Fortune*, September 20, 1993, p. 74.

22. Bunting, Glenn F. "Town Hall Meetings Put Senators on the Map with New Constituents." *Los Angeles Times*, February 14, 1993, A3, A38-39.

23. Gordon, pp. 17-20.

24. Michels, Antony J. "More Employees Evaluate the Boss." *Fortune*, July 29, 1991, p. 13.

25. Rice, Faye. "Champions of communication." *Fortune*, June 3, 1991, p. 112.

26. Fraser, Jill Andresky. "Women, power and the new GE; General Electric Co. Cover Story." *Working Woman*, December, 1992, Vol. 17, No. 12, p. 58.

27. Billard, Mary. "Do women make better managers?" *Working Woman*, March 1992, Vol. 17, No. 3, p. 68.

28. Broder, David S. "Clinton Deals Himself a Tough Hand. *Los Angeles Times*, October 4, 1993, B9.

29. Holusha, John. "Grace Pastiak's Web of Inclusion." *The New York Times,* May 5, 1991, Sec. 3, 1. The company reported a loss of $968,000 for the first quarter, compared with a profit of $2.54 million last year.

30. Harte, Susan. "Business report on the workplace: Gender affects leadership style, expert suggests." July 5, 1992, *Atlanta Journal/Constitution*, C2.

Chapter 7

1. Craib, Jr., Donald F. "Allstate's Communication Strategy: It's a Tool for Growth." *Communication World*, May, 1986, pp. 24-26.

2. Stewart, Thomas A. "GE Keeps Those Ideas Coming." *Fortune*, August 12, 1991, pp. 41-49.

3. "A Big Company That Works." *Business Week*, May 4, 1992, pp. 124-132.

4. "Out of the Frying Pan." *INC.*, December, 1991, p. 157.

5. Hyde, Jack. "Hicks B. Waldron, Chairman & CEO, Avon Products Inc." Leadership Profile Series, *Sky*, Feburary, 1988, pp. 28-32.

6. Ibid.

7. "CEOs Perceive 5 Shortcomings of PR Practitioners." *pr reporter*, July 12, 1993, p. 4.

8. Lengel, Robert H. and Daft, Richard L. "The Selection of Communication Media as an Executive Skill." *The Academy of Management EXECUTIVE*, Vol. II, No. 3, 1988, pp. 225-232.

9. Pincus, J. David and Rayfield, Robert E. "The Emerging role of Top Management Communication: 'Turning On' Employee Commitment." *Personnel Management:Communications*, Prentice-Hall, 1985, pp. 1291-1296.

10. Orman, Dave. "Still Prime Time After All This Time." *ARCO Spark*, October 1988, p. 3.

11. "And That's the Way It Is ..." *Los Angeles Times*, "Footnotes" column, September 25, 1989, Sec. IV, p. 1.

Chapter 8

1. Howard-Cooper, Howard. "For Lucas, Winning Is Secondary." *Los Angeles Times*, February 15, 1993, C1, C9; Starr, Mark and Carroll, Ginny. "Sinking a Long Shot." Newsweek, March 1, 1993, pp. 65-66.

2. Carlzon, Jan. *Moments of Truth*. Cambridge, MA: Ballinger Publishing Co., 1987.

3. Byrne, John. "The Rebel Shaking Up Exxon." *Business Week*, July 18, 1988, pp. 104-111.

4. Miles, Gregory L. "Forging the New Bethlehem." *Business Week*, June 5, 1989, pp. 108-110.

Chapter 9

1. Norwood, Robyn. "A Happy Visitor." *Los Angeles Times*, August 12, 1992, C1, C6.

2. Lindgren, Kristina. "Candid Style Key to UCI's New Leader." *Los Angeles Times*, June 20, 1993, A1, A22-23.

3. Cole, Jeff. "New CEO at Hughes Studied Its Managers, Got Them on His Side." *The Wall Street Journal*, March 30, 1993, A1, A6.

4. In an excerpt from *Control Your Destiny or Somebody Else Will* by Noel M. Tichy and Stratford Sherman, New York: Bantam Doubleday Dell, 1993, in *Fortune*, January 25, 1993, pp. 86-93; also in "Reviews of Jack Welch's Book Show It Can Be Useful Counseling Tool." *pr repoter*, July 19, 1993, p. 4.

5. Kanter, Rosabeth Moss. "The New Managerial Work." *Harvard Business Review*, November-December, 1989, pp. 85-92.

6. Dumaine, Brian. "What The Leaders Of Tomorrow See." *Fortune*, July 3, 1989, pp. 48-62.

7. O'Connor, Terri. "Communication Styles of Female Business Executives: A Way to Break Through the Glass Ceiling." Final M.A. project paper, M.A. program in communications at California State University, Fullerton. Ms. O'Connor is communication director at Cypress College, Cypress, Calif.

8. Bennett, Amanda. "The Chief Executives In Year 2000 Will Be Experienced Abroad." *The Wall Street Journal*, February 27, 1989, A1, A4.

9. Dumaine, pp. 48-62.

10. Harper, Stephen C. "The challenges facing CEOs: past, present and future. *Academy of Management EXECUTIVE*, Vol. 6, No. 3, 1992, pp. 7-25.

11. In Ingber, Dina, "Inside the Executive Mind." *Success!*, December, 1984, pp. 33-37.

12. Ibid.

13. Ibid.

14. Lawrence, John F. "Human Touch in a Boss Shows Touch of Class." *Los Angeles Times*, June 7, 1987, D1.

15. "Managing: A Study in Neglect." *Los Angeles Times*, May 23, 1988, Sec. IV, pp. 10-11.

16. In Main, Jeremy. "B-Schools Get A Global Vision." *Fortune*, July 17, 1989, pp. 78, 80, 85-86.

17. Ibid.

18. Munter, Mary. "Trends in Management Communication at Graduate Schools." *Journal of Business Communication*, 1983, Vol. 20, No. 1, pp. 5-11.

19. In Greising, David. "Chicago B-Schools Go Touchy-Feely." *Business Week*, November 27, 1989, p. 140; and in Main, Jeremy. pp. 78, 80, 85-86.

20. Putka, Gary. "It's Unlikely Holders of This Sheepskin Will Act Like Sheep." *The Wall Street Journal*, November 12, 1992, A1.

21. Deutschman, Alan. "The Trouble with MBAs." *Fortune*, July 29, 1991, pp. 67-80.

22. Thomas, Emory. "Business Grads Now Must Be Communicators." *Atlanta Business Chronicle*, October 10, 1988, 5B; personal letter and copies of syllabi for "Business 561: Communication for Managers" and "Business 562: Communication Strategies" from Cathy Pinson, MBA student at Emory Business School and graduate assistant to Dr. Sherron Kenton, January 9, 1990.

23. Bongiorno, Lori. "Corporate America's New Lesson Plan." *Business Week*, October 25, 1993, pp. 102-106.

24. Byrne, John A. "The Limits of Power." *Business Week*, October 23, 1987, pp. 33-35.

25. Bennett, A1, A4.

26. Weber, Jonathan. "Hewlett-Packard Splits Power Between 2 Chiefs." *Los Angeles Times*, October 6, 1990, D3.

27. Lublin, Joann S. "Shareholders Campaign to Dilute Power of Chief Executives by Splitting Top Jobs." *The Wall Street Journal*, April 1, 1992, B1, B5.

28. Schachter, Jim. "The Title Game." *Los Angeles Times*, March 4, 1989, Sec. IV, p. 1.

29. Bennett, A1, A4.

30. Weber, Jonathan. "Fisher Leaves Motorola in Good Shape." *Los Angeles Times*, October 29, 1993, D1, D5.

Appendix

The following are the top executives who participated in one-on-one interviews as part of the research for this book. The titles are those held by the executives at the time of the interview and the cities are the sites at which the interviews took place.

Bruce Burtch, president, The William Bentley Agency, San Francisco, Cal.

Tom Clausen, chairman and CEO, Bank of America, San Francisco, Cal.

Dr. Jewel Plummer Cobb, president, California State University, Fullerton, Cal.

Bill Davila, president and CEO, Vons Grocery Co., El Monte, Cal.

Robert Dockson, chairman, California Federal Savings, Los Angeles, Cal.

Redmond Doms, managing principal, Karsden Real Estate Co., Santa Monica, Cal.

Berit Durler, president, Old Stone Bank of CA, Newport Beach, Cal.

Dr. Noel Hinners, associate deputy administrator for institution, NASA, Washington, D.C.

Carl Karcher, president and CEO, Carl Karcher Enterprises, Anaheim, Cal.

Norm Leaper, president, International Association of Business Communicators, San Francisco, Cal.

Bob Ludka, president and CEO, Randomex, Inc., Yorba Linda, Cal.

David Price, CEO, American Golf Corporation, Santa Monica, Cal.

Tom Priselac, senior VP and COO, Cedars-Sinai Medical Center, Los Angeles, Cal.

Phil Quigley, president and CEO, Pacific Bell Telephone Companies, San Francisco, Cal.

Henry Rogers, chairman of executive committee, Rogers & Cowan Public Relations, Brentwood, Cal.

Carl Sardegna, president, Blue Cross/Blue Shield of Maryland, Towson, Md.

Dick Schlosberg, president and COO, Los Angeles Times, Los Angeles, Cal.

Sandy Sigoloff, chairman and CEO, Wickes Companies, Santa Monica, Cal.

Herb Stein, chairman, **Phil Stein,** COO, H&E Hardware Stores, Victorville, Cal.

Alexander Trowbridge, president, National Association of Manufacturers, Washington, D.C.

Jim Verney, president (leader), Winchell's Donut House, La Habra, Cal.

Hicks Waldron, CEO, Avon Products, New York, N.Y.

Richard Warren, chief administrator, Washington Hospital, Fremont, Cal.

Charles Wick, director, United States Information Agency, Washington, D.C.

Walter Williams, CEO, Bethlehem Steel Company, Bethlehem, Pa.

Index

About the Authors

J. DAVID PINCUS, Ph.D., APR, is director of the MBA program and Research Professor of Communication in the College of Business Administration at the University of Arkansas, Fayetteville. Prior to that, he was a tenured full professor in the public relations sequence of the Department of Communications at California State University, Fullerton.

Before receiving his Ph.D. in organizational communication at the University of Maryland in 1984, he worked as the first corporate-wide employee communication director for Marriott Corporation and headed the communication departments for two national trade associations in the Washington, D.C., area. Since that time, he has served as consultant to a variety of companies, including IBM, Sheraton, Wm. M. Mercer, Foster Higgins, the California Society of CPAs, and the Maryland Center for Quality of Worklife.

Starting in the early 1980s, Dr. Pincus has conducted a systematic series of research projects exploring the impact of management communication—particularly that of CEOs—on employees and organizational effectiveness. This body of research, ranging from national studies to one-on-one interviews with CEOs, has served as the basis for many of his published works, which have appeared in a variety of professional and scholarly journals, among them *Communication World, Public Relations Review, Employee Responsibilities and Rights Journal, Journal of Accountancy, The Journal of Public Relations Research,* and *Association Management.*

His ground-breaking work has been honored by the Institute for Public Relations Research and Education, which named him winner of its prestigious Pathfinder Award in 1994, and the Public Relations Society of America Foundation, which tapped him recipient of the 1995 Jackson, Jackson & Wagner Behavioral Science Prize.

In 1987–1988, Dr. Pincus served as Visiting Professor of Business Communication in the School of Business Administration at the University of Southern California, where he taught in the MBA and Executive MBA programs.

J. NICHOLAS DEBONIS, Ph.D., is an Atlanta-based marketing and communication consultant to Fortune 500 firms, and a teacher at Emory University's business school. Since 1980 he has conducted nearly 500 business seminars throughout the United States and Canada.